Introductory logic and sets for computer scientists

INTERNATIONAL COMPUTER SCIENCE SERIES

Consulting Editor: **A D McGettrick**   *University of Strathclyde*

SELECTED TITLES IN THE SERIES

Introductory logic and sets for computer scientists

Nimal Nissanke

University of Reading

ADDISON WESLEY LONGMAN

Harlow, England ● Reading, Massachusetts ● Menlo Park, California ● New York

Don Mills, Ontario ● Amsterdam ● Bonn ● Sydney ● Singapore ● Tokyo

Madrid ● San Juan ● Milan ● Mexico City ● Seoul ● Taipei

Pearson Education Limited
Edinburgh Gate
Harlow
Essex CM20 2JE
England

and Associated Companies throughout the world

Visit us on the World Wide Web at:
http://www.pearsoneduc.com

Cover designed by The Senate, London
Text design by Claire Brodmann
Typeset in Stone Serif by 32
Produced by Pearson Education Asia Pte Ltd.
Printed and bound by Antony Rowe Ltd, Eastbourne

First published 1999

ISBN 0-201-17957-1

British Library Cataloguing-in-Publication Data
A catalogue record for this book is available from the British Library

Library of Congress Cataloging-in-Publication Data
Nissanke, Nimal.
    Introductory logic and sets for computer scientist/Nimal Nissanke.
        p.   cm. -- (International computer science series)
    Includes bibliographical references and index.
    ISBN 0-201-17957-1 (pbk.)
    1. Computer logic.   2. Set theory.   I. Title.   II. Series.
QA76.9.L63N57 1999
004'.01'5113 --dc21   98-28534
                                                      CIP

Transferred to digital print on demand, 2006

For Samaya and Hikaru

my dearest children

Contents

Preface

....

With the rapid and radical changes taking place both in the economy and society, many industrialized nations are facing new challenges in higher education. These include greater diversity in the academic background of students at entry into institutions, higher expectations on the part of students and ever-changing demands placed by society both towards achieving high standards and making higher education more accessible and more relevant to social and economic needs. A logical outcome in this respect has been the greater awareness of the need for alternative and more effective forms of delivery of educational material to students.

Today, increasing numbers of students take different routes to higher education. Vocational education and industrial training are some of the choices many students make early in their secondary education. With the subsequent realization of their academic potential and the desire to improve their long-term career opportunities, these students are returning to higher education in considerable numbers. Another category is the mature student who graduated some years ago and is working in industry, who is also returning to higher education in order to update his knowledge and to acquire new skills. As a result of these and other factors, students enter higher educational institutions today with diverse academic qualifications, and inevitably with disparate standards in academic achievements and skills in the basic subjects of secondary education, especially in mathematics. In addition, there are many who continue education during employment, in pursuit of professional or intellectual advancement. Those pursuing higher education at the workplace, albeit in a limited form, face similar problems to those faced by students at institutions. They all naturally require some flexibility in their studies, particularly with respect to time. The above also place rather unusual demands on teachers providing higher education.

One way to address the demand for flexible learning is to provide the students with educational material that facilitates and encourages a degree of independence in study. In practical terms, in addition to changes in cultural attitudes to learning, this calls for measures in teaching which are designed to sustain students' interest, build up their confidence and provide them with the means for self-evaluation. This text aims at achieving this in its subject area: logic and set theory. It also aims at being 'student-friendly', that is, by being direct and responsive to their expectations at different stages. The student is given the opportunity to select both the pace and depth of study. Such independence, as well as the assurance that a high standard is within the reach of every student, is felt vital for ensuring some uniformity in competence at the conclusion of the course.

The text is intended as a first course in the mathematical foundations of software engineering and, to an extent, computer science in general. The two areas covered, namely, logic and set theory, form the mathematical foundation of software specification languages, such as the Z notation (see Hayes, 1993; Potter *et al.*, 1991; Spivey, 1992; Woodcock and Davies, 1996) and VDM (Vienna Development Method; see Andrews and Ince, 1991; Jones, 1986; Jones and Shaw, 1990). These languages are aimed at providing a sound mathematical framework for the design and analysis of reliable and critical computer systems. Both languages possess largely similar capabilities and are of similar stature. They already form core courses in formal (mathematical) methods in software engineering at universities.

The adoption of computer science as an application domain for logic and set theory has been beneficial in two ways. First, since the text uses a subset of the Z notation, it has the benefits of using a well documented standard notation. The student will thus have access to other authoritative literature for further clarification of ideas, concepts and notations. Secondly, computer science being an applied science, the text makes it a point to amplify the applied nature of logic and set theory. As a result, the impression commonly associated with the subject matter, that it is a highly abstract discipline, is replaced, wherever possible, with common sense, and is explained with many examples drawn from everyday life which the students can easily relate to. The aim has been to build the mathematical skills through practical problem-solving and on the basis of sound understanding of concepts.

This book is suitable for first-year undergraduates as a text in logic and set theory at universities and as a resource for self-study at home or at the workplace. Chapters 1–8 and 10–16 would serve as a basic introduction to logic and set theory, whereas the remaining chapters suit specialised or more advanced courses. Thus the text can be adapted to the needs of different courses.

Nimal Nissanke
Reading, May 1998

Acknowledgements

I greatly benefited from a number of sources cited as references. They have been cited where most appropriate. The chapter quotations have different origins, but most can be found in Mackay and the *Concise dictionary of quotations* (Oxford University Press, 1994).

The material presented in this text is based on a course given at the University of Reading, UK. I am grateful to the students who have attended this course. They have contributed in numerous ways to the development of the approach being advocated and to the improvement of the form of presentation. I am indebted to Andrew Rae and Peter Samuels for sharing their ideas and experiences in relation to a similar effort at Brunel University, UK. I wish to thank Neil Robinson for assistance in the early phase of this work and Ali Abdallah, Hamdan Dammag, Sue Walmsley, Shirley Williams and Simeon Veloudis for comments, assistance and encouragement. I am extremely grateful to the anonymous reviewers of the manuscript; their comments have resulted in many improvements. I owe special thanks to Emma Mitchell, Michael Strang and Sarah Falconer of Addison Wesley Longman for their patience and professionalism in bringing this book into existence. I owe my greatest debt to my family: Machiko, Samaya and Hikaru.

Nimal Nissanke
Reading, May 1998

The publisher is grateful to the following copyright holders for permission to reproduce copyright material.

Dover Publications Inc for an extract from Madachy, J. S. (1979) *Madachy's Mathematical Recreations*. New York: Dover Publications Inc. (See Exercise 16.2, p. 250).

Encyclopaedia Britannica International Ltd for an extract from *Children's Britannica*. (See Exercise 1.2, p. 9).

Times Newspapers Limited, 1996 for permission to adapt the article by Steve Connor, 'The Lonely Planet' *Sunday Times*, 29 December 1996, © Times Newspapers Limited. (See Exercise 2.8, p. 21).

The publisher has made every effort to obtain permission to reproduce material in this book from the appropriate source. If there are any errors or omissions please contact the publisher who will make suitable acknowledgement in the reprint.

A note on the exercises

The exercises have been graded, with a number of stars alongside the exercise number indicating the degree of complexity of the exercise concerned. Grading is as follows:

Grade	Explanation
✳	These exercises are simple and are within everyone's ability.
✳ ✳	These exercises are slightly more complex. The ability to do them indicates a good understanding of the material.
✳ ✳ ✳	These are the hardest in this text. The ability to do them indicates a thorough understanding of the material. The reader should not be disappointed if unable to solve them successfully at the first attempt.

The answers for selected exercises are given in Appendix A. The answers for most of the exercises may be obtained from http://www.awl-he.com.

Chapter 1

An overview of logic

Topic: Logic

....

O Logic: Born gatekeeper to the Temple of Science,
Victim of capricious destiny,
Doomed hitherto to be drudge of pedants,
Come to the aid of thy master, Legislation

Jeremy Bentham
English philosopher, economist and theoretical jurist (1748–1832)

Objectives

On completion of this chapter you should be able to:

- Explain the link between logic and scientific disciplines.

- Explain the link between logic and computer science.

- Separate the form and content of an argument.

- Identify syllogistic, propositional and predicate logical systems.

This chapter is an overview of three logical systems. Two of them will be studied in detail later, but the aim here is to gain a broader view of their place in logic. The chapter begins with a discussion of the function of logic and concludes with a brief discussion of the wider context of our study, namely, on how logic is used in areas of computer science dealing with specification of requirements, program verification, and so on.

1.1 What is logic?

Although it may differ in form from one scientific discipline to another, logic lies at the heart of every such discipline: physicists use logic with extensive use of symbols and proofs and biologists with a less formal form of reasoning. Logic makes such disciplines *scientific*, by providing a way to deduce the vast amount of knowledge in each discipline from a relatively small number of explicitly stated facts or hypotheses. In order to make this kind of deduction, logic can be treated as a language, and this allows, first, the expression of knowledge concisely and precisely and, secondly, a way to reason about the consequences of that knowledge rigorously.

This is how logic is seen by both logicians and those outside logic. In addition, logicians take an uncompromising stand with respect to their role in logic. In order to play this role effectively, logicians deliberately avoid, by having a limited interest in any argument, becoming involved in the logic of the subject matter. Instead, they concentrate on the correctness of the *argument form*, irrespective of the discipline under study. Logicians are thus very different from, for example, judges, who pay attention to both facts and soundness of arguments placed before them at the same time.

Addressing the correctness of the form of any argument, and not its content, is the *function of logic* and, interestingly, also happens to be the most important aspiration shared by computer scientists in their pursuit of correctness. The study of argument forms is in essence two-fold: first, the analysis of an argument, that is, how to identify its structure, and secondly, how to make a judgement as to whether the argument is an acceptable or an unacceptable one. In logic, this acceptability is referred to as *validity* and, in computer science, as *correctness*.

Note that a program can be viewed as an argument. A description of a program basically says that given such-and-such inputs (data) it produces such-and-such output (results). Therefore, when we examine its correctness what we really examine is whether it is possible to sustain the argument that the program produces the right result, provided that the input data conform to a stated specification.

It is not strictly correct to advocate that the language of logic is essential for expressing knowledge and the reasoning about it. Natural language performs this function quite effectively; no artificial language could challenge natural language with respect to expressiveness, flexibility, richness and beauty. However, the same qualities disqualify natural language from being used in science, where precision and clarity are paramount.

1.2   Logic in real arguments

Quite often, we hear arguments such as

Argument I
If I play cricket or I go to work, but not both, then I will not be going shopping. Therefore, if I go shopping then neither would I play cricket nor would I go to work.

and less often ones like

Argument II
An object remaining stationary or moving at a constant velocity means that there is no external force acting upon it. Therefore, if there is a force acting upon the object, either it is not stationary or it is not moving at a constant velocity.

The above two arguments belong to widely differing areas of discourse: the former to ordinary life and the latter to mechanics. Despite the difference in the content, the underlying logic of the arguments is, however, the same. This becomes clear if we separate the subject matter and the logical structure of the arguments. We do this by using symbols for the meanings expressed by the various clauses. In the case of the above two arguments, let p, q and r stand for the following:

Argument I
p: **I play cricket.**
q: **I go to work.**

r: **I go shopping.**

Argument II
p: **The object is stationary.**
q: **The object is moving at a constant velocity.**
r: **There is an external force acting upon the object.**

Then, the two arguments may be written as follows:

If p or q, but not p and q, then not r.
Therefore, if r then either not p or not q.

What we now have is an abstract form, free from any subject matter. Nevertheless, it is in a form which allows reasoning about the acceptability, namely, the validity, of the argument quite independently from the factual truth of the clauses which make up the original argument. As a result, the correctness of the argument may now be addressed in two stages and from two independent perspectives: the correctness of the abstract argument purely from the logical point of view, and the correctness, or the material (factual) truth, of the argument from the point of view of the application domain. Computer scientists look to this separation of concerns, and to their subsequent independent treatment, as an important strategy for developing computer systems in a disciplined manner.

1.3 Arguments and deduction

An argument is in essence a claim. As it is subjected to a logical analysis, the argument may be seen as a relationship between statements. The statements are ordered in such a way that some of these sentences, referred to as *premises*, serve as the basis for accepting another statement of the argument, singled out as the *conclusion*. If the conclusion is justified, relying solely on the basis of those premises, the underlying form of reasoning is referred to as *deduction*. The other major form of reasoning is *induction*, whereby we make generalizations from particular instances of knowledge, on the basis of strong but inconclusive evidence. This book does not cover the latter kind of reasoning.

1.4 The logical systems

We consider briefly three logical systems. Our aim is to show the important aspects of modern logic. The three systems differ primarily in the way the sentences are analysed and, as a consequence, in our ability to reason about them formally.

Historically, the oldest system is associated with Aristotle, who identified a list of nineteen correct argument forms, called *syllogisms*. His logic was based on a simple analysis of sentences into subject–predicate form as shown in

1. All *men* are *mortal*.

2. No *man* is *immortal*.

Each of the above identifies one or more individuals and a property or a relationship unifying them. With such an analysis of sentences in place, a typical syllogism can be given in the following form:

Actual form	*Abstract form*
All Greek gods were jealous.	*All Gs were J.*
Zeus was a Greek god.	*Z was a G.*
Therefore, Zeus was jealous.	*Therefore, Z was J.*

Although it was adequate at the time, this form of reasoning was limited to very simple arguments and hindered the development of logic for some time.

The next important breakthrough in logic is attributable to the English mathematician George Boole. Boole is the author of what is widely known as *propositional logic*, which allows reasoning about arguments of a particular form, where certain types of statement (proposition) are regarded as the smallest building blocks for constructing arbitrarily complex statements. An example of a typical argument in this system is:

Actual form	*Abstract form*
Alexandria is a port or a holiday resort.	*P or H.*
Alexandria is not a port.	*Not P.*
Therefore, Alexandria is a holiday resort.	*Therefore, H.*

Boole's system uses symbols for simple whole sentences and, as a result, the advantage offered by syllogisms in identifying properties and relationships between things or individuals is lost. On the other hand, Boole's system overcomes the restriction of syllogisms to simple sentences – the limiting factor in syllogistic reasoning.

The third logical system, *predicate logic*, attributable to Gottlob Frege, in effect combined syllogistic and propositional reasoning and emerged as the leading system in modern logic. It retained the syllogistic analysis of sentences and extended the notion of *predicate* to include relationships between any number of individuals, things or objects. It incorporated the whole of Boole's propositional logic and, thus, the ability to reason about sentences of arbitrary complexity. Although it contains the notation to be introduced later, the example below is intended primarily to indicate the expressive power of predicate logic. Let us introduce the following predicates with the indicated meanings:

Predicate	Meaning
stationary (x)	**x is stationary.**
in-uniform-motion (x)	**x is in uniform motion.**
x is-acted-upon-by f	**x is acted upon by** *f***.**

It is possible to express as shown below even Newton's second law of motion (Argument II on page 2) – an idea known for complexity and requiring a precise understanding

$$\forall\, x :\; Object \bullet stationary\,(x) \oplus in\text{-}uniform\text{-}motion\,(x) \oplus$$

$$\exists\, f :\; Force \bullet x\ is\text{-}acted\text{-}upon\text{-}by\ f$$

where $\oplus$ is a symbol to be read as 'exclusive or', $\forall$ as 'for every' and $\exists$ as 'there exists'. Note that $\bullet$ is a separator. The above mathematical formula as a whole is to be read as

For every *x* **of** (a certain) **type** (referred to as) *Object***,** *x* **is stationary,** *x* **is in uniform motion or there is an** *f* **of type** *Force* **such that** *x* **is acted upon by** *f***.**

In summary, a feature that distinguishes propositional logic and predicate logic is that the former limits analysis of sentences to the recognition of such *connectives* as *and* and *or*, which play the role of glue in building complex sentences from simpler ones. On the other hand, predicate logic goes beyond and as far as the recognition of objects and relationships between them in sentences. As a result, predicate logic is a richer formalism with greater expressiveness and greater reasoning capabilities.

The task of Chapters 2–9 is to acquire a detailed acquaintance with the above concepts through a study of propositional and predicate logic. Before we embark on it, let us also examine the wider context of our study.

(1.5) Scientific theories and specifications

Logic is a common denominator of all sciences. Unlike sciences, which deal with material phenomena, and mathematics, which deals with abstract objects such as numbers and geometrical shapes, logic has a totally different kind of subject matter, namely, *arguments*. Arguments, in a non-emotive sense, lie at the heart of every science.

A coherent argument which is confined to the study of a particular problem is called a *theory*. Some well known examples are: the *theory of evolution*, dealing with the gradual development over long periods of time of complex living forms (species) from simpler ones, the *theory of relativity*, dealing with motion as a relative process and the profound effects it has on observations when motion takes place over large distances in space, and *genetics*, dealing with ways in which characteristics are passed from 'parents' to 'offspring' in living organisms and plants.

Such theories consist of a large body of highly structured (organized) knowledge. Textually, this knowledge is expressed as a collection of sentences. Some of this knowledge is taken for granted and its *truth* is not questioned within the theory. In mathematical theories, the latter kind of knowledge is expressed as *axioms*. The rest of the knowledge is commonly *deduced* from the former by appealing to undisputed rules and laws of *reasoning*. The axioms are thus the most fundamental and undisputed truths (facts) in a theory serving as its bedrock, upon which we pile up more and more other provable truths through deduction. As described earlier, each such deduction takes the form of an argument and consists of a set of *premises* and a *conclusion*. Following the same discussion, the purpose of logic is to ensure that such deductions are sound and the *form* of each argument is *correct*. That is why we need logic. However, some might dispute this relevance immediately, suggesting that such 'theories' are of remote interest in their work.

One does not need to be a great scientist to formulate a theory. Most of us do this in everyday life, albeit in more humble terms. A child building a sand-castle on the beach does so with a theory in the back of his mind. He knows that a canopy or a portico is too ambitious an extension to the castle. Although he may not be able to articulate it in such words, the child knows that the predictive power of the theory precludes such a structure because of the physical nature of the raw material – sand. On the other hand, if, instead, plasticine is used as the raw material, then within limits the idea would have worked. At a more serious level, a designer of a clock, a car, a bridge, an aeroplane or any other artifact has a more robust theory in mind, describing precisely how it works generally and predicting with great accuracy how it might work under extreme conditions.

We build theories in computer science too. When we wish to acquire or to develop a computer system or a software package, we first describe it. When such descriptions are complete enough to be contractually binding, we refer to them as *specifications*. Specifications are theories not only in the sense of such a complex idea as the theory of evolution, but also in the simple theory of the working of a toy.

We often speak of a program being correct or an implementation of a larger system being correct. Since correctness in computing is a notion with a precise meaning, and is closely tied to an associated specification, some specifications in computing are treated with extreme care.

This is especially true in critical systems, where the cost of any failure could have severe consequences in relation to human life (for example in patient-monitoring or aviation), success of the mission of the system (for example in the launch of a spacecraft), the environment (for example in nuclear power generation), property (for instance in air-crashes) and financial assets (such as in stocks and shares, and banking). It is quite common for the origins of such failures to be tracked down to ambiguities, vagueness and incompleteness in the original product specification. For this reason, specifications of such systems are beginning to take a precise form. This precision is gained through writing them in formal languages, which are invariably founded on logic. A major advantage of using such a formal language is the scope for rigorous reasoning or – in the technical terminology – *proofs*.

1.6 Mathematical models

Prior to construction of an artifact such as a car or a bridge, the designers build *models* in order to convince themselves, as well as others, through *experiments* and other forms of *reasoning* that their understanding and predictions are correct. The power of models is that they help us to visualize how a given object works or behaves at some chosen level of detail and thus avoid costly and risky 'experiments' in real life.

A model used by an architect concentrates on the functionality and aesthetics of a building. Such a model could be made out of plastic or a similar material but, despite the unsophisticated nature of the material, should be more than sufficient for demonstrating the spatial characteristics of the building. A model of the same building used by an engineer would go into further detail and describe the material structure of the building and its behaviour under extreme and operational conditions in the environment. In this respect, an engineer may resort to a physical model, using components which are scaled-down versions of the real ones and which have the appropriate degrees of strength and elasticity. Engineers construct such models using physically meaningful materials and methods. Alternatively, or as a supplement, the engineer may resort to an abstract model, using mathematical descriptions of how materials and structures behave. In the case of complex structures, computer models enable not only analysis but also detailed simulations.

The model appropriate to a particular study is thus a product of *abstraction*, whereby the study is limited to a particular level of detail. It also involves creativity since the choice of the kind of model and how the model is to be constructed for the particular scenario is left to the human.

There are areas of human activity where the only means of modelling is abstract and mathematical. Compared with our previous scenarios, this is what characterizes computing. A *computation* is the process of derivation of the possible values of a set of unknowns using a mathematical model. It can be a mental activity when we confine ourselves to pencil and paper; or it can be a physical process set in motion on a piece of equipment, an abacus, a calculator or a computer. Given a specification, a number of programmers may implement it differently, giving rise to different programs. Even the same programmer might come up with different programs for the same specification, ranging from prototypes to increasingly sophisticated programs employing different algorithms. Each such program is a model, but there can be other abstract models, which, unlike programs, cannot be 'executed' on a computer.

Whatever the *tool* being used, an engineer in a traditional branch of engineering performs engineering computations using an abstract mathematical model as described above. However, such branches have the benefit of working in continuous domains such as real numbers, which are amenable to precise descriptions using differential calculus, linear algebra and conventional geometry. Normally, the models envisaged by these descriptions do not involve abrupt changes in behaviour, and even when they do, such changes usually arise because of deficiencies in the model and can be rectified by switching to a more appropriate model.

In this respect, computations in discrete domains are qualitatively different. Typical examples of discrete domains are natural numbers and integers. A program that counts the number of entrants to a building always produces a whole number like 5 or 6, and never a number like 5.778. A switch is either on or off. An event is yet to take place, has successfully taken place, has failed or is yet to finish. At a larger granularity, discrete domains also include such massive objects as databases, networks and computers themselves.

Such programs and systems require a different kind of mathematics. The relevant branch of mathematics is founded basically on set theory and extends to many other areas in discrete mathematics including graph theory (which enables the study of such things as networks and grids), modern algebra (which enables the systematic study of structurally complex abstract objects) and combinatorics (which enables the study of complexity of computations).

In dealing with discrete systems, it is possible to build mathematical models of significant value using just objects such as *sets*, *relations* and *functions*, which are studied under set theory in Chapter 11 and onward. Sets are collections of objects taken in isolation. Relations are sets where elements exhibit relationships in the ordinary sense, such as someone being older than someone else or a number being exactly divisible by another number. Relations will be represented by sets of, say, pairs or triples of simpler objects. Going a step further, functions can be seen as relations, where elements exhibit certain unique relationships with one another. They are all sets of one sort or another.

Once a mathematical model is built using sets or whatever, then any reasoning about its behaviour has to be done using laws about the same mathematical objects. The language of this reasoning is logic. Thus, analogous to differential calculus in continuous domains, set theory enables the construction of mathematical models encountered in discrete domains using such objects as sets, relations and functions with well understood properties and relationships. On the other hand, logic enables reasoning about such models, and through such observations, about the real artifacts.

(1.7) Limitations of our study

There are different kinds of logic with different capabilities. As is already clear, the system of logic introduced in this text is called *predicate logic*. Our stepping stone to its study – classical *propositional logic* – is a typical example with many cousins. The system of propositional logic that we will study differs from other kinds basically in that it confines itself to the study of sentences which are either true or false, and excludes sentences having an intermediate truth value or a truth value which depends on, among other things, beliefs and *modalities*. A typical modality we often come across is hidden in words such as *possibility* and *necessity*, *sometimes* and *always*. As a consequence, we will not be able to infer, for example, from a sentence such as '**it always rains in London on May Day**' that '**it sometimes rains in London on May Day**'.

Exercise 1.1 ✳

Discuss briefly the function and the form of usage of logic in natural language, the sciences in general, and computer science in particular.

Exercise 1.2 ✳ ✳

Extract the linguistic form of argument (that is, without adhering to any particular logical system) of the following piece of text by eliminating its subject matter with symbols for simple sentences.

Mechanical work is done whenever a force moves an object, the force being the push or pull needed to move it. Work is done only if the object is moved – for example, when a man is asked to lift a heavy object onto a shelf and he succeeds in doing so. If it is too heavy for him to lift he cannot be said to have done any useful work at all, no matter how much he strains.

(from *Children's Britannica*)

[Hint: Paraphrase the domain-specific phrases, with additional words if necessary, in order to expose the sentences with a common meaning. Also, retain the domain-independent English words without any change.]

Chapter 2

Propositions and propositional connectives

Topic: Propositional logic

There are no whole truths; all truths are half-truths.
It is trying to treat them as whole truths that plays the devil.

Alfred Whitehead
English mathematician and philosopher (1861–1947)

Objectives

On completion of this chapter you should be able to:

● Explain what a proposition is.

● Explain the meaning of propositional connectives.

● Formalize logic statements written in natural language.

● Interpret logical formulae as statements in natural language.

● Identify ambiguity and vagueness in natural language.

Propositions are a fundamental concept in logic. Documents describing computer systems as well as claims and counterclaims about how they work contain propositions. In order to reason about them formally, propositions have to be extracted from their sources. This is not always as straightforward as it may seem because the same proposition can be expressed in a variety of ways in natural language. Moreover, ambiguities and imprecision of natural language make this task even more difficult. This chapter is about how to identify different propositions and how to clarify their meanings.

2.1 Propositions

Description   Proposition

A *proposition* is the underlying meaning of a *declarative sentence* – a sentence which is either true or false.

The truth or falsehood of a proposition may be characterized by assigning it one of the two possible *truth values*: T for true and F for false.

Example 2.1

Consider which of the following are propositions.

1. **Mammals are warm-blooded.**
   This is a true fact and is a proposition.

2. **The sun orbits the earth.**
   This is a false proposition, believed to be true by the ancient civilizations.

3. **Every second, the sun converts 4 million tons of itself into energy.**
   This is a scientific fact and a proposition. Obviously, our interest here is in the order of magnitude.

4. **An earthquake of magnitude 7.5 on the Richter scale hits California every 75 years.**
   This is also a proposition but its truth value is uncertain in absolute terms. Depending on available knowledge, seismologists can admit it as a true proposition or dismiss as a false proposition.

5. **John is taller than Juan.**
   This is a proposition.

6. **Juan is shorter than John.**
   Although it is a different sentence, this is exactly the same proposition as the one above. Remember, propositions concern only the meaning and not how they are written down.

7. **John is not shorter than Juan.**
   This is a complex proposition and is different from the sentence 5 above.

8. **Over millions of years, they build up on top of one another to form a reef.**
   This has a *variable* – the word 'they'. The truth value of the sentence depends on what 'they' are. The sentence is therefore not a proposition since its truth value relies on a variable. If the context were known, which in this case is a discussion of coral reefs, this may be treated as a proposition.

9. Can the Arctic hare change the colour of its coat to match its surroundings?

This is a question and no truth value can be assigned. It is therefore not a proposition. We would similarly discount commands, exclamations and any other form of sentence to which no truth value can be assigned.

10. The evergreen forests of Canada consist of spruce, pine and fir trees.

This is a complex proposition.

Terminology

* Propositions such as those in sentences 1–6 of Example 2.1 are the most basic type of proposition. They are referred to as *prime propositions*. They are also known as simple, atomic or elementary propositions. Prime propositions are the basic building blocks from which we can construct more complex expressions known as *compound propositions*. Two examples of compound propositions are those in sentences 7 and 10 in Example 2.1.

* In some textbooks, as well as in Chapter 1, you may find propositions referred to as *statements*.

Exercise 2.1 ✳

Which of the following are propositions?

1. Pay your bills on time.
2. Long live the king!
3. The equator runs through the North and the South poles.
4. Prevention is better than cure.
5. In health care, prevention of diseases is better than their cure.
6. Why is prevention of diseases better than their cure?
7. All seals are carnivores.
8. The circumference of a circle is equal to twice its radius multiplied by π.
9. The circumference of a circle is equal to four times its diameter.

2.2 Connectives

The words that we use to join prime propositions together to form compound propositions are called *propositional connectives*. Some connectives used in English appear in Example 2.2.

Example 2.2

1. **In 1938 Hitler seized Austria, in 1939 he seized former Czechoslovakia *and* in 1941 he attacked the former USSR *while* still having a non-aggression pact with it.**
   [Note that there is an invisible *and* at the comma.]

2. ***Although* both Stanley *and* Gordon are *not* young, Stanley has a better chance of winning the next bowling tournament, *despite* Gordon's considerable experience.**

3. ***If* Polonius is *not* behind that curtain *then* Polonius is well.**

Exercise 2.2 ✳

Identify the prime propositions and words serving as connectives in the following sentences.

1. Edmund Hillary and Tenzing Norgay conquered Mount Everest.

2. Edmund Hillary and Tenzing Norgay were the first to conquer Mount Everest.

3. Indochina lies within the tropics and has hot summers but the winters in the north are cool.

4. A pen is to write with, a glass to drink out of and an arrow to attack someone from a distance. Thus, the purpose of an object determines its shape except for those things made for art or pleasure.

5. No matter how high you jump you cannot reach the moon, except by flying in a spacecraft.

6. If seals fall into the water then they almost always drown unless they are attached to floats.

In contrast, propositional logic has a standard set of connectives: *not, and, or, if ... then* and *if and only if*. These are represented by the symbols given in Table 2.1.

Table 2.1 Propositional logic connectives.

Name	Read as	Notation
negation	*not*	¬
conjunction	*and*	∧
disjunction	*or*	∨
implication	*if ... then ...*	⇒
equivalence (biconditional)	*if and only if*	⇔

These can represent a wide range of connectives in natural language and the symbols are intended to prevent unwarranted inferences from the use of words such as *and*, *or*, etc. instead.

The meaning of the symbols in Table 2.1 is expressed in English in the following Description.

Description   Propositional connectives

Negation	A negation $\neg\, p$ is true if and only if p is false.
Conjunction	A conjunction $p \wedge q$ is true if and only if both p and q are true.
Disjunction	A disjunction $p \vee q$ is true if and only if p is true or q is true. That is, either p or q is true or both are true.
Implication	An implication $p \Rightarrow q$ is false if and only if p is true and q is false.
Equivalence	An equivalence $p \Leftrightarrow q$ is true if and only if both p and q have the same truth value.

Terminology

- The formulae (a terminology we use for expressions) written on either side of a conjunction $\wedge$ are called *conjuncts*.

- The formulae written on either side of disjunction $\vee$ are called *disjuncts*.

- In an implication written in the form $p \Rightarrow q$, the formula p is referred to as the *antecedent* and q as the *consequence*.

Example 2.3

The sentences in Example 2.2 may be formalized as follows.

1. In 1938 Hitler seized Austria, in 1939 he seized former Czechoslovakia *and* in 1941 he attacked the former USSR *while* still having a non-aggression pact with it.

Prime propositions (in bold type indicate the choice of symbols for denoting propositions):

Symbol	Meaning
A	*In 1938 Hitler seized* **Austria**.
C	*In 1939 Hitler seized former* **Czechoslovakia**.
U	*In 1941 Hitler attacked the former* **USSR**.
P	*In 1941 Hitler had a non-aggression* **pact** *with the former USSR.*

Formalization:

$$A \wedge C \wedge U \wedge P$$

2. *Although* Stanley *and* Gordon are *not* young, Stanley has a better chance of winning the next bowling tournament, *despite* Gordon's considerable experience.

Prime propositions:

Symbol	**Meaning**
S	**Stanley** is young.
G	**Gordon** is young.
B	Stanley has a **better** chance of winning the next bowling tournament.
E	Gordon has considerable **experience** in bowling.

Formalization:

$$(\neg S) \wedge (\neg G) \wedge B \wedge E$$

3. *If* Polonius is *not* behind that curtain *then* Polonius is well.

Prime propositions:

Symbol	**Meaning**
C	Polonius is behind that **curtain**.
W	Polonius is **well**.

Formalization:

$$(\neg C) \Rightarrow W$$

4. Increased spending overheats the economy.

Prime propositions:

Symbol	**Meaning**
S	**Spending** increases.
E	**Economy** overheats.

Formalization:

$$S \Rightarrow E$$

5. Increased spending coupled with tax cuts overheats the economy.

Prime propositions:

Symbol	**Meaning**
S, E	As above.
C	There are tax **cuts**.

Formalization:

$$(S \wedge C) \Rightarrow E$$

Most of the above interpretations make sense, although, as we will see shortly, we may sometimes experience difficulties in relating them to our understanding in ordinary life. A part of the problem is that in natural language there are many phrases for saying the same thing. This applies also to words playing the role of connectives. In this respect, Table 2.2 is a collection of English phrases roughly corresponding to propositional connectives. It is only a rough guide to translation, that is, formalization into logic and interpretation in English, and should not be interpreted as a precise recipe.

> **Table 2.2** English phrases corresponding to propositional connectives.
>
> | Connective | Possible interpretations in English |
> | --- | --- |
> | $\neg p$ | not p, p does not hold, it is not the case that p, p is false |
> | $p \wedge q$ | p and q, p but q, not only p but q, p while q, p despite q, p yet q, p although q |
> | $p \vee q$ | p or q, p or q or both, p and/or q, p unless q |
> | $p \Rightarrow q$ | if p then q, q if p, p only if q, q when p, p is sufficient for q, q is necessary for p, p implies q, p materially implies q |
> | $p \Leftrightarrow q$ | p if and only if q (p iff q), p is necessary and sufficient for q, p exactly if q, p is materially equivalent to q |

Exercise 2.3 ✷

Rewrite the following formulae in English where p is 'the thief is young', q is 'the thief is hanged', r is 'the thief will grow old' and s is 'the thief will steal'.

1. $p \wedge q \Rightarrow \neg r \wedge \neg s$
2. $p \wedge q \Rightarrow \neg (r \vee s)$

What is the difference between the two sentences you have written?

Exercise 2.4 ✷✷✷

This exercise continues with the last two sentences in Example 2.3. Identify the prime propositions appearing in the sentences given below. Formalize the sentences in propositional logic if they are amenable to such a treatment, otherwise explain why they are not so.

1. Overheating economy is a synonym for rise in excess demand.
2. Inflation does not rise only if excess demand does not rise.
3. Tax cuts are a sign of declining inflation.
4. Cut taxes for stimulating (i.e. raising) spending!
5. Nothing can overheat the economy if spending is not rising.
6. Something leads to inflation unless spending is not reduced.
7. Does inflation rise with increased spending?
8. Inflation either rises or does not.
9. Increase in excess demand raises inflation provided that there is no rise in interest rate.
10. Rising inflation raises interest rate whereas the rising interest rate causes no rise in inflation.
11. Inflation either rises or declines, but not both.
12. Rising inflation is equivalent to not declining inflation.
13. Inflation rises only if it does not decline.

The following sections highlight some of the difficulties in understanding the exact meanings of propositional connectives as they appear in English.

2.2.1   Disjunction

In English, the word 'or' can often be ambiguous. It is important to be aware of the two possible meanings in logic: *inclusive 'or'* and *exclusive 'or'*.

(**Description**)   Inclusive 'or' and exclusive 'or'
_____

Inclusive 'or' is represented in logic by the connective $\vee$, whereas *exclusive 'or'* is represented by $(p \vee q) \wedge \neg (p \wedge q)$.

In some textbooks, exclusive 'or' is denoted by the symbol $\oplus$, with exactly the same meaning as described above.

(**Example 2.4**)
_____

1. **Your money or your life!**
   The 'or' here is clearly exclusive. If we answered 'Both, please', we would not be surprised at a refusal. (Note that the above is not a proposition – it is a threat.)
2. **The error is in the main program or in the sensor data.**
   If one is speaking about a single error, then the 'or' is exclusive, because one error cannot be in both.
3. **The main program or the sensor data are erroneous.**
   Here the 'or' is inclusive. It is perfectly possible that both the main program and the sensor data have errors.

2.2.2   Implication

We begin by looking at the meaning of implication in greater detail.

(**Example 2.5**)
_____

Consider the following sentence:

> **If Roland eats sweets then he will get fat.**   **(I)**

Here we have an implication, $p \Rightarrow q$, where p is '**Roland eats sweets**' and q is '**Roland gets fat**'. What does this mean exactly? We will analyse the sentence by considering all the possible assignments of truth values to the prime propositions.

1. p is true and q is true. In this case Roland eats sweets and gets fat, so (I) is clearly true.

2. *p* is true and *q* is false. Roland eats sweets and does not get fat. (I) is clearly false.

3. *p* is false and *q* is true. Roland does not eat sweets but does get fat. Is (I) true or false in this case?

   In fact, (I) is true since the speaker did not say what would happen if Roland did not eat sweets. Roland may get fat because of eating chips.

4. *p* is false and *q* is false. Roland does not eat sweets and does not get fat. For the same reason as in case (3) above, (I) is true.

In Example 2.5, we appealed to intuition to decide on the truth of the sentence in each case. Confirm this intuitive analysis later by checking it against the definition of implication given on page 28.

Terminology

Cases 3 and 4 in Example 2.5, where the first term of the implication is false, are examples of an implication being *vacuously true*.

Exercise 2.5 ✳

The following sign was seen posted behind a local bar:

> *The bar-staff do not mean to offend but if they think you are over 18 then they will not ask for identification.*

Comment on its truth when:

1. *'The bar-staff mean to offend'* is false.
2. *'The bar-staff think you are over 18'* is false.
3. *'The bar-staff ask for identification'* is false.

In ordinary language the implication may be introduced in different ways, affecting the nature of its truth in a quite subtle way. For example, the following sentences are implications, but their truth depends on logical grounds, linguistic factors and factual circumstances.

1. **If all students take maths and Jo is a student then Jo takes maths.**
   A statement which is true on logical grounds.

2. **If anyone goes to outer space then he/she is an astronaut.**
   The truth is based on the definition of the word 'astronaut'.

3. **If Heathrow becomes foggy then the flight is delayed.**
   A causal connection between states and events.

4. **If Jo is intelligent then she is also clever.**
   A relationship between contemporaneous states of affairs.

2.2.3   Sorting out equivalence and implication

One should always be aware of the difference between equivalence and implication. In English, it is not always clear which connective is intended.

(**Example 2.6**)

1. Eating hamburgers at a fast-food bar is equivalent to aiding the destruction of the world's rainforests.

This sentence looks like an equivalence, but if we swap the sentence round, we can see that something is wrong.

Aiding the destruction of the rainforest is equivalent to eating hamburgers at a fast-food bar.

In fact, the intended meaning is an implication:

If one eats hamburgers at a fast-food bar then one is aiding the destruction of the world's rainforests.

2. I will give you a lift to London, if you are going to London.

Although this appears to be an implication, the intended meaning is an equivalence.

(**Exercise 2.6** ✳)

In relation to Exercise 2.5, how could the bar-staff amend their sign so that under 18s will always expect to be asked for identification?

(**2.3**) **Ambiguity and imprecision**

Our exploration into the meanings of propositions has also been an exploration into intricacies in natural language. In the process, we begin to see how logic helps us to clarify the meanings of descriptions written, for example, in English. After all, one reason for our use of logic is to state precisely the requirements of computer systems.

Descriptions in natural language can be imprecise and ambiguous. They often rely on the 'common sense' of the reader to convey the correct meaning.

(**Description**)   Ambiguity and imprecision

An *ambiguous* sentence can have more than one distinct meaning. By contrast, an *imprecise* or *vague* sentence has only one meaning but, as a proposition, the distinction between the circumstances under which it is true and the circumstances under which it is false is not clear-cut.

Vagueness arises from the use of qualitative descriptions. Often we need to introduce some quantitative measure to remove vagueness. In contrast, an ambiguous sentence usually has several specific interpretations. Ambiguity has to be eliminated by querying the author of the sentence or by examining the context.

Imprecision and ambiguity in natural language are a major problem in scientific disciplines. Sentences written in logic, on the other hand, are precise and unambiguous. This is a very good reason for learning logic.

Example 2.7
_____

Imprecise sentences

1. **John is tall.**
   We do not know exactly what 'tall' means. A more precise description is **'John is over 2 metres tall.'**

2. **This computer is fast.**
   The meaning of 'fast' is imprecise – fast compared with what? A more precise description would be **'This computer executes 2 million instructions per second.'**

Ambiguous sentences

3. **David and John from Chelmsford are coming to visit.**
   Who is from Chelmsford? David and John or just John? It is impossible to know without further information.

4. **I know a much funnier man than Bill.**
   This may have one of two meanings: **I know a much funnier man than Bill does**, or **I know a much funnier man than Bill is**. Again, we cannot decide which meaning is correct without further information.

5. **The program prints the results or an error message.**
   This has more than one meaning. Could the program print both the results and an error message or one or the other on an exclusive basis?

6. **Don't leave animals in cars because they rapidly turn into ovens.**
   The immediate reading is far from the intended meaning!
   (From _News Quiz_, BBC Radio 4, 10 October, 1994.)

Exercise 2.7 ✳✳
_____

Identify any ambiguity and/or imprecision in the following sentences.

1. Discrete mathematics should be fun.

2. Discrete mathematics is funny.

3. This exercise does not take more than ten minutes.

4. Jane disapproves of Harold's cooking.

5. Major will meet Adams in Birmingham.

6. What is the length of the coast of Britain?

7. While John is out of the house he does not want anyone using his telephone.

8. While Daphne is gone, she does not want anyone to leave the car.

Exercise 2.8 ✷

Identify prime propositions and propositional connectives in the following argument. Discuss the soundness of its facts and any gaps and ambiguities in its reasoning.

It takes 100,000 years to cross our galaxy, the Milky Way, in a spacecraft travelling at the speed of light. For 4.5 billion years, our own star, the Sun, has sent out a constant stream of light and energy that has powered the evolution of life on at least one of its nine planets. In another 5 billion years it will begin to swell up into a Red Giant star, engulfing our pale blue dot and vaporising all life on it.

Around many of the stars in the Milky Way there would have been planets very much like the Earth, with water, an atmosphere and all the other ingredients for the evolution of life and intelligence. If there were technologically aware civilisations on them, like ours, then they must have realised, just as we have, what would eventually happen to their own stars.

Given what we know about the rate of technological development, they should have been able to build colonising spaceships to other, safer solar systems during the thousands – possibly millions – of years between predicting the end of their planet and it actually occurring.

Therefore, if intelligent life existed on other planets then our galaxy should be awash with colonising aliens and we should by now have seen them. The fact that we haven't suggests that there aren't other intelligent civilizations.

(Based on an article in the *Sunday Times*, 29 December 1996)

Exercise 2.9 ✷✷

Here are some general questions.

1. What do you think are the advantages of using propositional logic for descriptions?

2. What do you think are the disadvantages of using propositional logic for descriptions?

3. Can you think of any benefits of ambiguity and vagueness in natural language?

Chapter 3

Propositional logic as a language

Topic: Propositional logic

··

How can one talk about 'understanding' a proposition and 'not understanding'
a proposition?
Surely it's not a proposition until it's understood?

Ludwig Wittgenstein
Austrian-born English philosopher (1889–1951)

Objectives

On completion of this chapter you should be able to:

● Write and identify grammatically correct formulae in propositional logic.

● Understand the meaning of grammatically correct formulae.

● Use truth tables.

● Identify tautologies, contradictions and contingent propositions.

● Identify logical equivalences and implications.

● Represent digital circuits as Boolean expressions.

● Interpret Boolean expressions as digital circuits.

The primary concern of the previous chapter was how propositions relate to the application with respect to their meanings. In this chapter we deliberately move away from such application-oriented concerns and lay the foundation for a more abstract treatment of propositions. The motivation for this is formal reasoning about arguments – the subject of the next two chapters.

Much can be said about the meanings of propositions purely within the confines of logic. Some propositions imply others, and some are totally independent. As seen in the previous chapter, complex propositions can be built from simpler ones. Some propositions are mere statements of facts, which can be either true or false, while others have a fixed truth value irrespective of the subject matter. Although we continue to take an interest in what propositions mean from the application point of view, this chapter presents essentially a formal framework for the study of meanings of propositions purely from the logical perspective. This framework has direct applications in computing, for example, in the design of digital circuits, which is a topic dealt with at the end of this chapter.

3.1 About formal languages

Propositional logic is best studied as a formal language. The most widely known formal languages are programming languages. No programming language allows the programmer to write just anything he or she wants. The programmer must obey precise rules as to the symbols that can be used and in which order the symbols can be put together to form program instructions that a machine can interpret as intended.

The same applies to logic, except that the symbols used in logic are rather unusual and that the machine intended for its 'execution' is our brain. Otherwise, programming languages and logic share many things in common.

A formal language, and for that matter any language, consists basically of three ingredients:

1. A set of permitted symbols, that is, the *alphabet*.

2. Rules defining the right order of symbols in sentences, that is, the *syntax*.

3. Assignment of meaning to correctly written sentences, that is, the *semantics*.

Although they are not formal languages, let us first identify the above in relation to natural languages. In English, for example, the alphabet corresponds, at the lowest level, to letters and, at a higher level, to all English words. The syntax corresponds to the English grammar on how to write sentences correctly using words and punctuation. The semantics is defined in terms of the meanings of words, as defined in a dictionary, and the meanings of sentences, which we acquire through learning and education.

In programming languages, the alphabet consists normally of alphanumeric characters supported on computer keyboards. The grammar, that is, permitted sequences of those symbols to form 'words', and 'words' in turn to form 'instructions', is given by various means such as syntax diagrams and the BNF (Backus–Naur Formalism) notation. Since ours is not a study of programming languages, no example of these is given here, but examples can be found in many books, especially in those devoted to specific programming languages. Although the precise grammar of programming languages may be found in such sources, the most common way of explaining the meanings of programs, that is, the semantics, is through examples and in natural language. This is because most programming languages are too rich in capabilities and, as a result, require a great deal of effort if their meanings are to be defined precisely. The only language which can give that precision is mathematics, requiring expertise in both defining and understanding such descriptions. This is not to say that it cannot be done. On the contrary, there are programming languages with formally defined semantics.

The study of propositional logic as a formal language, at least in a very simplistic way as it is done here, can therefore give us an insight into formal languages of immediate relevance to computer programming.

3.2 Grammar of propositional logic

The grammar of propositional logic is defined using an *alphabet* and *syntax*, which are considered separately below.

3.2.1 The alphabet

The alphabet consists of the following:

1. Symbols for denoting propositions: *identifiers*.
   Logicians usually use single letters such as A, B, C or p, q, r.
   Sometimes subscripts are used, as in x_1, x_2.

2. Punctuation symbols
   Brackets: (,)

3. Propositional connectives
   $\neg$, $\wedge$, $\vee$, $\Rightarrow$, $\Leftrightarrow$
   From the previous chapter, we are already familiar with the intended use of these symbols.

Terminology

Sentences written using the alphabet symbols listed above are called *formulae*.

Example 3.1

1. $A \Rightarrow B \wedge \neg C$ is a formula.

2. $A\neg \Rightarrow \wedge \wedge C$ is a formula.

3. cat $\wedge$ dog (where cat and dog are English words) is not a formula since 'cat' and 'dog' have not been introduced as propositional identifiers.

3.2.2 The syntax

The syntax provides us with a set of rules for generating arbitrarily complex formulae. If a formula does not obey these rules it has no further use. These rules, or the syntax of propositional formulae as they are often called, are defined formally in the Definition.

Definition   Syntax of propositional logic

1. An identifier is a proposition (e.g. A, B, p, q).

2. If p and q are propositions then so are $\neg p$, (p), $p \wedge q$, $p \vee q$, $p \Rightarrow q$, $p \Leftrightarrow q$.

Note the recursive, or self-referential, character of the rules in the Definition with respect to propositions. That is, propositions are defined using other propositions. As a result, we can construct a formula *iteratively* or analyse it *recursively*.

For example, given propositions A, B and C, we notice from rule (2) that

$$A \Rightarrow C$$

is a grammatically correct formula and, therefore,

$$A \Rightarrow C \vee B$$

is a grammatically correct formula and, therefore,

$$A \Rightarrow C \vee B \Leftrightarrow A$$

is a grammatically correct formula and so forth. The above is an example of iterative generation of formulae.

On the other hand, we could analyse the last formula *recursively*, in effect reversing the above process. Assuming now that the formula

$$A \Rightarrow C \vee B \Leftrightarrow A$$

is given, we note from rule (2) that it is written grammatically correctly provided that each of the formulae

$$C \vee B \Leftrightarrow A, \quad A \Rightarrow C \vee B, \quad A \Rightarrow C, \quad B \Leftrightarrow A$$

is written grammatically correctly. In order to justify this, we have to examine whether the formulae which make up the latter are written grammatically correctly. Thus we question whether each of the formulae

$$C \vee B, \quad B \Leftrightarrow A, \quad A \Rightarrow C, \quad C \vee B, \quad A, \quad B, \quad C$$

is written grammatically correctly, eventually questioning whether A, B and C are correctly written. Being a set of identifiers permitted by the rule (1), the formulae A, B and C are correctly written and, hence, we conclude that the original formula is correctly written. This kind of analysis of formulae is also done by compilers (translators) that generate low-level machine-oriented languages, in particular assembly languages, from high-level programming languages. It is known in compiling as *syntax analysis*.

Generally, there is potentially an infinite number of arbitrary prime propositions denoted by identifiers. All other propositions can be built from them using propositional connectives but strictly observing the above grammatical rules.

Example 3.2

Given certain propositions, A, B and C, the above rules in effect allow us to build formulae such as the following by placing propositional connectives in grammatically correct places.

1. $A \vee B \Rightarrow \neg B \wedge C$
2. $\neg (C \wedge \neg C) \Leftrightarrow \neg A \vee B \wedge C$
3. $A \vee B \Rightarrow \neg B \wedge C \Rightarrow \neg (C \wedge \neg C) \Leftrightarrow \neg A \vee B \wedge C$
4. $A \vee B \Rightarrow \neg (B \wedge C) \Rightarrow \neg (B \vee \neg B) \Leftrightarrow \neg (A \vee B) \wedge C$

Terminology

Formulae that contain only the symbols of the agreed alphabet and obey the grammatical rules given in the Definition are called *well-formed formulae*. A common abbreviation is *wffs* (pronounced 'woofs').

Exercise 3.1 ✳

Which of the following are well-formed formulae?

1. $A \Rightarrow B \wedge \neg C$
2. $A \neg \Rightarrow \wedge \wedge C$
3. $p \wedge (q \vee r)$
4. $p \vee 2 \vee 3$
5. $p \vee p \Leftrightarrow p$
6. $p \wedge \neg q$
7. $p \vee \Rightarrow q$
8. $(p \vee q) \wedge$
9. $(p \wedge q) \vee ((q \wedge r)) \Leftrightarrow s \Rightarrow t$
10. p
11. $*\&p!$
12. $(p \vee q) \wedge \neg (p \wedge q)$
13. $p \wedge (q \wedge \neg q)$

3.2.3   Brackets: to insert them or not?

It is obvious from Example 3.2 that even a moderately long formula looks like a long train of symbols. Such a 'flat' structure can be ambiguous when we have to deal with its meaning. For example, is the formula $A \wedge B \vee C$ supposed to represent

$$(A \wedge B) \vee C \quad \text{or} \quad A \wedge (B \vee C)?$$

The way to resolve such an ambiguity is to use brackets, but a large number of brackets in a long formula can sometimes be an irritant.

In order to overcome this, let us extend the syntax with a certain convention on how to associate propositional variables with adjacent connectives. This convention is based on the *precedence* order of the connectives, which is:

Connective	Precedence
$\neg$	*highest*
$\wedge$	
$\vee$	
$\Rightarrow$	
$\Leftrightarrow$	*lowest*

According to this, the formula $A \wedge B \vee C$ in our example has to be interpreted as $(A \wedge B) \vee C$, and not as $A \wedge (B \vee C)$, because $\wedge$ has a higher precedence than $\vee$.

Precedence rules enable us to drop some of the brackets in complex formulae, thus improving readability. Remember the ordering of the connectives:

Brackets
Negation
Conjunction
Disjunction
Implication
Equivalence

We will see in Section 3.6 how this helps in the evaluation of the truth values of formulae.

Example 3.3

Precedence rules are not totally new to us – they exist in arithmetic. Here is an example. Multiplication ($\times$) has a higher precedence than addition (+). So, $2 \times 2 + 3$ means $(2 \times 2) + 3$ which equals 7, and not $2 \times (2 + 3)$ which would equal 10.

The results of getting the precedence wrong in propositional logic are just as disastrous as in arithmetic. Consider the following complex formula in propositional logic:

$$(((\neg p) \wedge q) \Rightarrow ((\neg s) \wedge (\neg t))) \Leftrightarrow ((\neg v) \vee w)$$

The formula is quite difficult to read as it stands, but if we use precedence rules to remove all the unnecessary brackets we obtain:

$$\neg p \wedge q \Rightarrow \neg s \wedge \neg t \Leftrightarrow \neg v \vee w$$

which is arguably more readable. However, we must now remember the precedence ordering of the connectives.

Exercise 3.2 ✳

1. Remove the unnecessary brackets from the following formulae.
   (a) $(p \vee (\neg q)) \Rightarrow r$
   (b) $(\neg p) \Leftrightarrow (q \Rightarrow r)$
   (c) $((\neg p) \Leftrightarrow q) \Rightarrow r$
   (d) $p \wedge (q \vee r)$

2. Insert brackets into following formulae so that we do not have to rely on precedence rules on connectives in the interpretation of formulae.
   (a) $\neg p \wedge \neg q \Rightarrow \neg r$
   (b) $\neg p \wedge (q \Rightarrow r)$
   (c) $p \Rightarrow q \vee (r \wedge \neg s)$
   (d) $p \wedge (q \vee r \Rightarrow s) \vee t \Leftrightarrow u$

(3.3) The semantics

Semantics deal with the meaning of compound propositions. Note that meanings
given to the individual prime propositions are of no concern in logic. This is because,
as discussed in Chapter 1, the purpose of logic is to reason about arguments and,
therefore, collections of propositions without getting involved in their factual truth.

Since compound propositions can be arbitrarily complex, we need some rules to
work out the truth value of any compound proposition, knowing the truth values
of its simpler parts (constituent propositions). These have been presented in
English in Section 2.2. Here we attempt a more symbolic approach.

As mentioned in Section 2.1, we use the symbol T to talk about the *property* of a
given proposition being true. Likewise we use the symbol F to talk about the *property*
of a given proposition being false. We return to a discussion about these two symbols
in Section 3.6. Here is an example illustrating this approach.

(**Example 3.4**)

Another way to present the meaning given to $\wedge$ in Section 2.2 is using the
following table. In effect, it gives a rule for determining the meaning of $p \wedge q$, for
all possible assignments of truth values to some arbitrary propositions p and q.

p	q	$p \wedge q$
T	T	T
T	F	F
F	T	F
F	F	F

We can ascertain from this table that $p \wedge q$ is true only when both p is true and q
is true. In all other cases $p \wedge q$ is false.

It is possible to present the meaning of other connectives in a similar manner.

(**Definition**) Propositional connectives

The meaning of each propositional connective is given in the following table:

p	q	$\neg p$	$p \wedge q$	$p \vee q$	$p \Rightarrow q$	$p \Leftrightarrow q$
T	T	F	T	T	T	T
T	F	F	F	T	F	F
F	T	T	F	T	T	F
F	F	T	F	F	T	T

We consult the table of propositional connectives when determining the truth value of any given formula. It is a kind of a dictionary for interpreting complex formulae knowing their simpler parts. Thus, the table in the Definition is not a truth table, which is the subject of the next section.

3.4 Truth tables

Truth tables are a concise way of computing the truth values of compound propositions, given the truth values of constituent prime propositions. In constructing a truth table, we consult the table given under the above Definition as a reference source.

Example 3.5

Compute the truth values for $(p \vee q) \Rightarrow ((p \wedge q) \vee q)$.

1. Break the formula into all its possible subformulae. In this case, the subformulae in the order of increasing complexity are:

    $p \vee q$

    $p \wedge q$

    $(p \wedge q) \vee q$

    $(p \vee q) \Rightarrow ((p \wedge q) \vee q)$

2. Construct a table allowing a column for each prime proposition and each of the compound propositions listed above.

3. Allow for enough rows to contain all possible combinations of truth values for the prime propositions. Since we have only two prime propositions we need only four rows. [How many rows do we need if we have n prime propositions?]

4. Allocate columns to subformulae from left to right, in the order of increasing complexity. At this stage, the truth table looks like this:

p	q	$p \vee q$	$p \wedge q$	$(p \wedge q) \vee q$	$(p \vee q) \Rightarrow ((p \wedge q) \vee q)$
T	T				
T	F				
F	T				
F	F				

5. Now fill in each column, using the table on page 28 for reference.

p	q	$p \vee q$	$p \wedge q$	$(p \wedge q) \vee q$	$(p \vee q) \Rightarrow ((p \wedge q) \vee q)$
T	T	T	T	T	T
T	F	T	F	F	F
F	T	T	F	T	T
F	F	F	F	F	T

6. The above is the truth table for the formulae

$$p \vee q \Rightarrow ((p \wedge q) \vee q)$$

Each row in this table gives the truth value of the above formula for a specific assignment of truth values to its prime propositions.

7. For example, if p is known to be true and q is known to be false, then we read the truth value of our formula from the second row of the truth table under the assignment of the truth value T to p and the truth value F to q. Thus, we see that it is false.

Exercise 3.3 ✳

Construct truth tables for the following compound propositions.

1. $\neg p \vee q$
2. $\neg (p \wedge q)$
3. $\neg p \vee \neg q$
4. $p \Rightarrow (q \wedge r)$
5. $p \vee (q \wedge r) \Rightarrow (p \wedge q) \vee r$

Exercise 3.4 ✳

Fill in the truth table below for the connective *exclusive 'or'* introduced in Section 2.2.1.

p	q	$p \vee q$	$p \wedge q$	$\neg (p \wedge q)$	$(p \vee q) \wedge \neg (p \wedge q)$
T	T				
T	F				
F	T				
F	F				

Exercise 3.5 ✳ ✳

Establish the circumstances under which the answers to Exercises 2.5 and 2.6 are true. Substantiate your answer using a truth table.

3.5 Tautologies, contradictions and contingent propositions

An important classification of propositions is based on the truth values each proposition can take under all possible interpretations of its constituent prime propositions. This classification leads to three different kinds of propositions: *tautologies*, *contradictions* and *contingent propositions*.

Among them, tautologies are an important class of propositions from the point of view of logic. As will be seen in Chapter 5, tautologies are closely related to the *valid argument forms* – patterns of arguments whose correctness is not in question.

In essence, the truth value of a tautology or a contradiction can be determined solely within logic, whereas the truth value of a contingent proposition has to be determined outside logic by observations or scientific enquiry.

Definition   Tautology

A *tautology* is a compound proposition which is true under all possible assignments of truth values to its prime propositions.

From the Definition, then, a tautology is a formula which has all Ts in the final column of its truth table.

Example 3.6

Show that $p \lor \neg p$ is a tautology.

We demonstrate this by constructing the truth table:

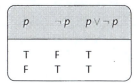

p	$\neg p$	$p \lor \neg p$
T	F	T
F	T	T

Terminology

Tautologies are also referred to as *valid propositions*.

Definition   Contradiction

A *contradiction* is a compound proposition which is false under all possible assignments of truth values to its prime propositions.

From the Definition, then, a contradiction is a formula which has all Fs in the final column of its truth table.

Example 3.7

Show that $p \wedge \neg p$ is a contradiction.

We demonstrate this by constructing the truth table:

p	$\neg p$	$p \wedge \neg p$
T	F	F
F	T	F

Terminology

Contradictions are also referred to as *inconsistent propositions* or *identically false propositions*.

Definition   Contingent proposition

A *contingent* proposition is one which is neither a tautology nor a contradiction.

From the Definition, then, a contingent proposition is a formula which has a mixture of Ts and Fs in the final column of its truth table.

Example 3.8

Show that $p \Rightarrow \neg p$ is a contingent proposition.

We demonstrate this by constructing the truth table:

p	$\neg p$	$p \Rightarrow \neg p$
T	F	F
F	T	T

It is not possible to make a general statement about the truth value of a contingent proposition. We always need to know the truth values of all or some of its prime propositions in order to comment on the truth value of the proposition as a whole.

Exercise 3.6 ✳

Determine whether each of the following is a tautology, a contradiction or a contingent proposition.

1. $p \Rightarrow p$
2. $p \wedge \neg\, p$
3. $p \wedge (q \vee p)$
4. $p \wedge \neg\, (q \Rightarrow p)$
5. $p \Rightarrow (q \Rightarrow p)$
6. $p \Rightarrow q \Leftrightarrow \neg\, p \vee q$
7. $p \wedge q \wedge \neg\, q$
8. $p \vee q \wedge \neg\, q$
9. $p \vee q \vee \neg\, q$
10. $p \Leftrightarrow (\neg\, p \wedge q)$

Let us briefly note the significance of the above classification in relation to mathematical theories (descriptions, specifications) of applications. Since they are identically true, sometimes trivially and sometimes in less obvious ways, tautologies do not provide any additional information in any mathematical theory and, therefore, may be eliminated from the theory without affecting its overall meaning. We inherit them anyway from the logical system in which the given mathematical theory is expressed.

By contrast, contradictions are important from the point of view of both logic and the application theory. Contradictory statements slip into specifications quite easily. Contradictions result in inconsistent theories where, as a result, every formula happens to be true, that is, every formula coexists with its negation, the relevant with the irrelevant, and so forth. An inconsistent theory is therefore a pretty useless theory, so it is important to be able to detect them, especially in mathematical specifications because, otherwise, the whole enterprise of mathematical reasoning becomes meaningless.

Contingent propositions express factual or material truth. In specifications some contingent propositions are explicitly stated as requirements, while others follow implicitly from the explicitly stated requirements. Note that software or system requirements are established by a 'requirement analysis', which is a software engineering activity aimed at establishing user requirements. Both categories of contingent proposition are important from the point of 'requirement validation' – a software engineering activity aimed at establishing whether the documented or inferred requirements match the user's own requirements.

3.6 Notations: T vs *true* and F vs *false*

Note that both T and F, introduced on pages 11 and 28, are not symbols belonging to the logical system we are discussing, so we should never write expressions like $A \wedge T$ or $F \wedge T$. Both T and F are just abbreviations: T for 'a given proposition being true' and F for 'a given proposition being false'.

However, quite often we need to write long formulae which are identically true or which are identically false. For these the previous section introduced the terminology 'tautology' and 'contradiction'. In order to make the distinction between references to meanings and references to some unspecified tautologies and contradictions, we introduce two more symbols, **true** and **false**, as abbreviations: **true** for any formula which happens to be identically true, and **false** for any formula which happens to be identically false. For example,

$$\left. \begin{array}{r} A \vee \neg A \\ A \wedge B \Rightarrow B \wedge A \\ \neg (A \wedge B) \Rightarrow \neg B \vee \neg A \end{array} \right\} \textit{true}$$

are some formulae which come under **true**, whereas

$$\left. \begin{array}{r} A \wedge \neg A \\ A \Leftrightarrow \neg A \\ A \wedge B \wedge \neg A \end{array} \right\} \textit{false}$$

are some formulae which come under **false**.

With the above symbols, we are permitted to write, for example, expressions like $A \wedge \textit{true}$ or $\textit{false} \wedge \textit{true}$, because **true** and **false** stand for some unknown formulae which just happen to be identically true and false respectively.

Example 3.9

This exercise is related to the material in Section 3.2.3. Consider the following expression. Is it true or false?

$$\textit{true} \vee \textit{false} \Rightarrow \neg (\textit{true} \wedge \textit{true}) \Leftrightarrow \textit{true} \wedge \textit{false}$$

Using the precedence rules and the table on page 28 defining the meaning of the propositional connectives, we can evaluate the truth value of the expression one step at a time, starting with the brackets, as follows:

Brackets   Evaluate the contents of any brackets first. So we get:
                 $\textit{true} \vee \textit{false} \Rightarrow \neg \textit{true} \Leftrightarrow \textit{true} \wedge \textit{false}$
Negation $\textit{true} \vee \textit{false} \Rightarrow \textit{false} \Leftrightarrow \textit{true} \wedge \textit{false}$
Conjunction $\textit{true} \vee \textit{false} \Rightarrow \textit{false} \Leftrightarrow \textit{false}$
Disjunction $\textit{true} \Rightarrow \textit{false} \Leftrightarrow \textit{false}$
Implication $\textit{false} \Leftrightarrow \textit{false}$
Equivalence $\textit{true}$

Hence, the truth value of the expression as a whole is true.

In summary, when we say that 'the proposition A has a truth value T' what we mean is that the proposition A is true. On the other hand, **true** stands for an unspecified formula which is identically true. A similar description applies to F and **false**. We write T and F in truth tables, because there we deal with semantics, and we write **true** and **false** in formulae, because there we deal with syntax.

Evaluate the truth values of the following formulae as either T (for true) or F (for false).

1. *true* ∧ *false*

2. *false* ∨ *true*

3. *false* ⇒ *false*

4. *true* ∨ *true*

5. ¬ *false* ∧ *true*

6. ¬ ¬ *false* ∨ *false*

7. (*true* ∧ *false*) ∨ (¬ *false* ∧ ¬ *false*)

8. *true* ⇒ *true* ∧ ¬ *true*

9. ¬ (*true* ∧ ¬ *false*) ⇔ *true* ⇒ *false* ∨ *true*

3.7 Logical equivalence and logical implication

It is important to appreciate the meaning of logical equivalence and logical implication before beginning the topic on proofs in propositional logic in Chapter 4.

Description Logical equivalence

Two formulae are *logically equivalent* if and only if their equivalence is a tautology or, in other words, they have identical truth values under all possible assignments of truth values to their prime propositions.

The symbol used for logical equivalence is ⟺.

Example 3.10

Consider the following formulae.

1. $p \wedge q \Leftrightarrow q \wedge p$. This is a tautology (check it!). We could therefore write $p \wedge q \Longleftrightarrow q \wedge p$. Whatever truth values are assigned to the prime propositions, p and q, the formula $p \wedge q \Leftrightarrow q \wedge p$ is always true.

2. $p \Leftrightarrow q$. The truth of this formula entirely depends on the truth of p and q. It is a contingent proposition and, therefore, is not a logical equivalence.

(**Description**) Logical implication
_____

> A formula p is said to *logically imply* a formula q if and only if the implication
> $p \Rightarrow q$ is a tautology.

_____

The symbol used for logical implication is $\Rightarrow$.

(**Example 3.11**)
_____

Consider the following formulae.

1. $p \wedge q \Rightarrow q$. This is a tautology (check it!). We could therefore write $p \wedge q \Rrightarrow q$. Whatever truth values are assigned to the prime propositions, p and q, the formula $p \wedge q \Rightarrow q$ is always true.

2. $p \Rightarrow q \vee r$. The truth of this formula depends entirely upon the truth of p, q and r. It is a contingent proposition and therefore not a logical implication.

(**Example 3.12**)
_____

The following examples demonstrate the nature of truth of some sentences.

1. **Napoleon would have remained Emperor if and only if he had won the Borodin Battle.**
   A plausible material equivalence.

2. **Napoleon would have won the Borodin Battle if and only if Kutuzov won it.**
   Material equivalence. It happens to be a contradiction in the given historical context since Napoleon and Kutuzov were actually opponents.

3. **Eclipses occur if and only if the moon comes in between the Sun and the Earth.**
   Material equivalence. It is a true statement with respect to our solar system.

4. **Kutuzov won the Borodin Battle if and only if it was not the case that Kutuzov did not win the Borodin Battle.**
   Logical equivalence and is a tautology.

5. **Kutuzov won the Borodin Battle if and only if Kutuzov did not win the Borodin Battle.**
   An equivalence, but is a logical contradiction.

_____

Note

The symbols $\Leftrightarrow$ and $\Rightarrow$ are not part of the language of propositional logic. Recall that they did not appear in the syntax definition. Each of them conveys two pieces of knowledge. First, that we are dealing with an equivalence or an implication as understood under $\Leftrightarrow$ or $\Rightarrow$, which are part of the syntax. Secondly, that the formula concerned is identically true, whereby we are making a statement about semantics. We write $p \Leftrightarrow q$ or $p \Rightarrow q$ to convey both these pieces of information.

3.8 An application: digital circuits

A variant of propositional logic, known as *Boolean algebra*, serves as the theoretical framework for the design of digital circuits at the so-called digital logic level – the hardware level of computers and various electronic devices. The term 'Boolean algebra' should remind us of George Boole, the author of propositional logic mentioned in Chapter 1. A detailed discussion of Boolean algebra appears in Chapter 19.

3.8.1 Gates

Digital circuits are made out of tiny primitive devices called *gates*, which are capable of computing various logical functions. Their inputs and outputs are binary digital values, usually represented by digits 0 and 1. At the physical level, 1 corresponds to an electrical pulse, the emission and duration (width) of which in time is controlled precisely by a clock. On the other hand, 0 corresponds to the absence of such a pulse.

Figure 3.1 shows the symbols for three such gates, *not*, *and* and *or*, along with a description of their function using truth tables expressed, not with familiar truth values T and F, but instead with binary digits 1 and 0 respectively. The *and* gate, for example, is a device which produces an output 1 when both its two inputs A and B are 1s and produces 0 otherwise. The associated truth table depicts this intended behaviour. For all three types of gate, the figure also shows the relationship of the input and output variables A, B and O in propositional logic, treating them as propositional variables. Needless to say, there is a remarkable similarity between the propositional connectives $\neg$, $\wedge$ and $\vee$ on one hand and the gates *not*, *and* and *or* on the other, except for the rather superficial use of 1 and 0 instead of T and F. What, then, is the difference?

One of the differences is that gates distinguish between input signals and the output signal, whereas formulae in propositional logic have no such notion. In other words, the inputs are knowns and the output is an unknown dependent on the inputs. Another difference is that there is a signal propagation delay through the gate between the time of arrival of input signals (pulses) and the generation of the output signal. This is not very significant in the case of primitive gates, but must be considered in the case of large circuits built by cascading such primitive gates. Propositional formulae thus describe the state of gates and digital devices after they become stable following changes in input signals.

Digital logic:

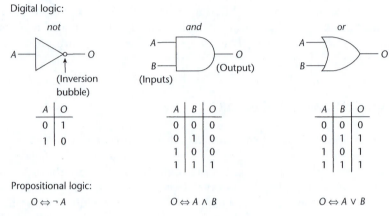

Propositional logic:

$O \Leftrightarrow \neg A$ $O \Leftrightarrow A \wedge B$ $O \Leftrightarrow A \vee B$

Figure 3.1 Gates *not, and* and *or:* symbols and truth tables

Digital logic:

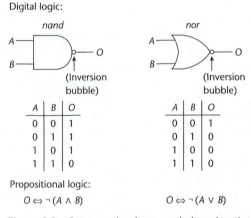

Propositional logic:

$O \Leftrightarrow \neg (A \wedge B)$ $O \Leftrightarrow \neg (A \vee B)$

Figure 3.2 Gates *nand* and *nor:* symbols and truth tables of gate function

Note also that there are no gates corresponding to propositional connectives $\Rightarrow$ and $\Leftrightarrow$, but this can be easily justified on the grounds that they are not really primitive connectives and can be defined in terms of other connectives and, therefore, are abbreviations for formulae written using connectives $\neg$, $\wedge$ or $\neg$, $\vee$. (This is the subject of question 5 in Exercise 4.11.) Therefore, given a need for gates corresponding to $\Rightarrow$ and $\Leftrightarrow$, they can be built using the primitive gates.

Despite lacking any standard gates for $\Rightarrow$ and $\Leftrightarrow$, digital logic uses two other gates as primitive building blocks: *nand* and *nor* gates, shown in Figure 3.2. In fact, these two gates are used in practice more often than their counterparts *and* and *or* because they require fewer transistors: *nand* and *nor* require two transistors each, whereas *and* and *or* need three each.

3.8.2   Designing circuits

Let us now consider how electronics engineers use the gates described above to develop higher-level devices for various applications. Consider, for example, a control device intended to monitor and control a physical process such as a boiler. We consider two such examples – a gas burner and a patient monitoring system – in Examples 3.13 and 3.14.

Example 3.13

A gas burner consists of a gas valve controlling the flow of gas to the burner, a sensor indicating whether the flame is burning, a sensor monitoring any gas leakage and a watchdog timer monitoring leakage durations. Gas can leak when the gas valve is closed. Gas is also assumed to leak when the gas valve is open but the flame is not burning. A safety-critical requirement is that the gas valve is closed in both cases of gas leakage when the accumulated duration exceeds a specified fraction of time over a certain given period of time. This information is provided here by the watchdog timer. Note that closing the gas valve is a *fail-safe* operation – an operation that eliminates the exposure to risks associated with any gas leakage.

In a scenario such as this, certain combinations of states cannot prevail. For example, without a leakage or gas flow, it does not make sense if the watchdog timer is activated. Let us ignore such interactions and dependencies for the time being. The states of the gas burner of interest to safety concerns can be described as follows:

Inputs/outputs	Meaning
G	**Gas** valve is open.
B	Flame is **burning**.
L	Gas is **leaking**.
W	**Watchdog** timer raises alarm.
C	Request the gas valve to be **closed**.

The monitoring part, that is, sensors, samples the values of certain *state variables* and enables the control device to establish the current state of the process. The device is provided with this information as some inputs G, B, L and W. The designer of the device is provided by the process engineers with the values of G, B, L and W that should invoke the activator, which in this case closes the valve. So the device must produce an appropriate value for the output C which can be fed into the actuator as an input.

A device producing just one output in this manner is called a *recognizer*, because the task is to 'recognize' in the input states the need for a further action. The information provided by the process engineer for such a recognizer may then be presented as an *input/output table*. Table 3.1 is such a table for instructing the valve closure.

Table 3.1 Instructions for valve closure for Example 3.13.

Line	Inputs				Output
	G	B	L	W	C
1	0	0	0	0	0
2	0	0	0	1	0
3	0	0	1	0	0
4	0	0	1	1	1
5	0	1	0	0	0
6	0	1	0	1	0
7	0	1	1	0	0
8	0	1	1	1	0
9	1	0	0	0	0
10	1	0	0	1	1
11	1	0	1	0	0
12	1	0	1	1	1
13	1	1	0	0	0
14	1	1	0	1	0
15	1	1	1	0	0
16	1	1	1	1	0

The above input/output table specifies precisely the circumstances under which the valve must be closed. According to row 10, for example, a request for closing the valve is to be made if the gas is flowing but not burning, even if there is no leakage.

Note that certain combinations of inputs such as those on rows 9 and 10, may never occur or may be unrealistic. In such cases the actual value of the output may be irrelevant from the point of view of the application. For the purpose of illustrating the application of digital logic let us now consider a simpler scenario.

Example 3.14

A patient monitoring system, which monitors a patient with a particular disorder, is provided with patient's temperature, blood pressure and pulse rate. The following table gives threshold values of these parameters requiring the raising of an alarm for medical assistance.

Description of states

Inputs/outputs	Meaning
A	Patient's temperature is in the range 36–40 °C.
B	Patient's systolic blood pressure is outside the range 80–160 mm.
C	Patient's pulse rate is outside the range 60–120 beats per minute.
O	Raising the alarm is necessary.

Input/output table for the recognizer

The idea is that the alarm is to be raised for $O = 1$, which occurs only for the values of A, B and C in the highlighted rows of Table 3.2. Thus, according to the fourth row indicated by $\leftarrow$, the alarm is to be raised when both blood pressure and pulse rates are outside the relevant ranges of values. In real life this kind of information is provided to the circuit designer by the medical expert.

The first step in developing a circuit is to work out for it the required logic. This can be done in several ways. We propose a logic based on a truth table, the construction of which has been guided by the formula

$$(\neg A \wedge B \wedge C) \vee (A \wedge \neg B \wedge C) \vee (A \wedge B \wedge \neg C) \vee (A \wedge B \wedge C)$$

where each disjunct corresponds to a row where the output O is 1. The solution given below does not match exactly the above formula. (We justify the solution adopted in the next chapter.)

Table 3.2   I/O table for Example 3.14.

A	B	C	O	
0	0	0	0	
0	0	1	0	
0	1	0	0	
0	1	1	1	$\leftarrow$
1	0	0	0	
1	0	1	1	
1	1	0	1	
1	1	1	1	

Truth table for a particular design of the recognizer

Table 3.3 may now be used in developing, as shown in Figure 3.3, an equivalent graphical layout for the circuit.

According to this diagram, each of the inputs A, B and C is fed into two gates. The *and* gates 1, 2 and 3 perform the logical function enumerated under columns 4, 5, and 6 respectively in the truth table. The *or* gate 4 performs

Table 3.3   Truth table for a particular design in Example 3.14

A	B	C	and (A,B)	and (A,C)	and (B,C)	or (and (A, B), and (A, C))	O = or(or(and (A, B), and (A, C)), and (B, C))
1	2	3	4	5	6	7	8
0	0	0	0	0	0	0	0
0	0	1	0	0	0	0	0
0	1	0	0	0	0	0	0
0	1	1	0	0	1	0	1
1	0	0	0	0	0	0	0
1	0	1	0	1	0	1	1
1	1	0	1	0	0	1	1
1	1	1	1	1	1	1	1

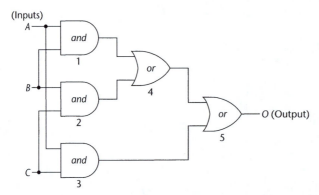

Figure 3.3   A digital circuit for the patient monitoring system of Example 3.14.

the logical function given by column 7 using the outputs produced by gates 1 and 2. The *or* gate 5 then produces the final output according to column 8 by using the outputs produced by gates 3 and 4.

Exercise 3.8 ✳

Reconstruct the input/output tables used in the design of the digital circuits shown in Figures 3.4–3.6.

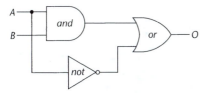

Figure 3.4   First digital circuit for Exercise 3.8.

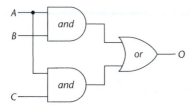

Figure 3.5   Second digital circuit for Exercise 3.8.

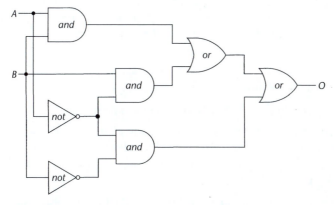

Figure 3.6   Third digital circuit for Exercise 3.8.

Exercise 3.9 ✳✳

Construct a digital circuit for each of the following input/output tables.

1. A recognizer with two inputs.

A	B	O
0	0	0
0	1	1
1	0	1
1	1	0

What does this digital circuit compute?

2. A recognizer with three inputs.

A	B	C	O
0	0	0	1
0	0	1	0
0	1	0	1
0	1	1	0
1	0	0	0
1	0	1	1
1	1	0	0
1	1	1	0

Suggest an application where this digital circuit could have a use.

Exercise 3.10 ✳✳✳

Think of an application and a recognizer involving just three inputs for performing a particular task of the application. Produce the input/output table for the desired recognizer and construct a digital circuit implementing it.

Exercise 3.11 ✳✳

Here are some general questions.

1. Can a prime proposition be a tautology or a contradiction?
2. What is the difference between formulae in general and well-formed formulae? Is it possible to determine the truth value of an ill-formed formula?
3. What is the distinction between the table in the definition on page 28 and the table in Example 3.5?
4. Why do computer scientists need to know about tautologies, contradictions and contingent contradictions?
5. 'Syntax is more important than semantics'. Discuss this statement.

Chapter 4

Transformational proofs

Topic: Proofs in propositional logic

If we take in our hand any volume; of divinity or school metaphysics, for instance; let us ask:

Does it contain any abstract reasoning concerning quantity or number? No. Does it contain any experimental reasoning, concerning matter of fact and existence? No.

Commit it then to the flames: for it can contain nothing but sophistry and illusion.

David Hume

Scottish philosopher, historian and economist (1711–76)

Objectives

On completion of this chapter you should be able to:

- Prove the equivalence of formulae using truth tables.
- Remember and use the laws of equivalence.
- Carry out a transformational proof.
- Simplify conditionals in computer programs.
- Simplify digital circuits.

In natural language we are often able to express the same idea in several different ways. The same is true in logic as well as in programming. However, since in logic the meaning is concealed by symbols, it is not always easy to establish whether two formulae are identical in meaning. Transformational proof is the kind of reasoning which allows just that in such situations.

Transformational proofs have other uses too. Conditionals in programs and Boolean expressions relating inputs and outputs of digital circuits are just two areas with immediate applications of such proofs, which often enable the simplification of the relevant logical formulae. The last two sections of this chapter demonstrate how this can be done.

4.1 Logical laws and how to establish them

Chapter 3 discussed the equivalence of propositions and tautologies. Continuing this discussion here, we will learn how to demonstrate that any given two formulae are logically equivalent. There are two approaches: using truth tables and transformational proofs.

4.1.1   Truth tables and logical laws

The notion of logical law is based on the notion of logical equivalence, introduced in Chapter 3. Let us restate in a slightly different form the definition of logical equivalence given there.

(**Description**)   Logical equivalence

Two formulae are *logically equivalent* if and only if they are identical in meaning.

The Description means that we can use any two logically equivalent formulae interchangeably. Given an occurrence of one, we can replace it with its logically equivalent counterpart without affecting the meaning of the original formula. This is what we intend to exploit when transforming formulae into simpler forms.

Recall that, in a truth table incorporating logically equivalent formulae, those formulae have identical columns. We can use this property to establish some basic logical equivalences to be used as logical laws. Some candidate logical laws are given in Examples 4.1 and 4.2.

(**Example 4.1**)

1. $p \Leftrightarrow p \vee p$

   Demonstration of this logical equivalence is by the truth table:

p	$p \vee p$
T	T
F	F

2. $p \vee q \Leftrightarrow q \vee p$

   Demonstration of this logical equivalence is by the truth table (examine the last two columns):

p	q	$p \vee q$	$q \vee p$
T	T	T	T
T	F	T	T
F	T	T	T
F	F	F	F

Another way to show that two formulae are logically equivalent is to show that the equivalence of the formulae is a tautology (recall the definition on page 35). This is demonstrated in Example 4.2.

Example 4.2

$(p \vee q) \vee r \Leftrightarrow p \vee (q \vee r)$

We can demonstrate this by showing that $(p \vee q) \vee r \Leftrightarrow p \vee (q \vee r)$ is a tautology. Table 4.1 sets out the truth table.

Table 4.1   Truth table for Example 4.2.

p	q	r	$p \vee q$	$(p \vee q) \vee r$	$q \vee r$	$p \vee (q \vee r)$	$(p \vee q) \vee r \Leftrightarrow$ $p \vee (q \vee r)$
T	T	T	T	T	T	T	T
T	T	F	T	T	T	T	T
T	F	T	T	T	T	T	T
T	F	F	T	T	F	T	T
F	T	T	T	T	T	T	T
F	T	F	T	T	T	T	T
F	F	T	F	T	T	T	T
F	F	F	F	F	F	F	T

Indeed it is a tautology because the last column of Table 4.1 contains only Ts.

Exercise 4.1 ✳

Using truth tables, demonstrate the following logical equivalences.

1. $\neg (\neg p) \Leftrightarrow p$
2. $p \Rightarrow q \Leftrightarrow \neg p \vee q$
3. $\neg (p \wedge q) \Leftrightarrow \neg p \vee \neg q$
4. $p \Leftrightarrow q \Leftrightarrow (p \Rightarrow q) \wedge (q \Rightarrow p)$

4.1.2   New logical laws from the already known ones

As Example 4.2 may have demonstrated, the use of truth tables becomes increasingly tedious as the number of variables increases. With four variables, there will be 2^4 rows, that is, 16 rows. With five variables there will be 2^5, or 32 rows, and so on. It has become necessary to find an alternative.

Once we agree upon a small number of logical equivalences, as we are about to do, it is possible to use them to establish further equivalences. Why not use this as an alternative?

First, let us list the equivalences we have established so far and give them some names (Table 4.2).

Table 4.2 Some laws of logic.

Logical equivalence	Its name as a law
$p \Leftrightarrow p \vee p$	Idempotence of $\vee$
$p \vee q \Leftrightarrow q \vee p$	Commutativity of $\vee$
$(p \vee q) \vee r \Leftrightarrow p \vee (q \vee r)$	Associativity of $\vee$
$\neg(\neg p) \Leftrightarrow p$	Negation law
$p \Rightarrow q \Leftrightarrow \neg p \vee q$	Law of implication
$\neg(p \wedge q) \Leftrightarrow \neg p \vee \neg q$	De Morgan's first law
$p \Leftrightarrow q \Leftrightarrow (p \Rightarrow q) \wedge (q \Rightarrow p)$	Law of equivalence

The laws in Table 4.2 allow us to transform a formula into a different form. Example 4.3 shows how to use them to *prove* some more logical equivalences.

Example 4.3

1. The following is a proof that $\neg(p \vee q) \Leftrightarrow \neg p \wedge \neg q$ (De Morgan's second law). Start from the formula on the left-hand side of $\Leftrightarrow$ as follows:

$$\neg(p \vee q) \Leftrightarrow \neg(\neg(\neg p) \vee \neg(\neg q)) \qquad \text{negation law}$$
$$\Leftrightarrow \neg(\neg(\neg p \wedge \neg q)) \qquad \text{De Morgan's first law}$$
$$\Leftrightarrow \neg p \wedge \neg q \qquad \text{negation law}$$

2. Next, a proof that $p \wedge p \Leftrightarrow p$ (idempotence of $\wedge$):

$$p \wedge p \Leftrightarrow \neg(\neg p) \wedge \neg(\neg p) \qquad \text{negation law}$$
$$\Leftrightarrow \neg(\neg p \vee \neg p) \qquad \text{De Morgan's second law}$$
$$\Leftrightarrow \neg(\neg p) \qquad \text{idempotence of } \vee$$
$$\Leftrightarrow p \qquad \text{negation law}$$

3. Now, a proof that $p \wedge q \Leftrightarrow q \wedge p$ (commutativity of $\wedge$):

$$p \wedge q \Leftrightarrow \neg(\neg p) \wedge \neg(\neg q) \qquad \text{negation law}$$
$$\Leftrightarrow \neg(\neg p \vee \neg q) \qquad \text{De Morgan's second law}$$
$$\Leftrightarrow \neg(\neg q \vee \neg p) \qquad \text{commutativity of } \vee$$
$$\Leftrightarrow \neg(\neg q) \wedge \neg(\neg p) \qquad \text{De Morgan's second law}$$
$$\Leftrightarrow q \wedge p \qquad \text{negation law}$$

Exercise 4.2 ✳✳

The following logical equivalences have been proved using the laws we have established so far (including those in the above examples). Provide the *names of the laws* used in each step of the proofs below.

1. $p \Leftrightarrow q \Longleftrightarrow q \Leftrightarrow p$ (commutativity of $\Leftrightarrow$)

Proof

$$
\begin{aligned}
p \Leftrightarrow q &\Longleftrightarrow (p \Rightarrow q) \wedge (q \Rightarrow p) \\
&\Longleftrightarrow (q \Rightarrow p) \wedge (p \Rightarrow q) \\
&\Longleftrightarrow q \Leftrightarrow p
\end{aligned}
$$

....
....
....

2. $p \Rightarrow q \Longleftrightarrow \neg q \Rightarrow \neg p$ (contrapositive law)

Proof

$$
\begin{aligned}
p \Rightarrow q &\Longleftrightarrow \neg p \vee q \\
&\Longleftrightarrow q \vee \neg p \\
&\Longleftrightarrow \neg(\neg q) \vee \neg p \\
&\Longleftrightarrow \neg q \Rightarrow \neg p
\end{aligned}
$$

....
....
....
....

3. $p \wedge (q \wedge r) \Longleftrightarrow (p \wedge q) \wedge r$ (associativity of $\wedge$)

Proof

$$
\begin{aligned}
p \wedge (q \wedge r) & \\
&\Longleftrightarrow p \wedge \neg\neg(q \wedge r) \\
&\Longleftrightarrow p \wedge \neg(\neg q \vee \neg r) \\
&\Longleftrightarrow \neg\neg(p \wedge (\neg(\neg q \vee \neg r))) \\
&\Longleftrightarrow \neg(\neg p \vee \neg(\neg(\neg q \vee \neg r))) \\
&\Longleftrightarrow \neg(\neg p \vee (\neg q \vee \neg r)) \\
&\Longleftrightarrow \neg((\neg p \vee \neg q) \vee \neg r) \\
&\Longleftrightarrow \neg(\neg(p \wedge q) \vee \neg r) \\
&\Longleftrightarrow \neg\neg(p \wedge q) \wedge \neg\neg r \\
&\Longleftrightarrow (p \wedge q) \wedge r
\end{aligned}
$$

....
....
....
....
....
....
....
....
....

(4.2) The logical laws listed

(Description) Logical laws

Logical laws are a collection of specially chosen logical equivalences.

Below is a complete list of the equivalence laws used later in proofs. We have already established many of them. If in doubt of any, try them as exercises.

Most of these laws are intuitive. Those which may require a special effort to remember are marked with a ◀ on the right.

Commutative laws

$$
\begin{aligned}
p \wedge q &\Longleftrightarrow q \wedge p & \textbf{(4.1)} \\
p \vee q &\Longleftrightarrow q \vee p & \textbf{(4.2)} \\
(p \Leftrightarrow q) &\Longleftrightarrow (q \Leftrightarrow p) & \textbf{(4.3)}
\end{aligned}
$$

That is, the order of the propositions appearing on either side of $\wedge$, $\vee$ and $\Leftrightarrow$ is immaterial. [Note that the connective $\Rightarrow$ does not appear under these laws. Why?]

Associative laws

$$p \wedge (q \wedge r) \Longleftrightarrow (p \wedge q) \wedge r \qquad \textbf{(4.4)}$$
$$p \vee (q \vee r) \Longleftrightarrow (p \vee q) \vee r \qquad \textbf{(4.5)}$$

That is, the order of evaluation of a series of conjunctions or a series of disjunctions is immaterial.

Distributive laws

$$p \vee (q \wedge r) \Longleftrightarrow (p \vee q) \wedge (p \vee r) \qquad \textbf{(4.6)}$$
$$p \wedge (q \vee r) \Longleftrightarrow (p \wedge q) \vee (p \wedge r) \qquad \textbf{(4.7)}$$

Remember these laws by drawing a parallel with the following in arithmetic:

$$a \times (b + c) = a \times b + a \times c$$

De Morgan's laws

$$\neg (p \wedge q) \Longleftrightarrow \neg p \vee \neg q \qquad \blacktriangleleft \textbf{(4.8)}$$
$$\neg (p \vee q) \Longleftrightarrow \neg p \wedge \neg q \qquad \blacktriangleleft \textbf{(4.9)}$$

The laws to get rid of too many negatives in speech! For example, if someone is saying that 'I am neither x nor y', that person is really saying that 'I am not x and I am not y', which, according to (4.9), is equivalent to 'It is not the case that I am x or y'.

Law of negation

$$\neg (\neg p) \Longleftrightarrow p \qquad \textbf{(4.10)}$$

A doubly negated proposition is identical to the original proposition.

Law of excluded middle

$$p \vee \neg p \Longleftrightarrow \textbf{true} \qquad \textbf{(4.11)}$$

Every proposition has a truth value, namely, T or F. This is a fundamental premise in classical logic.

Law of contradiction

$$p \wedge \neg p \Longleftrightarrow \textbf{false} \qquad \textbf{(4.12)}$$

No proposition can be both true and false.

Law of implication

$$p \Rightarrow q \Leftrightarrow \neg p \vee q \qquad \qquad \blacktriangleleft \text{(4.13)}$$

Implication is really an abbreviation of a slightly more complex looking formula.

Contrapositive law

$$p \Rightarrow q \Leftrightarrow \neg q \Rightarrow \neg p \qquad \qquad \blacktriangleleft \text{(4.14)}$$

This shows why the implication did not appear under the commutative laws given above.

Law of equivalence

$$(p \Leftrightarrow q) \Leftrightarrow (p \Rightarrow q) \wedge (q \Rightarrow p) \qquad \qquad \text{(4.15)}$$

Equivalence is really an abbreviation for a fairly long formula involving two implications. For this reason, equivalence is often called a *bi-implication*.

Idempotence

$$p \vee p \Leftrightarrow p \qquad \qquad \text{(4.16)}$$
$$p \wedge p \Leftrightarrow p \qquad \qquad \text{(4.17)}$$

Two laws to remove redundancies in sentences.

Laws of simplification I

$$p \wedge \textbf{true} \Leftrightarrow p \qquad \qquad \text{(4.18)}$$
$$p \vee \textbf{true} \Leftrightarrow \textbf{true} \qquad \qquad \text{(4.19)}$$
$$p \wedge \textbf{false} \Leftrightarrow \textbf{false} \qquad \qquad \text{(4.20)}$$
$$p \vee \textbf{false} \Leftrightarrow p \qquad \qquad \text{(4.21)}$$

These show the special status of **true** and **false** in logic. See also Example 4.4.

Laws of simplification II

$$p \vee (p \wedge q) \Leftrightarrow p \qquad \qquad \blacktriangleleft \text{(4.22)}$$
$$p \wedge (p \vee q) \Leftrightarrow p \qquad \qquad \blacktriangleleft \text{(4.23)}$$

Although they are marked as difficult to remember, these two laws are fairly intuitive. Consider, for example, formula (4.22). The formula on the left-hand side is a disjunction where each disjunct contains p. That is, the left-hand side implies the right-hand side. If we consider the formula on the right-hand side, we see that p implies the formula p taken in disjunction with any other formula, including $p \wedge q$. The two implications confirm the logical equivalence.

Note, however, following our discussion in Section 3.6 of the previous chapter, we do not write T but *true* in formulae such as (4.11), (4.18) and (4.19). The same applies to F and *false* in formulae (4.12), (4.20) and (4.21). Example 4.4 is intended to reinforce this distinction.

Example 4.4

Demonstration of formula (4.18): $p \land true \Leftrightarrow p$

p	$true$	$p \land true$	$p \land true \Leftrightarrow p$
T	T	T	T
F	T	F	T

Since the final column has only Ts, the relevant equivalence is a logical equivalence expressing a law.

4.3 On the art of proofs

On page 48 we saw some simple proofs using logical laws. It is time now to consider why these proofs work. There are two rules implicit in this kind of proof:

1. *Rule of substitution*
   We can always substitute a logically equivalent formula for a sub-formula embedded in a much larger formula without affecting its meaning.

2. *Rule of transitivity*

   if $p \Leftrightarrow q$ and $q \Leftrightarrow r$ then $p \Leftrightarrow r$

   If every step in a proof is carried out using a logical equivalence, then every pair of formulae appearing anywhere in the chain of the complete proof are logically equivalent to each another.

The best way to learn how to do this kind of proof is to practise. One must become familiar with the logical laws and learn which ones to apply under different circumstances. However, keep the following points in mind:

1. The solution may require translating between formulae containing different connectives.

2. Where formulae seem very complex, it is often a good idea to treat a complex subformula as a single fictitious variable. This will help you to identify the general structure (form) of the formula. Then look for a law with a matching form.

Example 4.5

Prove that the following formula is a tautology.

$$\neg q \wedge (p \Rightarrow q) \Rightarrow \neg p$$

Proof

Our task is to show that the formula is logically equivalent to **true**. Here is a series of transformations doing that.

$$\neg q \wedge (p \Rightarrow q) \Rightarrow \neg p$$

$\Leftrightarrow \neg q \wedge (\neg p \vee q) \Rightarrow \neg p$	implication law
$\Leftrightarrow (\neg q \wedge \neg p) \vee (\neg q \wedge q) \Rightarrow \neg p$	distributivity
$\Leftrightarrow (\neg q \wedge \neg p) \vee$ **false** $\Rightarrow \neg p$	contradiction
$\Leftrightarrow \neg q \wedge \neg p \Rightarrow \neg p$	simplification
$\Leftrightarrow \neg (q \vee p) \Rightarrow \neg p$	De Morgan's law
$\Leftrightarrow \neg (\neg (q \vee p)) \vee \neg p$	implication law
$\Leftrightarrow (q \vee p) \vee \neg p$	negation law
$\Leftrightarrow q \vee (p \vee \neg p)$	associativity
$\Leftrightarrow q \vee$ **true**	simplification
$\Leftrightarrow$ **true**	simplification

This law is called *modus tollens* and is discussed in Chapter 5.

Exercise 4.3 ✳✳

Complete the missing annotation and steps in the following proofs.

1. $p \Rightarrow (q \Rightarrow r) \Leftrightarrow (p \Rightarrow q) \Rightarrow (p \Rightarrow r)$

   Proof:

$$p \Rightarrow (q \Rightarrow r)$$

$\Leftrightarrow p \Rightarrow (\neg q \vee r)$	....
$\Leftrightarrow$	implication law
$\Leftrightarrow (\neg p \vee \neg q) \vee r$	....
$\Leftrightarrow ($**true** $\wedge (\neg p \vee \neg q)) \vee r$	....
$\Leftrightarrow ((\neg p \vee p) \wedge (\neg p \vee \neg q)) \vee r$	....
$\Leftrightarrow$	distributivity
$\Leftrightarrow ((p \wedge \neg q) \vee \neg p) \vee r$	....
$\Leftrightarrow$	associativity
$\Leftrightarrow \neg \neg (p \wedge \neg q) \vee (\neg p \vee r)$	....
$\Leftrightarrow \neg (\neg p \vee \neg \neg q) \vee (\neg p \vee r)$	....
$\Leftrightarrow \neg (\neg p \vee q) \vee (\neg p \vee r)$	....
$\Leftrightarrow$	negation law
$\Leftrightarrow (\neg p \vee q) \Rightarrow (\neg p \vee r)$	implication law
$\Leftrightarrow$	....
$\Leftrightarrow (p \Rightarrow q) \Rightarrow (p \Rightarrow r)$	....

2. $p \wedge (p \Rightarrow q) \Rightarrow q \Leftrightarrow$ *true*

Proof:

$p \wedge (p \Rightarrow q) \Rightarrow q$
$\Leftrightarrow$ ....   implication law
$\Leftrightarrow (p \wedge \neg p) \vee (p \wedge q) \Rightarrow q$ ....
$\Leftrightarrow$ ....   simplification
$\Leftrightarrow$ ....   simplification
$\Leftrightarrow \neg (p \wedge q) \vee q$ ....
$\Leftrightarrow$ ....
$\Leftrightarrow (\neg p \vee \neg q) \vee q$ negation law
$\Leftrightarrow$ ....   associativity
$\Leftrightarrow$ ....   excluded middle
$\Leftrightarrow$ *true*   simplification

Exercise 4.4 ✳✳

Complete the missing annotation and steps in the following proofs.

1. $(p \vee q) \wedge (\neg p \vee q) \Leftrightarrow q$

Proof:

$(p \vee q) \wedge (\neg p \vee q)$
$\Leftrightarrow (q \vee p) \wedge (\neg p \vee q)$ ....
$\Leftrightarrow (q \vee p) \wedge (q \vee \neg p)$ ....
$\Leftrightarrow$ ....   distributivity
$\Leftrightarrow$ ....
$\Leftrightarrow q$ ....

2. $(p \vee q) \vee (\neg p \wedge \neg q) \Leftrightarrow$ *true*

Proof:

$(p \vee q) \vee (\neg p \wedge \neg q)$
$\Leftrightarrow$ ....   De Morgan's law
$\Leftrightarrow$ ....
$\Leftrightarrow$ ....
$\Leftrightarrow$ *true*   ....

Exercise 4.5 ✳✳

Prove the following logical equivalences.

1. $(p \vee q) \wedge (\neg p \wedge \neg q) \Leftrightarrow$ *false*

2. $\neg (\neg (p \vee q) \vee \neg (p \vee r)) \Leftrightarrow p \vee (q \wedge r)$

3. $(p \vee q) \wedge \neg (p \wedge q) \Leftrightarrow (p \wedge \neg q) \vee (\neg p \wedge q)$

4. $(\neg (p \wedge q) \vee (p \vee q)) \wedge (\neg (p \vee q) \vee (p \wedge q)) \Leftrightarrow (\neg p \wedge \neg q) \vee (p \wedge q)$

Show that the following pairs of sentences are logically equivalent.

1. (Use prime propositions C, B and W)
   (a) *If you are not a crustacean then you have bones or you would wriggle along the ground.*
   (b) *If you are not a crustacean and you do not have bones then you would wriggle along the ground.*

2. (Use prime propositions L, W and C)
   (a) *If you are not lazy then you work hard or you are clever and lazy.*
   (b) *You work hard or you are lazy.*

4.3   An application: programming

4.3.1   The conditional in programming languages

Here we examine one of the common commands in programming languages – the conditional command. Its most familiar form is

    if ... then ... else ...

Given a condition P, the command 'if P then S_1 else S_2' means that if P is true then execute the command (program) S_1, else execute the command S_2. Note also that there is a difference between 'if ... then ... else ...' in programming and the implication written in some texts in the style 'if ... then ...'. The former is a command in a programming language while the latter is a declarative statement in logic. Hence, there is a need to exercise some care when translating statements between programs and logic.

The conditional command may also be nested. For example, the following is also a valid command:

    if P then S_1
       else if Q then S_2
          else if R then S_3
             else S_4 **(4.24)**

Thus, the nesting of the conditional command can take very complex forms. For example, it is not very obvious whether, according to the above code, S_4 will be executed under the condition

$$\neg (P \wedge Q \wedge R) \qquad \textbf{(4.25)}$$

or under the condition

$$\neg P \wedge \neg Q \wedge \neg R \qquad \textbf{(4.26)}$$

From the De Morgan law (4.8), we know that the former is identical to

$$\neg P \vee \neg Q \vee \neg R \qquad \textbf{(4.27)}$$

which is a weaker condition than the correct interpretation (4.26) implicit in the code of (4.24).

Such confusions arise when the code is written in the style of (4.24) with several levels of nesting. This could be avoided by writing the code in the following way:

```
if        P              then    S₁
else if   ¬P∧Q           then    S₂
else if   ¬P∧¬Q∧R        then    S₃
else if   ¬P∧¬Q∧¬R       then    S₄
```
$$\text{(4.28)}$$

This uses a 'cascade' of `if` P_1 `then` S_1 `else if` P_2 `then` ... `elseif` P_n `then` S_n. The above code makes explicit the circumstances under which each of the programs S_1, S_2, S_3 and S_4 are to be executed.

4.3.2 The conditional in the guarded command language

An analogous command exists in the *Guarded Command Language* (GCL) due to Edsger Dijkstra (1976), a pioneer in the study of program correctness. GCL is a generalization of conventional imperative programming languages. It consists of a number of programming language constructs, or commands, which are identical or close to those found in other common programming languages, and is a part of a notation widely used in mathematical reasoning about programs. The idea is to develop programs first in GCL rigorously and then to translate them into a conventional programming language. This is considered a straightforward task.

The conditional command in GCL, known usually as *alternation*, takes the general form

```
if    G₁ → prog₁
[]    G₂ → prog₂
      ⋮
[]    Gₙ → progₙ
fi
```
$$\text{(4.29)}$$

G_1, G_2, ..., G_n in the above are called the *guards* and $prog_1$, $prog_2$, ..., $prog_n$ the associated *guarded commands*.

Informally, the alternation command is executed in GCL in the following manner:

1. One of the guarded commands associated with a true guard is chosen non-deterministically (arbitrarily) for execution.

2. If none of the guards are true, then the alternation command as a whole is aborted.

The guards in an alternation command do not have to be disjoint. However, it is essential that the commands associated with guards with any common enabling state do not result in contradictory states after their execution. Also, a good design should prevent failure of the command in the case of a non-exhaustive set of guards by appropriate measures, for example, using an additional branch having as its guard the negated conjunction of existing guards and `skip` (a program which does nothing but successfully terminates) or an error handling facility as its command.

It can be seen that the program (4.24) can be expressed in GCL as

$$
\begin{array}{llll}
\text{if} & P & \rightarrow S_1 \\
[] & \neg P \wedge Q & \rightarrow S_2 \\
[] & \neg P \wedge \neg Q \wedge R & \rightarrow S_3 \\
[] & \neg P \wedge \neg Q \wedge \neg R & \rightarrow S_4 \\
\text{fi}
\end{array}
\tag{4.30}
$$

Thus, the alternation command in GCL is concise, clearer and more general. It offers more, since it is also a framework for mathematical program verification and program development by *refinement* – an approach that allows the development of code by a series of mathematically verifiable small steps.

Exercise 4.7 ✳ ✳ ✳

The following are some programming statements written in the syntax of a pseudo-programming language close to Pascal, Modula-2 or C. Simplify them using propositional logic and express the simplified version in the pseudo-programming language and in GCL.

In these statements, A and B are some propositions and **true** and **false** are two arbitrary propositional formulae which are respectively identically true and false and S_i for $i = 1, 2, 3$ are some programs.

1. if **true** then S_1

2. if A then if B then S_1
$\qquad\qquad\qquad$ else S_2
$\qquad$ else S_3

3. if A then if $(A$ and $B)$ then S_1
$\qquad\qquad\qquad$ else if $(\text{not } B)$ then S_2

4. if A then if $(A$ or $B)$ then S_1
$\qquad\qquad\qquad$ else skip
$\qquad\qquad$ else if $((B$ or $(\text{not } A))$ and **false**$)$ then S_2

As mentioned earlier, `skip` is a program which does nothing but successfully terminates.

5. if $(A$ or **true**$)$ then if $(A$ and **true**$)$ then if S_1
$\qquad\qquad\qquad\qquad\qquad$ else S_1
$\qquad\qquad$ else S_2

An application: digital circuits

In the design of digital circuits, the logical laws given in Section 4.13 have several uses. An obvious use is in the simplification of circuits. Example 4.6 illustrates this in relation to the problem we attempted in Exercise 3.14. The design of digital circuits is not always driven by simplicity of the circuit. There can be other factors. Sometimes the design of a large circuit may be influenced by the preference for some repetitiveness in its subcircuits and sometimes by a desired number of different types of gate to be used. Whatever the goal, once the desired functionality is established in the form of a formula in propositional logic, the criteria appropriate to a given design may be met by manipulating the formula using logical laws. We now know that any transformation of a formula done by applying logical laws does not affect the meaning, which in this case is the circuit functionality.

Example 4.6

The following formula was presented in Exercise 3.14.

$$(\neg A \wedge B \wedge C) \vee (A \wedge \neg B \wedge C) \vee (A \wedge B \wedge \neg C) \vee (A \wedge B \wedge C)$$

As a solution, the digital circuit of Figure 3.3 was proposed. Although the two are related, the circuit has a much simpler structure. How is this justified?

Justification is by simplifying the above formula as follows:

$$
\begin{aligned}
& (\neg A \wedge B \wedge C) \vee (A \wedge \neg B \wedge C) \vee (A \wedge B \wedge \neg C) \vee (A \wedge B \wedge C) \qquad\qquad \text{given} \\
\Leftrightarrow\ & ((\neg A \wedge B \wedge C) \vee (A \wedge B \wedge C)) \vee \\
& ((A \wedge \neg B \wedge C) \vee (A \wedge B \wedge C)) \vee \\
& ((A \wedge B \wedge \neg C) \vee (A \wedge B \wedge C)) \qquad\qquad \text{commutativity and idempotence} \\
\Leftrightarrow\ & ((\neg A \vee A) \wedge (B \wedge C)) \vee \\
& ((\neg B \vee B) \wedge (A \wedge C)) \vee \\
& ((\neg C \vee C) \wedge (A \wedge B)) \qquad\qquad \text{commutativity and distributivity} \\
\Leftrightarrow\ & (\textbf{true} \wedge (B \wedge C)) \vee (\textbf{true} \wedge (A \wedge C)) \vee (\textbf{true} \wedge (A \wedge B)) \qquad \text{excluded middle} \\
\Leftrightarrow\ & (B \wedge C) \vee (A \wedge C) \vee (A \wedge B) \qquad\qquad \text{simplification}
\end{aligned}
$$

It may be noted that the last formula matches exactly the circuit shown in Figure 3.3.

Exercise 4.8 ✳

By a transformational proof, derive a functionally equivalent circuit to the one given in Figure 3.5 in Exercise 3.8.

Exercise 4.9 ✳✳

By transforming the formula derived in Example 4.6 or otherwise, derive a digital circuit functionally equivalent to the one given in Figure 3.3 but using *nand* gates only.

Exercise 4.10 ✳✳✳

The answer to Exercise 3.8 should indicate that the digital circuits shown in Figures 3.4 and 3.6 have the same functionality.

1. Prove the functional equivalence of the two circuits.

2. Using the above proof or otherwise, derive the simplest (with the least number of gates) functionally equivalent circuit to those given in Figures 3.4 and 3.6.

Exercise 4.11 ✳ ✳ ✳

Here are some general questions.

1. You have come across the words 'demonstrate' and 'prove' in relation to establishing equivalences. Is there a difference between their usage? If so, explain why.

2. Explain what it means for a connective to be associative and commutative.

3. Identify any propositional connectives that are not associative. Justify your answer with the help of truth tables.

4. The connective ∧ is *distributive over* ∨ since

$$p \wedge (q \vee r) \Longleftrightarrow (p \wedge q) \vee (p \wedge r)$$

Find a pair of connectives such that the first connective is not distributive over the other. Justify your answer with the help of a truth table.

5. Is it possible to formulate propositional logic with fewer connectives than we have used? Explain how.

Chapter 5

Deductive proofs

Topic: Proofs in propositional logic

Logical consequences are the scarecrows of fools and the beacons of wise men.

T. H. Huxley
English biologist (1825–1895)

Objectives

On completion of this chapter you should be able to:

- Define the notion of validity of an argument.

- Establish the validity of an argument using truth tables.

- Demonstrate the invalidity of an argument.

- Remember and use inference laws.

- Establish the validity of an argument by providing a proof.

- Reason about theories that can be expressed using prime propositions.

Proofs are not just about how to transform a formula to an equivalent one. They are really about how to establish the *validity* of arguments, which, as mentioned in Section 1.1 of Chapter 1, is the prime concern of logic. Therefore, compared with transformational proofs covered in the previous chapter, the kind of proof introduced in this chapter has a more general applicability.

   As far as the relevance of proof in computing is concerned, it is sufficient to note that questions about specifications and claims made in programming are arguments as well. Therefore, it is legitimate to ask for the *proof* at the end of a requirements validation exercise (validation of user requirements documented in a specification) or a verification of correctness of a computer program.

5.1) Arguments

Description) Argument

An *argument* is a collection of propositions, one of which, referred to as the *conclusion*, is justified by the others, referred to as the *premises*.

The following is an argument in natural language.

On the basis that every adult is eligible to vote and John is an adult, we conclude that John is eligible to vote.

The same argument can be written in a different form:

1. Every adult is eligible to vote.	premise
2. John is an adult.	premise
3. Therefore, John is eligible to vote.	conclusion

Description   Deductive arguments

If the conclusion of an argument is wholly justified by the premises, the argument is said to be *deductive*.

Deductive arguments reason about knowledge that is implicit, or seems to be implicit, in an already known body of knowledge. Part of this known body of knowledge is explicitly stated and the rest must have been established by prior reasoning. *Inductive* arguments reason about more general new knowledge from a small number of particular facts or observations.

Example 5.2

The following is a *deductive* argument:

1. All Rugby players drink too much.

2. Jenny is a Rugby player.

3. Therefore, Jenny drinks too much.

The following is an *inductive* argument:

1. All those taking part in these league matches are a fair sample of Rugby players.

2. They all drink too much.

3. Therefore, all Rugby players drink too much.

Induction is a special form of reasoning in its own right. Whether it concerns the boiling point of water or the size of the population of a particular species of animals in the wild, they are all estimated on the basis of inductive principles.

Inductive generalizations are based on observations about a *fair sample* of individuals or experiments. The premise that the observations constitute a fair sample is pivotal to the validity of an inductive argument. The first piece of evidence to the contrary could be fatal.

Although this text does not cover induction any further, it does cover a related topic – *mathematical induction* – in Chapter 10.

5.2 Validity

Validity is the logician's term for the correctness or the soundness of an argument.

Description) Validity

If the conclusion of a deductive argument is always true whenever all its premises are true then the argument is said to be *valid*. Otherwise the argument is said to be *invalid*.

An obvious implication of the definition of validity given in the Description is that when establishing the validity of an argument, one must take the premises for granted. That is, we should not question them. This is because our concern is whether the conclusion follows logically from the premises and not whether the premises or, for that matter, the conclusion, are factually true. Factual truth of the premises and the conclusion is left for the scientist, the journalist and, in the case of computing, for the 'requirement analyst'.

Example 5.3)

The following is a valid argument:

1. If the patient has a pulse then the patient's heart is pumping.	premise
2. The patient has a pulse.	premise
3. Therefore, the patient's heart is pumping.	conclusion

The conclusion is true whenever the premises are true. The argument is therefore a valid one.

It is possible for an argument to be valid but have a false conclusion.

Example 5.4)

1. If I buy cable TV, I will have access to a hundred free channels.	premise
2. I buy cable TV.	premise
3. I have access to a hundred free channels.	conclusion

This argument is valid, even though it has led us to a false conclusion, because of a factually false premise.

It is also possible for an argument to be invalid but have factually true premises and a factually true conclusion.

Example 5.5

> **1. If I win the lottery then I am lucky.**   premise
>
> **2. I do not win the lottery.**   premise
>
> **3. Therefore, I am not lucky.**   conclusion

The point made here is that the argument is unsound, although we may sympathise with the predicament of the author of the argument.

5.3 Demonstrating validity using truth tables

Thus far we have explored the validity of arguments relying just on our intuition. We now turn our attention to more formal ways of establishing validity.

Our first approach is based on the use of truth tables. If it can be shown that whenever the premises are true the conclusion is also true, then the argument is valid (recall the definition of validity).

Example 5.6

We will use one of our previous examples.

> **1. If the patient has a pulse then the patient's heart is**
> **pumping.**   premise
>
> **2. The patient has a pulse.**   premise
>
> **3. Therefore, the patient's heart is pumping.**   conclusion

Let p be '**The patient has a pulse**', and q be '**The patient's heart is pumping**'. We can express the argument formally as:

1. $p \Rightarrow q$ premise

2. p premise

3. Therefore, q conclusion

The following truth table demonstrates the validity of this argument.

Prime propositions		Premises		Conclusion
p	q	$p \Rightarrow q$	p	q
T	T	T	T	T
T	F	F	T	F
F	T	T	F	T
F	F	T	F	F

Remember, we need to examine only the rows in which the premises are all true. As highlighted in the truth table, there is only one such row in the given truth table.

Another way of looking at an argument is as an implication. If we can show that the premises logically imply the conclusion, that is, that the implication is a tautology, then the argument is valid.

Example 5.7

The argument in the previous example can be rewritten as

$$((p \Rightarrow q) \wedge p) \Rightarrow q$$

[We have written all its premises as a conjunction in the antecedent of the implication. The conclusion appears as the consequent of the implication.] An extension of the previous truth table shows that this is a tautology.

p	q	$p \Rightarrow q$	$(p \Rightarrow q) \wedge p$	$((p \Rightarrow q) \wedge p) \Rightarrow q$
T	T	T	T	T
T	F	F	F	T
F	T	T	F	T
F	F	T	F	T

Therefore, $((p \Rightarrow q) \wedge p) \Rightarrow q$, which is the required tautology.

5.4 Demonstrating invalidity

Description Invalidity

An argument is *invalid* if and only if there is at least one assignment of truth values in which the premises are true, but the conclusion is false.

Example 5.8

Let us revisit a previous example.

1. If I win the lottery then I am lucky.	premise
2. I do not win the lottery.	premise
3. Therefore, I am not lucky.	conclusion

Let p be '**I win the lottery**' and q be '**I am lucky**'. The argument is thus:

1. $p \Rightarrow q$	premise
2. $\neg p$	premise
3. Therefore, $\neg q$	conclusion

There is *only one way* to demonstrate the invalidity of an argument and that is by using a truth table.

Prime propositions		Premises		Conclusion
p	q	$p \Rightarrow q$	$\neg p$	$\neg q$
T	T	T	F	F
T	F	F	F	T
F	T	T	T	F
F	F	T	T	T

It is not necessary to produce the whole truth table. We need to produce just one row of it (or just one assignment of truth values) which shows that the conclusion is false despite all premises being true.

Exercise 5.1 ✳

Demonstrate the invalidity of the following arguments.

1. $p \vee q$
$\neg p$
Therefore, $\neg q$

2. $p \Leftrightarrow q$
$p \Rightarrow r$
r
Therefore, p

3. $p \vee q$
q
Therefore, p

4. $p \Rightarrow q$
$q \Rightarrow p$
Therefore, $p \wedge q$

Note

As a result of this and the previous sections, we now have a second use of truth tables, namely, for establishing the validity and the invalidity of arguments.

(5.5) Proving validity using deductive proofs

When the number of prime propositions in an argument is more than, say, two or three, using truth tables for demonstrating validity becomes tedious. With as few as five prime propositions we would have to construct a truth table with 32 rows. Thus, the use of truth tables for establishing validity is not generally very practical.

Furthermore, so far we have worked out the validity of arguments relying solely on our *understanding* of truth and falsehood. Although we should not be against this in principle, there are reasons for a more detached approach.

For these reasons, we now turn our attention to a different approach – an approach not only based on understanding of truth but also containing a strong element of *reasoning*. This process of reasoning is going to be quite formal, making it at the same time more mechanical. In the age of computers, this is perhaps an added virtue. This alternative approach is based on what is called *deductive proof*.

(**Description**) Deductive proof

Deductive proof is an approach to establishing the validity of an argument by using a series of simpler arguments that are known to be valid.

The 'simpler arguments' referred to in the Description of deductive proof are known as the *inference rules*.

(5.6) Inference rules

5.6.1   What are they?

We have already met logical laws (in Chapter 4) which we used to conduct special kind of proofs – transformational proofs or proofs of equivalences. Here, we introduce a new set of rules which, along with the logical laws, will enable us to carry out deductive proofs – a more general kind of proof.

(**Description**) Inference rule

An inference rule is a primitive valid argument form. Each inference rule enables the elimination or the introduction of a logical connective.

Recall that the logical laws were really logical equivalences. Similarly, most inference rules may be seen as logical implications.

Below is a full list of inference rules. First, though, a note about the presentation of rules. Each rule has an identification such as $\wedge \_I$ and $\wedge \_E$, involving:

⬤ a connective (such as ∧), and

◗ the letter *I* indicating that the rule is intended to introduce the relevant connective, or

⬤ the letter *E* indicating that the rule is intended for eliminating the connective.

There are two parts in the body of the rule which are separated by a horizontal line.

◗ Above the line is a list of formulae that must already appear in the proof in order to apply the inference rule. Each such formula is just a pattern. Each propositional variable in the formula may stand for an arbitrarily complex compound proposition in the actual proof.

◗ Below the line is what may be deduced by the application of the inference rule. This means that if the proof already contains a set of formulae matching those given above the line, then one can insert a new formula into the proof which matches the formula given below the line.

The following example illustrates just the use of the above notation.

Example 5.9

The following inference rule,

$$p$$
$$q$$
$$\overline{p \wedge q}$$

is referred to as ∧ __*I* since it introduces a ∧ connective. According to this rule, if *p* has been already established in the proof and *q* has also been established, then we can deduce $p \wedge q$.

The validity of inference rules can be established using truth tables. Example 5.10 is an illustration.

Example 5.10

The following truth table demonstrates the validity of *modus tollens* – an inference rule listed in Section 5.6.2.

Prime propositions		Premises		Conclusion
p	*q*	$p \Rightarrow q$	¬ *q*	¬ *p*
T	T	T	F	F
T	F	F	T	F
F	T	T	F	T
F	F	T	T	T

Recall also that we demonstrated the validity of *Modus Tollens* in Example 4.5 using a transformational proof.

5.6.2   The inference rules listed

Below is a complete list of inference rules used in this book.

Conjunction: $\wedge\_I$

$$\frac{\begin{array}{c}p\\q\end{array}}{p\wedge q}$$

Simplification: $\wedge\_E$

$$\frac{p\wedge q}{p} \qquad \text{inspired by}$$

$$p\wedge q\Rightarrow p$$

Addition: $\vee\_I$

$$\frac{p}{p\vee q} \qquad \text{inspired by}$$

$$p\Rightarrow p\vee q$$

Disjunctive syllogism: $\vee\_E$

$$\frac{\begin{array}{c}p\vee q\\\neg p\end{array}}{q} \qquad \text{inspired by}$$

$$(p\vee q)\wedge\neg p\Rightarrow q$$

Modus ponens: $\Rightarrow\_E$

$$\frac{\begin{array}{c}p\Rightarrow q\\p\end{array}}{q} \qquad \text{inspired by}$$

$$(p\Rightarrow q)\wedge p\Rightarrow q$$

Modus tollens: $\Rightarrow\_E$

$$\frac{\begin{array}{c}p\Rightarrow q\\\neg q\end{array}}{\neg p} \qquad \text{inspired by}$$

$$(p\Rightarrow q)\wedge\neg q\Rightarrow\neg p$$

Contradiction: ¬_E

$$p$$
$$\underline{\neg\, p}$$
$$q$$

inspired by

$$p \wedge \neg\, p \Rightarrow q$$

Double negation: ¬_E

$$\underline{\neg\,\neg\, p}$$
$$p$$

inspired by ⇔

$$\neg\,\neg\, p \Rightarrow p$$

Transitivity of equivalence: ⇔_I

$$p \Leftrightarrow q$$
$$\underline{q \Leftrightarrow r}$$
$$p \Leftrightarrow r$$

inspired by

$$((p \Leftrightarrow q) \wedge (q \Leftrightarrow r)) \Rightarrow (p \Leftrightarrow r)$$

Laws of equivalence: ⇔_E

$$\underline{p \Leftrightarrow q}$$
$$p \Rightarrow q$$

inspired by

$$(p \Leftrightarrow q) \Rightarrow (p \Rightarrow q)$$

$$\underline{p \Leftrightarrow q}$$
$$q \Rightarrow p$$

and

$$(p \Leftrightarrow q) \Rightarrow (q \Rightarrow p)$$

Next below are two *special inference rules*. They are special because we cannot justify them using the approach studied so far, that is, the approach based on the notion of validity of arguments. Instead we have to justify them by *intuitive reasoning* and on the basis of *provability* – a concept belonging to our language of reasoning.

The notation ⊢ used in these inference rules means that the formula on its right is *provable* from the formulae on its left.

Deduction theorem: ⇒ _I

$$\underline{p, \ldots, r, \boxed{s} \;\; \vdash t}$$
$$p, \ldots, r \vdash s \Rightarrow t$$

Note that the highlighted $\boxed{s}$ in the first line is a formula distinguished as an *assumption*. The above rule states that if t is provable from the formulae $p, \ldots, r$ and the assumption s, then $s \Rightarrow t$ may be inserted into the proof as a formula provable from just $p, \ldots, r$. In other words, the *deduction theorem* says that in order to establish $s \Rightarrow t$, assume s, deduce t and discharge the assumption by writing $s \Rightarrow t$.

Reductio ad absurdum: ¬_I

$$p, \ldots, q, \; \boxed{r} \vdash s$$
$$p, \ldots, q, \; \boxed{r} \vdash \neg s$$
$$\overline{p, \ldots, q \vdash \neg r}$$

Note that, as in the previous inference rule, the highlighted $\boxed{r}$ in the first line is a formula distinguished as an *assumption*. *Reductio ad absurdum* (meaning *'reduction to absurdity'* in Latin) is also used to conduct proofs by introducing an assumption. It states that in order to prove $\neg r$, assume r and deduce a contradiction. It can be justified on the grounds of the logical implication

$$(r \Rightarrow s) \wedge (r \Rightarrow \neg s) \Rrightarrow \neg r$$

Terminology

- Proofs carried out using the deduction theorem are called *conditional proofs*.
- Proofs carried out using *reductio ad absurdum* are called *indirect proofs*, or sometimes, *proofs by contradiction*.

Conditional and indirect proofs are in fact two well known proof strategies. There is more about them in Sections 5.7.4 and 5.7.5.

Exercise 5.2 ✳

Demonstrate the validity of the following inference rules.

1. Disjunctive syllogism: ∨_E

   $$p \vee q$$
   $$\neg p$$
   $$\overline{q}$$

2. Addition: ∨_I

   $$p$$
   $$\overline{p \vee q}$$

3. Simplification: ∧_E

   $$\overline{p \wedge q}$$
   $$p$$

Here are some further inference rules commonly found in many texts on logic. Although these two rules have not been cited in the main list, they are convenient shorthand for several lines of proofs. As can be seen, they are quite intuitive. If it is not the case, verify their validity using truth tables as exercises.

Hypothetical syllogism

$$p \Rightarrow q$$
$$q \Rightarrow r$$
$$\overline{p \Rightarrow r}$$

This says that if p implies q and q implies r, then it can be logically concluded that p implies r.

Constructive dilemma

$$p \Rightarrow q$$
$$r \Rightarrow s$$
$$p \vee r$$
$$\overline{q \vee s}$$

This rule says that if the disjunction of the antecedents of two implications holds, then the disjunction of their conclusions must also hold.

5.7 On the art of proofs

5.7.1 Presentation of proofs

Proofs are a highly disciplined way of reasoning. Part of this discipline lies in having to explain even the minutest step. This forces constant questioning, giving proof its greatest strength. A proof without justifications is as error prone as an informal proof. It is imperative therefore that proofs are properly commented so that the reasoning behind them is absolutely clear.

Note that each step must be justified by a logical law or an inference rule. For this purpose, each step of a proof should be numbered and annotated with:

- the previous lines of the proof justifying the step, and

- the name of the logical law or the inference rule used.

In the case of reasoning involving an assumption, it is a good idea to indent the lines appropriately to highlight the assumption's scope.

5.7.2 Use of logical laws

Part of the proof may involve transformations of formulae into equivalent formulae. The guidelines given in Section 4.2 still apply.

Sometimes it is worth transforming the goal into a different form using a logical law. You may then have a better idea of what to aim for.

Example 5.11 below illustrates also the use of an inference rule. There is more about such rules in Section 5.7.3. See step 4 which eliminates the clause containing a q.

Example 5.11

From the premise $(p \wedge q) \vee r$, derive $\neg p \Rightarrow r$.

1. $(p \wedge q) \vee r$	premise
2. $r \vee (p \wedge q)$	from 1, commutativity
3. $(r \vee p) \wedge (r \vee q)$	from 2, distributivity
4. $r \vee p$	from 3, $\wedge\_E$
5. $p \vee r$	from 4, commutativity
6. $\neg\neg p \vee r$	from 5, negation law
7. $\neg p \Rightarrow r$	from 6, implication law

Example 5.11 will be used again to show two special proof strategies, namely, conditional proofs in Section 5.7.4 and indirect proofs in Section 5.7.5.

5.7.3   Setting subgoals

Doing proofs is quite often a task of setting subgoals. It is also a highly creative task guided more by intuition than anything else. Obviously, as in any creative activity, the experience matters enormously.

Examine the goal carefully. The goal may be broken into subgoals, and they in turn into other subgoals. If there appear to be no further subgoals to be proven, then in essence the proof has already been accomplished.

It is impossible to give an exhaustive set of rules on how to go about setting subgoals. Those in Table 5.1 are just a few.

Table 5.1   Setting subgoals.

Goal	Possible subgoals	Inspired by
$p \wedge q$	Both p and q	Inference rule $\wedge\_I$
$p \vee q$	Either p or q	Inference rule $\vee\_I$
$p \Rightarrow q$	Either $\neg p$ or q	Law of implication
$p \Rightarrow q$	q, after assuming p	Conditional proof (see Section 5.7.4)
$p \Leftrightarrow q$	Both $p \Rightarrow q$ and $q \Rightarrow p$	Law of equivalence and inference rule $\wedge\_I$
$p \Leftrightarrow q$	Both $p \Leftrightarrow r$ and $r \Leftrightarrow q$ for some r	Transitivity of equivalence and inference rule $\wedge\_I$
p	$q \Rightarrow p$ and q for some q	Inference rule $\Rightarrow\_E$ (*modus ponens*)
p	$p \wedge q$ for some q	Inference rule $\wedge\_E$
p	$p \vee q$ and $\neg q$ for some q	Inference rule $\vee\_E$

Example 5.12

Here is the chain of subgoals for Example 5.11.

The goal	$\neg p \Rightarrow r$	*which*
leads to subgoal	$\neg \neg p \vee r$	*which*
leads to subgoal	$r \vee p$	*which*
leads to subgoal	$(r \vee p) \wedge (r \vee q)$	*etc.*

5.7.4   Proof strategies: conditional proof

When the goal is an implication, or it can be transformed to an implication, a conditional proof may be quite a promising strategy.

Conditional proofs are based on the following idea. If we wish to prove an implication such as $p \Rightarrow q$, we first assume p, and then using this assumption, deduce q. This amounts to saying that if p were to be true then q must also be true. On the other hand, if p were to be false then nothing may be said of q, whether q is true or false. This situation is not different from that implied by the formula $p \Rightarrow q$, where we do not care whether q is true or false, should p happen to be false. This is exactly what the deduction theorem points out. The deduction theorem takes advantage of this similarity. Thus, we finally use the deduction theorem to discharge the assumption by inserting $p \Rightarrow q$, which is the goal, into the proof.

Example 5.13

Here is Example 5.11 again, but this time using a conditional proof.

1. $(p \wedge q) \vee r$ premise
2. $\neg (\neg p \vee \neg q) \vee r$ from 1, double negation & De Morgan
3. $\neg p \vee \neg q \Rightarrow r$ implication law
     4. $\neg p$ assumption
     5. $\neg p \vee \neg q$ from 4, $\vee \_I$
     6. r from 3 & 5 $\Rightarrow \_E$ (*modus ponens*)
7. $\neg p \Rightarrow r$ from 4, 5, 6, $\Rightarrow \_I$

Note here the use of indentation where the assumption holds. Line 7 *discharges* the assumption. Also note the use of $\vee \_I$ in step 5 to introduce a propositional variable.

5.7.5   Proof strategies: indirect proof

Indirect proof is another effective proof strategy. It is based on the inference rule *reductio ad absurdum*. It may particularly suit situations where the goal typically consists of a single propositional variable. Obviously, it can be generalized easily to situations where the goal is a compound proposition, as in the case of Example 5.14.

The reasoning behind indirect proofs is as follows. If we wish to prove a certain formula (the goal), we first adopt its negation as an assumption and then show that this assumption leads to a contradiction. That is, we show that for some formula p, we can deduce both p and $\neg p$. The fact that a contradiction arises as a consequence of our assumption is taken as sufficient grounds to justify that the negation of the assumption must hold. It is obvious that the negation of the assumption is identical to the double negation of the goal, which is identical to the goal.

(**Example 5.14**)

Example 5.11 is revisited once again, but this time for showing an indirect proof.

1. $(p \wedge q) \vee r$ premise
2. $(p \vee r) \wedge (q \vee r)$ from 1, commutativity & distributivity
3. $p \vee r$ from 2, $\wedge\_E$
     4. $\neg(\neg p \Rightarrow r)$ assumption
     5. $\neg(p \vee r)$ from 4, law of implication & negation
6. $\neg\neg(\neg p \Rightarrow r)$ from 3, 4, 5, $\Rightarrow\_I$ (*reductio ad absurdum*)
                           (contradiction of line 5 with line 3)
7. $\neg p \Rightarrow r$ from 6, double negation

Indirect proofs should not be taken as a universal rule applicable to all situations involving just a prime proposition or single propositional variable. Such a proof may be attempted in a number of different ways – see Section 5.7.3 for other possible tactics.

An illuminating proof by contradiction may be found in Section 17.3.2.

5.7.6   Formal proofs of natural language arguments

When proving the validity of an argument presented in a natural language such as English, translate it first to logic, retaining its form as close as possible to the original. At this stage, do not think about the proof. What is important is getting the argument right. Once this is completed, address the validity of the argument. Note that, for the time being, you are advised not to attempt the proof immediately. Treat these two stages as totally separate.

Once formalized in logic, examine the argument again. If the argument appears to be unsound, it may well be an invalid argument. If you have the slightest doubt, you are well advised first to check it for invalidity. Invalid arguments do not have proofs.

We have discussed how to establish the invalidity of an argument in Section 5.4. In the case of a simple argument involving a small number of prime propositions, this may be done with the help of a truth table. In the case of more complex arguments, search by other means for a counterexample that substantiates your intuition. Once you are satisfied that the argument is valid, then attempt the proof.

Example 5.15

Is the following argument valid?

If you eat carefully then you will have a healthy digestive system. If you exercise regularly you will be very fit. If you have a healthy digestive system or you are very fit, you will live to a ripe old age. You do not live to a ripe old age. Therefore, you did not eat carefully and you did not exercise regularly.

First, identify the prime propositions:

Symbol	Meaning
A	You eat carefully.
B	You have a healthy digestive system.
C	You exercise regularly.
D	You are very fit.
E	You live to a ripe old age.

Now, formalize the argument in logic:

$A \Rightarrow B$
$C \Rightarrow D$
$B \vee D \Rightarrow E$
$\neg E$
Therefore, $\neg A \wedge \neg C$

Finally, since the argument appears to be a valid one, we attempt its proof. We begin by writing out the premises:

1. $A \Rightarrow B$ premise
2. $C \Rightarrow D$ premise
3. $B \vee D \Rightarrow E$ premise
4. $\neg E$ premise

Here, we will use an indirect proof in two parts. First we assume A, in order to deduce $\neg A$:

5. A assumption
6. B from 1 & 5, $\Rightarrow \_E$ (*modus ponens*)
7. $B \vee D$ from 6, $\vee \_I$
8. E from 3 & 7, $\Rightarrow \_E$ (*modus ponens*)
             (contradiction with line 4)
9. $\neg A$ from 4, 5 and 8, $\Rightarrow \_I$ (*reductio ad absurdum*)

Secondly, we use a similar approach but assuming C, in order to deduce $\neg C$:

10. C assumption

11. D from 2 & 10, $\Rightarrow$ _E (*modus ponens*)

12. $D \vee B$ from 11, $\vee$ _I

13. $B \vee D$ from 12, commutativity

14. E from 3 & 13, $\Rightarrow$ _E (*modus ponens*)
                   (contradiction with line 4)

15. $\neg C$ from 4, 10 and 14, $\Rightarrow$ _I (*reductio ad absurdum*)

Finally, we combine the results of the two parts to get the conclusion:

16. $\neg A \wedge \neg C$ from 9 & 15, $\wedge$ _I

Exercise 5.3 ✳

There follows a different version of the above proof. Annotate each step of the proof:

1. $A \Rightarrow B$ premise

2. $C \Rightarrow D$ premise

3. $B \vee D \Rightarrow E$ premise

4. $\neg E$ premise

5. $\neg (B \vee D)$ ....

6. $\neg B \wedge \neg D$ ....

7. $\neg B$ ....

8. $\neg A$ ....

9. $\neg D$ ....

10. $\neg C$ ....

11. $\neg A \wedge \neg C$ ....

Exercise 5.4 ✳✳

Fill in the gaps in the following proofs.

1.   1. $A \Rightarrow \neg B$ premise

     2. $(B \vee C) \vee D$ premise

     3. $\neg C \vee D \Rightarrow A$ premise

     4. $\neg C$ premise

     5. ....

     6. A ....

     7. ....

     8. $\neg B \wedge \neg C$ ....

     9. ....

     10. D ....

2. This next proof shows that $p \Rightarrow q \wedge q \Rightarrow r \Rightarrow p \Rightarrow r$. This is *hypothetical syllogism* – an inference rule we cited on page 71, but not included in our list of rules.

    1. $A \Rightarrow B$ premise

    2. $B \Rightarrow C$ premise

    3. ....

    4. B ....

    5. ....

    6. $A \Rightarrow C$ ....

You may use the above result in the next question.

3.   1. $\neg A \Rightarrow (B \Rightarrow C)$ premise

    2. $D \vee \neg C \vee E$ premise

    3. $A \Rightarrow D$ premise

    4. $\neg D$ premise

    5. ....

    6. $B \Rightarrow C$ ....

    7. ....

    8. $\neg D \Rightarrow (C \Rightarrow E)$ ....

    9. ....

  10. $B \Rightarrow E$ ....

Exercise 5.5 ✱✱

Are the following arguments valid? Provide a proof in each case.

1. If you give your order by telephone or fax then we will deal with it promptly and efficiently. Your goods will arrive on the next day only if we deal with your order promptly or we use Zippo couriers. Therefore, if you give your order by telephone your goods will arrive on the next day.

2. If I visit the Grand Canyon, I will see one of the most amazing sights in the world. But, if I do not visit the Grand Canyon, if I do not see one of the most amazing sights in the world, my neighbours will not be impressed. I have not seen one of the most amazing sights in the world. Therefore, if my neighbours are impressed then they are just pretending.

Exercise 5.6 ✱✱✱

There are two types of people in a certain world – saints, who always tell the truth, and liars, who never tell the truth. Everyone is either a saint or a liar, but not both Decide in each of the following cases whether the speaker is a liar or a saint. (It may be difficult to say in some cases.)

1. 'I am a saint or a liar.'

2. 'Jane and I are both liars.' – Also, is Jane a saint or a liar?

3. 'I am a liar or Matthew is a liar.'

4. 'I am a saint.'

5. 'I am a liar.'

6. 'If I am a saint then I can say that I am a liar.'

5.8 An application: reasoning in theories

Section 1.5 of Chapter 1 discussed the relevance of the notion of *theory* in the context of specifications of requirements of computer systems. A theory in computing is not necessarily a specification of requirements. It could be a description of a behaviour of a process (program), the state of a program at any given state, or any situation. A description or a specification does not confine itself literally to what is presented in writing or verbally. The implications of such a description may sometimes be just the obvious, but often concern the non-trivial and matters of far-reaching importance.

Logic is an ideal language to reason about theories where precision and rigour matter. Exercise 5.7 demonstrates the use of logic in the construction of mathematical theories and formal reasoning.

Exercise 5.7 ✳✳✳

A document dealing with possible emergencies of an unmanned interplanetary space vehicle contains the following sentences:

(a) If misalignment of the clocks of the robot implies a shortage of its power then there will be a delay in the descent of the buggy to the Martian surface.

(b) Misalignment of the clocks of the robot prevents commands from Mission Control reaching the robot and delays the descent of the buggy to the Martian surface.

(c) If the solar batteries are fully drained during the Martian night or there is a delay in the descent of the buggy to the Martian surface then there is a power shortage in the robot.

In the context of the scenario described, comment on the truth of the claims listed below. Provide proofs of validity for propositions which happen to be true and formal refutation for others.

1. There is a delay in the descent of the buggy to the Martian surface.

2. Solar batteries are fully drained during the Martian night or there is a delay in the descent of the buggy to the Martian surface, but the clocks of the robot are misaligned.

3. There is a power shortage in the robot.

Exercise 5.8 ✳ ✳ ✳

Here are some general questions.

1. Is validity just a logical notion or has it got any relevance in everyday conversations and arguments? Explain your answer.

2. Given a choice, what is your preferred way of establishing the validity of an argument? Justify your answer.

3. In relation to establishing the validity of an argument, is it possible to achieve anything with a formal proof that cannot be done with a truth table, or are truth tables more 'powerful' than proofs?

Chapter 6

Predicates and quantifiers

Topic: Predicate logic

....

The limits of my language mean the limits of my world.

Ludwig Wittgenstein
Austrian-born English philosopher (1889–1951)

Objectives

On completion of this chapter you should be able to:

- Explain the need for predicate logic.
- Describe what a predicate is.
- Use quantifiers.
- Express simple arguments in predicate logic.
- Specify programs as abstract programs using *pre* and *post* conditions.
- Interpret program specifications.

As was noted in Chapter 1, propositional logic has certain limitations despite its prominence in logic. These limitations stem from the fact that it confines itself to the study of propositions with no regard to what they are about. As a consequence, propositional logic is unsuitable for reasoning about material and abstract objects such as people, books, bank accounts, numbers, or whatever. These limitations are overcome in *predicate logic* – a richer, more powerful, logical system.

Predicate logic brings along with it the notions of *values* and *variables*. These notions are also shared by programs and this enables us to discuss various aspects of programs. Section 6.8 illustrates this with respect to program specification.

6.1 The need for predicate logic

Consider the following argument from Chapter 5:

Every adult is eligible to vote.
John is an adult.
Therefore, John is eligible to vote. (I)

According to propositional logic, this is an invalid argument, because if we identify the prime propositions and then write down the argument in symbolic form, it becomes

A

B

Therefore, *C*

Obviously, the above is invalid in propositional logic. Even a truth table is unnecessary to dismiss it. There is also neither an inference rule nor a logical law allowing the deduction of *C* from *A* and *B*. Yet, according to our intuition, argument (I) does sound perfectly reasonable. The reason for this 'apparent invalidity' is that we have lost something in the process of translating the argument from natural language to propositional logic. Once we have introduced symbols *A*, *B* and *C* for the prime propositions, we have lost for ever the 'inside view' of the propositions concerned. This is because the machinery of propositional logic is incapable of penetrating the barrier created by the symbols of prime propositions.

In order to deal with this kind of situation, we need to extend propositional logic. The resulting system of logic is called *predicate logic*, with its name originating from its most fundamental concept – the notion of *predicate*.

6.2 Predicates

We can talk about objects (things) in terms of their *attributes* or *properties* and their *relationships* with each other. In natural language, things appear as nouns and include, for example, words such as fish, people, John, planet, the number 5, rocks or Abraham Lincoln. Attributes and relationships can be written using adjectives, adverbs and verbs.

Example 6.1

Some attributes of an individual named John are:

John is a human being.
John is an adult.
John speaks slowly.
John rides horses.

Predicates correspond to attributes (properties) or relationships and, when used in conjunction with individuals, enable us to assert that certain properties or certain relationships hold for certain individuals.

In predicate logic, we use symbols for predicates. The idea is similar to the use of symbols in propositional logic for propositions.

Example 6.2

Some predicates which define the attributes expressed in the sentences in Example 6.1 are:

___ *is_a_human*
___ *is_an_adult*
___ *speaks_slowly*
___ *rides_horses*

For example, *speaks_slowly* in Example 6.2 is a symbol denoting a property. The long underscore preceding it indicates where the name of the individual should appear. The short underscore shows continuity of the identifier chosen for the symbol.

In addition, as in Example 6.3, we may also wish to define a relationship between a number of objects.

Example 6.3

Here are some predicates which define relationships between two objects:

___ *loves* ___
___ *is_greater_than* ___
___ $\leqslant$ ___

In these examples, *loves* is taken to mean the relationship referred to as 'love' in ordinary life between individuals, *is_greater_than* to mean a notion of one thing being 'greater' than another thing, and $\leqslant$ being the 'less than or equal to' symbol as used in relation to numbers.

In Examples 6.2 and 6.3 the long underscore is used to indicate the expected position of objects in predicates. An alternative notation is to use variables such as *x* and *y*. Variables are especially useful when we wish to make explicit that different positions refer to different objects. Note that, for example, *x loves x* and *x loves y* conveys more information than the notation ___ *loves*___ because, following the informal definition given in Example 6.3, *x loves x* means that the individual referred to as *x* loves him/herself, whereas *x loves y* means that the individual referred to as *x* loves the individual referred to as *y*, who could also be *x* him/herself.

Example 6.4

This is an example illustrating predicates that use variables.

x loves x
x loves y
x is_greater_than y
$a \leqslant b$

$$x \; speaks\_slowly$$
$$x \; is\_an\_adult$$
$$\sqrt{x+y+z} = t$$

We can also write predicates like 'functions' in mathematics, because predicates return truth values when their variables are replaced with individuals. A more detailed study of 'functions' will follow later in Chapter 16

Example 6.5

Here are some predicates written in functional notation.

loves (x, y)
greater_than (x, y)
speaks_slowly (x)
adult (x)
square_root_of_sum_of (x, y, z, t)

Description) Predicate

A *predicate* is a symbol denoting the meaning of an attribute (property) of an object or the meaning of a relationship between two or more objects.

Terminology

- A predicate that takes a single object as an argument is called a *unary predicate*.

- A predicate that takes two objects as arguments is called a *binary predicate*.

- In general, if the number of arguments that a predicate takes is *n*, then that predicate is referred to as an *n-ary* predicate.

6.3) **Unary predicates**

In order to understand the role of predicates, propositional connectives and quantifiers in predicate logic, we first examine unary predicates.

Description) Unary predicate

A *unary predicate* is a predicate involving just one object. It expresses a property or an attribute of the object.

Example 6.6

Each of the following predicates expresses a property about an individual referred to by the variable x.

Predicate	Informal meaning
adult(x)	x is an adult.
child(x)	x is a child.
tall(x)	x is tall.
short(x)	x is short.
clever(x)	x is clever.

Exercise 6.1 ✳

Propose suitable unary predicates for expressing the following sentences.

1. Iceland is cold but not all countries are cold.

2. Some countries are warm and are holiday resorts.

3. No country is a holiday resort unless it is by the sea.

4. Northern European countries are cold but beautiful.

5. Beautiful holiday resorts are all in European countries.

6.4   Predicate logic and propositional logic

We noted earlier that predicate logic is an extension of propositional logic. This means that everything we learned in Chapters 2–5 remains applicable. Propositions, propositional connectives and propositional proofs will continue to play their role.

Let us examine briefly how predicates fit in with propositional logic. An important new feature is that predicates, where all or some variables have been replaced by specific individuals, replace identifiers used in propositional logic for prime propositions. Thus, predicates behave almost as if they were prime propositions. We can thus use basic predicates to build more 'complex predicates' – formulae involving one or more predicates and propositional connectives. However, a predicate does not become a fully fledged proposition unless all its variables have been replaced by specific individuals or constants.

Example 6.7

This example illustrates the use of predicates with propositional connectives.

Predicate/proposition	Informal meaning
1. adult(x) $\land$ tall(x)	x is a tall adult.
2. child(x) $\land$ clever(x)	x is a clever child.
3. child(x) $\land$ clever(x) $\Rightarrow$ short(x)	x is short, if he/she is a clever child.

4. *adult*(**John**) ∧ (*short*) **John**) ∨ ¬ *clever*(**John**))	John is an adult and he is short or is not clever.
5. $x < y$	x is less than y.
6. $5 < y$	5 is less than y.
7. $5 < 3$	5 is less than 3.

Note that formulae (1), (2) and (3) in Example 6.7 are still predicates but are rather complex ones. Formula (4) is a proposition because one can assign a truth value to it because all its variables have been replaced by a constant (an individual). Formulae (5) and (6) are predicates, (5) being a binary predicate while (6) is a unary predicate. By contrast, formula (7) is a proposition because both its place holders now contain constants.

Furthermore, compared with formulae encountered when operating solely within propositional logic, formulae (4) and (7) are more 'powerful' propositions in the sense that we have now partially regained the 'inside view' shielded in propositional logic by propositional symbols; see Section 6.1. We regain the rest of this 'inside view' in the next section.

6.5 Quantifiers

How can we make propositions from formulae (1), (2) and (3) of Example 6.7 without replacing variables with specific individuals? The answer is: attach ∀ or ∃ in front.

∀ and ∃ are called *quantifiers*. ∀x is to be read as 'for every x' and ∃x as 'for some x'. Each quantifier results in a different meaning.

Example 6.8

Let us revisit Example 6.7 to illustrate how quantifiers affect the meaning of formulae (1) and (3) there.

Predicate/proposition	**Informal meaning**
1. ∀x • *adult*(x) ∧ *tall*(x)	Everybody is a tall adult.
2. ∃x • *adult*(x) ∧ *tall*(x)	There is at least one tall adult.
3. ∀x • *child*(x) ∧ *clever*(x) ⇒ *short*(x)	Every clever child is short.
4. ∃x • *child*(x) ∧ *clever*(x) ⇒ *short*(x)	There is someone who is short, if he/she is a clever child.

The bullet • is used as a separator between, on one hand, the quantifier and the variable it introduces and, on the other, the formula to which the given 'quantification' applies. Although there are variables in each of the above formulae, each formula is a proposition.

Note that intervening brackets can radically alter the meaning. As in propositional logic, brackets override the convention on precedence rules introduced in Section 3.2.3 for connectives.

Example 6.9

Consider the formula (3) in Example 6.8 with an extra pair of brackets, as:

$$(\forall x \bullet child(x) \wedge clever(x)) \Rightarrow short(x)$$

This now means that 'if everybody is a clever child then x is short'. Thus, the newly added pair of brackets has completely changed the meaning of the sentence.

The new formula in Example 6.9 is not a proposition. Why is that?

Description   Quantifiers

Quantifiers are symbols used to indicate whether a variable applies to all objects or some objects. Predicate logic provides us with two quantifiers.

Symbol	Read as	Name
$\forall$	for all	Universal quantifier
$\exists$	there exists	Existential quantifier

Quantifiers basically qualify the nature of variables being used in two different ways.

Exercise 6.2 ✳✳

Express the following in colloquial English as precisely as possible. [Note: Sentences starting with phrases such as 'For every x there is ...' are not colloquial because of the style and the use of a variable x, which can be avoided.]

1. $\forall x \bullet adult(x) \vee child(x)$
2. $(\forall x \bullet adult(x)) \vee (\exists x \bullet child(x))$
3. $\forall x \bullet (adult(x) \vee \exists x \bullet child(x))$
4. $(\forall x \bullet adult(x)) \vee (\forall x \bullet child(x))$
5. $\neg \exists x \bullet short(x) \wedge clever(x) \wedge child(x)$
6. $(\neg \exists x \bullet short(x)) \Rightarrow (\forall x \bullet clever(x) \wedge child(x))$
7. $\forall x \bullet adult(x) \wedge child(x) \Rightarrow short(John) \wedge tall(John)$

Exercise 6.3 ✳✳

1. Express these in predicate logic as closely as possible to the original meaning.
   (a) Everybody is tall but there are children.
   (b) Tall children are not clever if there are short adults.
   (c) Short children are definitely clever.

(d) Although all adults are tall, they are not clever.

(e) Some adults are clever exactly when none of the children are clever.

2. Express the sentences in Exercise 6.1 on page 84 in predicate logic.

Exercise 6.4 ✶✶

1. Using appropriate unary predicates, express these in predicate logic.
    (a) All first-year students are clever.
    (b) No one can be clever without being hardworking.
    (c) Clever students work hard.
    (d) Those who do not work hard are lazy.
    (e) The lazy students are exactly those who do not work hard.
    (f) Not being lazy is equivalent to being hardworking.
    (g) Although all students are hardworking there are some who are lazy if they do not work hard.

2. With reference to question 1, what extra information can you deduce if:
    (i)   sentences (a) and (c) are true;
    (ii) sentence (d) is true and (e) is false;
    (iii) sentence (d) is true and (f) is true;
    (iv) sentences (a) and (b) are true.

6.6 Elementary reasoning in predicate logic

We now have the means to express arguments in predicate logic. By looking first at Example 6.10, let us briefly examine how we can reason in predicate logic.

Example 6.10

Recall the argument from page 80.

Every adult is eligible to vote. (1)

John is an adult. (2)

Therefore, John is eligible to vote. (3)

Letting *adult(x)* mean '*x* is an adult' and *eligible(x)* mean '*x* is eligible to vote', we can now write this argument as

$\forall x \bullet adult(x) \Rightarrow eligible(x)$
adult (John)
Therefore, *eligible (John)*

Notice that the predicate in the first formula of Example 6.10, that is $adult(x) \Rightarrow eligible(x)$, applies to any *x* and, therefore, it should apply to *John* as well. This leads to

$adult(John) \Rightarrow eligible(John)$

Now we can reason in propositional logic. Applying *modus ponens* to the above formula and to formula (2) of Example 6.10, we obtain the conclusion given in formula (3) of the example.

Exercise 6.5 ✳ ✳

1. Express the following arguments in colloquial English.
   (a) $\forall x \bullet planet(x) \Rightarrow round(x)$
   (b) $planet(\textbf{Pluto})$
       Therefore, $round(\textbf{Pluto})$
   (b) $\exists x \bullet planet(x) \wedge bright(x)$
       $\forall x \bullet planet(x) \wedge bright(x) \Rightarrow small(x)$
       Therefore, $\exists x \bullet bright(x) \wedge small(x)$

2. Express the following arguments in predicate logic.
   (a) Distant planets are cold. Pluto is a distant planet. Therefore, Pluto is cold.
   (b) Some small planets are hot. Venus is hot. Therefore, Venus is a small planet.
   (c) Small hot planets orbit close to the Sun. Venus and Mercury are both small hot planets. Therefore, if Mercury orbits close to the Sun then so does Venus.

6.7 Predicates with higher arities

A predicate can involve any number of objects. For example, binary predicates involve two objects, ternary predicates three objects and so on.

Description: *n*-ary predicate

An *n*-ary predicate is a predicate involving *n* objects expressing a relationship among them.

The unary predicates from Example 6.1 do not allow the expression of relationships between individuals. However, when talking about individuals, it may be necessary to talk about people loving/hating/respecting each other, being jealous of specific individuals, being taller/cleverer/shorter, and so on.

Example 6.11

Some binary predicates are:

$loves(x, y)$ – x loves y.
$respects(x, y)$ – x respects y.
$cleverer(x, y)$ – x is cleverer than y.

As before, one can use propositional connectives and quantifiers to express complex ideas.

Example 6.12

$\forall x \bullet child(x) \wedge clever(x) \Rightarrow \exists y \bullet loves(y, x)$	Clever children are loved.
$\forall x \bullet child(x) \wedge clever(x) \Rightarrow \exists y \bullet adult(y)$ $\wedge loves(y, x)$	Clever children are loved by adults.
$\forall x \bullet clever(x) \Rightarrow \exists y \bullet cleverer(x, y)$	One cannot be clever without being cleverer than someone.
$tall(\textbf{Jane}) \wedge \neg \exists x \bullet loves(x, \textbf{Jane})$ $\wedge \forall x \bullet respects(x, \textbf{Jane})$	Jane is tall and nobody loves her although everybody respects her.

Exercise 6.6 ✳ ✳

Express the following formulae in colloquial English.

1. $\exists x \bullet cleverer\,(x, \textbf{John}) \wedge short(\textbf{John}) \wedge respects(\textbf{Jane}, x)$
2. $\forall x \bullet \forall y \bullet loves(x, y) \wedge tall(y) \Rightarrow respects(x, y)$
3. $\exists x \bullet \forall y \bullet loves(x, y)$
4. $\neg \forall x \bullet \forall y \bullet loves(x, y)$
5. $\forall x \bullet \forall y \bullet loves(x, y) \Rightarrow loves(y, x)$
6. $\exists x \bullet loves(x, \textbf{Jane}) \wedge \neg respects(\textbf{Jane}, x)$
7. $\exists x \bullet \forall y \bullet \neg respects(y, x)$
8. $\exists x \bullet \neg \exists y \bullet loves(y, x) \vee respects(y, x)$

Exercise 6.7 ✳ ✳

Express the following sentences in predicate logic.

1. One cannot love without respecting.
2. One who loves him/herself loves only clever children.
3. One cannot be cleverer than someone without being clever in the first place.
4. John is not known for loving and respecting.
5. Love can only be between adults and children.
6. Mutual respect is not found among tall adults.

Exercise 6.8 ✳ ✳

Using appropriate predicates, express the following in predicate logic.

1. London stores only supply stores outside of London.
2. No store supplies itself.
3. There are no stores in Grimsby but there are some in Halifax.
4. Stores do not supply stores that are supplied by stores which they supply.

5. There is no more than one store in any one place.

6. Stores which supply each other are always in the same place.

Exercise 6.9 ✳✳✳

Using appropriate predicates, express the following in predicate logic.

1. London is 30 miles away from Reading.

2. The store which is furthest away from London is in Edinburgh.

3. The distance between any two places is unique.

4. Stores supply other stores only if they are within a 30 mile radius.

6.8   An application: program specification

A computer program written in imperative sequential style consists of a sequence of commands. There are different kinds of command, most common among them being the assignment, sequential composition, conditional command (alternation) and repetition (iteration). The following is an example:

```
var
    q, r : integer;
begin
    q := 0;
    r := m;
    while (r ⩾ n) do
        begin
            q := q + 1;
            r := r − n;
        end
end
```
(6.1)

But, what does it do? The purpose of the above program is not very obvious because programs themselves are not suitable for explaining their purpose, certainly not to humans, although programs make perfect sense to machines which execute them.

Often, we need to communicate the purpose of programs to others. A customer may place an order with a software developer for a particular program by describing just its purpose. Likewise, the manager of a software development team may delegate the development of a particular program to a programmer by describing its purpose without giving any clue as to how it is to be implemented. A member of a software development team may document concisely what a particular program computes in a user manual, deliberately avoiding any discussion of the details which are of no interest to its user. Clearly, in all such cases it is not necessary to describe what every bit of the program does or how the program works as a whole. What is required is a statement about *what the program does* as a complete entity, namely, a *specification*.

A program specification basically says what the program computes for different combinations of admissible input data. Program specifications written in mathematics, that is, *formally*, make these statements in such a way that the specification concerned has a precise meaning.

Mathematical program specifications are expressed as a pair of predicates using program variables as *objects*. Each predicate expresses a relationship among the values of program variables at a relevant reference point in the program. There are two such relevant reference points in program specification: just before the first executable statement, referred as to as the *before state*, and just after the last executable statement, referred as to as the *after state*. One of the predicates, commonly referred to as the precondition and denoted as *pre*, defines the admissible values of the program variables for its execution in the before state. The other predicate, commonly referred to as the postcondition and denoted as *post*, defines the values of the program variables in the after state, provided that the program variables satisfy the predicate *pre* in the before state.

Tony Hoare, a pioneering advocate of using mathematics for reasoning and development of programs, invented the following notation for program specification

$\{pre\}\ S\ \{post\}$

which is a predicate about a program S asserting that

If the execution of S is begun in a state satisfying *pre* then it is guaranteed to terminate in a finite amount of time in a state satisfying *post*.

We emphasize that the formula $\{pre\}\ S\ \{post\}$ is a predicate about the program S. Like any other formula in predicate logic, the predicate $\{pre\}\ S\ \{post\}$ can be either true or false, meaning that S meets its specification or does not.

Returning to the program code (6.1), given at the beginning of this section, we note that it computes the quotient q and the remainder r when the integer m is divided by the integer n. Note, as a specific example, that if $m = 37$ and $n = 5$ then $q = 7$ and $r = 2$. In the general case, if q and r denote respectively the quotient and the remainder resulting from dividing the integer m by the integer n, then

$m = q \times n + r$ and $0 \leqslant r < n$

Note that both these expressions are predicates, which q, r, m and n must satisfy simultaneously. Therefore, the expression

$m = q \times n + r \wedge 0 \leqslant r < n$

must be true if and when the program terminates. Thus, this is the postcondition of the program we are dealing with. On the other hand, the program must always work irrespective of the values of q, r, m and n, provided that they are all integers. This aspect can be taken care of by making proper use of types and by using an identically true precondition. Denoting by the identifier *Quotient_Prog* any program having the same functionality as the code (6.1), we thus arrive at its specification in Hoare style as

$\{\mathbf{true}\}\ Quotient\_Prog\ \{m = q \times n + r \wedge 0 \leqslant r < n\}$ **(6.2)**

The predicate $\{pre\}\ S\ \{post\}$ can be used in different ways. The first use is to treat it as a specification for developing S, in which case S is supposed to be unknown, that is, S is yet to be developed. On the other hand, if S is already known (already developed) and the predicates *pre* and *post* are given, the task of establishing whether the predicate $\{pre\}\ S\ \{post\}$ is true or false is to be regarded as a task of *program verification*, that is, verifying whether S meets the specification given in terms of *pre* and *post*. Thus, program verification is the second use.

A third use is program annotation (a kind of documentation) in the following style:

```
var
    q, r : integer;
{true}                                              ◄
begin
    q := 0;
    r := m;
    while (r ⩾ n) do
        begin
            q := q + 1;
            r := r − n;
        end
end
{m = q × n + r ∧ 0 ⩽ r < n}                         ◄
```

From this we make assertions about the state of the underlying machine with respect to the relevant program variables as the program execution reaches the points marked by ◄. This kind of use of the predicate $\{pre\}\ S\ \{post\}$ corresponds to a *claim*, which can be relied upon by other users.

An alternative to the above approach based on Hoare's predicate about programs is to think of program specifications as a kind of highly abstract program. This is an approach used in *program refinement*, that is, the development of correct programs from formally specified programs by a series of small verifiable programming steps using rigorous rules (see Morgan (1994)). Viewing program specifications as *abstract programs* is justified on the grounds that a program specification is in essence a way of instructing a 'powerful' hypothetical machine capable of executing high-level instructions, that is, instructions potentially consisting of mathematical operators which cannot be executed directly using conventional programming languages. Thus, abstract programs can express commands in a manner close to human thinking.

(**Description**)   Abstract programs

Program specifications may be viewed as a high-level *abstract program*

$$w : [pre, post]$$

with the meaning

Alter the values of the program (state) variables w such that the after state satisfies the postcondition post, *provided that the before state satisfies the precondition* pre.

It is important to realize that the command in the Description is an abstract program and requires just what is stated; nothing more and nothing less.

Returning to the code (6.1) on page 90, denoted subsequently also as *Quotient_Prog*, for computing the quotient q and the remainder r, the program specification in the new style may be given as

$$Quotient\_Prog \stackrel{def}{=} q, r : [\textbf{\textit{true}}, m = q \times n + r \wedge 0 \leqslant r < n] \qquad (6.3)$$

Obviously, a specification given in either form (6.2) or (6.3) is clearer about what the code (6.1) computes than (6.1) itself conveys.

Here is a summary of terminology and conventions associated with abstract programs.

1. w is known as the *frame* and is usually a set of program variables whose values may be altered by the program. In general, w is written as a list of variables, with adjacent variables delimited by commas ','.

2. The precondition *pre* is a well-formed (grammatically correct) formula written in predicate logic with respect to the values of the program variables in the before state.

3. The postcondition *post* is a well-formed formula in predicate logic written with respect to the values of variables both in the before state and in the after state.

   Note that we use the subscript 0 for certain variables in *post* in order to refer to their values in the before state. For example, if x is a program variable appearing in w, x's value in the before state is referred to in *post* as x_0.

4. The frame lists only the variables with both 'read and write access'. This means that, if necessary, their values may be accessed and be altered. Those variables appearing in either *pre* or *post* but not in w are allowed only 'read-only access'. This means that their values may be accessed but cannot be altered.

(**Example 6.13**)

The following are abstract programs intended for certain specific actions.

Abstract Program	Description
$x : [\textbf{\textit{true}}, \ x > y]$	Make x greater than y but without altering y
$x : [\textbf{\textit{true}}, \ y^2 = x]$	Make x the square of y without altering y
$y : [x \geqslant 0, \ y^2 = x]$	Make y equal to the square root of x without altering x, provided that x is not negative
$x, y : [\textbf{\textit{true}}, \ y^2 = x]$	Choose x and y such that x is the square of y
$x : [b^2 - 4 \times a \times c \geqslant 0, \ a \times x^2 + b \times x + c = 0]$	Make x equal to one of the roots of the quadratic equation $ax^2 + bx + c = 0$, provided that the latter has real roots, but without affecting the program variables a, b and c
$a, b, c : [\textbf{\textit{true}}, \ a \times x^2 + b \times x + c = 0]$	Determine a, b and c such that x is one of the roots of the quadratic equation $ax^2 + bx + c = 0$, but without affecting the program variable x

Example 6.14

Below are some abstract 'data processing' programs using information about a set of individuals and the predicates $loves(x, y)$, $respects(x, y)$ and $cleverer(x, y)$ introduced in Example 6.11.

Abstract program	Description
$x : [y = \textbf{John} \lor y = \textbf{Mary}, x \text{ loves } y]$	Without altering y, choose x such that the individual referred to by x loves the individual referred to by y, provided that y refers (initially) to **John** or **Mary**
$x : [\textbf{true}, loves(x, x) \land respects(x, x)]$	Make x refers to an individual who loves and respects him/herself.
$x.y : [\textbf{true}. \ loves(x, y) \lor$ $\neg \ respects(x, y) \Rightarrow cleverer(x, y)]$	Choose x and y such that x is cleverer than y if x loves y or x does not respect y. Note that here the programmer is free to choose any values for x and y if x does not love y but x respects y

Exercise 6.10 ✳✳

The variables x and y in the following abstract programs denote integers, and $abs(x)$ is a function returning the absolute value of x as its result. Explain what these abstract programs are supposed to compute.

1. $x : [\textbf{true}, x = y + 1]$
2. $x : [x < y, x > x_0 \land x > y]$
3. $x : [x < y, x = x_0 + y]$
4. $x : [y \geqslant 0, x^2 = y]$
5. $x : [\textbf{true}, x^3 = x]$
6. $x : [\textbf{true}, x^3 = abs(x)]$
7. $x : [\textbf{true}. \ x^3 = abs(x_0)]$
8. $x : [x < 0, x^3 = x \land x \geqslant 0]$
9. $x : [x < y + 5 \land y \neq 0, x > x_0 \land x > y]$
10. $x : [x < y \land y \neq 0, x = 2 \times abs(y)]$
11. $x : [x + y \neq 0, x_0 \leqslant 0 \Rightarrow x > -x_0 + y + 1 \land x_0 > 0 \Rightarrow x = x_0 + y]$

Exercise 6.11 ✳✳

Using appropriate predicates, specify the following as abstract programs. In the case of any ambiguity, answer on the basis of a clearly stated assumption. Note that a, b, c, x and y in the informal program specifications denote integers. Unless the question specifically asks for it, do not alter the value of any variable.

1. A program which computes as x the lesser of the absolute initial values of x and y.

2. A program which computes as x the sum of initial values of x and y if the initial value of x is negative.

3. A program which computes as x the sum of initial values of x and y, provided that the initial value of x is negative.

4. A program which computes as x the cube of its initial value, provided that x is initially negative.

5. A program to check whether a, b and c could be the lengths of the sides of a right-angled triangle.

6. A program that sets the values of x and y to be in the same ratio as that of a and b if c equals the initial value of x, but otherwise, chooses x and y such that their sum is zero.

7. A program that sets the values of x and y to the roots (solutions) of the equation given below. Unless both roots of the equations are the same, x and y must be different.

$$a \times z^2 + b \times z + c = 0$$

Note that the above equation has two roots given by

$$\frac{-b \pm \sqrt{b^2 - 4ac}}{2a}$$

Exercise 6.12 ✳✳✳

This is a follow-up to Example 6.14. Specify the following as abstract programs:

1. A program that chooses as x an individual loved and respected by y, provided that x is not cleverer than y.

2. A program that chooses as x an individual loved and respected by y, provided that the individual initially recorded as x is not cleverer than y.

3. A program that chooses as x and y two mutually respecting distinct individuals.

4. A program that checks whether x and y are two mutually respecting distinct individuals.

5. A program that chooses for x an individual who respects *John* and whom *John* loves.

Exercise 6.13 ✳✳

Here are some general questions.

1. What are the limitations of propositional logic? How does predicate logic overcome them?

2. What are the various symbols used in predicate logic? What are the symbols common to propositional logic and predicate logic and what are the symbols unique to each?

3. What is the relationship between program verification and program refinement?

Chapter 7

Further predicate logic

Topic: Predicate logic

···

Perfect freedom is reserved for the man who lives by his own work and in that work does what he wants to do.

R. G. Collingwood
English historian and philosopher (1889–1943)

Objectives

On completion of this chapter you should be able to:

- Identify bound and free variables in formulae.

- Use and remember the scoping rules defined in this chapter.

- Express the type of variables in predicate logic.

- Relate free and bound variables in predicate logic to global and local variables in programs.

Predicates are inextricably linked with variables, which provide us with the means to refer, and cross-refer, to various known and unspecified objects. However, variables we see on paper and variables playing the role of place-holders for different things in predicates are quite different. This chapter concentrates first on the role of variables in predicates. Later on, it introduces certain practices in software engineering.

7.1 Scope of quantifiers

The same variable appearing in different places in a given formula in predicate logic may mean different things. Consider, for example

$$\forall x \bullet distant(x) \wedge planet(x) \Rightarrow \exists x \bullet moon(x)$$

Here, x occurs in three predicates; the first two occurrences refer to one object and the third refers to another object. The object referred to by each occurrence of a variable has to be worked out according to some agreed rules. These rules are referred to as *scoping rules* and are related to the *scope of quantifiers*.

Description Scope of quantifiers

The *scope of a quantifier* in a formula is the extent over which the quantifier applies in the given formula.

In the absence of intervening brackets, we assume that the scope of any quantifier extends to the end of the line (or of several lines if properly indented). We use brackets to enforce any other pattern of scoping.

Example 7.1

In $\forall x \bullet child(x) \wedge clever(x) \Rightarrow \exists y \bullet loves(y, x)$ brackets are implicit as follows:

$$\forall x \bullet (child(x) \wedge clever(x) \Rightarrow \exists y \bullet loves(y, x))$$

This is supposed to mean **'clever children are loved'**.
  On the other hand, the brackets in

$$(\forall x \bullet child(x) \wedge clever(x)) \Rightarrow \exists y \bullet loves(y, x)$$

alter the scope of the quantifier $\forall$. The last occurrence of x no longer comes under the scope of $\forall$ and, for that matter, under the scope of any quantifier. It now means **'If all are clever children then x is loved by someone'**.

Exercise 7.1 ✳✳

Express the following formulae in colloquial English, using $employs(x, y)$ to mean x employs y, $smart(x)$ to mean x is smart and $clever(x)$ to mean x is clever.

1. $\forall x \bullet \exists y \bullet employs(x, y) \Rightarrow smart(y) \wedge clever(y)$
2. $\forall x \bullet \exists y \bullet employs(x, y) \Rightarrow smart(y) \wedge clever(x)$
3. $(\forall x \bullet \exists y \bullet employs(x, y) \Rightarrow smart(y)) \wedge clever(x)$
4. $\forall x \bullet (\exists y \bullet employs(x, y)) \Rightarrow smart(y) \wedge clever(x)$
5. $\forall x \bullet employs(x, y) \Rightarrow \exists y \bullet smart(y) \wedge clever(x)$
6. $\forall x \bullet employs(x, y) \Rightarrow \exists y \bullet smart(y) \wedge clever(y)$
7. $\forall x \bullet employs(x, x) \Rightarrow \exists y \bullet smart(x) \wedge clever(y)$
8. $\forall x \bullet employs(x, x) \Rightarrow \exists x \bullet smart(x) \wedge clever(x)$
9. $(\forall z \bullet \exists s \bullet employs(z, s) \Rightarrow smart(s)) \wedge clever(x)$

Exercise 7.2 ✳✳

Express the following in predicate logic using suitable predicates.

1. Employees are always smart.
2. Smart employees have clever employers.
3. If everybody is employed by someone and x is smart then y is clever.
4. If everybody is smart and employed then x is clever.

5. Smart employees are always clever.

6. If everybody is smart and someone is self-employed then that someone is clever.

7. If everybody is smart and someone is self-employed then they are clever.

7.2 Bound and free variables

Bound and free variables are two important concepts determining the meaning of formulae in predicate logic.

Description — Bound and free variables

A *bound variable* in a formula is an occurrence of a variable which has been introduced by a quantifier in that formula and lies within the scope of that quantifier.

A *free variable* in a formula is an occurrence of a variable which does not lie within the scope of any of the quantifiers appearing in that formula. Thus, free variables have no quantifiers introducing them within the given formula.

Note the distinction between the 'occurrence of a variable' and the 'names of variables'. Generally, x is just a variable name. Its use in a predicate makes x a variable. x may appear in different places in a formula and each appearance of x is a different occurrence of x. The point to remember is that different occurrences of x may not necessarily stand in for the same variable. As a consequence, different variables may be shown on paper by the same variable name.

Example 7.2

This is an example illustrating bound and free occurrences of variables.

Formula	Variable status
child(x)	There is only one occurrence of x and it is free.
$\forall x \bullet child(x) \wedge clever(x)$	Both occurrences of x are bound by the same quantifier and stand in for the same variable.
$(\forall x \bullet child(x)) \wedge clever(x)$	The first occurrence of x is bound and the second occurrence of x is free. The two occurrences stand in for two different variables.

In the formulae below, we will indicate variable binding by putting a number on top of each variable. Thus, every $\overset{1}{x}$ is associated with the same quantifier and, therefore, stands in for the same variable. If in any formula, $\overset{1}{x}$ and $\overset{2}{x}$ appear, they stand in for different bound variables, although shown by the same x. In the case of free variables, we write, for example, $\overset{free}{x}$ to mean that that particular occurrence is a free occurrence of x.

$$\forall \overset{1}{x} \bullet child(\overset{1}{x}) \wedge \ clever(\overset{1}{x}) \Rightarrow \exists \overset{1}{y} \bullet loves\left(\overset{1}{y}, \overset{1}{x}\right)$$

$$\left(\forall \overset{1}{x} \bullet child(\overset{1}{x}) \wedge \ clever(\overset{1}{x})\right) \Rightarrow \exists \overset{1}{y} \bullet loves\left(\overset{1}{y}, \overset{free}{x}\right)$$

Important note

Bound variables are dummy variables and the names used for them do not matter as long as the same pattern of bound variables is maintained. The *meaning does not depend on the names of bound variables* but on the pattern of their distribution in the formula.

Example 7.3

1. The sentences

   $$\forall x \bullet child(x) \wedge clever(x) \Rightarrow \exists y \bullet loves(y, x)$$
   $$\forall p \bullet child(p) \wedge clever(p) \Rightarrow \exists r \bullet loves(r, p)$$

   mean exactly the same thing, whereas

   $$(\forall p \bullet child(p)) \wedge clever(p) \Rightarrow \exists x \bullet loves(x, x)$$

   means something totally different from the above two.

2. The sentences

   $$(\forall x \bullet \exists y \bullet employs(x, y) \Rightarrow smart(y)) \wedge clever(x)$$
   $$(\forall z \bullet \exists s \bullet employs(z, s) \Rightarrow smart(s)) \wedge clever(x)$$

   mean exactly the same thing, although they have different bound variables.

Important note

Free variables denote unknowns or unspecified objects. Therefore, *their replacement alters the meaning*.

Example 7.4

1. $(\forall x \bullet child(x) \wedge clever(x)) \Rightarrow \exists y \bullet loves(y, x)$
2. $(\forall x \bullet child(x) \wedge clever(x)) \Rightarrow \exists y \bullet loves(y, z)$

Sentence (1) means '**if all are clever children then x is loved**', while (2) means that '**if all are clever children then z is loved**'.

Exercise 7.3 ✻ ✻

1. Identify the variable binding in the formulae in Exercise 7.1.

2. Identify the variable binding in your answers to Exercise 7.2.

Exercise 7.4 ✻ ✻

Identify the bound and free variables in the following formulae.

1. $\exists x \bullet y$ taller_than x

2. $\exists x \bullet \exists y \bullet x$ taller_than $y \wedge y$ taller_than z

3. $\forall z \bullet \exists x \bullet \exists y \bullet x$ taller_than $y \wedge y$ taller_than z

4. $\exists x \bullet y$ shorter_than z

5. $\forall y \bullet \forall z \bullet z$ shorter_than y

7.3 Types of values

In the treatment of objects, we have so far been following classical logic, where the concern is usually just one kind of thing. This is captured implicitly by having a specific *domain of discourse* in mind, which could be the human beings, numbers, or every conceivable thing relevant to a particular discussion.

Logic, as used in software engineering, adopts a slightly different approach by being explicit about the kinds of thing we are dealing with. This is because clarity is paramount in software engineering, particularly in mathematical approaches, and is not taken for granted.

In our study so far, we have not given much thought to whether a variable can be replaced by any object. For example, could we use any object for x in the predicate *loves*(x, *John*)? We can sensibly substitute **Fido** for x, but obviously not an inanimate object such as **The Eiffel Tower**. Arguably, it does not make much sense.

Thus, when a variable is quantified, we should associate with it a *type*, or a *domain*, to indicate the sort of thing the variable is representing. We associate a type R with a variable x by writing $x : R$, meaning that 'x has the type R'. This is done immediately after the introduction of a variable by a quantifier. Thus, to say there exists an x of type R, we write $\exists x : R$.

Example 7.5

This example illustrates the use of types in formulae. (Note that *Person* denotes the set of all people.)

Formula	*Informal meaning*
$\forall y : Person \bullet mortal(y)$	Everybody is mortal.
$\exists x : Person \bullet x$ loves **John**	Somebody loves John.
$\neg \exists x : Person \bullet x \neq$ **John** $\wedge$ x speaks_slowly	Nobody, except John, speaks slowly.

Terminology

- Formulae involving explicitly typed variables are referred to as *typed formulae*.
- There are some frequently used notations in mathematics for domains. They are almost like standard types. These are:

$\mathbb{N}$ Natural numbers, $\mathbb{N} = \{0, 1, 2, 3, \ldots\}$
$\mathbb{Z}$ Integers
$\mathbb{Q}$ Rational numbers
$\mathbb{R}$ Real numbers

Example 7.6

Here are some propositions about natural numbers.

1. All natural numbers are greater than zero:

   $\forall x : \mathbb{N} \bullet x > 0$

2. There is a natural number that is greater than 5:

   $\exists x : \mathbb{N} \bullet x > 5$

3. All natural numbers are the sum of two natural numbers:

   $\forall x : \mathbb{N} \bullet \exists a : \mathbb{N} \bullet \exists b : \mathbb{N} \bullet a + b = x$

4. Every natural number has a successor:

   $\forall x : \mathbb{N} \bullet \exists y : \mathbb{N} \bullet x + 1 = y$

5. (Comment on the truth value of the following):

   $\exists y : \mathbb{N} \bullet \forall x : \mathbb{N} \bullet x + y = y$

Exercise 7.5 ✳✳✳

Using the following predicates:

$actor(x)$ x is an actor
$rich(x)$ x is rich
$collect(x, y)$ x collects y
$superior(x, y)$ x is superior to y
$valuable(x)$ x is valuable

and appropriate types, express the following as typed formulae. If you are unable to express any sensibly, explain why.

1. Rich actors collect valuables.
2. Valuables are superior to something.
3. Every superior thing has a collector if it is valuable.
4. All collected things are superior valuables.
5. Nobody collects anything which is inferior to something.
6. Some valuables are neither superior to others nor inferior.
7. Some superior actors are neither rich nor valuables.
8. Some rich actors collect other actors.

7.4 Some conventions

We introduce below some conventions used in a popular specification language known as Z. Specification languages generally pay considerable attention to making specifications readable because they are written, after all, for communication among humans. We concentrate only on how the Z notation improves readability of formulae. There are, of course, other features used for facilitating communication, but these are not dealt with here. [Unenthusiastic readers may skip the remainder of this chapter without much loss.]

7.4.1   Merging of type declarations

The following conventions are intended for *simpler writing* of typed formulae.

1. If x and y are of the same type, say R, and are both introduced by two or more consecutive $\forall$s, then we write

   $\forall x, y : R \bullet \ldots$

   instead of the longer

   $\forall x : R \bullet \forall y : R \bullet \ldots$

   Thus, the first is an abbreviation for the second. An analogous abbreviation applies to $\exists$.

2. If x and y are of different types, say R and S, and are introduced by two or more consecutive $\forall$s, then we write

   $\forall x : R; y : S \bullet \ldots$

   instead of

   $\forall x : R \bullet \forall y : S \bullet \ldots$

   Again, the first is an abbreviation for the second. A similar abbreviation applies to $\exists$.

7.4.2   Constraints on values of variables

Suppose that, in addition to type information, we wish to restrict the objects to which a formula is applicable. In this case, we attach a constraint immediately after the type declaration. This is done as follows.

Universal quantifier

If, for example, we wish to state that only players who win more than five games are qualified for the national team, we may state it as

   $\forall x : Player \mid x \text{ wins } 5 \bullet qualified(x)$

using the predicates

x *wins* n	x wins more than n games
qualified(x)	x is qualified for the national team

This is just a way of writing and has nothing to do with logic on its own. The above is to be interpreted in logic as an *implication*:

$$\forall x : Player \bullet x \ wins \ 5 \Rightarrow qualified(x)$$

Generally, a constraint of the form

$$\forall x : X \mid p(x) \bullet q(x)$$

involving a universal quantifier, where $p(x)$ is referred to as a constraint on the values of x for which q holds, is to be interpreted as

$$\forall x : X \bullet p(x) \Rightarrow q(x)$$

Thus, the first is an abbreviation for the second.

Existential quantifier

A constraint having the same syntax as above may be attached to the existential quantifier, but its interpretation is *different* from that used in relation to universal quantification.

Suppose that we wish to express that there is a player who wins less than or equal to five games but is still qualified for the national team. This may be written as

$$\exists x : Player \mid \neg \ x \ wins \ 5 \bullet qualified(x)$$

and is to be understood in logic as a conjunction:

$$\exists x : Player \bullet \neg \ x \ wins \ 5 \wedge qualified(x)$$

Here, a constraint of the general form

$$\exists x : X \mid p(x) \bullet q(x)$$

is to be interpreted as

$$\exists x : X \bullet p(x) \wedge q(x)$$

Again, the first is an abbreviation for the second.

Example 7.7

Given the predicates

x attends y	person *x* attends course *y*
x registered_for y	person *x* is registered for course *y*
external(x)	*x* is an external student

the following illustrate the use of constraints.

1. All students who are registered for computer science (**CS**) attend mathematics (**Maths**).

   $$\forall x : Person \mid x \ registered\_for \ \textbf{CS} \bullet x \ attends \ \textbf{Maths}$$

2. Students who are registered for computer science but do not attend the course on computer science are external students.

   $$\forall x : Person \mid x \ registered\_for \ \textbf{CS} \wedge \neg \ x \ attends \ \textbf{CS} \bullet external(x)$$

3. There are students among external computer science students who do mathematics and philosophy (**Phil**).

   $\exists x : Person \mid x\ attends\ \textbf{CS} \wedge external(x) \bullet x\ attends\ \textbf{Maths} \wedge x\ attends\ \textbf{Phil}$

   (Note that the English sentence is slightly ambiguous.)

4. Some students attending philosophy do not attend computer science but are registered for computer science.

   $\exists x : Person \mid x\ attends\ \textbf{Phil} \bullet \neg\ x\ attends\ \textbf{CS} \wedge x\ registered\_for\ \textbf{CS}$

Exercise 7.6 ✳ ✳

Translate the following into predicate logic.

1. Those doing computer science do not attend mathematics unless they are registered for mathematics.
2. Some computer science students registered for mathematics do not attend mathematics.
3. There is a student doing philosophy who is registered for everything.
4. A student registered for nothing attends mathematics and computer science.
5. Among those who are registered for philosophy there are some students who attend mathematics but never computer science.

Exercise 7.7 ✳ ✳

For each of the following, identify the scope of the quantifiers and translate the formulae into English. (Infer the meaning of predicates from the words used for them.)

1. $\forall x, y : Lecturer \bullet sarcastic(x) \vee cynical(y)$
2. $(\forall x, y : Lecturer \bullet sarcastic(x)) \vee cynical(y)$
3. $(\forall x : Lecturer \mid sarcastic(x) \bullet \exists y : Student \bullet annoyed(y))$
4. $\exists u : University \bullet \forall x : Student \mid cynical(x) \bullet (\exists y : Lecturer \bullet annoyed(y)) \wedge attends(x, u)$
5. $\exists u : University \bullet (\forall x : Student \mid cynical(x) \bullet (\exists y : Lecturer \bullet annoyed(y))) \wedge attends(x, u)$
6. $\exists u : University \bullet \forall x : Student \mid cynical(x) \bullet (\exists y : Lecturer \bullet annoyed(y) \wedge attends(x, u))$

7.5 Comparison with variable usage in programming

The discussion in Sections 7.1 and 7.2 has some relevance to programming. This is because scope of quantifiers and status of variables applies also to programs, albeit in a different way. Consider a fragment of a program with the following form:

```
begin
var
    x, y : integer;
    ⋮
    x := 4;
    y := 2;
    ⋮
    begin
    var
        x : integer        ◀ A
        ⋮
        x := 5;
        x := x × y;
        ⋮
    end                    ◀ B
    ⋮
    x := x × y;
    ⋮
end
```

scope of second x

scope of first x

The program consists of two 'blocks' of code, one embedded inside the other. Each block refers to a certain variable x, but the two xs are two different variables denoting, in general, different values. As the program execution reaches the point marked by A, the inner block overrides the context of the outer block. When the program execution reaches the point marked by B, the context of the outer block is restored. Thus, the underlying machine treats the two xs as two different variables by physically storing their values at different locations of the memory.

Compare the above with the following formula:

$$\forall x, y \bullet \overbrace{p(x) \wedge (z(\underbrace{\exists x \bullet q(x,y)) \vee r(x,y))}}$$

In this formula the scope of the first x, indicated by the under-brace, is overridden by the scope of the second x, indicated by the over-brace.

The situation in the above program fragment is similar to that in the above formula. Different blocks in a program using a common variable name are conceptually similar to different scopes of a common variable name in a formula.

The inner block in the program fragment treats its x as a local variable and has no access to the x in the outer block. However, since there is no y declared within it, the inner block treats y as a global variable. The inner block can refer to y (or has access to it), but cannot affect its value. Print statements for x inserted soon after each multiplication would therefore produce two different values, 10 and 8 respectively, assuming neither x nor y are affected by any other computations. If we exercise the freedom to use the terminology in logic, within the inner block x is a 'bound variable', whereas y is a 'free variable'.

This similarity can be extended to abstract programs, discussed in Section 6.8 of Chapter 6. We illustrate this by using the abstract programs of Example 6.13.

Example 7.8

Let us first extend the abstract programs in Example 6.13 with variable declarations to emphasize the point that some are local variables. In this context, obviously, the 'bound' variables are local variables and 'free' variables are global variables.

Abstract program	*Variable status*
var $x \bullet x : [\textbf{true}, x > y]$	x is 'bound' and y is 'free'
var $x \bullet x : [\textbf{true}, y^2 = x]$	x is 'bound' and y is 'free'
var $y \bullet y : [x \geqslant 0, y^2 = x]$	x is 'free' and y is 'bound'
var $x, y \bullet x, y : [\textbf{true}, y^2 = x]$	Both x and y are 'bound'
var $x \bullet x : [b^2 - 4 \times a \times c \geqslant 0,$ $a \times x^2 + b \times x + c = 0]$	x is 'bound', but a, b and c are 'free'
var $a, b, c \bullet a, b, c : [\textbf{true},$ $a \times x^2 + b \times x + c = 0]$	a, b and c are 'bound', but x is 'free'

Exercise 7.8 ✳

After introducing variable declarations as appropriate, identify the status of variables in abstract programs produced as answers to Exercise 6.11 as 'bound' and 'free' variables.

7.6 Comparison with variable usage in mathematics

The concepts of bound and free variables have their origins, as well as a wider relevance, in ordinary mathematics. This section provides some familiar examples.

With respect to the integral below, for example,

$$\int_0^y x \, y \, dx$$

we may observe that

1. $\int$ is the operation symbol.

2. dx introduces the integration variable x. [In the terminology introduced in this chapter, the variable x is said to be *bound* to the integration operator and is a *dummy* variable in the sense that the value of the integral does not depend on x.]

3. xy is the formula under the scope of the integration operator.

4. y is called a *free* variable since it is free to assume any value as permitted by the context outside the integral.

The same state of affairs may be seen in other contexts, for example, in the summation,

$$\sum_{n=0}^{5} a_n \, x^{n-1}$$

where n is bound and the a_i and x are free. However, there can also be mixed situations such as,

$$ax + \int_0^y y \sin x \, dx$$

where a, y and the first occurrence of x are free and the second occurrence of x is bound.

Thus, the role of variables varies according to how they relate to the mathematical operators embedded in expressions. If a variable has been introduced as a subsidiary variable for the purpose of defining how a certain value is to be computed, then that variable is said to be *bound* within the *scope* of the relevant operator.

Chapter 8

Interpretation of formulae

Topic: Predicate logic

···

Mathematics may be defined as the subject in which we never know what we are talking about, nor whether what we are saying is true.

Bertrand Russell
English logician and philosopher (1872–1970)

Objectives

On completion of this chapter you should be able to:

- Establish the truth value of formulae in predicate logic.
- Reason informally in predicate logic.

In Chapter 3, we established the truth values of formulae in propositional logic using truth tables. In this chapter we study how to establish the same in predicate logic.

There is a major distinction between the two systems. In propositional logic, we had propositional variables (symbols) taking only truth values. In predicate logic, we deal with individuals, their properties and relationships between them. Some predicates may be true of certain individuals and false of others. Thus, truth values apply to predicates instantiated with individuals.

As a result, we cannot construct, as in propositional logic, a truth table starting from prime propositions. We have to develop a new kind of 'truth table' starting not from prime propositions, but from individuals.

8.1 Interpretation of universal quantification

Let us assume that we are dealing with a finite domain of individuals. In this case, we may expand universal quantification into a finite number of conjunctions.

Definition Universal quantification
───

$$\forall x : X \bullet p(x) \Longleftrightarrow p(x_1) \land p(x_2) \land \ldots \land p(x_n)$$

where $x_1, x_2, \ldots, x_n$ are the names of all the individuals in the set X.

Example 8.1

Let the human society H consist of the individuals *Adam*, *Eve*, *Rosalyn*, *Pele*, *Mario* only, and let the following propositions hold true:

male(*Adam*)	*greedy*(*Adam*)	*kind*(*Mario*)
male(*Pele*)	*greedy*(*Pele*)	*kind*(*Eve*)
male(*Mario*)		

Let these predicates be false of the individuals not mentioned above. Is the following formula true in the given context?

$$\forall x : H \bullet male(x) \Rightarrow greedy(x) \vee kind(x)$$

The truth of this formula may be established as T by constructing a table like the one shown in Table 8.1.

Table 8.1   'Truth table' for Example 8.1.

x	$male(x)$	$greedy(x)$	$kind(x)$	$greedy(x)$ $\vee$ $kind(x)$	$male(x) \Rightarrow$ $greedy(x) \vee$ $kind(x)$	$\forall x : H \bullet$ $male(x) \Rightarrow$ $greedy(x) \vee$ $kind(x)$
Adam	T	T	F	T	T	—
Eve	F	F	T	T	T	—
Rosalyn	F	F	F	F	T	—
Pele	T	T	F	T	T	—
Mario	T	F	T	T	T	—
						T

On the other hand, it is clear from Table 8.1 that

$$\forall x : H \bullet greedy(x) \vee kind(x)$$

is a false formula.

Exercise 8.1 ✳ ✳

Evaluate the truth of the following formulae for the scenario given in Example 8.1.

1. $\forall x : H \bullet \neg\, male(x) \Rightarrow kind(x)$
2. $\forall x : H \bullet greedy(x) \Leftrightarrow male(x) \wedge \neg\, kind(x)$
3. $\forall x : H \mid kind(x) \bullet \neg\, male(x) \vee x = \textbf{\textit{Mario}}$

8.2 Interpretation of existential quantification

In a finite domain of individuals, existential quantification may be expanded into a finite number of disjunctions.

Definition) Existential quantification

$$\exists x : X \bullet p(x) \Longleftrightarrow p(x_1) \lor p(x_2) \lor \ldots \lor p(x_n)$$

where $x_1, x_2, \ldots, x_n$ are the names of all the individuals in the set X.

Example 8.2)

Returning to the previous example, consider the truth value of

$$\exists x : H \bullet male(x) \land (\neg\, greedy(x) \Rightarrow kind(x))$$

x	$male(x)$	$greedy(x)$	$kind(x)$	$\neg\, greedy(x)$	$\neg\, greedy(x)$ $\Rightarrow kind(x)$	$male(x) \land$ $(\neg\, greedy(x)$ $\Rightarrow kind(x))$	$\exists x : H \bullet$ $male(x) \land$ $(\neg\, greedy(x)$ $\Rightarrow kind(x))$
Adam	T	T	F	F	T	T	—
Eve	F	F	T	T	T	F	—
Rosalyn	F	F	F	T	F	F	—
Pele	T	T	F	F	T	T	—
Mario	T	F	T	T	T	T	—
							T

Exercise 8.2 ✳✳)

Evaluate the truth of the following formulae for the scenario given in Example 8.1.

1. $\exists x : H \bullet male(x) \land (greedy(x) \lor \neg\, kind(x))$
2. $(\exists x : H \bullet \neg\, male(x) \land kind(x)) \Rightarrow (\forall x : H \bullet male(x) \Rightarrow \neg\, kind(x))$
3. $\exists x : H \mid greedy(x) \bullet \neg\, x = \textbf{Adam} \land male(x)$

8.3 Theorems in predicate logic and proofs

The expansion of quantifiers into a series of conjunctions (or disjunctions) cannot be done when one is dealing with infinite domains. In this case, establishing the truth value of a universally quantified formula requires proofs – a topic covered in the next two chapters. Here we outline how to reason informally about formulae.

Certain logical equivalences and logical implications hold in predicate logic. These are usually referred to as *theorems*, since their proofs do not involve any premises. An example is

$$\forall x \bullet p(x) \wedge q(x) \iff (\forall x \bullet p(x)) \wedge (\forall x \bullet q(x)) \tag{8.1}$$

A proper proof of this requires us to know how to handle variables in predicate logic. This topic is covered in the next chapter. Our reasoning here about the logical truth of the above is therefore informal.

We can consider the above as two implications:

$$\forall x \bullet p(x) \wedge q(x) \Rightarrow (\forall x \bullet p(x)) \wedge (\forall x \bullet q(x)) \tag{8.2}$$

$$(\forall x \bullet p(x)) \wedge (\forall x \bullet q(x)) \Rightarrow \forall x \bullet p(x) \wedge q(x) \tag{8.3}$$

and reason about them individually. Consider implication (8.2) first. If we can assume that

$$\forall x \bullet p(x) \wedge q(x) \tag{8.4}$$

then prove that

$$(\forall x \bullet p(x)) \wedge (\forall x \bullet q(x)) \tag{8.5}$$

holds, then we would have proved (8.2) to be a logical implication since the proof involves no other premises.

Hence, let us assume (8.4). Then

$$p(x) \wedge q(x) \tag{8.6}$$

is true for any x. Similarly $p(x)$ is true for any x and so is $q(x)$. Therefore, we can conclude

$$\forall x \bullet p(x)$$

$$\forall x \bullet q(x) \tag{8.7}$$

individually, from where we establish (8.5). Thus (8.2) is a logical implication. Turning to the proof of the implication (8.3), we assume (8.5), from where we obtain (8.7). From (8.7), we can deduce that $p(x)$ holds for every x and that $q(x)$ also holds. It follows that

$$p(x) \wedge q(x)$$

is true for every x. The same can be rewritten as

$$\forall x \bullet p(x) \wedge q(x)$$

which is the conclusion of (8.3) and hence the proof of (8.3). Again, since our reasoning does not involve other premises, (8.3) is a logical implication. This concludes the proof of the logical equivalence (8.1).

8.4 Useful theorems in predicate logic

The following are useful theorems in predicate logic.

1. $\forall x \bullet p(x) \wedge q(x) \Longleftrightarrow (\forall x \bullet p(x)) \wedge (\forall x \bullet q(x))$
2. $\exists x \bullet p(x) \vee q(x) \Longleftrightarrow (\exists x \bullet p(x)) \vee (\exists x \bullet q(x))$
3. $\neg \exists x \bullet p(x) \Longleftrightarrow \forall x \bullet \neg p(x)$
   This theorem concerns the propagation of negation through the quantifier $\exists$.
4. $\neg \forall x \bullet p(x) \Longleftrightarrow \exists x \bullet \neg p(x)$
   This theorem concerns the propagation of negation through the quantifier $\forall$.
5. $(\forall x \bullet p(x)) \vee (\forall x \bullet q(x)) \Longrightarrow \forall x \bullet p(x) \vee q(x)$
6. $\exists x \bullet p(x) \wedge q(x) \Longrightarrow (\exists x \bullet p(x)) \wedge (\exists x \bullet q(x))$
7. $\exists x \bullet p(y) \wedge q(x) \Longrightarrow p(y) \wedge (\exists x \bullet q(x))$
   if x does not occur free in $p(y)$. An analogous theorem holds for $\forall$.
8. $\exists x, y \bullet p(x, y) \Longrightarrow \exists y, x \bullet p(x, y)$
   Variable declarations may be interchanged if they have been introduced by the same quantifier. An analogous theorem holds for $\forall$.

However, note the following:

$$\forall x \bullet (p(x) \vee q(x)) \not\Longleftrightarrow (\forall x \bullet p(x)) \vee (\forall x \bullet q(x))$$

$$\exists x \bullet (p(x) \wedge q(x)) \not\Longleftrightarrow (\exists x \bullet p(x)) \wedge (\exists x \bullet q(x))$$

Some logical implications hold between the left- and right-hand sides of above. Establish them as exercises.

Exercise 8.3 ✳✳✳

1. Give informal proofs for the following theorems.
   (a) $\exists x \bullet p(x) \vee q(x) \Longleftrightarrow (\exists x \bullet p(x)) \vee (\exists x \bullet q(x))$
   (b) $\forall x \bullet \neg p(x) \Longleftrightarrow \neg \exists x \bullet p(x)$

2. Are the following formulae logically equivalent? Give an informal proof of your answer.
   $\forall y \bullet \exists x \bullet p(x, y)$
   $\exists x \bullet \forall y \bullet p(x, y)$

Chapter 9

Proofs in predicate logic

Topic: Predicate logic

In questions of science the authority of a thousand is not worth the humble reasoning of a single individual.

Galileo Galilei
Italian mathematician, astronomer and physicist
(1564–1642)

Objectives

On completion of this chapter you should be able to:

- Identify genuine variables and variables standing for unknowns.

- Introduce quantifiers in order to make explicit, if necessary, which are genuine variables and which are unknowns.

- Describe the role of different inference rules used in predicate logic, including those it inherits from propositional logic.

- Justify variable handling rules applicable to elimination and introduction of quantifiers.

- Conduct proofs in predicate logic.

- Refine abstract programs by other abstract programs and by assignment.

Our study of proofs in propositional logic in Chapters 4 and 5 dealt with arguments expressed in terms of prime propositions. This chapter extends the discussion to include reasoning about relationships among individuals or objects involved in arguments.

The notions of values and variables have enabled us to establish a link between predicate logic and programs. The benefit of this link lies, really, in the ability to reason about programs formally. Furthermore, since our interest is not confined to programming but covers activities such as specification and design, proofs in predicate logic have far wider applications in computing. Such an application is the development of programs from their abstract specifications by a process of successive *refinement*. An introduction to this topic is given towards the end of this chapter.

Despite its general importance, this text does not rely heavily on the material in this chapter as a prerequisite for the study of the remainder. Therefore, a decision to skip this chapter initially should not cause many difficulties in the study of subsequent chapters.

(9.1) Recapitulation

Let us first recapitulate the aspects of predicate logic which are of immediate relevance to our study of proofs in predicate logic.

As we have seen, predicate logic is an extension of propositional logic. In other words, it incorporates propositional logic fully within it. It differs from propositional logic by having the following:

- symbols that uniquely identify specific individuals or *constants* and denote nothing else;
- symbols which play the role of *variables* denoting unspecified individuals;
- predicate symbols, constants and variables, which together yield *predicates*;
- two symbols ∀ and ∃, called *quantifiers*, for forming propositions out of predicates.

These features concern the syntax of predicate logic. In this new enterprise, since predicates take over the role of propositional variables, propositional logic has a slightly modified role. However, propositional connectives such as ∧ and ∨ continue to play the role of 'glue' for building complex formulae out of simpler ones.

When it comes to interpretation, predicate logic treats the formulae that can be built using the above features in the following manner:

- It treats predicates with constants only (that is, predicates not containing variables) as propositions which are either true or false.
- It treats formulae with quantifiers but with no free variables as propositions.
- It treats formulae with quantifiers but with free variables simply as predicates, albeit with a more complex appearance.

(9.2) Formulae in propositional form

This chapter aims to explain how predicate logic reasons about the validity of arguments expressed using formulae in predicate logic. Here, predicate logic retains intact the capability of propositional logic to reason about the validity of arguments expressed in propositional style. However, it now has to reason about the validity not in terms of propositional symbols, but in terms of individuals and their relationships, while fully respecting the framework of proof it borrowed from propositional logic.

Table 9.1 Examples of formulae in propositional form.

Formula	Main connective	Whether in propositional form
1. $kind(x) \land adult(x)$	$\land$	Yes (For reasoning about x being *kind* or an *adult*)
2. $kind(x)$	none	Yes (For reasoning about x being *kind*. Note that predicates play the role of propositions)
3. $\forall x \bullet kind(x) \land adult(x)$	$\forall$	No (For reasoning about any individual being *kind* or *adult*)
4 $kind(y) \lor$ $\boxed{\forall x \bullet kind(x) \land adult(x)}$	$\lor$	Yes (For reasoning about y being *kind* or the set of individuals involved in the second disjunct as a whole)
5. $\boxed{\forall x \bullet kind(x) \land adult(x)}$	none	Yes (For reasoning about the formula as a whole with no interest in the individuals and the relationships involved. Note that this formula represents a proposition)

Let us consider how predicate logic achieves this. In order to be able to use inference rules of propositional logic, the main connective of the formulae to be reasoned about must be a propositional connective. Obviously, this depends on the individuals and the relationships to be reasoned about. Let us refer to formulae in this form as formulae in *propositional form*. Table 9.1 presents some examples of formulae in propositional form.

Commonly, formulae in propositional form do not contain quantifiers. However, this is not necessarily the case. For example, when it is unnecessary to use information hidden within it, a quantified formula may itself may be used in place of a proposition. An example of such an instance is the formula under item (4) in the table. In short, a formula is in propositional form not because of what it is but because of inferences we wish to make from it.

As mentioned in Table 9.1, the formula

$$\forall x \bullet kind(x) \land adult(x)$$

is not in a form that can be manipulated in propositional style for reasoning about any individual being *kind* or *adult*. However, if we can eliminate $\forall$ from the above, the formula reduces to a propositional form and enables such reasoning. This suggests the need for some means in predicate logic to remove and, subsequently, to reintroduce the two quantifiers $\forall$ and $\exists$.

Once all the formulae in a given argument are reduced to the propositional form, it is possible to manipulate them using inference rules and logical laws of propositional logic as if these formulae were propositions. We can make as much reasoning as possible in propositional logic at this level and, depending on the goal, reintroduce any quantifiers at the very end of reasoning.

The above outlines how predicate logic extends the apparatus of reasoning in propositional logic. In doing so, predicate logic introduces four inference rules to the system: a rule for eliminating each of the two quantifiers $\forall$ and $\exists$, and another pair of rules for introducing each one of them.

However, these rules are not as simple as those in propositional logic. This is because there are other symbols, denoting constants and variables, brought to the system by predicate logic. It so happens that these symbols need to be handled with great care when eliminating and introducing $\forall$ and $\exists$. As a result, the four new inference rules may appear to have more to do with variable handling than any reasoning. This is a false impression given by a long list of occasionally non-intuitive rules on variable handling. As will be seen shortly, the variable handling and reasoning are closely linked.

9.3 Unknowns and genuine variables

In addition to the classification of variables into bound and free variables considered in Chapter 7, here is another classification of variables. Both these classifications will help us to understand why certain symbols have to be handled with care.

Consider the following two equations:

$$x + 5 = 9 \tag{9.1}$$

$$x + x = 2x \tag{9.2}$$

which are also predicates. Both these equations use the same symbol x as a variable. In (9.1), x denotes a specific individual, which is the number 4. In (9.2), x applies to all numbers and is not restricted to one or more specific individuals. Although it has the same variable name, x thus has a different status in each of the two equations. In (9.1), x is an *unknown* referring to a specific value which can be determined from the equation. By contrast, x in (9.2) is a *variable* in the true sense of the word.

Here are some slightly more complex examples.

$$x^2 - 3x + 2 = 0 \tag{9.3}$$

$$x^2 + 2xy + y^2 = (x + y)^2 \tag{9.4}$$

$$ax^2 + bx + c = 0 \tag{9.5}$$

In (9.3), x is an unknown and may denote either or both 1 and 2. In (9.4), x and y can be any pair of numbers. The status of a, b, c and x in (9.5) is rather tricky. Our familiarity with it in elementary algebra as the general form of a quadratic equation immediately prompts us to treat x as an unknown and a, b, c as arbitrary numbers. However, such a stand is nothing more than a presumption.

Let us examine the source of this apparent context dependence of variable status in the above formulae. It lies in the common practice in mathematics of not making explicit the quantification of variables. A closer examination should convince us that the above equations carry some 'invisible' quantifiers. These may be made explicit as,

$$\exists x \bullet x + 5 = 9 \tag{9.6}$$

$$\forall x \bullet x + x = 2x \tag{9.7}$$

$$\exists x \bullet x^2 - 3x + 2 = 0 \tag{9.8}$$

$$\forall x, y \bullet x^2 + 2xy + y^2 = (x + y)^2 \tag{9.9}$$

$$\forall a, b, c \bullet \exists x \bullet ax^2 + bx + c = 0 \tag{9.10}$$

Proposition (9.10), for example, makes absolutely clear the usage of a, b, c and x as intended in quadratic equations in elementary algebra, but in the domain of complex numbers. This is another example where predicate logic enables us to overcome ambiguities – in this case, in mathematics itself.

The quantifiers must be introduced in such a manner that the resulting formula is a true proposition. Replacement of $\exists$ in (9.8) with $\forall$, for example, results in a false proposition, which cannot be satisfied for every x. In the case of (9.10), among the other possible quantifications

$$\exists a, b, c \bullet \exists x \bullet ax^2 + bx + c = 0 \tag{9.11}$$

$$\forall a, b, c \bullet \forall x \bullet ax^2 + bx + c = 0 \tag{9.12}$$

proposition (9.11) is true and (9.12) is false.

(**Description**)   Genuine variables and unknowns

A *genuine variable* is a free variable, the universal quantification of which yields a true formula.

An *unknown* is a free variable, the existential quantification of which yields a true formula.

We are not concerned with cases where the quantification in the above results in a false proposition, since it precludes the possibility of assigning an individual (a constant) at all to the variable concerned.

(**Exercise 9.1** ✳)

Identify the unknowns and genuine variables in the following formulae or sentences and make their status explicit by introducing quantifiers as appropriate. Note that 'sin' and 'cos' are trigonometric functions and 'even' and 'odd' are predicates on integers with the obvious meanings.

1. $\sin(x) = \frac{1}{2}$

2. $\sin^2(x) + \cos^2(x) = 1$

3. $\sin^2(x) + \cos^2(y) = 1$

4. $\dfrac{a}{b} = 4$

5. $\dfrac{a}{b} = \dfrac{c}{d} \Rightarrow a \times d = b \times c$

6. $even(n) \lor odd(n)$

7. $even(n) \Leftrightarrow odd(n+1)$

8. $0 + 1 + 2 + 3 + \ldots + n = \dfrac{n(n+1)}{2}$

9. $ax^2 + bx + c = 0 \Rightarrow x = \dfrac{-b + \sqrt{b^2 - 4ac}}{2a} \lor x = \dfrac{-b - \sqrt{b^2 - 4ac}}{2a}$

10. Every even number is the sum of two prime numbers.
    (This is known as Goldbach's conjecture.)

Exercise 9.2 ✳✳

1. Using appropriate predicates, state the following conjectures about prime numbers. [You may use a function named *square(x)* defined on natural numbers (non-negative integers) and returning the square of its argument *x*.]

   (a) Every even number is the difference between two prime numbers.
   (b) Every even number is the difference between two consecutive prime numbers.
   (c) Given that *n* is a natural number, there exists at least one prime number between n^2 and $(n^2 - n)$.
   (d) There are at least four prime numbers between the squares of consecutive prime numbers greater than 3.

2. Identify the status of variables used in each of the formulae in the answer to question 1.

9.4 Notation for new inference rules

Section 9.2 mentioned the new inference rules in predicate logic: a rule for eliminating each of the two quantifiers $\forall$ and $\exists$, and another pair of rules for introducing each one of them.

Description   Notation for quantifier elimination and introduction

We use the following notation for inference rules:

● $\forall\_E$, the rule for eliminating the universal quantifier $\forall$

● $\forall\_I$, the rule for introducing the universal quantifier $\forall$

We use an analogous pair of symbols for eliminating and introducing $\exists$.

The notation in the Description is similar to that used in propositional logic for eliminating and introducing propositional connectives.

Terminology

▪ The terms *instantiation* and *elimination* are often used interchangeably as synonyms.

❋ Similarly, the term *generalization* is a synonym for the *introduction* of ∀ and the term *specialization* for the *introduction* of ∃.

9.5) What to guard against

The purpose of this section is to understand the reasoning behind the various rules on variable handling in proofs in predicate logic. In doing so we follow the approach and style adopted by Kahane (1973).

9.5.1   Freeing variables from the universal quantifier

Freeing variables when eliminating ∀ is perhaps the least problematic case of all. This is because the variables so released are genuine variables. Starting with the case of a constant a, we note that if the formula

$$\forall x \bullet p(x)$$

already appears in the proof, we may insert $p(a)$ into the proof as a new valid inference. This is shown in Figure 9.1 for an individual called *RobinHood* (a symbol denoting the legendary figure Robin Hood) and a predicate *kind* with the obvious meaning. Likewise, we may justify the inference

$$\forall x \bullet kind(x)$$

Therefore, $kind(y)$ **(9.13)**

y being a genuine variable or an unknown.

Here is another issue. When freeing a variable as a result of elimination of ∀, is it really necessary to make sure that there is not already a free occurrence of the same variable name? This appears to be an unnecessary restriction, preventing perfectly sound inferences. The following example, where $loves(x, y)$ means that x loves y, illustrates this point:

1. $\exists x \bullet \forall y \bullet loves(y, x)$ premise
2. $\forall y \bullet loves(y, x)$ from 1, ∃_E
3. $loves(x, x)$ from 2, ∀_E   ◀ valid (although more free occurrences than the number freed)
4. $\exists x \bullet loves(x, x)$ from 3, ∃_I

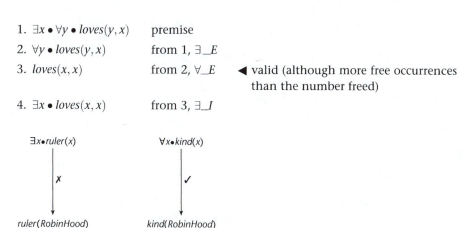

$\exists x \bullet ruler(x)$ $\forall x \bullet kind(x)$

$ruler(RobinHood)$ $kind(RobinHood)$

Figure 9.1   Inferences about constants.

It may be noted that although the elimination of ∀ in line 3 freed only one occurrence of *x*, there are two occurrences of *x* in the resulting formula. From the fact that there is at least one person who is loved by everyone, there is no difficulty in agreeing with the conclusion that there is at least one person who loves him/herself.

Note

The above proof uses rules such as ∃_*E* and ∃_*I* which are yet to be discussed. The justification for doing this is that the reasoning underlying a given rule can be better understood by demonstrating incorrect inferences that result in a complete proof as a consequence of an injudicious application of the rule.

9.5.2   Freeing variables from the existential quantifier

When dealing with variables freed by the elimination of ∃, we have especially to bear in mind the distinctions made in Section 9.3 about the status of variables, namely, about unknowns and genuine variables.

Taken in complete isolation, the inference

∃*x* • *kind*(*x*)

Therefore, *kind*(*y*)   **(9.14)**

is a valid inference, although *y* is an unknown and is not, as in (9.13), a genuine variable.

However, inferences of this sort could lead to incorrect inferences in a number of cases. First, given that *a* is a constant, it is incorrect to conclude from

∃*x* • *p*(*x*)

that *p*(*a*) is true, that is, *p* holds for *a*. This is illustrated in Figure 9.1.

(**Rule 1 on variable handling**)   _____

Do not assume that a property holds for a particular individual on the basis that it holds for at least one individual. That is, when eliminating the quantifier ∃, do not instantiate its variable with a constant.

Rule 1 is a fairly obvious rule, but there are less obvious ones, as the one relevant in the following 'proof':

1. ∃*x* • *ruler*(*x*)   premise
2. ∃*x* • *thief*(*x*)   premise
3. *ruler*(*y*)   from 1, ∃_*E*
4. *thief*(*y*)   from 2, ∃_*E*   ◄ invalid step
5. *ruler*(*y*) ∧ *thief*(*y*)   from 3 and 4, ∧_*I*
6. ∃*x* • *ruler*(*y*) ∧ *thief*(*y*)   from 5, ∃_*I*

In this 'proof', from two separate propositions about the existence of a ruler and the existence of a thief, we incorrectly conclude that there is a ruler who also happens to be a thief. Let us trace where we went wrong. In step 3, by eliminating ∃ from the formula in line 1, we correctly conclude that the individual y is a ruler. Note that y is a variable name that we have chosen and is an unknown. Then in step 4, when eliminating ∃ from the formula in line 2, we incorrectly conclude that the same unknown individual y is a thief.

Conceptually, the reason for the incorrect inference in step 4 is therefore a mix-up of two different unknown variables because of the use of a single variable name.

(Rule 2 on variable handling)

When eliminating the quantifier ∃, do not instantiate its variable with an existing free variable.

For the above reason, the right order of inferences in a proof involving the premises

$\forall x \bullet kind(x)$
$\exists x \bullet thief(x)$

is

1. $\forall x \bullet kind(x)$ premise
2. $\exists x \bullet thief(x)$ premise
3. $thief(y)$ from 2, ∃_E
4. $kind(y)$ from 1, ∀_E
     ⋮

and not

1. $\forall x \bullet kind(x)$ premise
2. $\exists x \bullet thief(x)$ premise
3. $kind(y)$ from 1, ∀_E
4. $thief(y)$ from 2, ∃_E ◀ invalid step
     ⋮

although, in this particular case, the order would have been immaterial as far as the outcome is concerned.

The incorrect 'proof' given earlier is illustrated in Figure 9.2, which also shows a proof with a sequence of correct inferences.

9.5.3   Introduction of the universal quantifier

Introduction of ∀ signifies a universal generalization. In order to generalize that a certain property holds for all individuals, we must consider an arbitrary element x

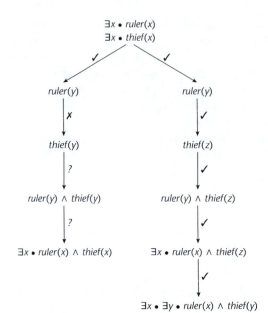

Figure 9.2   Inferences about unknowns.

(an element with no qualification at all about its choice) and prove that the property concerned is true of *x*. If this can be done, it is only on the basis of the arbitrary nature of *x* that we can claim that the property holds for all individuals.

The requirement on the arbitrary nature of the variable to be quantified precludes the choice of several kinds of symbol for generalization. These are as follows.

Given that $p(a)$ is true for a constant *a*, the insertion of the line

$$\forall x \bullet p(x)$$

in a proof is an invalid inference. This is illustrated in Figure 9.3.

Rule 3 on variable handling

Do not generalize, that is, introduce the quantifier $\forall$, on the basis of an individual (a constant).

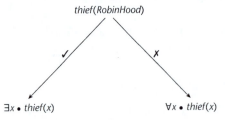

Figure 9.3   Inferences from constants.

Needless to say, as with constants, generalizations on the basis of unknowns, that is, variables freed by elimination of ∃s, are not allowed.

(Rule 4 on variable handling)

Do not generalize, that is, introduce the quantifier ∀, on the basis of an unknown.

Consider now the following 'proof', where the predicate *parent*(*y*, *x*) means that *y* is a parent of *x*.

1. ∀*x* • ∃*y* • *parent*(*y*, *x*)   premise
2. ∃*y* • *parent*(*y*, *x*)   from 1, ∀_*E*
3. *parent*(*y*, *x*)   from 2, ∃_*E*
4. ∀*x* • *parent*(*y*, *x*)   from 3, ∀_*I*   ◀ invalid step
5. ∃*y* • ∀*x* • *parent*(*y*, *x*)   from 4, ∃_*I*

The above 'proof' obeys the rule given in the previous section for ∃ since the elimination of ∃ in step 3 instantiates its freed variable with a fresh free variable. Yet the 'proof' does not make sense. It starts off with the premise that 'everybody has a parent' and concludes that 'there is someone who is everybody's parent'. Where have we gone wrong now? Obviously, steps 2 and 3 are correct. Step 4 seems to be reasonable too because all it does is to requantify with ∀ the variable *x* – a genuine variable previously released by the elimination of a ∀. However, this is the step leading to the incorrect inference and we must disallow such inferences. The problem is on what grounds to disallow such inferences. The only conceivable reason is that step 4 makes a generalization on the basis of the formula on line 3 obtained by elimination of ∃, that is, the formula on line 3 is 'contaminated' by mere association with ∃. Figure 9.4 is an illustration of the above 'proof'.

∀*x* • ∃*y* • *parent*(*x*, *y*)

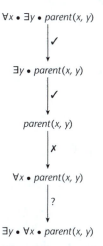

∃*y* • *parent*(*x*, *y*)

parent(*x*, *y*)

∀*x* • *parent*(*x*, *y*)

∃*y* • ∀*x* • *parent*(*x*, *y*)

Figure 9.4 generalization on the basis of a 'contaminated' genuine variable.

> **Rule 5 on variable handling**
>
> Do not generalize on the basis of a variable appearing in a formula obtained by eliminating the quantifier $\exists$, irrespective of whether that variable is a genuine variable.

9.5.4   Introduction of the existential quantifier

Contrary to the case with the universal quantifier, on the basis that a is a constant and $p(a)$ already appears in the proof, the line

$$\exists x \bullet p(x)$$

may be inserted into the proof as a new valid inference. This is also illustrated in Figure 9.3.

In Section 9.5.1, we concluded that it is unnecessary to make sure that the number of freed occurrences of a variable by elimination of $\forall$ need not be the same as the total number of free occurrences of the same variable name after the elimination. A similar freedom applies to $\exists$ but in the reverse process of quantifier introduction.

Here is an example, using the predicate $loves(x,y)$ to mean that x loves y.

1. $\forall y \bullet loves(y, y)$ premise

2. $loves(x, x)$ from 1, $\forall\_E$

3. $\exists y \bullet loves(x, y)$ from 2, $\exists\_I$ ◄ valid (although fewer bound occurrences than the number originally free)

4. $\forall y \bullet \exists x \bullet loves(y, x)$ from 3, $\forall\_I$

Thus, if everyone loves him/herself, then everyone loves someone.

9.5.5   Generalizations from assumptions

Consider the 'proof', where $gold(x)$ means that x is made out of gold.

1. $gold(x)$ assumption

2. $\forall y \bullet gold(y)$ from 1, $\forall\_I$ ◄ invalid step

3. $gold(x) \Rightarrow \forall y \bullet gold(y)$ from 1 & 2, $\Rightarrow\_I$

4. $\forall x \bullet (gold(x) \Rightarrow \forall y \bullet gold(y))$ from 3, $\forall\_I$

Here, from an assumption, we have concluded that if anything is gold then everything is gold. The problem is that in step 2 we have generalized using the variable x appearing in an assumption within the scope of that assumption, that is, before discharging it. The same proof is illustrated in Figure 9.5. In order to disallow such inferences, we must adopt Rule 6 on variable handling.

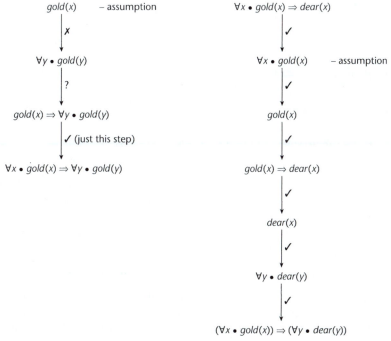

Figure 9.5 Inferences from assumptions.

(**Rule 6 on variable handling**)

Within the scope of an assumption, do not generalize on the basis of a variable appearing in the assumption.

However, a generalization based on the same variable after discharging the assumption is permitted. See Figure 9.5 for illustrations.

9.5.6 Inadvertent binding of newly freed variables

When freeing variables, one of our concerns so far has been to make sure, if necessary, that a freed variable does not clash with any existing free variable. Obviously, this is not a restriction we must always observe, but one that applies to elimination of $\exists$. What happens, though, if a freed variable clashes with a variable which is still bound by a quantifier?

Such a 'freed' variable does not really become free and, instead, gets bound in the process of 'freeing'. A consequence of such an inadvertent binding can be seen in the following 'proof' (see Figure 9.6(a)), where, as before, the predicate $parent(y, x)$ means that y is a parent of x.

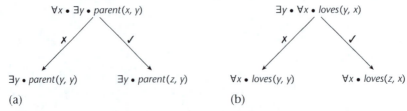

Figure 9.6   Inadvertent binding of newly freed variables.

1. $\forall x \bullet \exists y \bullet parent(y, x)$ premise

2. $\exists y \bullet parent(y, y)$ from 1, $\forall\_E$ ◀ invalid step

The choice of y for the newly freed variable leads to the conclusion that there is someone who is the parent of him/herself, which is obviously absurd. This proof is illustrated in Figure 9.6(a). A similar conclusion is drawn from the following 'proof' (see Figure 9.6(b)):

1. $\exists y \bullet \forall x \bullet loves(y, x)$ premise

2. $\forall x \bullet loves(x, x)$ from 1, $\forall\_E$ ◀ invalid step

This states that everyone loves him/herself, from the premise that there is someone who loves everyone. This conclusion is not as disastrous as in the previous 'proof', and indeed might be the case, but the point is that it cannot be inferred from the given premise.

> **Rule 7 on variable handling**
>
> Every instantiation, whether following the elimination of a $\forall$ or a $\exists$, must always be done with a free variable.

9.5.7   Unintended binding of newly quantified variables

The above kind of inadvertent binding could happen in the process of quantification of variables too. Consider the following 'proof':

1. $\forall x \bullet \exists y \bullet parent(y, x)$ premise

2. $\exists y \bullet parent(y, x)$ from 1, $\forall\_E$

3. $\forall y \bullet \exists y \bullet parent(y, y)$ from 2, $\forall\_I$ ◀ invalid step

We have managed to infer, from a premise that everyone has a parent, that there is someone who is a parent of him/herself; see Figure 9.7(a). Here is a similar scenario involving the existential quantification. Note that the predicate $boss(x, y)$ is true if and only if the individual x is a manager (boss) of the individual y.

1. $\forall x \bullet \exists y \bullet boss(y, x)$ premise

2. $\exists y \bullet boss(y, x)$ from 1, $\forall\_E$

3. $\exists y \bullet \exists y \bullet boss(y, y)$ from 2, $\exists\_I$ ◀ invalid step

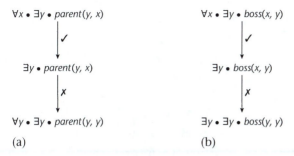

$\forall x \bullet \exists y \bullet parent(y, x)$

✓

$\exists y \bullet parent(y, x)$

✗

$\forall y \bullet \exists y \bullet parent(y, y)$

(a)

$\forall x \bullet \exists y \bullet boss(x, y)$

✓

$\exists y \bullet boss(x, y)$

✗

$\exists y \bullet \exists y \bullet boss(y, y)$

(b)

Figure 9.7   Unintended binding of newly quantified variables.

From the premise that there is a manager for everybody, the above 'proof' leads us to the conclusion that there are some who are managers of themselves (see Figure 9.7(b)). Although this is not unreasonable, the given premise does not warrant on its own the inference of the given conclusion. Again, what has happened is the binding of a newly quantified variable by an unintended quantifier.

Rule 8 on variable handling

Beware of binding of any newly quantified variable, that is, as a result of the introduction of either ∀ or ∃, by an unintended quantifier.

Exercise 9.3 ✳ ✳

Given below is an 'aimless proof' with some invalid inferences. Comment on the correctness of each step, assuming that all lines justifying it have been arrived at correctly. In the case of any incorrect inference, give reasons separately.

The 'proof' uses the predicates *master* and *serves* with the following meanings:

x master   is true if and only if the individual x is a master.
x serves y   is true if and only if the individual x serves the individual y.

The symbols a, b, c, etc. are constants or specific individuals, whereas u, v, w, x, y, z are genuine variables or unknowns.

			Correct/incorrect
1.	*a master*	premise	
2.	$\forall x \bullet x\ master$ $\Rightarrow \exists y \bullet y \neq x \land y\ serves\ x$	premise	
3.	$\forall x \bullet x\ master$	from 1, $\forall\_I$	....
4.	$\exists y \bullet y \neq x \land y\ serves\ x$	from 2 & 3 $\Rightarrow \_E$	....

Correct/incorrect

5(a) *y master*
  $\Rightarrow \exists y \bullet y \neq y \wedge y$ *serves* y from 2, $\forall\_E$ ....

5(b) *z master*
  $\Rightarrow \exists y \bullet z \neq y \wedge y$ *serves* z from 2, $\forall\_E$ ....

5(c) *z master*
  $\Rightarrow \exists y \bullet z \neq y \wedge y$ *serves* x from 2, $\forall\_E$ ....

6.   *z master*   an assumption

7. $\exists y \bullet z \neq y \wedge y$ *serves* z from 4 & 6, $\Rightarrow\_E$ ....

8(a) $z \neq y \wedge y$ *serves* z from 7, $\exists\_E$ ....

8(b) $z \neq a \wedge a$ *serves* z from 7, $\exists\_E$ ....

8(c) $z \neq z \wedge z$ *serves* z from 7, $\exists\_E$ ....

8(d) $z \neq w \wedge w$ *serves* z from 7, $\exists\_E$ ....

8(e) $z \neq v \wedge w$ *serves* z from 7, $\exists\_E$ ....

9. w *serves* z from 8(d)–8(e), $\wedge\_E$ ....

10(a) $\forall y \bullet y$ *serves* z from 9, $\forall\_E$ ....

10(b) $\forall z \bullet w$ *serves* z from 9, $\forall\_I$ ....

10(c) $\forall z \bullet z \neq z \wedge z$ *serves* z from 8(d) $\forall\_I$ ....

11(a) $\exists x \bullet x$ *serves* w from 9, $\exists\_I$ ....

11(b) $\exists x \bullet v$ *serves* x from 9, $\exists\_I$ ....

11(c) $\exists w \bullet w$ *serves* w from 9, $\exists\_I$ ....

12(a) *z master* $\Rightarrow \exists x \bullet x$ *serves* z from 6 & 11(a) $\Rightarrow\_I$ ....

12(b) *z master*
  $\Rightarrow \exists y \bullet z \neq y \wedge y$ *serves* z from 6 & 7, $\Rightarrow\_I$ ....

13(a) $\forall y \bullet (y$ *master* $\Rightarrow \exists x \bullet x$ *serves* $y)$ from 12(a), $\forall\_I$ ....

13(b) $\forall y \bullet y$ *master*
  $\Rightarrow \exists y \bullet y \neq y \wedge y$ *serves* y from 12(b), $\forall\_I$ ....

$\vdots$

Example 9.1

Masters and slaves in a society are all adult men. However, it is not the case that all persons in this society are adult men. Prove that there are some who are not masters.

Proof

Let us use the predicates, *master* _ , *slave* _ , *adult* _ , *man* _ .
Then:

1. $\forall x \bullet (master\ x \vee slave\ x \Rightarrow adult\ x \wedge man\ x)$ premise
2. $\neg \forall x \bullet adult\ x \wedge man\ x$ premise

3. $\exists x \bullet \neg (adult\ x \wedge man\ x)$ from 2, theorem 4 listed in Section 8.4

4. $\neg (adult\ x \wedge man\ x)$ from 3, $\exists\_E$

5. $master\ x \vee slave\ x \Rightarrow adult\ x \wedge man\ x$ from 1, $\forall\_E$

6. $\neg (master\ x \vee slave\ x)$ from 4 & 5, $\Rightarrow\_E$

7. $\neg (master\ x) \wedge \neg (slave\ x)$ from 6, De Morgan's law

8. $\neg (master\ x)$ from 7, $\wedge\_E$

9. $\exists y \bullet \neg master\ y$ from 8; $\exists\_I$

Hence, the proof.

Example 9.2

Continuing Example 9.1, assume now that all masters and slaves are adults. However, there is at least one person who is neither a master nor a slave. Also, not all persons are young or not slaves. Show that there are some adults in this society.

Proof

Let us introduce a further predicate: $young$ __.

1. $\forall x \bullet master\ x \vee slave\ x \Rightarrow adult\ x$ premise

2. $\exists y \bullet \neg (master\ y) \wedge \neg (slave\ y)$ premise

3. $\neg \forall z \bullet young\ z \vee \neg (slave\ z)$ premise

4. $\exists z \bullet \neg (young\ z \vee \neg (slave\ z))$ from 3, theorem 4 listed in Section 8.4

5. $\neg (young\ z \vee \neg (slave\ z))$ from 4, $\exists\_E$

6. $\neg (young\ z) \wedge \neg \neg (slave\ z)$ from 5, De Morgan's law

7. $\neg \neg (slave\ z)$ from 6, $\wedge\_E$

8. $slave\ z$ from 7, $\neg\_E$

9. $slave\ z \vee master\ z$ from 8, $\vee\_I$

10. $master\ z \vee slave\ z$ from 9, commutativity

11. $master\ z \vee slave\ z \Rightarrow adult\ z$ from 1, $\forall\_E$

12. $adult\ z$ from 10 & 11, $\Rightarrow\_E$

13. $\exists x \bullet adult\ x$ from 12, $\exists\_I$

Hence, the proof.

9.6 Theorems in predicate logic

In Section 8.4, we considered the validity of theorems in predicate logic on an informal basis, giving, in addition, a list of important theorems. Let us return to this topic in order to see how such proofs can be conducted formally.

As mentioned in Chapter 5, the formulae derivable without using premises are called theorems. The theorems in predicate logic concern the interrelationships which hold under all circumstances among logical connectives, predicates and quantifiers and they supplement the armoury of propositional tautologies which we studied in Chapters 3 and 4. However, as was seen in Chapter 8, these theorems *cannot* be established using truth tables. When dealing with large or infinite domains of values, proofs are the only viable means of reasoning about the validity of formulae in predicate logic.

Proof of theorems is similar to proof of consequences from premises, except that, since such proofs do not consist of any premises, the first line has to be inserted by ourselves. The insertion of the first line often amounts to making an assumption with the hope of discharging it later on, as soon as the goal is reached. We are familiar with this approach through proof strategies such as conditional and indirect proofs, discussed in Chapter 5.

Example 9.3

Assuming that the underlying domain of values has at least one element, that is, it is not empty, show the validity of the following:

$$(\exists x \bullet p(x) \Rightarrow q(a)) \Longleftrightarrow ((\forall x \bullet p(x)) \Rightarrow q(a))$$

where a is a constant or a free variable.

Proof

In order to prove the above, let us try to prove separately the following two implications:

$$(\exists x \bullet p(x) \Rightarrow q(a)) \Rightarrow ((\forall x \bullet p(x)) \Rightarrow q(a))$$

and

$$((\forall x \bullet p(x)) \Rightarrow q(a)) \Rightarrow (\exists x \bullet p(x) \Rightarrow q(a))$$

Proof of the first implication:

1.	$\exists x \bullet (p(x) \Rightarrow q(a))$	assumption
2.	$\forall x \bullet p(x)$	assumption
3.	$p(x) \Rightarrow q(a)$	from 1, $\exists\_E$
4.	$p(x)$	from 2, $\forall\_E$
5.	$q(a)$	from 3 & 4, $\Rightarrow\_E$
6.	$(\forall x \bullet p(x)) \Rightarrow q(a)$	from 2 & 5, $\Rightarrow\_I$ (discharging the second assumption)
7.	$\exists x \bullet p(x) \Rightarrow q(a)) \Rightarrow ((\forall x \bullet p(x)) \Rightarrow q(a))$	from 1 & 6, $\Rightarrow\_I$ (discharging the first assumption)

Proof of the second implication consists of an indirect proof embedded in a conditional proof.

8. $(\forall x \bullet p(x)) \Rightarrow q(a)$ assumption

9. $\forall x \bullet p(x) \wedge \neg q(a)$ assumption

10. $(\forall x \bullet p(x)) \wedge \neg q(a)$ from 9, theorem 7 listed in Section 8.4

11. $\forall x \bullet p(x)$ from 10, $\wedge\_E$

12. $\neg q(a)$ from 10, $\wedge\_E$

13. $q(a)$ from 8 & 11, $\Rightarrow\_E$

14. $\neg q(a) \wedge q(a)$ from 12 & 13, $\wedge\_I$

15.   *false*   from 14, contradiction

16. $\neg (\forall x \bullet p(x) \wedge \neg q(a))$ from 9 & 15, $\neg\_I$

17. $\exists x \bullet \neg (p(x) \wedge \neg q(a))$ from 16, theorem 4 listed in Section 8.4

18. $\exists x \bullet \neg p(x) \vee \neg \neg q(a)$ from 17, De Morgan

19. $\exists x \bullet \neg p(x) \vee q(a)$ from 18, double negation

20. $\exists x \bullet p(x) \Rightarrow q(a)$ from 19, implication

21. $((\forall x \bullet p(x)) \Rightarrow q(a)) \Rightarrow (\exists x \bullet p(x) \Rightarrow q(a))$ from 8 & 20, $\Rightarrow\_I$

Thus, we arrive at the bi-implication:

22. $(\exists x \bullet p(x) \Rightarrow q(a)) \Leftrightarrow ((\forall x \bullet p(x)) \Rightarrow q(a))$ from 1 & 21, $\Leftrightarrow\_I$

From the above proof, and noting that it does not contain any premises and that the result no longer depends on any of the assumptions used in the proof, we conclude that the formula in line 22 is a logical equivalence. Hence, the required result.

Exercise 9.4 ✳ ✳ ✳

In each of the following, prove the last formula assuming the rest. Note that p, q and r are some unary predicates.

1. $\forall x \bullet (p(x) \vee r(x) \Rightarrow \neg q(x))$
   $\exists x \bullet \neg (\neg p(x) \wedge \neg r(x))$
   $\exists x \bullet \neg q(x)$

2. $\forall x \bullet (p(x) \Rightarrow \neg q(x))$
   $\exists x \bullet (r(x) \wedge q(x))$
   $\exists x \bullet (r(x) \wedge \neg p(x))$

3. $\forall x \bullet (q(x) \Rightarrow p(x))$
   $\exists x \bullet (r(x) \wedge \neg p(x))$
   $\forall x \bullet (\neg p(x) \vee q(x))$
   $\exists x \bullet (r(x) \wedge \neg p(x))$

Exercise 9.5 ✳✳✳

Establish the following or give counterexamples for those which cannot be proven.

1. $(\forall x \bullet p(x) \Rightarrow q(x)) \Rrightarrow (\forall x \bullet p(x) \Rightarrow \forall x \bullet q(x))$
2. $(\exists x \bullet p(y) \wedge q(x)) \Leftrightarrow p(y) \wedge \exists x \bullet q(x)$
3. $\neg \exists x \bullet \forall y \bullet p(x, y) \Leftrightarrow \forall x, y \bullet \neg p(x, y)$
4. $(\exists x \bullet (p(x) \wedge q(x))) \Rrightarrow (\exists x \bullet p(x)) \wedge (\exists x \bullet q(x))$

Exercise 9.6 ✳✳✳

Establish the validity (or the invalidity) of the following arguments.

1. **Princes are rich and they like only sports cars. Dennis is rich and he likes both his Porsche and the Mini. Porsche is a sports car and the Mini is not. Therefore, Dennis is not a prince.**
2. **Anyone who cares about others is not selfish. Anyone who cares only about himself is selfish. Therefore, everybody cares about someone.**
3. **Some visitors attend all events. No visitors attend outdoor events. Therefore, there are no outdoor events.**

Exercise 9.7 ✳✳✳

Recall Exercise 5.6. Here is a related one.

There are two types of people in a certain world – optimists and pessimists. Everyone is either an optimist or a pessimist, but not both. They communicate with one another only by asking questions in a highly disciplined manner and by utterances of the two words 'yes' and 'no'. The optimists only ask questions in such a way that the correct answer is always 'yes'. The pessimists, on the other hand, ask questions the correct answers to which are always 'no'.

From the following questions, deduce the type of the person asking each question and other persons referred to in the question. Note that P referred to in any given question is a specific person.

1. 'Am I a pessimist?'
2. 'Am I an optimist?'
3. 'Are both P and myself pessimists?'
4. Pointing to someone standing nearby, 'Is at least one of us a pessimist?'
5. Pointing to someone standing nearby, 'Are we of different types?'
6. 'Am I of the type who could ask whether I am a pessimist?'
7. 'Am I of the type who could ask the question I am asking now?'
8. 'Are you of the type who could ask me whether I am an optimist?'
9. 'Are you of the type who could ask whether at least one of us is a pessimist?'
10. 'Are you of the type who could ask P whether he/she is of the type who could ask whether you two are of different types?'

9.7 An application: program refinement

When introducing formal specification of programs in Section 6.8 of Chapter 6, we mentioned a formal technique called successive *refinement* for developing programs. This section elaborates on this and shows how refinement can be applied to developing programs and the role of proof in refinement. We illustrate refinement only in a rather limited sense and using very simple examples. Our aim is to concentrate on some of the ideas behind refinement rather than to demonstrate the power of refinement.

9.7.1 Programming as refinement

At the specification stage of any software, we must be conscious of the fact that a given problem may have a number of different solutions and, if that is the case, to leave them as options open to the implementer. Implementation of a specification as an executable program necessarily involves various design decisions. In the process of making such design decisions, the implementer reduces the potential solutions to a single solution.

Given that x is of the type integer, consider as an example a program for computing x such that

$$x^3 - 3x^2 + 2x = 0$$

Let it also be the case that x is expected to be initially 0 or 6. The required program may be specified as the abstract program

$$x : [x = 0 \lor x = 6, \ x^3 - 3x^2 + 2x = 0] \tag{9.15}$$

Here, the specifier has left open a number of suitable values as solutions for x. Some of them follow from the factorization

$$x^3 - 3x^2 + 2x = 0 \Leftrightarrow x(x-1)(x-2) = 0$$

The programmer may 'refine' the abstract program (9.15) to a concrete executable program or 'code' in a number of different ways. Some examples are the individual assignments

$$x := 0$$
$$x := 1$$
$$x := 2$$
$$x := x/3$$
$$x := x/6 \tag{9.16}$$

The programs listed in (9.16) are each considered a valid or correct refinement of (9.15) for two reasons. First, each uses a correct value for x in the mathematical sense and, thus, fulfils what is required in (9.15). Secondly, no program variables other than x are affected and, thus, no programming principle is violated.

The two kinds of program (9.15) and (9.16) are extremely important in refinement. As was mentioned in Section 6.8 of Chapter 6, programming begins with a specification such as (9.15), which is a statement oriented towards the humans. It is clear and precise about its purpose and is written in a language which facilitates further reasoning about what is required. Programming ends with an instruction such as (9.16). The latter is specific about what to do, but conveys no information about what is required, why it is done in that manner or why it is done at all. The purpose of refinement is to transform an intelligible command such as (9.15) by rigorous means to a program such as (9.16), which is machine-oriented and executable. However, there are other notions of refinement too!

In practical programming, for a problem of complexity (9.15), a solution of the form (9.16) is sufficient. For illustrative purposes, however, let us examine other ways for 'implementing' (9.15) and, in particular, in the form of abstract programs such as

$$x : [x = 0 \lor x = 6, x^2 - x = 0] \tag{9.17}$$

$$x : [\textbf{\textit{true}}, x^3 - 3x^2 + 2x = 0] \tag{9.18}$$

$$x : [\textbf{\textit{true}}, x^2 - x = 0] \tag{9.19}$$

Comparison of the above with (9.15) shows that, in some ways, each of the programs (9.17)–(9.19) too meets the requirements expected in (9.15). The aim of refinement is to transform systematically a program given in the form (9.15) to code such as (9.16), where necessary, through the kinds of intermediate program given in (9.17)–(9.19). Thus, refinement opens up the possibility of implementing a specification through a number of 'design' steps.

Since refinement involves both specifications and code, frameworks that advocate refinement as a disciplined approach to programming must treat them both uniformly. It is for this reason that Morgan (1994) refers to both kinds as *programs*. As a consequence, it is possible to define a whole spectrum of many other programs, lying in between the extremes such as (9.15) and (9.16) above. The most abstract in this spectrum are *specifications* in the conventional sense. Their 'abstractness' arises from two sources: first, from the fact that specifications are silent on possible solutions and implementations, and secondly, because of their bias towards mathematics in order to gain precision and clarity. In the process of refinement, the programmer gradually replaces these abstract specifications either in full, or partially, with more concrete programs until all are reduced to the most concrete form at the other end of the spectrum, that is, the *code*.

Given two programs S and S' such that S' is delivered by the developer in response to a customer request for S, we use the predicate

$$S \sqsubseteq S'$$

to mean that S' fulfils the customer's expectations as conceived in S. The above is to be read as S' **refines** S. This relation allows program development to be seen as a series of successive refinements such that in each step clarity is traded off for executability. The converse, which is *abstraction*, is true of the reverse process. This is shown diagrammatically in Figure 9.8, where S serves as the specification, S' serves as the final program, possibly the code, and each S_i represents some intermediate version between S and S'.

Increasing clarity

$$S \sqsubseteq S_1 \sqsubseteq S_2 \sqsubseteq S_3 \cdots\cdots\cdots \sqsubseteq S_n \sqsubseteq S'$$

Increasing executability

Figure 9.8 Refinement process.

Ensuring for every adjacent pair of programs S_i and S_j that $S_i \sqsubseteq S_j$ holds on mathematical grounds is a complex task. It involves an examination of the mathematical relationship between each meaningful pair of programs S_i and S_j. The word 'meaningful' here usually refers to a higher degree of executability of S_j compared with S_i.

In general, the two programs S_i and S_j may differ from each other in many different ways. For example, S_j may refine S_i by being an appropriate assignment, a composition of more than one program, an alternation or an iterative command. Furthermore, compared with S_i, S_j could be a program with a less constrained precondition about the initial state, or with a more constrained postcondition on its final state.

Therefore, it is necessary to examine each such case separately and establish the exact logical relationship between S_i and S_j in order for S_j to be a valid refinement of S_i. *Refinement rules* embody this kind of logical relationship between programs belonging to different kinds. Each rule tells us how to do the relevant refinement and, if applicable, what needs to be proved in order to justify it. The latter is often referred to as *proof obligations* to be discharged by the programmer.

For the simple reason that ours is not a dedicated study of program refinement, we will just consider a few of these rules.

9.7.2   Refinement by abstract programs

Let us return to an examination of the relationship between program (9.15) on one hand, and the programs listed in (9.17)–(9.19) on the other. For convenience, let us reproduce them again. First, the specification:

$$x : [x = 0 \lor x = 6, x^3 - 3x^2 + 2x = 0] \tag{9.15}$$

and then its 'implementations':

$$x : [x = 0 \lor x = 6, x^2 - x = 0] \tag{9.17}$$

$$x : [\textbf{\textit{true}}, x^3 - 3x^2 + 2x = 0] \tag{9.18}$$

$$x : [\textbf{\textit{true}}, x^2 - x = 0] \tag{9.19}$$

Compared with (9.15), program (9.17) says more about the final value of the frame variable x, that is, (9.17) constrains x in the postcondition. In other words, (9.17) *strengthens* or tightens the postcondition of (9.15). By contrast, by removing the restriction on x in the precondition, program (9.18) *weakens* the precondition of (9.15), or widens the possible initial values of the program variables. Yet, both programs deliver a result that satisfies the postcondition of (9.15). The program (9.19), on the other hand, combines the virtues of both programs (9.17) and (9.18).

On the other hand, it is important to note that the programs (9.17)–(9.19) fulfil the customer requirements as expressed in (9.15). In the case of (9.17), the implementer has taken advantage of options left open in the customer requirements expressed in (9.15). In the case of (9.18), the customer has been offered a program with more capabilities than asked for. In either case, there are no grounds for the customer not to accept these two programs delivered by the implementer. In this sense, these programs, as well as (9.19), are refinements of (9.15).

The validity of such refinements may be justified formally by refinement rules 1 and 2:

Refinement rule 1   Strengthening of postcondition

$$w : [pre,\ post] \sqsubseteq w : [pre,\ post'] \tag{9.20}$$

provided that

$$post' \Rrightarrow post \tag{9.21}$$

Refinement rule 2   Weakening of precondition

$$w : [pre,\ post] \sqsubseteq w : [pre',\ post] \tag{9.22}$$

provided that

$$pre \Rrightarrow pre' \tag{9.23}$$

The refinement of (9.15) by (9.17) is an example of strengthening of postcondition. It is a valid refinement since it satisfies (9.21), which becomes

$$x^2 - x = 0 \Rrightarrow x^3 - 3x^2 + 2x = 0 \tag{9.24}$$

On the other hand, the refinement of (9.15) by (9.18) is an example of weakening of precondition. It is also a valid refinement since it satisfies (9.23), that is,

$$x = 0 \lor x = 6 \Rrightarrow \mathbf{true} \tag{9.25}$$

The refinement of (9.15) by (9.19) affects both pre- and postconditions. This belongs to the form

$$w : [pre,\ post] \sqsubseteq w : [pre',\ post']$$

where both the pre- and postconditions of the refining program are different from those of the original program. For its validity, the refinement must therefore satisfy both rules (9.21) and (9.23) given above. In this particular case, the two rules require the same formulae as (9.24) and (9.25).

Now consider another program,

$$x : [x = 0 \lor x = 6,\ x = x_0/3] \tag{9.26}$$

as a refinement of (9.15). For the above to be a valid refinement, according to (9.21), the following

$$x = x_0/3 \Rightarrow x^3 - 3x^2 + 2x = 0 \tag{9.27}$$

should be a logical implication. However, this is not the case when formula (9.27) is taken in isolation. As a counterexample, consider the case when $x_0 = 15$. However, program (9.26) is a valid refinement of (9.15) because it has been suggested by relying on the values of x assured by the precondition. This apparent limitation of (9.21) is remedied by the more general rule given in (9.29).

Refinement rule 3   Strengthening of postcondition relying on precondition

$$w : [pre, \, post] \sqsubseteq w : [pre', \, post'] \tag{9.28}$$

provided that

$$pre'[w \setminus w_0] \wedge post' \Rightarrow post \tag{9.29}$$

In (9.29), $pre'[w \setminus w_0]$ denotes the formula pre' with all occurrences of variables w replaced by their corresponding initial values w_0. Application of this revised rule to the refinement of (9.15) by (9.26) leads to

$$(x = 0 \vee x = 6[x \setminus x_0]) \wedge x = x_0/3 \Rightarrow x^3 - 3x^2 + 2x = 0$$
$$\Leftrightarrow (x_0 = 0 \vee x_0 = 6) \wedge x = x_0/3 \Rightarrow x^3 - 3x^2 + 2x = 0$$

It is easy to prove that the above formula is indeed a logical implication. Therefore, the rule (9.29) confirms the validity of the refinement concerned.

Exercise 9.8 ✳✳

In the abstract programs below, n is an integer variable and abs is an integer function which returns the absolute value of its argument.

Among the following abstract programs $prog_1, \ldots, prog_7$, identify pairs of programs such that one program in each pair is a refinement of the other. Explain your reasoning.

$prog_1 = n : [n < 0, n^3 = n]$
$prog_2 = n : [\mathbf{true}, n^3 = n_0]$
$prog_3 = n : [n < 0, n^3 = n \wedge n \geqslant 0]$
$prog_4 = n : [\mathbf{true}, n^3 = n]$
$prog_5 = n : [\mathbf{true}, n_0^3 = n]$
$prog_6 = n : [n < 0, n^3 = abs(n)]$
$prog_7 = n : [\mathbf{true}, n^3 = abs(n)]$

9.7.3   Refinement by assignment

The *assignment* is one of those commands which can be represented as an abstract program immediately, namely, as

$$x := E \stackrel{def}{=} x : [\textbf{\textit{true}}, x = (E[x \setminus x_0])]$$

where '$\stackrel{def}{=}$' stands for equality by definition, and $E[x \setminus x_0]$ is the expression (term) obtained by replacing all occurrences of x in E with x_0.

In considering refinement by assignment, let us examine the relationship between the program (9.15) on one hand, that is,

$$x : [x = 0 \vee x = 6, x^3 - 3x^2 + 2x = 0] \tag{9.15}$$

and some of its implementations in code,

$$x := 2 \tag{9.30}$$
$$x := x/3 \tag{9.31}$$
$$x := x/6 \tag{9.32}$$
$$x := x/2 \tag{9.33}$$

on the other hand. Note that programs (9.30)–(9.32) are the same as the last three programs in (9.16).

Clearly, program (9.30) is a valid refinement of (9.15) independently of its precondition because 2 is a root of the equation $x^3 - 3x^2 + 2x = 0$. By contrast, programs (9.31)–(9.32) do rely on the precondition of (9.15). If (9.31) is delivered as a refinement of (9.15), then it relies on x being initially 0 or 6. This is guaranteed by the precondition, so (9.32) is a valid refinement of (9.15). A similar argument applies to refinement by program (9.31). On the other hand, in order for program (9.33) to be a valid refinement of (9.15), x must be initially 0, 2 or 4. This is not assured by the precondition. Therefore, (9.33) is not a valid refinement of (9.15). Refinement rule 4 embodies the above reasoning formally.

$\boxed{\textbf{Refinement rule 4}}$ Refinement by assignment

$$w : [pre, post] \sqsubseteq w := E \tag{9.34}$$

provided that

$$pre \Rightarrow (post[w \setminus E]) \tag{9.35}$$

A more general condition is

$$pre \wedge w = w_0 \Rightarrow (post[w \setminus E]) \tag{9.36}$$

which applies to situations where *post* contains initial variables.

Let us now examine the working of Rule 4 in relation to programs (9.30)–(9.33) delivered as refinement of (9.15). According to (9.35), the validity of refinement by program (9.30) requires

$$x = 0 \lor x = 6 \Rightarrow (x^3 - 3x^2 + 2x = 0[x \setminus 2]) \tag{9.37}$$

to be a logical implication. According to the following proof, this is indeed the case:

$$x = 0 \lor x = 6 \Rightarrow (x^3 - 3x^2 + 2x = 0[x \setminus 2])$$

$$\Leftrightarrow x = 0 \lor x = 6 \Rightarrow 2^3 - 3 \times 2^2 + 2 \times 2 = 0$$

$$\Leftrightarrow x = 0 \lor x = 6 \Rightarrow 8 - 12 + 4 = 0$$

$$\Leftrightarrow x = 0 \lor x = 6 \Rightarrow \textit{true}$$

$$\Leftrightarrow \textit{true}$$

Turning our attention to program (9.31), we note that for it to be a valid refinement, the following has to be a logical implication:

$$x = 0 \lor x = 6 \Rightarrow (x^3 - 3x^2 + 2x = 0[x \setminus x/3]) \tag{9.38}$$

Relying on the factorization of $x^3 - 3x^2 + 2x$, (9.38) can be written as

$$x = 0 \lor x = 6 \Rightarrow (x(x - 1)(x - 2) = 0[x \setminus x/3])$$

$$\Leftrightarrow x = 0 \lor x = 6 \Rightarrow \left(\frac{x}{3}\right)\left(\left(\frac{x}{3}\right) - 1\right)\left(\left(\frac{x}{3}\right) - 2\right) = 0$$

It is possible to provide a case analysis for $x = 0$ and $x = 6$ separately, showing that the consequence of the above implication is identically true under both conditions. This will constitute a proof of (9.38) being a logical implication. Thus, it can be shown that (9.31) is a valid refinement of (9.15). A similar argument applies to (9.32).

Now let us turn to (9.33) which, according to our earlier informal reasoning, is not a valid refinement of (9.15). Application of rule (4) requires for its validity that

$$x = 0 \lor x = 6 \Rightarrow (x^3 - 3x^2 + 2x = 0[x \setminus x/2]) \tag{9.39}$$

should be a logical implication. Again, relying on the factorization mentioned earlier, (9.39) can be written as

$$x = 0 \lor x = 6 \Rightarrow (x(x - 1)(x - 2) = 0[x \setminus x/2])$$

$$\Leftrightarrow x = 0 \lor x = 6 \Rightarrow \left(\frac{x}{2}\right)\left(\left(\frac{x}{2}\right) - 1\right)\left(\left(\frac{x}{2}\right) - 2\right) = 0$$

As a counterexample demonstrating that (9.40) is not a logical implication, let us choose 6 for x. In this case, the antecedent is true but the conclusion is false since it results in $6 = 0$. Therefore, (9.33) is not a valid refinement of (9.15).

Exercise 9.9 ✳✳

Comment on the validity of the following refinements. Justify your conclusion by providing either a proof of validity of the refinement, a specific instance of program variables for which the refinement is invalid, or any other reasoning. Note that x and y in these refinements are integer variables.

1. $x : [x \geqslant 0 , x > 0] \sqsubseteq x := 5$

2. $x : [x \geqslant 0 , x = 1] \sqsubseteq x := 5$

3. $x : [x \geqslant 0 \land y > 0 , x > 0] \sqsubseteq x := x + y$

4. $x : [x \geqslant 0 , x = x_0 + 1] \sqsubseteq x := 2$

5. $x : [x \geqslant 0 , x = x_0 + 1] \sqsubseteq x := x + 1$

6. $x : [x \geqslant 0 , x = x_0 + y] \sqsubseteq x := x + y$

7. $x : [x \geqslant 0 , y = x_0 + x] \sqsubseteq x := x + y$

8. $x : [x \geqslant 0 , y = x_0 + y_0] \sqsubseteq x := x + x$

9. $x : [x \geqslant 0 , y = x_0 + y_0] \sqsubseteq y := x + x$

Exercise 9.10 ✳✳✳

Refine the following programs by a single assignment.

1. $x : [x < 0, x = \sqrt[3]{x_0}]$

2. $x : [x \neq 0, x = 1/\sqrt[3]{x_0}]$

3. $x : [2 \,|\, x, x > x_0 \land 6 \,|\, x]$

4. $x : [2 \,|\, x, x = 3 \times x_0]$

5. $x : [2 \,|\, x, 2 \,|\, x \land x \neq x_0]$

(Note that $m \,|\, n$ stands for 'm divides n exactly'.)

Chapter 10

Proof by mathematical induction

Topic: Mathematical induction

....

Mathematical induction often arises as the finishing step ... of an inductive research.

George Polya
American mathematician

Objectives

On completion of this chapter you should be able to:

- Describe the principle of mathematical induction.

- Prove the validity of formulae by mathematical induction.

- Describe the relevance of inductive reasoning in analysis of algorithms.

- Assess the complexity of simple algorithms.

We have so far studied two major forms of reasoning which we referred to as transformational proofs and deductive proofs. These two are commonly known as proof by *deduction*. This chapter introduces another kind of formal reasoning known as *mathematical induction*. It is not a 'mathematized' version of induction, which we mentioned in passing in Chapter 5. Mathematical induction is also a kind of reasoning with widespread application in computing, functional programming and algorithm analysis, to name a few. The last section of this chapter demonstrates its relevance to the latter.

10.1 What is mathematical induction?

One way to describe mathematical induction is as follows:

> Mathematical induction is a demonstrative procedure often useful in verifying conjectures at which we arrived by some inductive procedure. (Polya, 1954)

In the above, 'inductive procedure' means a kind of generalization based on observations of a fair sample of experiments (see page 61).

Mathematical induction specializes in proofs of observations about large, typically infinite, sets of objects. Given that the objects in the set can be indexed numerically, in simple cases such an observation may be expressed as a predicate involving a numerical variable. In our discussion, we use the notation $P(n)$ for referring to an arbitrary predicate involving a numerical variable n. The variable n may appear explicitly in the formulae or may be implicit. Note that, in general, the formulae may involve more than one such numerical variable.

Terminology

Conjectures are formulae which we believe to be true but are yet to be proven. Once proven such formulae attain the status of true propositions or *theorems*. Obviously, some conjectures may fail to achieve this status.

(**Example 10.1**)

Classic problems used for illustrating mathematical induction include the following conjectures on the summation operator Σ:

A common notation	Using Σ for summation
1. $P(n) \overset{def}{\Leftrightarrow} 1 + 2 + 3 + \ldots + n = \dfrac{n(n+1)}{2}$	$P(n) \overset{def}{\Leftrightarrow} \displaystyle\sum_{i=1}^{n} i = \dfrac{n(n+1)}{2}$
2. $P(n) \overset{def}{\Leftrightarrow} 1 + 2^2 + 3^2 + \ldots + n^2 = \dfrac{n(n+1)(2n+1)}{6}$	$P(n) \overset{def}{\Leftrightarrow} \displaystyle\sum_{i=1}^{n} i^2 = \dfrac{n(n+1)(2n+1)}{6}$
3. $P(n) \overset{def}{\Leftrightarrow} \dfrac{1}{3} + \dfrac{1}{15} + \dfrac{1}{35} + \ldots + \dfrac{1}{4n^2 - 1} = \dfrac{n}{2n+1}$	$P(n) \overset{def}{\Leftrightarrow} \displaystyle\sum_{i=1}^{n} \dfrac{1}{4i^2 - 1} = \dfrac{n}{2n+1}$

What we wish to prove is that formulae such as those in Example 10.1 denoted by $P(n)$ hold for all n. Until then, each formula has to be treated as a conjecture.

(10.2) Relationship with induction

Conjectures such as those in Example 10.1 arise from our observations. Our intellectual curiosity and challenges in practical problem solving often lead us to observing interesting patterns in various kinds of data. Conjectures are statements about such observations. How we arrive at such conjectures is a complex process of discovery guided largely by intuition and experience.

As we develop new theories, we often hypothesize whether a certain conjecture is true for all such data. We first explore the validity of our conjecture by straightforward testing against each item of data. Continuous success in our tests strengthens our confidence in the conjecture. The first failure, on the other hand, forces us back to the starting point of our investigation. On such occasions we may modify our conjecture to account for the experience. This is quite characteristic for an inductive phase of reasoning.

Suppose that a certain conjecture has withstood all our tests. The question is whether this would warrant our claiming it to be a true proposition. It does not, because the next test could be fatal. If we are dealing with data which are inherently finite, we might be able, in principle, to conduct the test exhaustively and thus claim the validity of the conjecture. However, if our observations can never be complete, how could we possibly give the final seal of approval to a conjecture with absolute confidence? The answer to this question lies in mathematical induction.

Example 10.2

In a general discussion on proof, Dunham (1994) gives an interesting example:

Conjecture: *Upon substituting a positive integer for* n *in the polynomial*

$$f(n) = n^7 - 28n^6 + 322n^5 - 1960n^4 + 6769n^3$$
$$- 13\,132n^2 - 13\,069n - 5040 \tag{10.1}$$

we always get the same positive integer back. Symbolically, the assertion states that

$$f(n) = n \tag{10.2}$$

for any whole number n. *Is it true?*

Dunham then goes on to illustrate the point. He gives some calculations of the form

$$f(1) = 1 - 28 + 322 - 1960 + 6769 - 13\,132 - 13\,069 - 5040 = 1$$
$$f(2) = 2^7 - 28 \times 2^6 + 322 \times 2^5 - 1960 \times 2^4 + 6769 \times 2^3 -$$
$$13\,132 \times 2^2 - 13\,069 \times 2 - 5040 = 2$$
$$\vdots$$
$$f(7) = 7^7 - 28 \times 7^6 + 322 \times 7^5 - 1960 \times 7^4 +$$
$$6769 \times 7^3 - 13\,132 \times 7^2 - 13\,069 \times 7 - 5040 = 7$$

each supporting the claim. However, he then considers the substitution of $n = 8$ which is shown to be fatal:

$$f(8) = 8^7 - 28 \times 8^6 + 322 \times 8^5 - 1960 \times 8^4 + 6769 \times 8^3 -$$
$$13\,132 \times 8^2 - 13\,069 \times 8 - 5040 = 5048$$

The lesson is, in Dunham's words, that 'a few cases aren't enough' and that repeated success in tests should never be taken as confirmation of an absolute truth.

The above is really an example contrived to show pitfalls in generalizations. The polynomial concerned has been obtained from

$$f(n) = n + (n-1)(n-2)(n-3)(n-4)(n-5)(n-6)(n-7) \tag{10.3}$$

We could have been really fooled if Dunham had had the courage to put his other version

$$f(n) = n + (n-1)(n-2)(n-3)\dots(n-1\,000\,000) \tag{10.4}$$

in the more natural form of a polynomial, namely, in the form (10.1) as a sum of terms with each involving a power of n. We would have had to test as many as $1\,000\,000$ cases, performing enormous calculations, to discover that $f(n)$ in this case does not yield n for all n.

Although Example 10.2 has been contrived, mathematics is full of proven, disproven and unproven conjectures. Among the prominent conjectures that have attracted the interest of mathematicians of all walks of life for centuries are Fermat's Last Theorem and Euler's conjecture (see Singh (1997)). Fermat's Last Theorem has at last been proven to be true, whereas Euler's conjecture, which states that there are no solutions to

$$x^4 + y^4 + z^4 = w^4$$

has been proven false. After two centuries of effort, lately involving computers, the following counterexample

$$2\,682\,440^4 + 15\,365\,639^4 + 187\,960^4 = 20\,615\,673^4$$

has demonstrated the invalidity of Euler's claim. As Singh also emphasizes, the first million checks is not sufficient to claim that a conjecture is true for all numbers.

10.3 The technique of mathematical induction

10.3.1 Prerequisites: ordering of data

The aim of mathematical induction is to test a conjecture against all appropriate items of a set of data without examining them exhaustively. This may be done if we can identify some numerical ordering in the data. That is, we must be able to say by pointing to each item of data that this is our first piece of data, this is the second, and so forth.

Example 10.3

Referring to Example 1, one may notice the following numerical patterns in data:

Numerical ordering of data					
	1	2	3	4	...	n
1.	1	2	3	4	...	n
2.	1	2^2	3^2	4^2	...	n^2
3.	$\dfrac{1}{3}$	$\dfrac{1}{15}$	$\dfrac{1}{35}$	$\dfrac{1}{63}$	...	$\dfrac{1}{4n^2-1}$

Note in Example 10.3 that the data may be represented in many different ways. Whatever the representation, we must be able to identify a unique element in the data as the 'smallest' element. At the same time, our ordering must encompass the whole set of data.

10.3.2   Prerequisites: underlying functions

The conjectures subjected to mathematical induction invariably involve certain mathematical functions or operators. The conjectures are really statements about properties of these functions. (There is more about functions in Chapter 16) Proofs may be required in order to substantiate less obvious such properties.

In the case of Example 10.1, the conjectures concern the summation operator Σ. This particular operator is so widely known that it hardly requires an introduction (a definition). However, usually this is not the case. In order to prove less obvious properties of the underlying functions, we must, however, know about their more 'primitive' properties. Some of these primitive properties commonly take the form of *recurrence relations*, or in more familiar computer science terminology, *recursive definitions*. Proofs by mathematical induction therefore implicitly rely on the availability of appropriate recursive definitions of the functions appearing in the conjecture.

Terminology

Recursive functions are those which are defined in terms of themselves and a certain terminating clause with an associated definition. A function f, taking a natural number as its argument, can be defined *recursively* by:

1. giving its value at 0 (terminating clause), and

2. for each non-zero number n, giving a rule or a definition for determining $f(n+1)$ in terms of $f(n)$.

Since the conjectures in Example 10.1 are written without using the summation operator Σ on the right-hand side, they are, in effect, non-recursive definitions of the functions involved. For example,

$$\sum_{i=1}^{n} i = \frac{n(n+1)}{2}$$

.

defines the summation operator Σ explicitly for a series of consecutive numbers from 1 to n. In contrast, the definition against (1) in Example 10.4 below defines the same operator recursively.

Example 10.4

Recursive functions for Σ applicable to conjectures in Example 10.1 are:

Function in the conjecture	Recursive definition
1. $\sum_{i=1}^{n} i = 1 + 2 + 3 + \ldots + n$	$\sum_{i=1}^{1} i = 1$
	$\sum_{i=1}^{n} i = n + \sum_{i=1}^{n-1} i$
2. $\sum_{i=1}^{n} i^2 = 1 + 2^2 + 3^2 + \ldots + n^2$	$\sum_{i=1}^{1} i^2 = 1$
	$\sum_{i=1}^{n} i^2 = n^2 + \sum_{i=1}^{n-1} i^2$
3. $\sum_{i=1}^{n} \dfrac{1}{4i^2 - 1} = \dfrac{1}{3} + \dfrac{1}{15} + \dfrac{1}{35} + \ldots + \dfrac{1}{4n^2 - 1}$	$\sum_{i=1}^{1} \dfrac{1}{4i^2 - 1} = \dfrac{1}{3}$
	$\sum_{i=1}^{n} \dfrac{1}{4i^2 - 1} = \dfrac{1}{4n^2 - 1} + \sum_{i=1}^{n-1} \dfrac{1}{4i^2 - 1}$

Note that in the recursive functions we are actually defining the meaning of the summation operator Σ as applicable to each of the three different series in Example 10.1.

Comparison of the recursive functions in Example 10.4 and the corresponding non-recursive explicit conjectures in Example 10.1 reveals that the recursive functions are clearer and do not require further justification. This is the reason for placing greater trust on the recursive definitions than on explicit non-recursive definitions in inductive proofs. However, the explicit versions are preferable when it comes to computing such functions.

In summary, functions can have two different kinds of definition: explicit non-recursive definition and alternative recursive functions. Commonly, many examples of mathematical induction are concerned with the proof of explicit definitions using recursive definitions. However, mathematical induction is generally concerned with the proof of various properties of functions, and not just with proofs about summations, using the recursive definitions of these functions. This provides us with another perspective of mathematical induction.

10.3.3   Principle of mathematical induction

Once the numerical order has been exposed as in Section 10.3.1, the conjecture may be tested against:

1. the data item corresponding to the lowest value of the numerical variable (usually $n = 0$ or $n = 1$), and

2. an arbitrary data item other than that considered in (1), assuming that the conjecture holds for its predecessor.

Let us assume that we have been able to accomplish both above. An immediate consequence of applying (2) to (1) is that the conjecture holds for $n = 1$, assuming that the lowest value of the numerical variable is $n = 0$. By applying (2) again to the latter we establish that the conjecture holds for $n = 2$. Repeated application of (2) in this manner confirms the validity of the conjecture for all values $n = 0, 1, 2, 3, 4, \ldots$, thus confirming the universal validity of the conjecture.

(Description)   Principle of mathematical induction
_____

Given that $P(n)$ is a conjecture involving a numerical variable n, $P(0)$ being the conjecture corresponding to the lowest term, if

1. $P(0)$ holds, and

2. for an arbitrary k

$$P(k) \Rightarrow P(k + 1)$$ **(10.5)**

then $P(n)$ holds for all n.

The above principle may be translated into a general proof strategy as follows.

(Description)   Proof strategy
_____

In order to show that $P(n)$ holds for all n, provide two separate subproofs as follows:

1. Base case: prove $P(0)$ holds.

2. Inductive case

    (a) *Induction hypothesis*: assume $P(k)$ holds for an arbitrary k.
    (b) *Inductive proof*: prove that $P(k + 1)$ holds on the basis of (a).

The proof strategy in the Description assumes that the base case corresponds to $n = 0$, that is, the inductive reasoning concerns the validity of formulae starting with the formula corresponding to $n = 0$. This may not necessarily be true, in which case, $P(0)$ should be replaced with the formula appropriate to the base case. For example, the proof in Example 10.5 uses $n = 1$ as the base case, whereas Example 10.6 uses $n = 2$.

(Example 10.5)
_____

Let us attempt a proof by mathematical induction of conjecture (1) in Example 10.1, namely,

$$P(n) \overset{def}{\Leftrightarrow} \sum_{i=1}^{n} i = \frac{n(n+1)}{2}$$

In order to highlight the unique features of mathematical induction, we prove the conjecture again afterwards by deduction.

Proof by mathematical induction

The recursive definition for the underlying function is:

$$\sum_{i=1}^{1} i = 1$$

$$\sum_{i=1}^{n} i = n + \sum_{i=1}^{n-1} i$$

Base case:

Proof of $P(1)$:

$$\frac{1(1+1)}{2} = \sum_{i=1}^{1} i \qquad \qquad P(n) \text{ for } n = 1$$

$$\Leftrightarrow \tfrac{2}{2} = 1 \qquad \qquad \text{arithmetic and recursive definition}$$

$$\Leftrightarrow \textbf{\textit{true}} \qquad \qquad \text{arithmetic}$$

Thus, the above fulfils the first requirement of the principle of mathematical induction.

Inductive case

Induction hypothesis: Assume $P(k)$, that is,

$$\sum_{i=1}^{k} i = \frac{k(k+1)}{2}$$

Inductive proof: Prove $P(k+1)$, that is,

$$\sum_{i=1}^{k+1} i = \frac{(k+1)(k+2)}{2}$$

Proof of the above:

1. $\displaystyle\sum_{i=1}^{k} i = \frac{k(k+1)}{2}$ assumption (induction hypothesis)

2. $\displaystyle\sum_{i=1}^{k+1} i = (k+1) + \sum_{i=1}^{k} i$ recursive definition

3. $\displaystyle\sum_{i=1}^{k+1} i = (k+1) + \frac{k(k+1)}{2}$ from 1 & 2

4. $\displaystyle\sum_{i=1}^{k+1} i = \frac{(k+1)(k+2)}{2}$ from 3, algebra

Hence, the proof by induction. It follows from the above that

$$\sum_{i=1}^{k} i = \frac{k(k+1)}{2} \Rightarrow \sum_{i=1}^{k+1} i = \frac{(k+1)(k+2)}{2}$$

which is the second requirement of the principle of mathematical induction.

Proof by deduction (a transformational proof)

$\dfrac{n(n+1)}{2} = \displaystyle\sum_{i=1}^{n} i$	conjecture to be proven
$\Leftrightarrow n(n+1) = \displaystyle\sum_{i=1}^{n} i + \sum_{i=1}^{n} i$	arithmetic
$\Leftrightarrow n(n+1) = \displaystyle\sum_{i=1}^{n} i + \sum_{i=1}^{n} (n+1-i)$	rearrangement of second summation
$\Leftrightarrow n(n+1) = \displaystyle\sum_{i=1}^{n} (i+n+1-i)$	distributivity of Σ over $+$
$\Leftrightarrow n(n+1) = (n+1) \displaystyle\sum_{i=1}^{n} 1$	arithmetic
$\Leftrightarrow n(n+1) = (n+1) \times n$	arithmetic (sum of n 1s)
$\Leftrightarrow$ **true**	identity of equals

Hence, the proof by deduction.

Although we have been able to prove the conjecture both by mathematical induction and by deduction, deduction is less promising as a proof strategy in the kind of problem being dealt with here.

Exercise 10.1 ✳

Prove the following by both induction and deduction.

$$1 + q + q^2 + \ldots + q^n = \frac{q^n - 1}{q - 1}$$

(Note that the series on the left-hand side is a *geometric series*).

Exercise 10.2 ✳✳

Prove the validity of the following by mathematical induction for all n, n denoting a natural number.

1. $\displaystyle\sum_{i=1}^{n} i^2 = \frac{n(n+1)(2n+1)}{6}$

2. $\displaystyle\sum_{i=1}^{n} \frac{1}{4i^2 - 1} = \frac{n}{2n+1}$

3. $\displaystyle\sum_{i=1}^{n} \frac{1}{i^2} \leqslant 2 - \frac{1}{n}$

Example 10.6

The Fibonacci numbers F_0, F_1, F_2, etc. form a sequence of numbers and have the pattern

$n : 0, 1, 2, 3, 4, 5, 6, \; 7, \; 8, \; \ldots$

$F_n : 0, 1, 1, 2, 3, 5, 8, 13, 21, \; \ldots$

They can be defined recursively by

$F_0 = 0$

$F_1 = 1$

$F_n = F_{n-1} + F_{n-2} \quad$ for all $n \geqslant 2$

We wish to derive a general formula for $F_n F_{n-2} - F_{n-1}^2$ in terms of n for all $n \geqslant 2$.

Let us first investigate whether there is a pattern in the values of $F_n F_{n-2} - F_{n-1}^2$ dependent on n.

n	F_{n-2}	F_{n-1}	F_n	$F_n F_{n-2} - F_{n-1}^2$	
2	0	1	1	$1 \times 0 - 1^2 =$	-1
3	1	1	2	$2 \times 1 - 1^2 =$	1
4	1	2	3	$3 \times 1 - 2^2 =$	-1
5	2	3	5	$5 \times 2 - 3^2 =$	1
6	3	5	8	$8 \times 3 - 5^2 =$	-1
$\vdots$	$\vdots$	$\vdots$	$\vdots$	$\vdots$	$\vdots$

The above is suggestive of the equality

$$F_n F_{n-2} - F_{n-1}^2 = (-1)^{n-1} \tag{10.6}$$

for the values of n that we have tested and is likely to be true for others. In order to show that equality (10.6) holds unequivocally for all $n \geqslant 2$, we resort to mathematical induction. Let

$$P(n) \stackrel{sdef}{\Leftrightarrow} F_n F_{n-2} - F_{n-1}^2 = (-1)^{n-1}$$

Base case

Proof of $P(2)$ (for $n = 2$):

$\begin{array}{ll} F_2 F_0 - F_1^2 & \text{LHS of } P(2) \text{ (i.e. } n = 2) \\ = 1 \times 0 - 1^2 & \text{definition of } F_0, F_1, F_2 \\ = -1 & \text{arithmetic} \\ = (-1)^{2-1} & \text{arithmetic} \end{array}$

Thus

$$F_2 F_0 - F_1^2 = (-1)^{2-1}$$

That is, $P(2)$ is true. Therefore, the first requirement of the principle of mathematical induction is satisfied.

Inductive case

Induction hypothesis: Assume $P(n)$ to be true for $n = k$. That is,

$$F_k F_{k-2} - F_{k-1}^2 = (-1)^{k-1}$$

Inductive proof: Prove $P(k+1)$ to be true. That is,

$$F_{k+1} F_{k-1} - F_k^2 = (-1)^k \tag{10.7}$$

Proof of the above:

$F_{k+1} F_{k-1} - F_k^2$	LHS of the above equality
$= (F_k + F_{k-1}) F_{k-1} - F_k^2$	recursive definition for F_{k+1}
$= F_k F_{k-1} + F_{k-1}^2 - F_k^2$	rearrangement (distributivity of $\times$ over $+$)
$= F_k F_{k-1} - F_k^2 + F_{k-1}^2$	rearrangement (commutativity of $+$ (and $-$))
$= F_k(F_{k-1} - F_k) + F_{k-1}^2$	rearrangement (distributivity of $\times$ over $+$)
$= -F_k F_{k-2} + F_{k-1}^2$	recursive definition for F_k
$= -(-1)^{k-1}$	induction hypothesis
$= (-1)^k$	arithmetic

Hence, the proof by induction for $P(n)$ for all $n \geqslant 2$.

Proofs conducted so far involved only one numerical variable, as denoted by n in $P(n)$. In general, the predicate P may involve a number of variables. Exercise 10.3, for example, concerns a predicate $P(m, n)$ involving two numerical variables m and n. In this case, induction may be conducted with respect to one variable, while keeping the other fixed.

Exercise 10.3 ✳✳✳

Continuing Example 10.6, show for all natural numbers $n, m \geqslant 2$ that

$$F_{n+m-2} = F_n F_{m-1} + F_{n-1} F_{m-2}$$

Example 10.7

We examine here how Dunham's contrived conjecture given in Example 10.2 withstands the 'test' of mathematical induction. Let us modify the problem slightly such that an exhaustive test of the conjecture would fail at some undisclosed number m. Let us also use the polynomial in the following form:

$$f(n) = n + (n-1)(n-2)(n-3) \ldots (n-m) \tag{10.8}$$

and not in its deceptive form of (10.1) as a sum of terms involving powers of n. The claim of Dunham's conjecture is

$$f(n) = n \quad \text{for all } n$$

In subjecting the above to mathematical induction, let

$$P(n) \overset{\text{def}}{\Leftrightarrow} f(n) = n$$

Base case

Proof of $P(1)$:

$$1 + (1-1)(1-2)(1-3)\ldots(1-m) \quad \text{RHS of (10.8) for } f(1) \text{ (i.e. } n=1)$$
$$= 1 + (0)(-1)(-2)\ldots(1-m) \quad \text{arithmetic}$$
$$= 1 + 0 \quad \text{arithmetic}$$
$$= 1 \quad \text{arithmetic}$$

Thus

$$f(1) = 1$$

That is, $P(1)$ is true. Therefore, as far as the first requirement of the principle of mathematical induction is concerned, it is satisfied.

Inductive case

In this case, we need to show that

$$f(k) = k \Rightarrow f(k+1) = k+1 \tag{10.9}$$

for all k. Obviously, had we been confident in an inductive proof of the conjecture, the antecedent of the implication, namely, $f(k) = k$, is what would have been adopted as the induction hypothesis. Note that the antecedent can be expressed in an equivalent form, namely,

$$k = k + (k-1)(k-2)(k-3)\ldots(k-m) \quad \text{induction hypothesis}$$
$$\Leftrightarrow (k-1)(k-2)(k-3)\ldots(k-m) = 0 \quad \text{cancellation of common term}$$
$$\Leftrightarrow k = 1 \lor k = 2 \lor k = 3 \lor \ldots \lor k = m \quad \text{roots of the above equation}$$

In other words, it is possible to paraphrase the implication (10.9) required by the inductive case into the equivalent form:

$$k = 1 \lor k = 2 \lor k = 3 \lor \ldots \lor k = m$$
$$\Rightarrow f(k+1) = (k+1) + k(k-1)(k-2)(k-3)\ldots(k-(m-1)) \tag{10.10}$$

for all k. It may be easily verified that

$$k = 1 \quad \Rightarrow f(2) = 2$$
$$k = 2 \quad \Rightarrow f(3) = 3$$
$$k = 3 \quad \Rightarrow f(4) = 4$$
$$\vdots \qquad \vdots$$
$$k = m-1 \Rightarrow f(m) = m$$

but

$$k = m \Rightarrow f(m+1) = (m+1) + m(m-1)(m-2)(m-3)\ldots \times 2 \times 1$$

In the case of f given in (10.1), the above shows that $f(8)$ is 5048 and not 8, as the conjecture predicts. In the more general case, the above gives rise to

$$k = m \Rightarrow f(m+1) \neq m+1$$

The last instance serves as the counterexample showing that implication (10.9) does not always hold, thus invalidating the inductive part of the principle of mathematical induction. This points to the fact that Dunham's conjecture does not withstand the scrutiny of mathematical induction.

One might argue that, in order to show the invalidity, we still had to conduct m tests. In a sense, this is true since the value of m could have been buried in a polynomial of the form (10.1) and, in the worst case, we would have had to conduct m tests. The point is that, although an exhaustive testing process aimed at confirming the conjecture would have required at most $m + 1$ tests to discover the failure, dismissal of the conjecture requires only one test and, in the worst case, m tests.

10.4 An application: algorithm analysis

An algorithm is a way to compute a solution for a given problem. A problem may be unique, but its solutions may not be. If a problem has a number of different solutions, each of which can be expressed as a different algorithm, a question which arises naturally is how to compare different algorithms supposedly solving the same problem. Algorithms can be compared with one another in different ways; for example, according to elegance, to understandability or to the measure of resources required by each algorithm. Our concern here is how to compare algorithms with respect to resources required by each algorithm, in particular how much time it might take to solve a problem of a certain size or how much memory it might require to store various intermediate results it computes in the process of solving the problem.

However, posing the question in the above form as to the time or memory required by the algorithm in absolute and precise terms is often unnecessary. An exception is, perhaps, safety-critical systems where the timing information is important for dealing with their time-critical aspects. However, what is required in most other cases is a rough guide to resource requirements.

10.4.1 Algorithmic complexity

The cost of a computation depends on two important factors: one determined by the technology used for carrying out the computation, and the other dependent on the manner in which the computation is conducted. Because of constant technological advances and because of the variability of computational costs across different machines even in the same technological age, it is more meaningful to compare algorithms on the basis of costs associated with their internal characteristics rather than external factors. Another important reason for ignoring the technology-dependent factors is that the demands of certain algorithms can be so great that, in principle, they can never be met, even with the most sophisticated machines. Therefore, consideration of computational costs in absolute terms could often be meaningless. This is because different algorithms exhibit different degrees of complexity. The purpose of *algorithm analysis* is to assess the *complexity* of an algorithm in terms of the time it takes or the memory (space) it requires depending on a characteristic measure of the problem. These two measures are often referred to as *time complexity* and *space complexity*.

Complexity analysis often uses results established by mathematical induction. Example 10.8 illustrates such an instance.

The following algorithm *MaxMin(S)* finds both the maximum and minimum elements of a given set *S* of numbers and returns the result as a pair of numbers. Let the first element in the pair be the maximum element of *S* and the second its minimum element. Let us assume that *MaxMin* uses two basic functions *max* and *min*, returning respectively the maximum and minimum elements of a set containing just two elements. Below is an informal description of *MaxMin* expressed in a pseudoprogramming language.

```
function MaxMin(S)
var
  S : set of integer;
      if (S has only two elements) then
          return (max(S), min(S))                              ◀ A
      else
          begin
          var max1, max2, min1, min2 : integer
              let
                 S₁, S₂ partitions S into two disjoint
                        subsets of equal size
                 MaxMin(S₁) = (max1, min1)                     ◀ B
                 MaxMin(S₂) = (max2, min2)                     ◀ C
              return (max({max1, max2}),min({min1, min2}))     ◀ D
          end
```

Note that {...} is a notation used to show the elements of a set. Our discussion in this section relies on sets, discussed in more detail in Chapter 11.

Because of the restriction imposed by *max* and *min*, the only way to solve the problem in the case of a set of an arbitrary size (size being the number of elements in the set concerned) is to break up the set successively until each decomposed set is small enough to use *max* and *min*. The above algorithm employs such a strategy, which is generally known as the '*divide and conquer*' strategy. How the algorithm works in the case of a set with eight elements is illustrated in Figure 10.1.

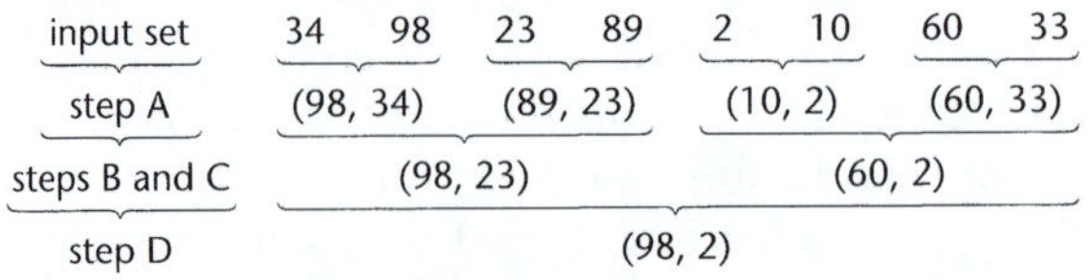

input set	34	98	23	89	2	10	60	33
step A	(98, 34)		(89, 23)		(10, 2)		(60, 33)	
steps B and C		(98, 23)			(60, 2)			
step D			(98, 2)					

Figure 10.1 The 'divide and conquer' strategy applied to a set of eight elements.

As a simplification, suppose that only comparisons of elements by *max* and *min* incur any cost and other computations of the algorithm are insignificant in terms of cost. Obviously, this approximation may not always be justified. Let the cost of comparison incurred with respect to a two-element set be unity in some appropriate unit of measurement.

As outlined earlier, our interest is in the cost of computation using the above algorithm as a function of the size of the set S, that is, the number of elements in S. Let the size of S be n and, as a further approximation and without much loss of generality, let $n = 2^m$ for some integer m. A practical consequence of this is that our analysis will be restricted to sets of sizes 2, 4, 8, 16, 32, 64, etc. If the actual size of a given set does not coincide exactly with any of these numbers, we can still gain some idea about the cost associated with it by considering sets of the two adjacent sizes. Therefore, our analysis will still be relevant.

Let the cost of a solution involving a set of size n be $T(n)$. Knowing how the algorithm works, it is possible to define $T(n)$ by means of the following *recurrence relations* or, in our familiar terminology, recursive equations:

$$T(n) = 1 \qquad \text{for } n = 2 \qquad\qquad \textbf{(10.11)}$$

$$\quad\; = 2T\left(\frac{n}{2}\right) + 2 \qquad \text{for } n > 2 \qquad\qquad \textbf{(10.12)}$$

According to these equations, the cost of solution for a set with two elements is 1 and the cost of solution for a set with n elements is twice the cost of solution for a set with $n/2$ elements plus the cost of two comparisons made in line (D) of the algorithm.

Although the above expresses the costs involved quite elegantly, it is not explicit about the form of dependence of $T(n)$ on n. The following is a derivation of an explicit expression for $T(n)$ in terms of n.

$T(2^m) = 2T(2^{m-1}) + 2$	(10.12) defining $T(n)$ for $n = 2^m$
$\qquad = 2(2T(2^{m-2}) + 2) + 2 = 2^2 T(2^{m-2}) + 2^2 + 2$	a further expansion: application of the same to the inner term $T(2^{m-1})$
$\qquad = 2^3 T(2^{m-3}) + 2^3 + 2^2 + 2$	
$\qquad \vdots$	more expansions
$\qquad = 2^{m-1} T(2) + 2^{m-1} + 2^{m-2} + \ldots + 2^3 + 2^2 + 2$	end of expansion
$\qquad = 2^{m-1} + 2 \underbrace{(1 + 2 + 2^2 + \ldots + 2^{m-3} + 2^{m-2})}_{\text{a geometric series}}$	rearrangement and since, according to (10.11), $T(2) = 1$
$\qquad = 2^{m-1} + 2\left(\dfrac{2^{m-1} - 1}{2 - 1}\right)$	sum of the geometric series substantiated by induction in Exercise 10.1
$\qquad = \frac{3}{2} 2^m - 2$	simplification
$\qquad = \frac{3}{2} n - 2$	substitution of $n = 2^m$

The derivation in Example 10.8 not only uses a result that can be established by mathematical induction, but itself too has an inductive flavour. Had we been able to guess the above result, namely

$$T(n) = \frac{3}{2}n - 2 \qquad\qquad (10.13)$$

for a few values of n such that each is a power of 2, it would have been possible to justify it by mathematical induction for every n which is a power of 2. Its proof is given in Example 10.9 to illustrate the wider relevance of mathematical induction in algorithm analysis.

(**Example 10.9**)

Proof of (10.13) for all n which is a power of two by mathematical induction. We use (10.11) and (10.12) as the recursive definition of $T(n)$.

Base case

Proof of (10.13) for $n = 2$

$$\begin{aligned}
& T(2) = 1 && \text{(10.11) of recursive definition} \\
\Leftrightarrow\ & T(2) = \tfrac{3}{2} \times 2 - 2 && \text{arithmetic}
\end{aligned}$$

Thus, the base case holds.

Inductive case

Induction hypothesis: Assume

$$T(k) = \tfrac{3}{2}k - 2$$

where k is a power of two.

Inductive proof: Prove

$$T(2k) = \tfrac{3}{2}(2k) - 2 = 3k - 2 \qquad\qquad (10.14)$$

[Note that if k is a power of two then the next power of 2 is $2k$.] Proof of (10.14):

1. $T(k) = \tfrac{3}{2}k - 2$ assumption (induction hypothesis)
2. $T(2k) = 2T(k) + 2$ (10.12) of recursive definition
3. $T(2k) = 2(\tfrac{3}{2}k - 2) + 2$ from 1 & 2
4. $T(2k) = 3k - 2$ from 3, algebra

Hence, the proof of (10.13) by induction.

10.4.2   Asymptotic complexity

Since we have chosen not to estimate running costs of algorithms in precise terms, the expressions of complexity of the form

$$T(n) = \tfrac{3}{2}n - 2$$

as derived in Example 10.8 for algorithm *MaxMin*, can be made more meaningful by ignoring various terms. For example, as n becomes large the contribution due to the term -2 in $T(n)$ becomes insignificant. Furthermore, the term $3/2$ in $T(n)$ is also not very meaningful since we do not deal with precise costs. (This factor is of use if we do deal with precise costs, but then we might need to consider other additional scaling factors too.)

In complexity analysis, therefore, we consider only the most dominant term involving n in $T(n)$, ignoring any multiplier not involving n and other less significant terms in $T(n)$. The idea is to express how the cost of an algorithm rises as the problem size increases, that is, *asymptotic complexity*. With respect to *MaxMin*, for example, the *Oh-notation* expressed as $O(n)$ conveys that the running cost of *MaxMin* rises linearly with increasing n. In general, there could be other expressions such as $O(n^2)$ and $O(n \log n)$ conveying that the costs increases as n^2 or as $n \log n$ respectively. Note that $O(n^2)$ is to be read as 'order n^2'.

Given $f(n)$ is a function of the problem size n, what does it really mean when we say that $T(n)$ is $O(f(n))$? Bearing in mind that in $f(n)$ we have already ignored any scaling multiplier, this means that there exists a real number c such that

$$T(n) \leqslant c\, f(n)$$

(Example 10.10)

Determine the order of growth of complexity of the function

$$T(n) = \tfrac{1}{1000} n^3 + 400n + 5000$$

where n is a positive integer.

$$T(n) = \tfrac{1}{1000} n^3 + 400n + 5000$$
$$\leqslant \tfrac{1}{1000} n^3 + 400n + 5000n^3$$
$$\leqslant \tfrac{1}{1000} n^3 + 400n^3 + 5000n^3$$
$$\leqslant n^3 + 400n^3 + 5000n^3$$
$$\leqslant 5401n^3$$

That is

$$\tfrac{1}{1000} n^3 + 400n + 5000 \leqslant c\, n^3$$

where $c = 5401$. Therefore, $T(n)$ is of $O(n^3)$. The point is that, no matter how small is its contribution initially, for large n the term $1/1000\, n^3$ catches up with the other terms in the time complexity function and, eventually, will far exceed their contribution.

(Exercise 10.4 ✴)

Express the following time complexity functions using the *Oh*–notation.

1. $5n - 2$
2. $2n(n + 1\,000\,000)$

3. $n(5 + \log n)$

4. $(n + 1)^5$

5. 1000

6. $1\,000\,000\,n^5 + (n + 3)^5$

7. $5n^2 \log n$

Terminology

Frequently occurring *Oh*–expressions have some common terms in English. These are listed in Table 10.1.

Consider now an algorithm consisting of two subalgorithms, which can be analysed separately. Is it possible to reason about the time complexity of the composite algorithm in terms of the two subalgorithms? The answer is yes. It is based on the following argument.

Let the time complexities of the two subalgorithms be $T_1(n)$ and $T_2(n)$, which are of the order $f(n)$ and $g(n)$ respectively. That is,

$$T_1(n) = c_1\, f(n) \qquad\qquad\qquad\qquad (10.15)$$

$$T_2(n) = c_2\, g(n) \qquad\qquad\qquad\qquad (10.16)$$

for some c_1 and c_2.

Let us assume that f and g are such that f is $O(g(n))$, that is, the growth rate of f is lower than, or identical to, that of g. Then, it follows from the definition of the *Oh*-notation that, for some constant c_f,

$$f(n) \leqslant c_f\, g(n) \qquad\qquad\qquad\qquad (10.17)$$

Provided that execution of the composite algorithm requires the execution of each of the two subalgorithms concerned at most m_1 and m_2 times respectively, the time complexity of the composite algorithm $T(n)$ may be estimated to be

$$T(n) \leqslant m_1\, T_1(n) + m_2\, T_2(n) \qquad\qquad\qquad (10.18)$$

Table 10.1   Some common *Oh-expressions.*

$T(n)$ is of …	Read as: $T(n)$ is of …
$O(1)$	constant order
$O(n)$	linear order (or order n)
$O(n^2)$	quadratic order (or order n^2)
$O(n^3)$	cubic order (or order n^3)
$O(\log n)$	logarithmic order (or order $\log n$)
$O(n \log n)$	order $n \log n$
$O(2^n)$	exponential order

This holds, for example, when the composite algorithm is written by composing the two subalgorithms sequentially and $m_1 = m_2 = 1$. It follows from the above that

$$
\begin{aligned}
T(n) &\leqslant m_1\, c_1\, f(n) + m_2\, c_2\, g(n) && \text{from (10.15), (10.16) and (10.18)} \\
&\leqslant m_1\, c_1\, c_f\, g(n) + m_2\, c_2\, g(n) && \text{from (10.17)} \\
&\leqslant (m_1\, c_1\, c_f + m_2\, c_2)\, g(n) \\
&= c\, g(n) && \text{(10.19)}
\end{aligned}
$$

where $c = m_1\, c_1\, c_f + m_2\, c_2$. Therefore, the time complexity of the composite algorithm is of $O(g(n))$. That is, 'divide and conquer' remains applicable in complexity analysis. Therefore, in the design of algorithms where complexity matters, it makes sense to focus attention on the subalgorithms possessing the most dominant complexity.

Exercise 10.5 ✳✳✳

The following algorithm sorts the elements of an array of length n in the ascending (non–decreasing) order. It is known as the *straight insertion* technique and sorts the array by scanning the array from one end and inserting one element at a time at the right place by shifting, if necessary, the elements in the already sorted part of the array. This is illustrated in Figure 10.2. Derive its complexity measures based on

1. the number of comparisons of array elements,
2. the number of moves (assignments) of array elements.

The algorithm may be expressed as

```
procedure StraightInsert;
var
      a : array of integer;        (of length n)
      i, j, x : integer;
begin
      i := 2;
      while i ⩽ n do
      begin                                      ◄
         x := a[i]; j := i; i := i + 1;
         while j ≠ 1 and x < a[j − 1] do
         begin
               a[j] := a[j − 1]; j := j − 1
         end;
         a[j] := x
      end
end
```

| 5 | 25 | 44 | 56 | 73 | 11 | 99 | 35 | 56 | An intermediate state of sorting |

  sorted part   yet to be sorted

| 6 | 11 | 25 | 44 | 56 | 73 | 99 | 35 | 56 | Next state of sorting |

  sorted part   yet to be sorted

Figure 10.2 How straight insertion works.

Table 10.2   How the algorithm *StraightInsert* sorts an array.

value of i at line marked ◄	Array values in the order of array indices								
	1	2	3	4	5	6	7	8	
	73	25	44	56	11	99	35	56	◁ index ◁ initial value
2	73	25	44	56	11	99	35	56	
3	25	73	44	56	11	99	35	56	
4	25	44	73	56	11	99	35	56	
5	25	44	56	73	11	99	35	56	
6	11	25	44	56	73	99	35	56	
7	11	25	44	56	73	99	35	56	
8	11	25	35	44	56	73	99	56	
9	11	25	35	44	56	56	73	99	

Table 10.2 is a detailed illustration of how the algorithm *StraightInsert* sorts an array of elements. Each row shows the state of the array at the beginning of each cycle of computation at the line marked by ◄.

Exercise 10.6 ✳ ✳

Here is another algorithm for sorting the elements of an array of length n in the ascending order. It is known as the *straight selection* technique and works by first locating the smallest element of the unsorted part of the array and interchanging it with the first element of the unsorted part. Derive an explicit definition for its complexity measure based on the number of comparisons of array elements by first deriving the recurrence relation for complexity.

```
procedure StraightSelect;
var
      a : array of integer;                          (of length n)
      i, j, k, x : integer;
begin
      i := 1;
      while i < n do
      begin                                          ◄
            x := a[i]; k := i; j := i + 1;
            while j ≤ n do
            begin
                  if a[j] < x then
                  begin
                        k := j; x := a[k]
                  end;
                  j := j + 1
            end;
            a[k] := a[i]; a[i] := x; i := i + 1
      end
end
```

Table 10.3   How the algorithm *StraightSelect* sorts an array.

value of i at line	Array values in the order of array indices							
	1	2	3	4	5	6	7	8
marked ◀	73	25	44	56	11	99	35	56
1	73	25	44	56	11	99	35	56
2	11	25	44	56	73	99	35	56
3	11	25	44	56	73	99	35	56
4	11	25	35	56	73	99	44	56
5	11	25	35	44	73	99	56	56
6	11	25	35	44	56	99	73	56
7	11	25	35	44	56	56	73	99

◁ index
◁ initial value

The working of the algorithm *StraightSelect* on the same array of elements as in the previous case is illustrated in Table 10.3. As before, each row shows the state of the array at the beginning of each array of the outer loop.

A divide and conquer strategy usually partitions a problem into two or more subproblems of approximately equal size. In this context, the Exercise 10.7 requires the generalization of the result established in Example 10.8 to deal with decomposition of a problem into an arbitrary number of subproblems.

Exercise 10.7 ✳✳✳

Given the recurrence relations defining the time complexity $T(n)$ of a problem of size n

$$T(n) = \begin{cases} b & \text{for } n = 1 \\ aT\left(\dfrac{n}{c}\right) + bn & \text{for } n > 1 \end{cases}$$

where a, b and c are positive constants, express $T(n)$ using the *Oh*-notation.

Exercise 10.8 ✳✳

Below is a third algorithm for sorting the elements of an array into ascending order. Using an appropriate recurrence relation and the result established in Exercise 10.7, derive a complexity measure of the algorithm based on the number of comparisons of array elements it makes depending on the array size n.

The algorithm is known as a *merge sort algorithm* and uses a subsidiary procedure *Merge*, which takes two sorted arrays as its arguments and produces a sorted array by merging the two sorted arrays in the appropriate manner. Figure 10.3 illustrates how *Merge* works.

Input1: *a*   15 15 33   40 46 47 65 67 86 ···
               ‹— already merged —› ‹— yet to be merged —›

Input2: *b*   8 9 11 20   66 70 72 76 79 80 ···
               ‹— already merged —› ‹— yet to be merged —›

Output: 5 8 9 11 15 20 33   ←   40
Merge(a, b)   ‹— already merged —›   next to be merged

Figure 10.3 How *Merge* works.

The algorithm *Merge* takes advantage of the fact that its two arguments are already sorted. In practical terms this means that, as it merges the two input arrays, the algorithm does not need to know the contents of arrays in full but just the elements at the current head of the subarrays remaining to be merged. This is particularly useful when dealing with data stored in the form of sorted files in external storage. For this reason, the algorithm is known as an *external sorting technique*.

The algorithm as a whole, *MergeSort*, is as follows:

```
procedure MergeSort(i, j);
var
      a : array of integer;                    (from index i to index j )
      i, j, k : integer;
begin
      if i = j then return a[i, j];                              ◀ A
      else
      begin
        k := (i + j − 1)/2;
        return Merge(MergeSort(i, k),
                            MergeSort(k + 1, j))                 ◀ B
      end
end
```

The working of the algorithm *MergeSort* is illustrated in Figure 10.4.

More detailed discussions about the algorithms given in exercises 10.5, 10.6 and 10.8 and other alternative algorithms may be found in many standard texts in algorithms and data structures, including that by Wirth (1986).

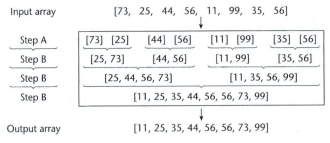

Input array   [73, 25, 44, 56, 11, 99, 35, 56]

Step A   [73] [25]   [44] [56]   [11] [99]   [35] [56]

Step B   [25, 73]   [44, 56]   [11, 99]   [35, 56]

Step B   [25, 44, 56, 73]   [11, 35, 56, 99]

Step B   [11, 25, 35, 44, 56, 56, 73, 99]

Output array   [11, 25, 35, 44, 56, 56, 73, 99]

Figure 10.4 How *MergeSort* works.

Chapter 11

Basic set theoretical concepts

Topic: Sets

....

To betray, you must first belong.

Kim Philby
British-born spy (1912–88)

Objectives

On completion of this chapter you should be able to:

● Explain what sets are.

● Define specific sets.

● Define set equality, the empty set, the universal set, subsets and the power set.

As outlined in Section 1.6 of Chapter 1, set theory is the other major item of our mathematical toolkit. With the knowledge of just classical logic and set theory, it is possible to study various aspects of computing rigorously. The major contribution of set theory is that its various mathematical objects enable the construction of mathematical models of all kinds of systems.

Furthermore, as discussed in Chapter 19, set theory is closely related to logic: so much so that many concepts in the two disciplines are almost interchangeable. Although at times it could be confusing, this link enables logic and set theory to complement each other's capabilities significantly, thus creating a powerful formalism for concise and precise representation of information and reasoning about it.

11.1 What are sets?

Sets are collections of objects or things. Some typical examples are a set of people, a set of shops, a set of languages, or a set of numbers. All these sets are characterized mathematically by

1. Their *elements* (alternative terms are *members*, *individuals*).

2. A *well-defined relation* between elements and sets under consideration. This relation is denoted by the symbol $\in$.

Given an object a and a set S, we write

$a \in S$ to mean that a is a member of the set S or a belongs to S.
$a \notin S$ to mean that a is not a member of the set S.

Note that the symbol $\notin$ may be defined in logic as

$$a \notin S \overset{def}{\Leftrightarrow} \neg (a \in S)$$

'Well-definedness' of the relation $\in$ requires us to be certain of the following:

1. The composition of S is definite, that is, given an element, we must be able to say definitely whether the element is in S or not.

2. All elements of the set S are mutually distinguishable. This is because otherwise there would be no means of identifying them. For example, in ordinary life it is impossible to talk about a set of snowflakes because its individuals lack any sensible means of identification.

11.2 How to define sets

There are two ways to define sets:

1. List the elements of sets. (This is referred to as *set enumeration.*)

2. Write a predicate (condition) on membership of elements. (This is referred to as *set comprehension.*)

When presenting sets in written form, both approaches enclose sets within curly braces $\{\ldots\}$.

Example 11.1

Here are some examples of set enumeration:

$\{$*Mercury, Venus, . . . , Pluto*$\}$	*The set of planets in the solar system.*
$\{$*France, Germany, UK, Italy*$\}$	*Set of rich countries of the European Union assuming that only France, Germany, UK and Italy belong to this category*
$\{0, 20, 40, 60, 80, 100\}$	*The set of natural numbers between 0 and 100 which are multiples of 20*

Having familiarized ourselves with the notation $\{\ldots\}$, let us state two important consequences of our understanding of $\in$:

1. There is no order of elements in a given set. That is, $\{a, b\}$ and $\{b, a\}$ are the same set.

2. There are no multiple occurrences of elements in a set. That is, $\{a, a, a\}$, $\{a, a\}$ and $\{a\}$ all denote the same set.

Example 11.2

Here are some examples of set comprehension.

$\{x \mid x \in EU \wedge rich(x)\}$ *Rich countries of the European Union as given in Example 11.1, provided that EU denotes the set of countries in the community and the predicate rich(x) is true only of France, Germany, UK and Italy among the countries in the EU.*

$\{n \mid n \in \mathbb{N} \wedge \exists k \bullet$
$k \in \mathbb{N} \wedge k \times 20 = n \wedge$
$0 \leqslant n \leqslant 100\}$ *The set of natural numbers between 0 and 100 that are multiples of 20*

We often regard certain sets consisting of all the objects of a given kind as a *type*. Because of lack of information about the actual representation of such objects, it is often unnecessary, and sometimes difficult, to define such sets at abstract levels of problem solving. As a consequence, the well–definedness of $\in$ becomes questionable. In such situations, the definition of elements in types may be deferred, distinguishing instead different types of values just by different type names. This is an approach used by specification languages in software engineering. For example, the specification language Z introduces such types in the following manner:

```
[DATE],
[Name]
```

or

```
[Date, Name]
```

denoting, for example, the sets of all possible dates and names and with the understanding that these sets are to be defined at a later stage. There is more about this in Section 12.7.

Exercise 11.1 ✳

1. Define the following sets by set enumeration and, where possible, by set comprehension.

   (a) Primary colours.

   (b) UN members with vetoing power on the Security Council.

   (c) Horror stories that frighten children.

   (d) A non-empty set of past and present women prime ministers in the world.

   (e) War veterans badly injured in the war.

   (f) The set of triangular numbers between 1 and 30. Every triangular number represents a number of objects that can be placed in a regular pattern of equilateral triangles. Figure 11.1 shows how this can be done for the first five triangular numbers T_i for values of *i* from 1 to 5.

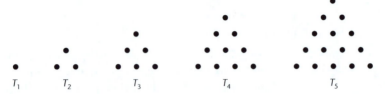

Figure 11.1   The first five triangular numbers for Exercise 11.1

2. Explain why any of the sets in question 1 could not have been defined formally.

11.3 Set equality

Set equality is a relationship between two given sets. Two sets are considered equal if and only if they have exactly the same elements. This is stated mathematically in the Definition.

Definition) Set equality (I)

$$A = B \Leftrightarrow (\forall x \bullet x \in A \Leftrightarrow x \in B)$$

where A and B denote two sets of elements.

The bi-implication in the Definition is useful for proving that two sets are identical. We will come across an example of its use in Section 12.4.

Exercise 11.2 ✳

1. Show that the following two sets are identical: the set of victorious superpower allies in the Second World War and the set of UN members with vetoing rights on the Security Council.

2. Show by an informal comparison that (a) and (b) below are the same:
   (a) The set of numbers between 1 and 20 which are squares of some number.
   (b) The set of numbers of objects required, as shown in Figure 11.2, for creating each time a roof-like symmetrical pattern by successively adding a row of 1, 3, 5 and 7 objects.

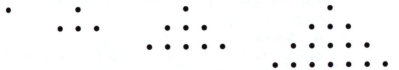

Figure 11.2   Diagram for Exercise 11.2

3. Show by mathematical induction that the equality established in question 2 holds if the two sets are extended to infinity. That is, the first set will contain all numbers each of which is a square of some number and, in constructing the second, the 'roof' patterns will include all rows from 1 to ∞.

(11.4) The empty set

The empty set is a unique set which is characterized by having no elements. It is denoted by $\varnothing$ or $\{\,\}$. One can conceive the empty set by referring to sets which are obviously empty. Some examples are:

$$\varnothing = \{x \mid x \neq x\}$$

$$\varnothing = \{n \mid n \in \mathbb{N} \wedge n > n\}$$

$\varnothing$ = The set of rivers where water always flows upstream.   **(11.1)**

Terminology

One can say that the sets in (11.1) are *logically* empty. However, there are many practical situations where the empty set occurs in a *factual* sense.

Example 11.3

Some sets which are factually empty are:

1. The set of African countries north of the Mediterranean Sea.

2. The set of European countries where the staple diet is rice.

(11.5) The universal set

The universal set consists of all the elements (objects) of concern in any discussion. It is applicable only when we are dealing with a single type of element, and in this case, the universal set and the underlying type, if it has been made explicit, are identical. The universal set is denoted by U.

Example 11.4

Some examples of universal sets in different contexts (discussions) are:

$\mathbb{N}$ *When counting in discrete domains*
$\mathbb{R}$ *When counting and measuring in continuous domains*
Alphabet   *When dealing with strings or sets of characters*

11.6 Subsets

11.6.1 Definition of a subset

Like set equality, subsets represent another possible relationship between any pair of sets. The set A is called a *subset* of the set B if and only if all elements of A are also elements of B. This is denoted as $A \subseteq B$.

Definition   Subsets (I)

The mathematical definition of a *subset* is:

$$A \subseteq B \Leftrightarrow (\forall x \bullet x \in A \Rightarrow x \in B)$$

where A and B are two sets.

Terminology

When $A \subseteq B$, A is said to be *contained* in B or B is said to *include* A.

Example 11.5

The two major states of the British Isles are a subset of the member states of the European Union. Letting

$$BritishIsleStates = \{\textbf{UK}, \textbf{RepublicIreland}\}$$

we write this as

$$BritishIsleStates \subseteq EU$$

Note that by definition,

$$A \not\subseteq B \overset{def}{\Leftrightarrow} \neg(A \subseteq B)$$

A set A is said to be a *proper subset* of B, written as $A \subset B$, if and only if A is a subset of B but is not equal to B, that is

$$A \subset B \overset{def}{\Leftrightarrow} A \subseteq B \wedge A \neq B$$

Example 11.6

Referring to Example 11.5,

$$\{\textbf{UK}, \textbf{Republic Ireland}, \textbf{Japan}\} \not\subseteq EU$$

Also, the two major states of the British Isles are a proper subset of the member states of the European Union. That is,

$$BritishIsleStates \subset EU$$

An alternative to the Definition given above would be to define a predicate $\varphi(x)$ that qualifies the elements of B which are elements of A. This results in a second definition for subsets.

Definition   Subsets (II)

$$A \subseteq B \Leftrightarrow (\forall x \bullet x \in A \Leftrightarrow x \in B \wedge \varphi(x))$$

Example 11.7

According to the second Definition of a subset,

BritishIsleStates $\subseteq EU$

if we take $\varphi(x)$ to be the predicate *inBritishArchipelago*(x) such that it is true of the Republic of Ireland and the UK.

Exercise 11.3 ✳

1. In relation to the sets used as Examples 11.1 and 11.2, identify the predicate $\varphi(x)$ such that:
   (a) The set of rich EU countries is a subset of the EU countries.
   (b) The set of natural numbers between 0 and 100 which are multiples of 20 is a subset of the natural numbers.

2. State, using only the subset relation, that:
   (a) European countries east of longitude 5 °E (meridian) are in the EU.
   (b) Not all Mediterranean countries are EU countries.
   (c) All EU countries are in the UN.
   (d) All European countries are in the UN but not in the EU (not true, since Switzerland is not in the UN).
   (e) All African countries north of the Mediterranean are in the EU.
   (f) The UN members include Switzerland.

11.6.2   Properties of the subset relation

Here is a list of the properties of the relation $\subseteq$.

1. The empty set is a subset of every set A. That is,

   $$\varnothing \subseteq A$$

   The truth above follows vacuously from the fact that $\varnothing$ has no elements.

2. Given a set A, A is a subset of itself. That is,

   $$A \subseteq A$$

   This property makes $\subseteq$ a *reflexive* relation (covered in Chapter 15).

3. Given any three sets A, B and C,

$$A \subseteq B \wedge B \subseteq C \Rightarrow A \subseteq C$$

This property makes $\subseteq$ a *transitive* relation (covered in Chapter 15).

11.6.3 Set equality and set inclusion

The concept of set inclusion enables an alternative definition of set equality to be given. This definition may be used for proving set equality (see Section 12.4 for an example).

Definition) Set equality (II)

Two sets are *equal* to each other if and only if each includes the other on a reciprocal (mutual) basis. That is,

$$(A = B) \Leftrightarrow A \subseteq B \wedge B \subseteq A$$

11.7 Size of sets

Definition) Size of sets

The *size* of any given set is the number of its elements. It is denoted by the symbol $\#$.

The notation $\#$ is meaningful only in the case of *finite sets* – sets where all the elements are countable from zero up to some natural number. Obviously, the following holds:

$$\#\varnothing = 0$$

Example 11.8

1. $\#\{blue, red, yellow\} = 3$
2. Consider a set of some current or former women prime ministers.

$$SomeWomenPMs = \{ \begin{matrix} Bandaranayake, & IndiraGandhi, & Thatcher, \\ GoldaMeir, & BenazirBhutto, & TansuCiller \end{matrix} \}$$

Then

$$\#SomeWomenPMs = 6$$

3. $\#\{n \in \mathbb{N} \mid 5 \leqslant n \leqslant 10\} = 6$

Terminology

A set consisting of just one element is called a *singleton* set.

11.8 Power set

(**Definition**) Power set

The *power set* of a given set is the set of all its subsets. A symbol used to denote the power set is $\mathbb{P}$. Given a set A, the power set of A is given by

$$\mathbb{P}A = \{a \mid a \subseteq A\}$$

Instead of the notation $\mathbb{P}$, we also use a special symbol $\mathbb{F}$ for the power set consisting of just the finite subsets of any given set.

(**Observations**)

Note that

1. $\#(\mathbb{P}A) = 2^{\#A}$

2. $\mathbb{P}A = \mathbb{F}A$, if A is a finite set

(**Example 11.9**)

$$\mathbb{P}\{p, q\} = \{\varnothing, \{p\}, \{q\}, \{p, q\}\}$$
$$\mathbb{P}\{p\} = \{\varnothing, \{p\}\}$$
$$\mathbb{P}\varnothing = \{\varnothing\}$$

(**Example 11.10**)

Given that

BritishIsles = **Britain**, **Ireland**, **Scilly**, **Hebrides**, **Orkney**, **Shetland**}

its power set is

$\mathbb{P}$ *BritishIsles* = $\{\varnothing, \{$**Britain**$\}, \{$**Ireland**$\}, \ldots,$
$\{$**Britain**, **Ireland**$\}, \ldots,$ *BritishIsles*$\}$

which is too big to enumerate because

$\#\mathbb{P}$ *BritishIsles* = $2^6 = 64$

Software specification languages treat the power set as a type, given that its operand set is also a type.

Example 11.11

Let us treat the set of British Isles given in Example 11.10 as a type. Then, the set

> {*Britain*, *Ireland*}

is of type $\mathbb{P}BritishIsles$. If we now wish to talk about a similar but arbitrary subset x of the British Isles, we declare x as

> $x : \mathbb{P}\,BritishIsles$

Exercise 11.4 ✳

Determine the power set of the following sets.

1. $\{a, b, c\}$
2. $\{\{1, 2\}, \{5\}, \{2, 3\}\}$
3. A set containing 3–4 European monarchies.

Exercise 11.5 ✳✳✳

How would you reason about the truth of the following?

> $\#(\mathbb{P}A) = 2^{\#A}$

For the time being, attempt an informal proof and, after studying Chapter 12, attempt a formal proof.

11.9 An extended notation for sets

This section extends the notation used in Section 11.2 for set abstraction. The purpose is to introduce, as in Sections 7.3 and 7.4, the notation used in the specification language Z.

Set abstraction involves a *term* and a predicate. A *term* is any expression corresponding to an *object* and not a predicate or a proposition. The notation used in Section 11.2 has the general syntax

> $\{\langle\text{term}\rangle \mid \langle\text{predicate}\rangle\}$

The extended syntax shown below requires in addition the type information about the variables appearing in the term.

> $\{\langle\text{term}\rangle \bullet \langle\text{signature}\rangle \mid \langle\text{predicate}\rangle\}$

The *signature* introduces variables appearing in the term and associates them with types. The above may be read as:

The set of objects as defined by the term *with variables declared in the* signature *such that they satisfy the predicate.*

The following is an alternative notation for the same.

> $\{\langle\text{signature}\rangle \mid \langle\text{predicate}\rangle \bullet \langle\text{term}\rangle\}$

Example 11.12

The examples used in Section 11.2 would become the following in the extended notation:

$\{x \bullet x : Country \mid x \in EU \land rich(x)\}$
Rich countries of the European Union, *Country* being a new type

$\{n \bullet n : \mathbb{N} \mid \exists k : \mathbb{N} \bullet k \times 20 = n \land 0 \leqslant n \leqslant 100\}$
The set of natural numbers between 0 and 100 that are multiples of 20

The term may not necessarily be a simple variable. It may be an arbitrarily complex expression, as Example 11.13 illustrates.

Example 11.13

The set of numbers each of which is a square of some prime number between 0 and 100 inclusively is the following set

$$primeSquared \stackrel{def}{=} \{n^2 \bullet n : \mathbb{N} \mid prime(n) \land n \leqslant 100\}$$

where '$\stackrel{def}{=}$' denotes the equality 'by definition'.

Note that the term may be omitted if it happens to be a simple variable. The term in Example 11.13 is not a variable on its own but an expression, that is, n^2. As will become clear in Chapter 12, the term may even be a 'pair' or a 'tuple' of elements and the signature may contain multiple type definitions.

Exercise 11.6 ✳

Define the sets in question 1 of Exercise 11.1 in the new notation.

Operations on sets

Topic: Sets

··

Nothing in the world is single;
All things, by a law divine,
In one spirit meet and mingle.

Percy Bysshe Shelley
English poet (1792–1822)

Objectives

On completion of this chapter you should be able to:

● Define and use binary set operations.

● Remember and prove laws about binary set operations.

● Define and use generalized set union and intersection.

● Define disjoint sets.

● Specify simple systems in the Z notation.

● Understand a formal specification written in the Z notation.

This chapter continues the study of basic set theoretic concepts started in the previous chapter. Its main purpose is to introduce certain common set theoretic operations. Some of these operations serve as the bridge between set theory and logic – a topic dealt with in greater detail in Chapter 19 on Boolean algebra. The chapter also introduces some of the basic ideas of the Z notation in relation to specification of systems.

12.1 Binary set operations

Each binary set operation produces a unique new set from any two given sets. In what follows, let A and B be sets of the same type.

Definition   Set union

The *union* of two sets is the set containing just the elements belonging to either set. It is denoted by $\cup$ and is defined mathematically as

$$A \cup B = \{x \mid x \in A \lor x \in B\}$$

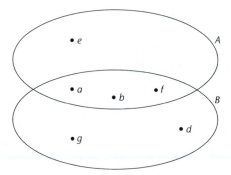

Figure 12.1   A Venn diagram for illustrating set operations.

Example 12.1

Let A and B be the sets

$$A = \{a,b,e,f\}$$
$$B = \{b,d,g,f,a\}$$

Then, as shown in Figure 12.1, the union of A and B is

$$A \cup B = \{a,b,d,e,f,g\}$$

Terminology

Diagrams such as Figure 12.1 showing sets and their elements are known as *Venn diagrams*.

Definition   Set intersection

The *intersection* of two sets is the set containing only those elements belonging to both sets. It is denoted by $\cap$ and is defined mathematically as

$$A \cap B = \{x \mid x \in A \wedge x \in B\}$$

Example 12.2

Referring to the example in Figure 12.1,

$$A \cap B = \{a,b,f\}$$

Note that the elements in $A \cap B$ are those inside the overlapping areas of sets A and B.

Observations

It may be shown in relation to set union and set intersection that

$$\#(A \cup B) = \#A + \#B - \#(A \cap B)$$

Definition) Set difference

The *difference* of a set with respect to another is the set containing only those elements belonging to the first set but not to the second set. It is defined mathematically as the subtraction,

$$A - B = \{x \mid x \in A \wedge x \notin B\}$$

Note that the order of the operand sets is important in the difference operation.

Example 12.3

Referring to the example in Figure 12.1.

$$A - B = \{e\}$$
$$B - A = \{d.g\}$$

Terminology

Set difference is also referred to as the *relative complement*.

Definition) Absolute complement

The *absolute complement* of a set is the difference of the universal set with respect to the given set. Given a set A, its absolute complement is denoted by A' and is defined as

$$A' = U - A = \{x \mid x \in U \wedge x \notin A\}$$

Example 12.4

Assuming $U = \{a, b, c, d, e, f, g, h\}$ for the sets shown in Figure 12.1, then

$$A' = \{c, d, g, h\}$$
$$B' = \{c, e, h\}$$
$$\emptyset' = U$$

Exercise 12.1 ✳

Given sets P, Q and R such that

$$P = \{x, t, m, s\}$$
$$Q = \{t, s, y\}$$
$$R = \{y, x\}$$
$$U = P \cup Q \cup R$$

find the following sets:

1. $(P \cap R) \cup Q$
2. $(R - Q) \cup P$
3. $R' \cap Q$
4. $(P \cup Q)'$
5. $P \cap R \cap Q$
6. $(P \cup Q) \cap (R \cup Q)$
7. $P' \cap Q'$
8. $P \cap Q \cap R$

12.2 Uses of sets

Set theoretic relations (equality, subsets) and operations (union, intersection, and so on) can be used for both

1. defining new sets (by manipulating sets), and
2. for expressing ideas about specific sets (using sets as a language).

When we use set theory as a language, we can practically abstain from using quantifiers in predicate logic completely and yet achieve the same expressiveness. Example 12.5 demonstrates both the above uses of set theoretic concepts as well as how to use sets in place of logical quantifiers.

Example 12.5

Imagine a library collection of books classified under different headings. Itemized below are some observations (or descriptions) in English about this collection. Let us formalize these descriptions using sets alone, that is, without using logical quantifiers.

Our *first task* is to identify the kinds of object and set involved. For this, first read the given English sentences. It follows from them that we are dealing with objects drawn from some type

  [*Book*]

denoting the set of all possible books, and with certain subsets of *Book*, namely,

  fiction, biographies, scientific, handbooks, travel, dictionaries, poetry, literary, English, foreign, languages : $\mathbb{P}$ *Books*

Using the above sets, it is possible to formalize the descriptions below as new sets (that is, the first use of sets mentioned above) or as predicates involving the above sets (that is, the second use of sets).

1. The set of non-fiction English books on travel:

  (*English* $\cap$ *travel*) − *fiction*

2. All handbooks are written in English:

   handbooks ⊆ *English*

3. Books written in English never appear under foreign language books:

   English ∩ *foreign* ∩ *languages* = ∅

   [Note that there is an ambiguity in the above English sentence. Do books written in English include English language books?]

4. The set of books classified as both handbooks and dictionaries.

   handbooks ∩ *dictionaries*

5. The set of books appearing in the handbook or dictionary collections:

   handbooks ∪ *dictionaries*

6. The set of science fiction books:

   scientific ∩ *fiction*

7. All non-scientific books on fiction, poetry and biographies are literary works:

   (*fiction* ∪ *poetry* ∪ *biographies*) − *scientific* ⊆ *literary*

Exercise 12.2 ✳✳

Using the sets in Example 12.5, determine or state the following.

1. The set of foreign books on languages.
2. No books on languages are to be classified as literary works.
3. No scientific book can be a literary work.
4. The set of scientific handbooks excluding dictionaries.
5. If any foreign literary works appear in the collection then they can only be on poetry.
6. Biographies are never to be treated as fiction.
7. All books must appear in scientific, literary or language collections.
8. No literary works are kept if there are no books on fiction.

Exercise 12.3 ✳✳

Using appropriate sets, formalize the following descriptions. The answers must not contain logical quantifiers.

1. Popular cars are exactly non-luxury cars.
2. Commercial vehicles and family cars are non-luxury cars.
3. There are luxury cars other than sports cars.
4. No sports car is a family car.

5. Some popular sports cars are inexpensive.

6. The set of expensive luxury cars excluding Rolls-Royces.

7. Popular cars are non-luxury cars.

8. The cars which are neither family cars nor commercial vehicles.

9. Luxury cars are exactly Rolls-Royces, sports cars and limousines.

10. If more than half of luxury cars are sports cars, then at least one-third must be limousines or there are some family sports cars.

Exercise 12.4

Refer to Chapter 6. Formalize the descriptions in Exercise 6.3 and question 1 of Exercise 6.4 using, as above, only sets but not quantifiers.

12.3 Set theoretic laws listed

Set theoretic operations are often interrelated and some operations exhibit interesting properties such as commutativity. Some of these observations must have been already evident in Exercise 12.1, where, for example, the sets in each of the following pairs of sets were found to be identical:

$(P \cap R) \cup Q$ and $(P \cup Q) \cap (R \cup Q)$
$P' \cap Q'$ and $(P \cup Q)'$

The following is a list of such observations, referred to often as *theorems* or *laws* on set operations. Each observation expresses an identity of two sets, most of them involving one or more set operations and some type-compatible but otherwise arbitrary sets. The reader is advised to compare these observations with logical laws given in Section 4.2. As in Chapter 4, the less intuitive observations are marked with a ◄.

Commutative laws

$$A \cap B = B \cap A \tag{12.1}$$

$$A \cup B = B \cup A \tag{12.2}$$

That is, it is immaterial whether to evaluate the intersection of the set A with the set B, or vice versa. The same applies to set union. Note the exception: commutativity is not applicable to set difference – see Example 12.3.

Associative laws

$$(A \cap B) \cap C = A \cap (B \cap C) \tag{12.3}$$

$$(A \cup B) \cup C = A \cup (B \cup C) \tag{12.4}$$

That is, the order of evaluation of a series of set intersections, or for that matter a series of set unions, is immaterial.

Distributive laws

$$(A \cup B) \cap C = (A \cap C) \cup (B \cap C) \qquad \textbf{(12.5)}$$

$$(A \cap B) \cup C = (A \cup C) \cap (B \cup C) \qquad \textbf{(12.6)}$$

Recall the parallel drawn in Section 4.2 between distributivity of, for example, $\vee$ over $\wedge$ and $\times$ over $+$ in arithmetic. These laws hold for set union and set intersection too.

De Morgan's laws

$$(A \cap B)' = A' \cup B' \qquad \blacktriangleleft \textbf{(12.7)}$$

$$(A \cup B)' = A' \cap B' \qquad \blacktriangleleft \textbf{(12.8)}$$

Identities involving $\varnothing$

$$A \cap \varnothing = \varnothing \qquad \textbf{(12.9)}$$

$$A \cup \varnothing = A \qquad \textbf{(12.10)}$$

$$A - \varnothing = A \qquad \textbf{(12.11)}$$

$$\varnothing - A = \varnothing \qquad \textbf{(12.12)}$$

$$\varnothing' = U \qquad \textbf{(12.13)}$$

It is worth noting the similarity between (12.9) and (12.10) on one hand, and (4.20) and (4.21) on the other. Another similarity is between (12.13) and the logical equivalence

$$\neg \textit{ false} \iff \textit{true}$$

Identities involving the universal set U

$$A \cap U = A \qquad \textbf{(12.14)}$$

$$A \cup U = U \qquad \textbf{(12.15)}$$

$$A - U = \varnothing \qquad \textbf{(12.16)}$$

$$U' = \varnothing \qquad \textbf{(12.17)}$$

Again, note the similarity between (12.14) and (12.15) on one hand, and (4.18) and (4.19) on the other. Note also the similarity of (12.17) with the logical equivalence

$$\neg \textit{ true} \iff \textit{false}$$

Laws about set intersection, union and inclusion

$$A \cap B \subseteq A \qquad \textbf{(12.18)}$$

$$A \subseteq A \cup B \qquad \textbf{(12.19)}$$

12.4 Set theoretic proofs

The validity of the observations about sets in Section 12.3 may be proven mathematically. Two proofs are demonstrated below. Proofs of various properties of sets relevant to a particular scenario may be conducted in a similar manner.

Proofs on sets are, in essence, conducted in predicate logic. For this, the relevant set theoretic relation or the operation has to be viewed in terms of the predicate defining it.

Example 12.6

Prove the following De Morgan law on sets:

$$(A \cup B)' = A' \cap B'$$

Guidance

This may be proved in two different ways, relying respectively on definitions given for set equality:

1. In terms of mutual belonging of every element to both sets (see Section 11.3).

2. In terms of reciprocal inclusion of the two sets in each other (see Section 11.6.3).

Proof based on approach 1

Consider an arbitrary element x belonging to the set on the left-hand side and prove that the belonging holds if and only if x belongs to the set on the right-hand side. Thus:

$x \in (A \cup B)'$

$\Leftrightarrow x \in U \wedge x \notin A \cup B$ definition of absolute complement

$\Leftrightarrow x \in U \wedge \neg (x \in A \cup B)$ definition of $\notin$

$\Leftrightarrow x \in U \wedge \neg (x \in A \vee x \in B)$ definition of set union

[We have thus translated fully the original set theoretic statement to logic. Now let us manipulate the above in logic.]

$\Leftrightarrow x \in U \wedge (x \notin A \wedge x \notin B)$ De Morgan law in logic

$\Leftrightarrow x \in U \wedge x \notin A \wedge x \in U \wedge x \notin B$ idempotence in logic

[Let us now translate the above back to set theory:]

$\Leftrightarrow x \in A' \wedge x \in B'$ definition of absolute complement

$\Leftrightarrow x \in A' \cap B'$ definition of set intersection

Note that the above is an unbroken chain of equivalences resulting in:

$$x \in (A \cup B)' \Leftrightarrow x \in A' \cap B'$$

Since x is chosen arbitrarily, the above is what is required for the following equality:

$$(A \cup B)' = A' \cap B'$$

Proof based on approach 2

Approach 2 allows the original goal to be divided into two subgoals:

$$(A \cup B)' \subseteq A' \cap B' \tag{12.20}$$

$$A' \cap B' \subseteq (A \cup B)' \tag{12.21}$$

Each of the above may be proved in predicate logic. Let us attempt only (12.20); (12.21) is left as an exercise for the reader.

In proving set inclusion, consider an arbitrary element x and show that

$$x \in (A \cup B)' \Rightarrow x \in A' \cap B'$$

Unlike in approach 1, we now have to prove an implication and not an equivalence. As a result, we may provide a deductive proof, and as the proof strategy, we adopt a conditional proof:

1. $x \in (A \cup B)'$ assumption
2. $x \in U \wedge x \notin A \cup B$ from 1, definition of absolute complement
3. $x \in U \wedge \neg (x \in A \cup B)$ from 2, definition of $\notin$
4. $x \in U \wedge \neg (x \in A \vee x \in B)$ from 3, definition of set union
5. $x \in U \wedge x \notin A \wedge x \notin B$ from 4, De Morgan's law in logic
6. $x \in U \wedge x \notin A \wedge x \in U \wedge x \notin B$ from 5, idempotence in logic
7. $x \in A' \wedge x \in B'$ from 6, definition of absolute complement
8. $x \in A' \cap B'$ from 7, definition of set intersection
9. $x \in (A \cup B)' \Rightarrow x \in A' \cap B'$ from 1 & 8, $\Rightarrow \_I$

Thus, the above is a proof of (12.20). A similar proof may be provided for (12.21), thus proving the required set equality.

Exercise 12.5 ✳ ✳

1. Prove the following set equalities.
   (a) $A \cup (B \cap C) = (A \cup B) \cap (A \cup C)$
   (b) $A \cup (A \cap B) = A$
   (c) $(A')' = A$

2. Prove the following subset relations.
   (a) $A \cap B \subseteq A$
   (b) $A \subseteq A \cup B$

Exercise 12.6 ✳ ✳ ✳

With reference to the Exercise 12.3 in Section 12.2, and assuming the following:

1. Commercial vehicles and family cars are non-luxury cars.

2. Sports cars are not commercial vehicles.

3. Some sports cars are family cars.

prove that there are non-luxury sports cars. The argument must be formalized using sets and without using logical quantifiers. The proof may be an informal proof.

12.5 Generalized set operations

Often, it is necessary to find either the union or the intersection of more than two sets. The generalized set intersection takes a set containing an arbitrary but finite number of sets of the same type and returns the 'grand intersection' of all of them. This syntactic information is contained in the following type definition:

$$\bigcap\_ : \mathbb{P}(\mathbb{P}X) \rightarrow \mathbb{P}X$$

Its meaning may be defined recursively as

$$\bigcap\{s\} = s$$
$$\bigcap(\{s\} \cup t) = s \cap (\bigcap t)$$

where s is a subset of X, that is, $s : \mathbb{P}X$, and t is a set of subsets of X, that is, $t : \mathbb{P}(\mathbb{P}X)$.

Example 12.7

Consider the set

$$t = \{\{a, b, c\}, \{b, e\}, \{d, b\}, \{c, e, a, b\}\}$$

and find the generalized intersection of all sets which are elements of t. Its Venn diagram is shown in Figure 12.2.

The generalized intersection contains only the elements common to all sets in t, that is, the ones in the shaded area of Figure 12.2. Thus

$$\bigcap t = \{b\}$$

The generalized set union may be defined in a similar manner to the generalized intersection, as follows:

$$\bigcup\_ : \mathbb{P}(\mathbb{P}X) \rightarrow \mathbb{P}X$$
$$\bigcup\{s\} = \{s\}$$
$$\bigcup\{s\} \cup t = s \cup (\bigcup t)$$

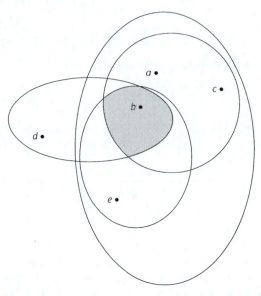

Figure 12.2   An example for generalized set operations.

Example 12.8

Referring to Example 12.7,

$$\bigcup t = \{a, b, c, d, e\}$$

That is, the generalized union gives a set containing the elements each of which is a member of at least one of the sets in t.

Exercise 12.7 ✳

1. Find the generalized union and the generalized intersection of the sets in the following set:

$$S = \{\{a, d, e, p\}, \{g, m, e, a\}, \{a, x, e\}, \{p, s, q, e, a\}\}$$

2. Referring to Example 12.5 and Exercise 12.2 in Section 12.2 and using the generalized set operations, determine or state the following:
   (a) Literary books are exactly the books on fiction, biographies, poetry and travel.
   (b) There are no books classified under fiction, poetry, travel and biographies.
   (c) Scientific books outnumber all other books.
   (d) Foreign books may not outnumber English books unless language books exceed three times other books.
   (e) The set of foreign poetry books of literary value are published in English.

12.6 Disjoint sets

Disjoint sets are sets with no common elements.

Definition) Disjoint sets

Two sets, say A and B, are said to be *disjoint* if and only if their intersection is empty. That is,

$$A \cap B = \varnothing$$

A collection of (indexed or differently named) sets $A_1, A_2, ..., A_k$ are said to be *pairwise disjoint* if and only if every distinct pair in the collection is disjoint. That is,

$$A_i \cap A_j = \varnothing \Leftrightarrow A_i \neq A_j$$

Example 12.9

Consider the sets

$$A = \{a, b, e\}, \quad B = \{d, f\}, \quad C = \{b, d\}, \quad D = \{h, k\}$$

Disjoint sets among the above are:

A and B
A and D
B and D
C and D

Two pairwise disjoint collections of sets are:

A, B and D
C and D

12.7 An application: formal system specification

12.7.1 Background

Section 1.5 of Chapter 1 discussed the role of specifications and their relationship with mathematical theories. Section 1.6 of the same chapter took this discussion further to include mathematical models as a form of visualization of such theories. In this section, we study how to construct mathematical models which could serve indirectly as mathematical specifications or theories.

Our medium of specification is the Z notation – a formal specification language widely used in computing. Prominent among the different approaches to mathematical (formal) specification are the *model-oriented approach* and *algebraic approach*. The Z notation belongs to the family of model-oriented languages, which rely on a mathematical model, constructed using such objects as sets, to convey what is required. By contrast, the algebraic approach relies on algebras, such as those discussed in Chapters 17 and 19, whereby the desired requirements are conveyed implicitly by interrelating system operations.

As far as the mathematical notation applicable to logic and set theory is concerned, this text has already been following the Z notation to a large extent. The main objective here, however, is to illustrate the basic ideas of formal specification of systems in Z. A fuller description of the Z notation and its use in specification may be found in Spivey (1992) and in many texts such as Woodcock and Davies (1996), Potter *et al.* (1991) and Diller (1990). Another well known model-oriented language is VDM, a description of which may be found in Jones (1986), Jones and Shaw (1990) and Andrews and Ince (1991).

Continuing our discussion from Section 1.5, let us briefly examine again the need for formal specification. History is full of incidents, where design faults have resulted in different kinds of failures of computer systems, sometimes with disastrous consequences at run-time, and other times with costly disputes and litigation about the responsibility for overspent budgets, overrun projects and systems not being able to deliver the service expected of them. These failures have often been traced back to the early stages of development and, in particular, to that stage dealing with specification of system requirements. At the root of specific failures are often misunderstandings of requirements. These misunderstandings result from:

1. misinterpretation of requirements because of *lack of clarity* and *precision*,
2. a tendency to compensate for missing information, that is, *incompleteness* of requirements,
3. the resolution of *inconsistencies*.

Such misunderstandings are often brought about by shortcomings in communication between the developer and the customer.

Formal specification addresses specifically these root causes, originating from specification of system requirements. Its primary objective is to express the system requirements *precisely* and *unambiguously*. Once formulated as a mathematical theory, specifications may be scrutinized for other attributes such as *completeness* and *internal consistency*. Thus, formal specification provides the developer and the customer with not only a sound basis for communication of system requirements but also a rigorous framework for studying the global and internal properties of the specification. Furthermore, once matters related to specification of requirements are settled, formal specifications can serve the purposes of design. This has been illustrated in Section 6.8 and Section 9.7 in relation to program development, which considered formal specification as the starting point.

In achieving the two most important attributes of specification, that is, precision and unambiguity, obviously there is no medium more powerful than mathematics. Formal specification languages recognize this fact. However, they also recognize that the conventional form of presentation of mathematical text is inadequate for the task. Note that specifications deal with large and complex systems, the development of which involves requirement analysts, specifiers, software designers and customers.

Therefore, specifications must be easily comprehensible by a range of professionals with different backgrounds. Furthermore, due to human fallibility in both formulating and interpreting them, a long list of unstructured mathematical sentences could itself be error-prone even to the trained mathematician. Thus, in terms of the final outcome, such a list could be as ineffective as a poor document written in natural language.

In order to overcome these deficiencies, formal specification languages incorporate an extended mathematical notation. Thus, they typically consist of two sublanguages, which, in the Z notation, represent the following:

1. A standard notation covering just predicate logic and set theory.

2. An extended notation, known as the *schema language*, for structuring specifications. The schema language is the sublanguage intended to facilitate communication of large pieces of mathematical text in a comprehensible manner.

The rest of this section illustrates the use of the Z notation and, in particular, the schema language, in system specification. As a case study, we consider the requirements of a library. Our knowledge of set theory is sufficient for an initial familiarization with formal specification. Knowing just the basic set theoretic concepts such as the empty set, power set, set union, etc., it is possible to formalize some of the simple features of our case study. We return to a more detailed formalization in Section 16.5.

12.7.2   Type definitions in Z

The basic types of values may be introduced into a specification in a number of different ways. Two basic ways among them are:

1. *Generic types.* Generic types introduce types of values without giving any formal definition. For example, two sets called *Book* and *Location*, which are to be used as types, may be introduced as follows:

    [*Book, Location*]

    Informally, *Book* consists of all possible instances of books, including copies of books, and *Location* their storage locations in the library.

2. *Free (enumerated) types.* Quite often, it is necessary to introduce types with explicitly named values. The names of such values are reserved for denoting those values only and, therefore, they may not be used for any other purpose. An example is:

    Status ::= **In** | **Out** | **Ref**

    where the values **In**, **Out** and **Ref** have the following meanings:

    In   is intended for marking books available for loan.

    Out   is intended for marking books on loan and, therefore, unavailable for borrowing.

Ref   is intended for marking books in the reference collection and, therefore, unavailable for borrowing.

No use will be made of types *Location* and *Status* until Section 16.5.

12.7.3   Schemas

A specification written in the Z notation is a collection of mathematical definitions, which may be presented in a number of ways. Some of these definitions are called *schemas*. For better comprehension and ease of mathematical manipulation, schemas are organized in the following manner. Each schema consists of the following:

1. *Schema name.* Naming a schema introduces a syntactic equality (equality by definition) of the schema name with the mathematical text enclosed in the schema. Given the need, the schema name may be replaced with the content of the schema, and vice versa.

2. *Signature part.* The signature part introduces components (identifiers) and declares their types (mathematical data structures such as sets, relations, functions and sequences; some of these concepts are covered in later chapters).

3. *Predicate part.* The predicate part introduces constraints on the values that the components in the signature part may take. These predicates may be referred to as data invariants (in data abstraction) or state invariants (in system specifications).

In visual presentations, schemas are presented in two forms: vertical layout and horizontal layout.

We use here mostly the vertical layout of schemas, which takes the form of a box subdivided by a horizontal line. This is illustrated in Example 12.10. In the vertical layout of schemata, several conventions apply, namely:

1. Implicit between type declarations on two successive lines is a semicolon, which signifies the continuation of the type declaration. Thus, type declarations may be broken at a semicolon and the semicolon may be omitted.

2. Likewise, implicit between predicates on two successive lines is a conjunction, signifying the continuation of the predicate. A lengthy predicate may therefore be broken at a conjunction and the connective ∧ may be omitted.

In the horizontal layout, a schema is enclosed within square brackets, with an intervening vertical bar separating the signature part from the predicate part.

12.7.4   Specification of system state

Let us illustrate first the use of schemas to describe the structure of a system and the constant aspects of its state, that is, those aspects which remain unchanged as the system evolves through its possible states.

Example 12.10

A specification for the stock of books of a library may be presented as follows.

```
__Lib_Stock_____

    stock, on_loan                          ⎫
    on_shelf, ref_coll   : 𝔽 Book           ⎬ ..    (signature part)
                                            ⎭
    ─────────────────────────────────────────
    stock = on_loan ∪ on_shelf              ⎫
    on_loan ∩ on_shelf = ∅                  ⎬ ..    (predicate part)
    ref_coll ⊆ on_shelf                     ⎭
_____
```

This schema captures the state of the library in relation to its stock. At this level of abstraction, the library consists of four components: *stock*, *on_loan*, *on_shelf* and *ref_coll*, each of which is a finite subset of *Book*. The intended use of these components is as follows. In a given state,

stock	denotes the complete set of books in the library stock.
on_loan	denotes the set of books currently on loan.
on_shelf	denotes the set of books currently available within the premises of the library.
ref_coll	denotes the set of books in the reference collection; these are unavailable for loan.

There are dependencies among the above components. As we begin to question them, we realize that *stock* could be the books on loan as well as those not on loan. On the other hand, the books within the premises may consist of the reference collection, that is, books never available for borrowing, and the books just happened to be not on loan. Obviously, the books on loan and the books within the premises must be totally separate.

The predicates in the above schema settle once and for all the 'could be's and the 'maybe's. The specification has made explicit a 'must be' too, so that no chances are taken with the reader's common sense.

Note how the schema in Example 12.10 expresses dependencies among its components using set theoretic concepts alone, just as in Example 12.5 and Exercises 12.2 and 12.3.

The schema *Lib_Stock* is a small specification. It concerns the structure of the library in terms of its different collections of books and the relationships that must always hold among them. The latter constitute the *system invariant* of the library. Such a specification is thus an expression of what are referred to in software engineering as system requirements. Usually, it is up to the *requirement analyst* to establish which requirements are really applicable. Production of a formal specification, however, often provides another opportunity to question their applicability, as well as whether there could be other requirements inadvertently missed out in the requirement analysis.

Although not relevant in Example 12.10, there could be constraints on individual components too.

12.7.5   Specification of system behaviour

A specification of any system requires the specification of:

1. the general state of the system;
2. its initial and, where applicable, terminal states;
3. state transformations under an agreed set of operations.

Specifications of the general state mentioned in (1) above may be captured through a schema by using it in the following manner:

(a) schema components representing the *state variables*;
(b) schema predicates representing the *state invariant*.

The earlier specification *Lib_Stock* illustrates the use of a schema in the context of (a) and (b) above. In order to describe the system evolution properly, we need the specifications for (2) and (3) listed above. This requires some additional notation, which is outlined below.

Our description below uses the term 'decoration'. An identifier is said to have been 'decorated' by postfixing a dash (a prime) at the end. This results in a new identifier with a matching name. A decorated identifier may be used as an identifier which is distinct from the original one. When used together, decorated and undecorated versions of an identifier refer to the values of the corresponding state variable in two adjacent states. Given such a pair of states, we refer to the first state in the pair as the *before state* and the second as the *after state*. Uses of decorated and undecorated identifiers and other notations are listed in Table 12.1.

Of particular interest in the specification of operations are the Δ and Ξ notations. In relation to our example, ΔLib_Stock is defined as

$$\Delta Lib\_Stock \triangleq Lib\_Stock \wedge Lib\_Stock'$$

which is a conjunction of two states. This is syntactically equivalent to a new schema, containing state variables and predicates as they appear in *Lib_Stock* and another corresponding set of state variables and predicates as in *Lib_Stock* but with all variables being decorated.

The above is an illustration of *schema conjunction* – an operation on schemas. In a conjunction of two schemas, their components are merged and the predicates are conjoined with the propositional connective $\wedge$. Similar operations exist for manipulating schemas in relation to other propositional connectives, with a corresponding effect on their predicates. Hence, there are other schema operations such as *schema disjunction*, *schema implication*, etc., which are all part of the schema language.

Note

The connectives written in the larger size conventionally apply to schemas. For example, $\bigwedge$ applies to schema conjunction, and $\bigvee$ to schema disjunction.

Table 12.1   Uses of decorated and undecorated identifiers.

Use	Convention
For identifying the *state before* the operation	Use the schema representing the given state in the original (undecorated) form. By convention, the undecorated schema components then refer to the values of individual state variables in the *before state*
For identifying the *state after* the operation	Decorate the schema representing the given state with a dash (prime). This is equivalent to implicitly decorating each state variable within the scope of the given schema with a dash as well. By convention, decorated (dashed) schema components refer to the values of *after state* variables
For identifying the *initial state* (a unique operation with only an 'after state')	Use the schema name with the subscript *init* to identify the initial state and define the initialization with the dashed schema name, dashed component names and, where applicable, any inputs
For identifying the *terminal state*	Use the schema as in 'before state'
For identifying the *inputs*	Postfix the identifier representing the input with a question mark '?'
For identifying the *outputs*	Postfix the identifier representing the output with an exclamation mark '!'

In terms of usage, the notation ΔLib_Stock identifies, by convention, two adjacent states of the system. *Lib_Stock* describes here the before state of the system concerned, and *Lib_Stock'* its immediate after state. The two states may in general be different, the difference signifying the expected transformation from the before state to the after state. The task of operation specification is then to describe this transformation by relating the dashed and non-dashed variables with appropriate predicates.

The Ξ notation also refers conventionally to two adjacent states, but the two states concerned are identical. Thus, ΞLib_Stock may be defined as

$$\Xi Lib\_Stock \triangleq Lib\_Stock \wedge Lib\_Stock' \mid Lib\_Stock = Lib\_Stock'$$

Unlike the Δ notation, the Ξ notation is used to define query operations or error handling operations, which involve no state transformations.

If applicable, each operation must be guarded by a precondition so that the user knows exactly when the operation may not succeed. The existence of a precondition requires, in general, the definition of two or more suboperations: (1) a *primary operation* bringing about the desired positive effect of the operation concerned, and (2) one or more *exception handling operations* to cater for scenarios when the primary operation fails. The intention is that exception handling operations do not affect the system state, but notify the user of the failure with an indication of the cause.

A *total operation* is an operation that never fails. Usually, it is an operation consisting of a primary operation, intended to have an effect on the system state, and one or more exception handling operations, taking effect when the primary operation fails. Obviously, exception handling operations should cover the possible failure scenarios of the primary operation exhaustively. In the schema language, a total operation is specified as a *disjunction* of the schema specifying the primary operation and the schemas specifying each of the exception handling operations.

Example 12.11 illustrates the use of the above conventions in the specification of an initialization operation and a more general system operation.

Example 12.11

Let us develop a specification for initialization of *Lib_Stock* system state, and an operation for taking new stocks of books. The latter includes an exception handling facility taking effect when the corresponding primary operation fails.

The initialization of the system described by the schema *Lib_Stock* can be defined as

$$Lib\_Stock_{init} \triangleq Lib\_Stock' \mid \underbrace{stock' = \emptyset}_{\text{new predicate}}$$

which also illustrates how to extend a schema with a new predicate. Note that initialization is a unique operation with only an after state. This explains the reason for using a dashed schema, and hence a dashed component. According to the above initialization specification, the library begins its life with an empty stock. Although we take such matters for granted from our common experience, it follows from the system invariant that other components, such as the set of books on loan, are also empty at the initialization state. When they happen to be non-trivial, such observations could be the subject of proofs.

Consider now the operation of stocktaking at the library. Obviously, a new stock is likely to be a collection of books. As far as the system is concerned, it is an input and, hence, we use the notation *new?*, the question mark signifying that it is an input.

Primary operation for taking new stocks

$$
\begin{array}{l}
\underline{\quad Add\_Stock_0 \quad} \\[4pt]
\Delta Lib\_Stock \quad \ldots\ldots \text{(inclusion of two schemas representing} \\
\hspace{5.2cm} \text{two adjacent states)} \\
new? : \mathbb{F}\, Book \quad \ldots\ldots \text{(an input)} \\[6pt]
\hline \\[-4pt]
new? : \neq \emptyset \\
new? \cap stock = \emptyset \quad \Big\} \ldots \text{(precondition)} \\
stock' = stock \cup new? \\
on\_loan' = on\_loan \quad \Big\} \ldots\ldots \text{(postcondition)}
\end{array}
$$

First, another note on the syntax of the schema language. Inclusion of the schema ΔLib_Stock results in the inheritance of all components and predicates in ΔLib_Stock by the schema Add_Stock_0. *Schema inclusion* is therefore another operation for manipulation of schemas. In fact, it permits the inclusion of any number of schemas in another schema.

In terms of the intended meaning of the schema ΔLib_Stock, its precondition states that the input value of *new?* must be a non-empty set of books but should not contain any books already in the library stock. On the other hand, the postcondition makes the effect of the operation clear, namely, that *stock* is updated with the addition of new stock while keeping the set of books on loan unaffected. By not including a predicate such as

$$ref\_coll' = ref\_coll$$

the specification has left open the possibility that the new stock may contain reference books. Similarly, by leaving out an analogous predicate involving *on_shelf*, the specification has taken care not to cause any violation of the system invariant. This is because, on one hand, according to *Lib_Stock*, the books in the set *stock'* must appear either under those on loan or under those on the library shelves. On the other hand, according to Add_Stock_0 above, the books on loan should not be affected by this operation. This leaves no option but to include the new books in the set *on_shelf'*.

Exception handling

The schema *Errorneous_New_Stock* specifies an alternative course of action when the precondition of the operation specified by Add_Stock_0 is not met, in other words, the operation Add_Stock_0 could fail. An error handling facility such as this should not affect the system state, but be informative to the user. For this purpose, let us introduce a new type *Report*, the values of which are error messages written as strings of characters.

```
┌─ Erroneous_New_Stock ────────────────────────────────
│  ΞLib_Stock      ...... (inclusion of two schemas representing two
│                          adjacent identical states)
│  new? : F Book   ...... (an input)
│  rep! : Report    ...... (an output)
├──────────────────────
│  (new? = ∅ ∨                      ⎫
│       new? ∩ stock ≠ ∅)           ⎬ (precondition)
│                                    ⎭
│  rep! =" Empty new stock          ⎫
│          or books in input are    ⎬ (the effect – an output only)
│          in existing stock too"   ⎭
└──────────────────────────────────────────────────────
```

Total operation

The total version of the stock taking operation is

$$Add\_Stock = Add\_Stock_0 \bigvee Errorneous\_New\_Stock$$

Exercise 12.8 ✳ ✳ ✳

Extend the specification developed in Example 12.11 with the introduction of the following operations:

1. An operation for lending a book from the library.

2. An operation for returning a borrowed book to the library.

3. An operation for disposing of a collection of books from the library stock.

4. An operation for checking whether a given book is available for loan. [Hint: Think of the Ξ notation.]

The above operations must be total operations.

Chapter 13

Relations: basic concepts

Topic: Relations

The human mind has to first construct forms, independently, before we can find them in things.

Albert Einstein
German–American physicist (1879–1955)

Objectives

On completion of this chapter you should be able to:

- Define the Cartesian product.
- Define mathematical relations.
- Relate mathematical relations to predicates.
- Define domain, range, field, identity relation and inverse relation.
- Relate mathematical relations to relations in relational databases, and vice versa.

Ordinary life is inconceivable without relationships between various things. We, humans relate to one another by blood, by friendship, by culture and by occupation. We relate to the world outside by having various interests in different things or by being dependent on them. Materials, atoms, plants, animals and numbers all likewise exhibit similar relationships.

Mathematical relations are an abstraction of all such relationships. They allow us to think of such relationships in highly abstract terms with the minimum amount of information required for the task in hand. Once represented as mathematical objects, relations can be mathematically manipulated and reasoned about with precision. The discussion on databases in Section 13.9 highlights the relevance of mathematical relations in computing, especially with respect to representation of information.

13.1 Pairs and tuples

As was discussed in Chapter 11, there is no order among the elements in a set. However, there are sets where it is natural to expect some ordering. Consider, for example, the set of one's parents. Here, we may wish to distinguish one element as the father and the other as the mother.

We use the term *tuple* for an arrangement of certain elements of a set in some order. The ordering is for the purpose of referring to elements only and does not reflect any preference or superiority, except, perhaps, informally. Tuples may be represented mathematically using ordinary sets. However, we do not attempt this and, instead, restrict ourselves to an informal understanding. The notation used universally for tuples is to list the elements in the desired order and enclose the list in parentheses (brackets).

Example 13.1

(*Gorbachev*, *Yeltsin*)	A tuple of two individuals, where **Gorbachev** is the first element and **Yeltsin** is the second.
(*Mercury*, *Venus*, *Earth*)	A tuple of planets, where **Mercury** is the first element, **Venus** is the second, **Earth** is the third.
(3, 7, 11, 13, 17)	A tuple of numbers.
(3, 11, 17, 13, 7)	A tuple of numbers, which is different from the above.

Terminology

A tuple containing just two elements is called a *pair*, one with three a *triple*, one with four a *quadruple*, etc.

Notation

In relation to ordered pairs, the following notations are identical:

$$(a, b) \stackrel{def}{=} a \mapsto b$$

where $\stackrel{def}{=}$ denotes the equality 'by definition'. A pair written in the form $a \mapsto b$ is often referred to as a *maplet*.

13.2 Cartesian product

Although it sounds like a highly technical term, the Cartesian product is a simple concept but fundamental to relations – the topic of this chapter. In its simplest form, the Cartesian product is a set operation which takes two sets and produces a set of ordered pairs of elements.

Definition   Cartesian product

Given two sets A and B, the *Cartesian product* is denoted by $A \times B$ and is defined as

$$A \times B \stackrel{def}{=} \{(a, b) \mid a \in A \land b \in B\}$$

The Definition tells us that $A \times B$ contains *all possible pairs* of elements such that the first in each pair belongs to A and the second to B. Note that,

$$A \times B \neq B \times A$$

unless $A = B$. That is, the Cartesian product is dependent on the order of appearance of A and B in the operation.

Example 13.2

Let us consider two sets of the individuals,

$$H = \{\textit{Eve, Adam, Pele, Mario, Rosi}\}$$
$$A = \{\textit{dog, cat, parrot, horse, fox}\}$$

H and A denoting respectively, say, a set of people and a set of species of animals. Then, the Cartesian product $H \times A$ is the following set:

$$
\begin{aligned}
H \times A = \{ & (\textit{Eve, dog}), (\textit{Eve, cat}), (\textit{Eve, parrot}), (\textit{Eve, horse}), \\
& (\textit{Eve, fox}), (\textit{Adam, dog}), (\textit{Adam, cat}), (\textit{Adam, parrot}), \\
& (\textit{Adam, horse}), (\textit{Adam, fox}), \dots (\text{all other pairs}), \dots \\
& (\textit{Rosi, dog}), (\textit{Rosi, cat}), (\textit{Rosi, parrot}), (\textit{Rosi, horse}), (\textit{Rosi, fox}) \}
\end{aligned}
$$

The concept of the Cartesian product may be extended to include the product of any number of sets. Thus, given k sets of the form $A_1, A_2, \dots, A_{k-1}, A_k$, it is possible to define a *k-fold product* as:

$$
A_1 \times A_2 \times \dots \times A_{k-1} \times A_k \overset{def}{=} \{(a_1, a_2, \dots, a_{k-1}, a_k) \mid \\
a_1 \in A_1 \wedge a_2 \in A_2 \wedge \dots \wedge a_{k-1} \in A_{k-1} \wedge a_k \in A_k\}
$$

By definition, A^k is the k-fold product of A itself. That is,

$$A^k \overset{def}{=} A \times A \times \dots \times A \quad (k \text{ times})$$

Note

The above notation for the k-fold Cartesian product of sets involving a numerical superscript is also used in Section 14.2 for *relational iteration*.

Exercise 13.1 ✳

Given the following sets:

$$shape = \{\textit{circle, triangle, polygon, rectangle}\}$$
$$size = \{\textit{tiny, small}\}$$
$$colour = \{\textit{black, white}\}$$

1. Determine the following Cartesian products:
   (a) *shape* $\times$ *size*
   (b) *size* $\times$ *shape*
   (c) *size*^{3}

2. Indicate the composition of the following Cartesian products:
   (a) *shape* × *size* × *colour*   (b) $(size \times colour)^2$

(13.3) Relations as sets

As mentioned earlier, mathematical relations are an abstraction of relations in ordinary life. Referring to the individuals in Example 13.2, we may relate certain people with certain animal species in order to signify a relationship such as **'someone having a certain species of animal as a pet'** or **'someone specialized (as a veterinary surgeon) to treat different species of animals'**. In each such case, what is required is to pair those who are so related, put them in a set and associate, by appropriately naming it, the resulting set with the intended relationship. This may result in sets such as:

$$hasPet = \{ \textbf{Eve} \mapsto \textbf{dog}, \textbf{Adam} \mapsto \textbf{parrot}, \textbf{Rosi} \mapsto \textbf{dog}, \textbf{Rosi} \mapsto \textbf{cat},$$
$$\textbf{Rosi} \mapsto \textbf{parrot} \} \tag{13.1}$$

$$treats = \{ \textbf{Eve} \mapsto \textbf{horse}, \textbf{Pele} \mapsto \textbf{cat}, \textbf{Pele} \mapsto \textbf{dog}, \textbf{Pele} \mapsto \textbf{horse},$$
$$\textbf{Rosi} \mapsto \textbf{parrot} \} \tag{13.2}$$

thus capturing some relationships familiar in ordinary life. Informally, $(x, y) \in hasPet$ is true if and only if the person x keeps at least one animal of the species y as a pet. Likewise, $(x, y) \in treats$ is true if and only if the person x specializes in the treatment of the species y. (Note that pairing of elements with the symbol is an alternative notation to brackets.)

The above are two examples of relations as understood in mathematics. It is also clear that the above relations are subsets of the Cartesian product $H \times A$. That is,

$$hasPet \subseteq H \times A$$
$$treats \subseteq H \times A$$

It follows that both the relations *hasPet* and *treats* are of the type

$$hasPet : \mathbb{P}(H \times A) \tag{13.3}$$

$$treats : \mathbb{P}(H \times A) \tag{13.4}$$

In the mathematical sense, the Cartesian product serves as the source of all kinds of relations. However, when using mathematics as a medium of representation, it is up to us to pick the right pairs of elements so that the resulting set represents an abstraction of the desired part of the reality. This explains the important role played by the Cartesian product in the theory of relations.

Terminology

- The relations (13.3) and (13.4) are said to be *from H to A*. In the case of a relation R from any given set A to itself, then R is said to be a *relation on A*.

- In analogy with predicates, a relation can be *unary*, *binary*, *ternary*, etc., depending on the number of elements (1, 2, 3, etc.) in its tuples.

Thus, the concept of relation applies to subsets of *n*-fold Cartesian products. In the case of a relation *R* which is a subset of an *n*-fold Cartesian product, *R* is referred to as an *n-ary relation*.

(**Definition**) Relation

A *relation* is a set of tuples, all belonging to the same Cartesian product. In the case of a binary relation *R* from a set *A* to a set *B*, then *R* is defined as a subset of the Cartesian product $A \times B$. That is,

$$R \subseteq A \times B$$

Notation

Given a relation *R* from a set *A* to a set *B*, the type of *R* may be defined in the Z notation in two alternative ways:

$R : \mathbb{P}(A \times B)$
$R : A \leftrightarrow B$

Note that the second is an abbreviation for the first and, hence, both are identical in meaning.

It is important to realize that mathematical relations are sets and, therefore, that they can be manipulated using set theoretic operations.

(**Example 13.3**)

Using the two relations *hasPet* and *treats*, we may construct other relations such as:

1. People related to animals by specializing in the treatment of their own pets:

   treatOwnPets = *treats* ∩ *hasPet*

2. People related to animals by not specializing in the treatment of their pets:

   treatNonPets = *treats* − *hasPet*

3. People related to animals by neither having them as pets nor being able to treat them:

   noTreatNoPet = (*treats* ∪ *hasPet*)′

(**Exercise 13.2** ✳)

Determine the following relations using the above and other appropriate relations.

1. People related to animals by having pets or specializing in their treatment.
2. People related to animals by having pets outside their specialization.

3. People related to animals by having as pets the animals they love.

4. People related to animals by being animal lovers but with no veterinary interest in them.

5. People related to animals by being animal lovers or pet keepers but specializing in their treatment.

6. People related to animals by not being animal lovers and specializing in their treatment but are pet keepers.

Example 13.4 and Exercise 13.3 illustrate relations of higher arities.

Example 13.4

Below are two ternary relations of identical type but intended for different uses.

$petKeeping : \mathbb{P}(H \times A \times \mathbb{N})$ $(h, p, n) \in petKeeping$ if and only if the **person h keeps n animals of species p as pets**.

$vetCharging : \mathbb{P}(H \times A \times \mathbb{N})$ $(h, p, n) \in vetCharging$ if and only if the **person h charges n pounds (dollars or whatever currency) for treating an animal of the species p.**

Exercise 13.3 ✳

Suggest relations and their types appropriate for the following uses:

1. The maximum number of animals of a given species to be kept by individual farmers as livestock.

2. A record of the number of animals of a given species treated by any individual veterinary surgeon between any two years.

3. A country by country population census of rare species of animals.

4. A record of veterinary surgeons, their clients and species of animals kept by the clients.

Note

As evident from Exercise 13.3, relations of higher arities have significant practical applications. Despite this, Chapters 14 and 15 are devoted exclusively to the study of *binary relations*.

13.4 Relations as predicates

In Section 12.2 we learned how to use sets as unary predicates. Exercise 12.4, for example, was concerned with the use of sets for a problem we solved earlier in

Chapter 6 using unary predicates. This section generalizes this approach to include relations (instead of simple sets) and predicates of identical arity. Returning to sets (13.1) and (13.2), we may capture the notions of **Eve** having a **dog** as a pet and **Rosi** being able to treat a **parrot** in two alternative ways but with identical meanings, as follows:

As predicates	As relations
*Eve hasPet **dog***	$(\textbf{\textit{Eve}}, \textbf{\textit{dog}}) \in hasPet$
Rosi** treats **parrot	$(\textbf{\textit{Rosi}}, \textbf{\textit{parrot}}) \in treats$

Note that *hasPet*, for example, is used as a predicate on the left-hand side and as a set on the right-hand side. Similarly, other complex meanings may be expressed by using different relations.

Example 13.5

Using the two relations, sets (13.1) and (13.2), we may assert the following.

1. No vet specializes in a species unless it is one of his/her pets:

   $treats \subseteq hasPet$

2. There is at least one vet specializing in some of his/her pets:

   $treats \cap hasPet \neq \emptyset$

3. There are some common animals in every vet's specialization and his/her pets:

   $\forall h : H \bullet \exists a : A \bullet (h, a) \in treats \cap hasPet$

4. People keep pets without being specialist vets:

   $hasPet - treats \neq \emptyset$

Exercise 13.4 ✳ ✳

Assert the following using the above and other appropriate relations but without using logical quantifiers.

1. There must be people keeping pets and treating them.
2. A vet's specialization invariably depends on his pets.
3. All pet keepers specialize in the treatment of their pets.
4. Pet keepers love their pets.
5. Those who love animals keep them as pets.
6. No one can be a vet unless that person loves animals under his/her specialization.
7. No one can be a vet unless that person loves animals.
8. Pet keepers are always the people who love or are able to treat animals.

Exercise 13.5 ✳ ✳

Assert the following using appropriate relations and without using logical quantifiers.

1. Readers' favourite books are those written by others.

2. There can be favourite books only if there are books written by people.

3. Authors' favourite books include their own books.

4. There are books not regarded by even their authors as favourite books.

5. John's and Jane's favourite books are Jeffrey Archer's books.

13.5 Graphical representation of relations

Relations may be better visualized if presented as graphs. A graph consists of the following:

1. A set of nodes representing the individuals appearing in the relation.

2. A set of arcs between pairs of these nodes such that each arc represents the pair of individuals related by the given relation.

Notes

1. If the relation is *from* one type of value *to* another type, the nodes are presented as shown in Figure 13.1.

2. Arrows are directed since pairs such as (a,b) and (b,a) may mean different things and the presence of one of them in the relation may not necessarily imply the presence of the other.

3. Figure 13.2 shows an alternative presentation for the case when the relation is defined *on* a single type of values.

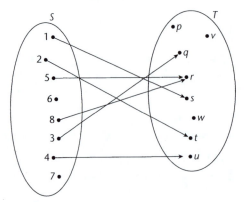

Figure 13.1 Graph of a relation between sets of disparate values.

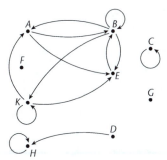

Figure 13.2 Graph of a relation on a set.

13.6 Domain, range and field

Domain, range and field allow the determination of the elements participating in a given relation. Given a relation R from a set A to a set B, each of these operations returns a set of elements taking part in R: the domain returns the elements of A, the range returns the elements of B and the field returns the elements of both A and B.

Definition   Domain, range and field

Given a relation R of the form

$[A, B]$
$R : A \leftrightarrow B$

the *domain* dom R, the *range* ran R and the *field* fld R of R are defined as the following sets:

dom $R = \{x : A \mid \exists\, y : B \bullet (x, y) \in R\}$
ran $R = \{y : B \mid \exists\, x : A \bullet (x, y) \in R\}$
fld $R = $ dom $R \cup$ ran R

Note from the Definition that the notion of *field* is of limited use, unless $A = B$.

Example 13.6

Referring to Example 13.3 in Section 13.3, the concepts of domain and range may be used to define other sets: the sets of pet keepers, pet species, veterinary surgeons and the species of veterinary surgeons' specializations. Similarly, the field may be used to determine the set of pets and their keepers, although we might generally argue against such use because of the disparity of types involved.

petKeepers $=$ dom *hasPet* $= \{$**Eve, Adam, Rosi**$\}$
vets $=$ dom *treats* $= \{$**Eve, Pele, Rosi**$\}$
pets $=$ ran *hasPet* $= \{$**dog, parrot, cat**$\}$
vetCaredAnimals $=$ ran *treats* $= \{$**horse, cat, dog, parrot**$\}$
petsAndKeepers $=$ fld *hasPet* $= \{$**Eve, Adam, Rosi, dog, parrot, cat**$\}$

Furthermore, continuing the theme in Example 13.3, we may now focus our attention on the actual sets of individuals rather than relations such as 'people related to animals by specializing ...' and so on:

1. People specializing in the treatment of their own pets:

$$vetsTreatingOwnPets = \text{dom }(treats \cap hasPet)$$

2. Species of pets with veterinary care available to them from pet keepers:

$$petsWithKeeperCare = \text{ran }(treats \cap hasPet)$$

3. Species of pets with veterinary care available to them:

$$petsWithVetCare = (\text{ran }treats) \cap (\text{ran }hasPet)$$

4. People specializing in the treatment of animals outside their pets:

$$vetsTreatingOutsideOwnPets = \text{dom }(treats \cap hasPet')$$

5. People specializing in the treatment of only other people's pets:

$$vetsTreatingOthersPets = (\text{dom }treats) - \text{dom }(treats \cap hasPet)$$

Exercise 13.6 ✳ ✳

Determine the following sets using the relations in your answer to Exercise 13.2.

1. People having pets or specializing in their treatment.
2. Veterinary surgeons having pets outside their specialization.
3. People having as pets the animals they love.
4. Animal lovers with no veterinary interest in animals.
5. Animal lovers and pet keepers with some veterinary expertise.
6. Pet keepers who are neither animal lovers nor specialists in the treatment of their pets.

Observations

Given that S and T are appropriate relations

$$\text{dom }(S \cup T) = \text{dom }S \cup \text{dom }T$$
$$\text{ran }(S \cup T) = \text{ran }S \cup \text{ran }T$$
$$\text{dom }(S \cap T) \subseteq \text{dom }S \cap \text{dom }T$$
$$\text{ran }(S \cap T) \subseteq \text{ran }S \cap \text{ran }T$$

13.7 Inverse relation

Often, it is possible to produce a new relation with a sensible meaning by simply reversing the order of pairs in a given binary relation. The operation does not alter the information content of the relation, but simply offers greater flexibility in terms of expression. What is gained is a different way of expression similar to, for example, 'older than' and 'younger than or of the same age as' in English.

Definition   Inverse relation

Given that

$$[A, B]$$
$$R : A \leftrightarrow B$$

the *inverse* $R^\sim$ of the relation R is defined as

$$R^\sim = \{(b, a) \bullet \ a : A; b : B \,|\, (a, b) \in R\}$$

Note

A common notation for the inverse relation is:

$$R^\sim \stackrel{def}{=} R^{-1}$$

Example 13.7

The inverse relations of the relations *hasPet* and *treats* in (13.1) and (13.2) in Section 13.3 are as follows:

petOwners = *hasPet*$^\sim$ = {**dog** $\mapsto$ **Eve**, **parrot** $\mapsto$ **Adam**, **dog** $\mapsto$ **Rosi**,
cat $\mapsto$ **Rosi**, **parrot** $\mapsto$ **Rosi**}

petCarers = *treats*$^\sim$ = {**horse** $\mapsto$ **Eve**, **cat** $\mapsto$ **Pele**, **dog** $\mapsto$ **Pele**, **horse** $\mapsto$ **Pele**,
parrot $\mapsto$ **Rosi**}

As indicated by the chosen names, the inverses may be used to convey the same information but with a slightly different 'meaning'.

Observations

Given that R is a relation,

$$(R^\sim)^\sim = R$$
$$\text{dom } (R^\sim) = \text{ran } R$$
$$\text{ran } (R^\sim) = \text{dom } R$$

Exercise 13.7 ✳

Prove two of the properties of binary relations given in the Observations.

(13.8) Identity relation

The identity relation gives the impression of a trivial mathematical concept, but it is as important as 0 in number theory. Without 0, for example, we cannot talk about the number 1, without 1 about the number 2, and so on (see Section 17.1.2). A similar role is played by this important 'member' in the 'theory of relations'.

(**Definition**) Identity relation

The *identity relation* on a set A, denoted by 'id A', is the relation obtained by pairing each and every element of A with itself. That is,

id $A \overset{def}{=} \{(a, a) \bullet a \in A\}$

(**Example 13.8**)

Given a set S

$S = \{a, b, c, d, e\}$

the identity relation on S is

id $S = \{a \mapsto a, \ b \mapsto b, \ c \mapsto c, \ d \mapsto d, \ e \mapsto e\}$

(**Exercise 13.8** ✳)

Produce a set theoretically valid statement about relations for each of the following expressions by inserting, as appropriate, a variable denoting a set or a relation, or a symbol (or name) denoting an operation on sets or relations, in place of each dotted blank. The symbols R. S in these expressions are variables standing for arbitrary relations from type X to type Y.

1. dom $S^{\sim} = \ldots S$
2. (id $X)^{\sim} = \ldots X$
3. $\ldots S^{\sim} = $ dom S
4. dom $(R \cup S) = (\ldots R) \cup (\ldots S)$
5. dom $(R \cap S) \ldots ($ dom $R) \cap ($ dom $S)$
6. dom $\ldots = \varnothing$
7. ran $\ldots = \varnothing$

(**Exercise 13.9** ✳✳✳)

The nodes of a power grid are classified according to whether they are electricity generating stations, suppliers of electricity to other nodes or consumers of electricity from the grid.

Using appropriate subsets of nodes and a relation on them, define or state the following using set theoretic (including relational) operations, but without using quantifiers.

1. The nodes which are both suppliers and consumers.

2. The nodes which are both suppliers and consumers but excluding those supplying themselves or consuming from themselves.

3. The nodes not supplying electricity to other nodes are consumers.

4. No node receives electricity from more than two supplier nodes.

5. The electricity generating nodes not supplying power to other nodes are called autonomous nodes.

6. Such autonomous nodes have a backup supply service from other nodes.

7. Autonomous nodes are consumers.

8. Autonomous nodes receive electricity only from one other node.

Also, assuming (3) and (5) to be true, deduce (7).

Exercise 13.10 ✳ ✳

Section 13.4 drew a parallel between predicates and relations and then went straight on to use set theoretic relations (such as subset relation) and operations (such as union) for expressing complex meanings.

What are the corresponding facilities in predicate logic with the same capability? Establish a list of such correspondences between predicate logic and set theory.

13.9 An application: relational model of databases

13.9.1 What are relational databases?

Databases are repositories of information that can be accessed and modified typically by a large number of users and applications. The diversity of potential users, as well as constant changes in applications with time, require databases to be flexible in terms of both the extent to which information is to be manipulated and the way in which the information is manipulated. This is because different users have different views of any database. Since some of these users could include other computerized applications, and because of the highly dynamic nature of certain applications in areas such as financial markets and airline reservations, databases have to be fast in terms of response. Furthermore, since different users access and modify data independently, maintenance of consistency of data becomes critically important. With the ever-growing role of information in day-to-day life, security is also an important factor affecting the extent of usage of databases. Whether they are functional or non-functional, the above are some of the requirements which are of direct concern to the user.

In addition, since modern databases such as those used in banking and commerce are quite extensive in terms of the amount of information they have to deal with, implementation issues are central to the design of databases. This is because the form of representation and storage have profound effects on efficiency and ease of use. Therefore, reconciliation of user concerns with implementation constraints depends on the provision of effective means of manipulation and retrieval of information. A major approach in this connection is based on the notion of *relational databases*.

13.9.2   Relations in the context of relational databases

As evident from the common approaches to recording information manually, tabular form is a simple and intuitive form of representation of information. The *relational model* of databases exploits this idea of *tabular* representation. A *relation* in the relational model consists of a *scheme* and an *extension*. The extension contains the actual data and takes the form of a collection of *tuples*, or *rows* in the terminology of conventional tables. Each tuple consists of a fixed number of items of data. As in conventional tables, the scheme plays the role of a 'header' for the content of data listed in the rows.

The information given in Table 13.1 is an illustration and concerns a record of certain hypothetical details of flights operated by an airline. A scheme consists of a number of *attributes*, each of which in turn consists of an *attribute name* and a *domain of values*. Basically, attribute names provide a way to refer to various items of data in each row, whereas the domain prescribes the type of value the corresponding item of data is permitted to take. For example, in Table 13.1, 'Departure time' is just the attribute name and, although not indicated in the table, is associated with time values as its domain.

Table 13.1   Relation *Flights*: flight itinerary information

Flight	Leg origin	Leg destination	Departure time	Arrival time	Vacancies	
						◄ scheme (attribute names only)
BA101	London	Paris	13:05	14:05	20	
BA101	Paris	Rome	15:00	16:00	45	⋮
BA101	Rome	Bombay	20:00	21:00	30	
BA101	Bombay	Singapore	22:00	04:00	90	◄ tuples in
BA220	Amsterdam	London	11:20	12:20	0	⋮
BA430	London	Dulles	13:30	22:00	100	extension
⋮	⋮	⋮	⋮	⋮	⋮	⋮

13.9.3   Comparison with mathematical relations

It is straightforward to represent the information in Table 13.1 as a mathematical relation. For this, let us introduce the domains of values used in relational algebra in the style we are already familiar with, namely:

[*FlightId, Place, Time*]

with symbols *FlightId*, *Place*, *Time* denoting, respectively, the sets of all flight identifiers, place names and appropriately represented time values. In relation to Table 13.1, these sets consist of the values as indicated in

$FlightId = \{BA101,\ BA220,\ BA430, \ldots\}$
$Place = \{London,\ Singapore,\ Amsterdam,\ Bombay,\ Paris,\ Dulles,\ Rome, \ldots\}$
$Time = \{0:00,\ 0:01,\ 0:02, \ldots\}$

$FlightItinerary : \mathbb{P}\ (FlightId \times Place \times Place \times Time \times Time \times \mathbb{N})$
$FlightItinerary = \{(BA101,\ London,\ Paris,\ 13:05,\ 4:05,\ 20),$
$\qquad\qquad\qquad (BA101,\ Paris,\ Rome,\ 15:00,\ 16:00,\ 45)$
$\qquad\qquad\qquad (BA101,\ Rome,\ Bombay,\ 20:00,\ 21:00,\ 30),$
$\qquad\qquad\qquad (BA101,\ Bombay,\ Singapore,\ 22:00,\ 04:00,\ 90)$
$\qquad\qquad\qquad (BA220,\ Amsterdam,\ London,\ 11:20,\ 12:20,\ 0),$
$\qquad\qquad\qquad (BA430,\ London,\ Dulles,\ 13:30,\ 22:00,\ 100), \ldots\}$

This example illustrates the close relationship between the concepts of relation in databases and mathematical relation. However, there are differences too. Table 13.2 provides a comparison.

Table 13.2 Comparison of mathematical relations and relations in databases.

Mathematical relations	Relations in databases
Relations are collections of tuples	Relations are collections of tuples but, in addition, have a notion of *scheme* associated with each relation
The order of elements in tuples is important because it is the position which determines what a particular item of data represents. The order of elements in tuples itself is determined by the order of the sets concerned in the relevant Cartesian product	The order of elements in tuples is irrelevant because it is the attribute which identifies what a particular data item represents. In visual representations of a relation, its columns of data can be interchanged, provided that the attributes too are interchanged accordingly
Relations are manipulated using set theoretic operations and other relational operations	Relations share the names of set theoretic operations applicable to mathematical relational operations with roughly the same meanings. A relational algebra supports several specialized operations for manipulating tables
Normally, tuples do not contain unknown values, although this can be overcome by introducing to each set a special *null value*	Missing entries in tuples under certain attributes are quite typical and take into account partial or incomplete knowledge about certain aspects. Operations in the algebra are equipped to deal with such unknowns

13.9.4   ## Modelling with relations

A *relational database* is a collection of relations, recording different kinds of information relevant to different operational aspects of an organization. The relevance is determined, as usual in mathematical modelling, by *abstraction* depending on the nature of problems being addressed.

An application-level operation usually requires information stored in more than one relation. For example, the operation for making a reservation of a place on a flight requires information about flights: flight times, seating capacity, occupancy over flight legs covered by passenger journey and so on. For better use of resources, such information is usually stored in different relations. For example, the information relevant to areservation may be stored in the following relations.

1. a relation recording the seating capacity of different carriers,

2. a relation recording the allocation of carriers to flights, and

3. a relation recording the state of passenger bookings on individual flights.

The aim of such a choice of relations is to avoid unnecessary replication of the same piece of information in different relations.

13.9.5   ## The need for relational operations

Design of a database must thus address two different issues: how the chosen information is to be represented as relations from the point of view of storage and how this information is to be presented to the user. From the point of view of storage, it may be imperative not to duplicate the information in different relations intended to be kept in storage. This is not only to reduce excessive storage requirement, but also to reduce the burden of maintaining consistency of multiple copies of the same piece of data. For the purpose of removing duplication of information, relational algebra provides for a technique known as *normalization* to rationalize information storage.

Decoupling of storage aspects from presentation aspects requires a *relational algebra*. The purpose of such an algebra is basically to bridge the mismatch between the relations as stored and the relations of interest to a user at a conceptual level. This involves interpreting user queries, expressed in a high-level language, in terms of stored relations for the purpose of retrieval, and then delivering the retrieved data in the form requested by the user.

With the above in mind, relational algebra provides a number of operations for manipulating relations when extracting information from the database or representing information in the form of relations prior to storage. Some of these operations are so akin to those on mathematical relations that they have the same names, such as *union* and *intersection*, but there are others such as *join* unique to relational databases.

Chapter 14

Advanced relational operations

Topic: Relations

··

Multiplication is vexation,
Division is as bad;
The rule of three doth puzzle me,
And practice drives me mad.

(Anonymous)

Objectives

On completion of this chapter you should be able to:

- Define relational composition and iteration, and work out these for specific relations.

- Define and use relational images.

- Modify a relation by limiting or excluding elements from its domain or from its range.

- Modify a relation by overwriting a subset of its pairs (relational overriding).

In this chapter we study some of the more advanced operations on relations. Note that these are exclusive to binary relations. The binary relations may be from one set to another or on a given set.

14.1 Relational composition

Given three sets A, B and C and two relations on them of the following form

$$R : A \leftrightarrow B \quad \text{and} \quad S : B \leftrightarrow C$$

it may be necessary sometimes to pair the elements of A and C in such a way that they are related through R and S via some intermediate elements in B. This is the use of relational composition.

Definition) Relational composition
_____

The *composition* of relations $R : A \leftrightarrow B$ and $S : B \leftrightarrow C$ is denoted by two alternative notations

$R \, ; S$ and $S \circ R$

and is defined as

$R \, ; S \overset{def}{=} S \circ R$

$\overset{def}{=} \{(a, c) \bullet a : A; c : C \mid \exists b : B \bullet (a, b) \in R \wedge (b, c) \in S\}$

where $\overset{def}{=}$ denotes the equality 'by definition'.

Terminology

- $R \, ; S$ is to be read as 'R followed by S'. This notation has its origin in the command for sequential composition '$;$' in programming languages.

- On the other hand, the notation $S \circ R$ originates from *composite functions* – a topic covered in Chapter 15. Given two functions f and g, $g(f(x))$ denotes the result of applying f to x first and then applying g to its result. The same may be obtained by applying $g \circ f$ to x, the composition operator '$\circ$' replacing/ removing the outer brackets in $g(f(x))$ as shown below:

$g(f(x))$
$\downarrow$
$g \circ f(x)$

Example 14.1)
_____

Consider three sets

[*Patient, Illness, Medicine*]

with the obvious meanings. Let the following be two relations

complaints : *Patient* $\leftrightarrow$ *Illness*
treatment : *Illness* $\leftrightarrow$ *Medicine*

with the following informal meanings:

$(p, x) \in$ *complaints*   *Patient p suffers from illness x.*
$(x, m) \in$ *treatment*   *Illness x may be treated with medicine m.*

If the two relations are available as a part of some 'mathematical' database, we may compute a new relation

medication : *Patient* $\leftrightarrow$ *Medicine*

with the meaning that

$(p, m) \in$ *medication*

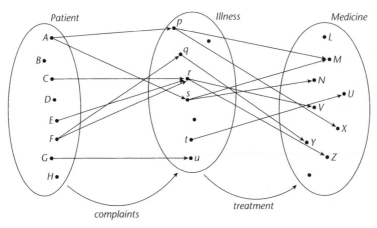

Figure 14.1   Example of relational composition.

is true if and only if the patient p may be treated with the medicine m. The relation *medication* may be defined as the relational composition

medication = complaints; treatment   (or = treatment ∘ complaints)

As an illustration, consider the following specific extensions of the two relations:

complaints = {(A, p), (C, r), (A, s), (E, r), (F, r), (F, q), (G, u)}

treatment = {(p, M), (p, X), (q, Y), (r, Z), (s, M), (s, N), (t, U), (r, V)}

Using the graph given in Figure 14.1, the medication that may be prescribed to various individuals may be established as:

medication = {(A, M), (A, N), (A, X), (C, V), (C, Z), (E, V), (E, Z),
             (F, Y), (F, V), (F, Z)}

Exercise 14.1 ✳

1. Given that the extensions of *complaints* and *treatment* are

   complaints = {(Jo, flu), (Yuri, ulcer), (Yuri, flu), (Rio, diabetes),
                (Tom, asthma), (Hilary, hayfever)}
   treatment = {(flu, paracetamol), (ulcer, omeprazole), (diabetes, insulin),
               (asthma, salbutamol), (hayfever, antihistamine)}

   Find the extension of the relation *medication* defined in Example 14.1.

2. Let us assume that we have some additional information on medicines which are not permitted for certain illnesses. Suggest a solution which associates patients with medicines that may not be prescribed to them.

3. Find the pairs of medicines that may clash with each other on the grounds that one of them is a treatment for a particular illness while the other is forbidden for the same illness.

4. Find the pairs of illnesses such that while the first may be treated by some medicine the second may be adversely affected by the same medicine.

5. Extend the database with patients' age and age–restricted medicines. Find the patients and medicines restricted on the grounds of their age.

6. Produce a relation associating patients with illnesses such that a medicine intended for the treatment of the illnesses concerned is restricted because of the patients' ages.

Observations

Given the arbitrary relations

$$R : A \leftrightarrow B, \quad S : B \leftrightarrow C \quad \text{and} \quad T : C \leftrightarrow D$$

the following hold:

$$R \mathbin{;} (S \mathbin{;} T) = (R \mathbin{;} S) \mathbin{;} T$$
$$(R \mathbin{;} S)^{\sim} = S^{\sim} \mathbin{;} R^{\sim}$$
$$\text{id}(\text{dom } R) = R \mathbin{;} R^{\sim}$$
$$\text{id}(\text{ran } R) = R^{\sim} \mathbin{;} R$$
$$\text{id } A \mathbin{;} R = R$$
$$R \mathbin{;} \text{id } B = R$$

Exercise 14.2 ✳✳

Prove the first two assertions in the Observations.

14.2 Iteration

In the previous section, we dealt with the composition of relations between sets of disparate values. Obviously, composition is also applicable to relations defined on a given set. In this case, composition may be repeated as many times as necessary, each time yielding some new information about the individuals engaged in the relation.

Definition   Iteration

Given a set A and a relation R on A, the nth *iteration* on R is the composition of R on itself n times. This may be defined recursively as

$$R^0 = \text{id } A$$
$$R^n = R \mathbin{;} R^{n-1}$$

Note

The notation involving a numerical superscript as in R^n is also used to denote the k-fold Cartesian product of sets; see Section 13.2.

Example 14.2

Consider a grid or a network, intended, for example, for power supply or communication purposes. The *adjacent* connections in the network may be given as a set of pairs (edges) of nodes in the network. Let the following set represent an abstraction of a specific network (see Figure 14.2), namely, its configuration:

$$net = \{(a,b),\ (b,c),\ (a,c),\ (c,a),\ (d,c),\ (d,e),\ (f,d),\ (e,f),\ (g,f),\ (e,h),\ (i,h),\ (i,j)\}$$

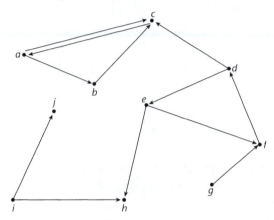

Figure 14.2 Example of relational iteration.

The intention is that the presence of a pair such as (a,b) in the set signifies that the node a can communicate with b directly. Note that the converse requires another pair (b,a) in the set.

Suppose that we now wish to establish the reachability of distant nodes on the assumption that the intermediate nodes on any path are able to act as forwarding stations. We can achieve this by using relational composition of *net* on itself as many times as each composition generates some new information. Iteration allows us to work this out gradually, just one extra composition each time.

The set net^2,

$$net^2 = net;\ net = \{(a,a),\ (c,c),\ (a,c),\ (b,a),\ (c,b),\ (d,a),\ (f,c),\ (f,e),$$
$$(d,f),\ (d,h),\ (g,d)\}$$

gives us the information on node reachability in two steps. (Note that the iteration may generate a pair which is already in the previous iteration.)

Similarly,

$$net^3 = net;\ net^2$$
$$= \{(a,a),\ (b,b),\ (a,b),\ (a,c),\ (b,c),\ (c,c),\ (d,d),\ (d,b),\ (c,a),\ (d,c),$$
$$(e,e),\ (f,f),\ (f,a),\ (f,h),\ (e,c),\ (g,c),\ (g,e)\}$$

giving node reachability in three steps. Likewise,

$$net^4 = net;\ net^3$$
$$= \{(b,a),\ (a,c),\ (a,a),\ (d,c),\ (f,b),\ (e,a),\ (g,a),\ (g,h),\ (a,c),\ (a,b),$$
$$(c,b),\ (d,a)\}$$

gives node reachability in four steps. One may carry on this process until each iteration generates no new information. Thus,

$$net^5 = net_; net^4 = \{(f,c),\ (e,b),\ (g,b),\ldots\}$$
$$net^6 = net_; net^5 = \varnothing$$

Although we have written '...' in net^5 and the empty set $\varnothing$ against net^6, strictly speaking, net^6 is not empty since each iteration takes us through further loops, perhaps, indefinitely. Thus, an empty set resulting from an iteration beyond a certain number of times may mean one of the two possibilities:

1. a genuine termination of new information, or

2. regeneration of already known information.

Exercise 14.3 ✷

The following represents the parenthood relationship among a certain set of individuals:

$$parent = \{(\textit{John, Leo}),\ (\textit{David, Mary}),\ (\textit{Mary, Leo}),\ (\textit{Mary, Jo}),\ (\textit{David, Pele}),$$
$$(\textit{Pele, Rosi}),\ (\textit{Jo, Ann}),\ (\textit{Rosi, Ann}),\ (\textit{Ann, Lincoln}),\ (\textit{Leo, Adam}),$$
$$(\textit{Ann, Ono}),\ (\textit{Leo, Eve})\}$$

Note that, in each pair, the second individual is a parent of the first. Find the individuals related by relationships such as grandparent, great-grandparent, great-great-grandparent and so on.

Observations

Given an arbitrary relation

$$R : X \leftrightarrow X$$

and $m, n : \mathbb{N}$, the following holds:

$$R^{m+n} = R^m; R^n$$
$$R^{m \times n} = (R^m)^n$$

Exercise 14.4 ✷✷✷

Prove the first law given in the Observations.

14.3 Relational image

Given a relation R from A to B and a subset S of individuals in the set A, it is sometimes necessary to find the set of individuals in B related to those in S through the relation R. Relational images serve this purpose.

Definition   Relational image

Given sets A and B and a relation R and a set S such that

$R : A \leftrightarrow B$

$S : \mathbb{P} A$

The *relational image* of S through R is denoted by $R(\!| S |\!)$ and is defined as

$R(\!| S |\!) \overset{def}{=} \{ y : B \mid \exists x : A \bullet (x, y) \in R \land x \in S \}$

Example 14.3

Referring to the relations *complaints*, *treatment* and *medication* in Example 14.1, we may find the illnesses of individuals A, C, D and F using the graph in Figure 14.3 as:

$complaints (\!| \{A, C, D, F\} |\!) = \{p, s, r, q\}$

Similarly, the medication suitable for them may be found as

$(complaints \, \text{\textfractionsolidus} \, treatment) (\!| \{A, C, D, F\} |\!) = \{M, N, X, V, Z, Y\}$

Exercise 14.5 ✳

1. Referring to Example 14.1, find the individuals receiving the medicines N, V, X and Z.

2. Referring to the same, find the medicines appropriate for illnesses p, r, t and u if they are also suitable for patients A, B, E, F and G.

3. Referring to Example 14.2, find the nodes reachable in three or more steps from nodes a, d, f and i.

4. Referring to Exercise 14.3, find the great-grandchildren of Eve, Ann, Rosi and Adam.

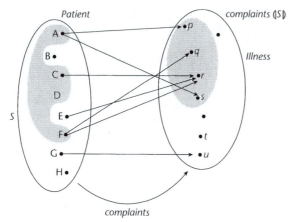

Figure 14.3   Example of relational image.

Given an arbitrary relation R and the sets A and B,

$$R : X \leftrightarrow Y \quad \text{and} \quad A, B : \mathbb{P}X$$

the following holds:

$$R (\!| A \cup B |\!) = R (\!| A |\!) \cup R (\!| B |\!)$$
$$R (\!| A \cap B |\!) = R (\!| A |\!) \cap R (\!| B |\!)$$
$$R (\!| \text{dom } R |\!) = \text{ran } R$$

Exercise 14.6 ✷ ✷

Prove the first of the assertions in the Observations.

14.4 Domain and range restriction and co-restriction

It is often necessary to modify binary relations in order to account for changes in individuals participating in them. One such modification is the subtraction or removal of all pairs that involve a given set of individuals. There are four different ways of removing pairs of elements in this manner, resulting in four different operations. These are:

1. *Domain restriction* – retaining exactly those pairs whose first elements are in the specified set.
2. *Domain co-restriction or domain subtraction* – removing exactly those pairs whose first elements are in the specified set.
3. *Range restriction* – retaining exactly those pairs whose second elements are in the specified set.
4. *Range co-restriction or range subtraction* – removing exactly those pairs whose second elements are in the specified set.

Let us attempt a more formal definition of these operations.

Definition   Domain restriction and domain co-restriction

Given a relation $R : A \leftrightarrow B$ and a set $S : \mathbb{P}A$, the *domain restriction* of R to S is denoted by $S \lhd R$ and is defined as

$$S \lhd R \stackrel{def}{=} \{(a, b) \bullet a : A; b : B \mid (a, b) \in R \land a \in S\}$$

Similarly, the *domain co-restriction* is denoted by $S \lhd\!\!\!- R$ and is defined as

$$S \lhd\!\!\!- R \stackrel{def}{=} \{(a, b) \bullet a : A; b : B \mid (a, b) \in R \land a \notin S\}$$

Example 14.4

Refer to Example 14.1. Suppose we wish to remove the participation of individuals C, E, G and D from the relation *complaints* in order to account for, say, discharging the patients from a clinic. We can achieve this in two ways as follows. Let, for example

$discharge : \mathbb{P}\ Patient$
$discharge = \{C, E, G, D\}$

The relation resulting from removing the individuals in *discharge* is

$discharge \lhd complaints$
$= discharge' \lhd complaints$
$= \{(A, p), (A, s), (F, r), (F, q)\}$

Exercise 14.7 ✳

1. Refer to Example 14.1.
   (a) Define a new relation from *treatment* by excluding all treatments for illnesses r, s and u.
   (b) Define a new relation from *Illness* to *Medicine* using *treatment* by excluding the illnesses suffered by the patients B, C, E and F given in *complaints*.

2. Recall Exercise 12.3 in Chapter 12. Imagine a database in the form of two binary relations for recording (1) vehicles and their registration numbers, and (2) vehicle registration numbers and vehicle owners.

   (a) Introduce the above two relations formally.
   (b) Define a new relation giving vehicles and registration numbers for luxury sports cars and Rolls-Royces.
   (c) Define a new relation giving vehicles and registration numbers for all vehicles other than commercial vehicles and limousines.
   (d) Define a new relation giving vehicles and the names of vehicle owners of luxury sports cars, luxury family cars and inexpensive popular sports cars.

Observations

Given an arbitrary relation R and the sets A and B,

$R : X \leftrightarrow Y$ and $A, B : \mathbb{P}\ X$

then the following hold:

$$A \lhd (B \lhd R) = (A \cap B) \lhd R$$
$$A \lhd (B \ntriangleleft R) = (A \cup B) \ntriangleleft R$$
$$(A \lhd R) \cup (A \ntriangleleft R) = R$$

Exercise 14.8 ✳✳

Prove the first or the second of the assertions in the Observations.

> **Definition**) Range restriction and co-restriction
>
> Given a relation $R : A \leftrightarrow B$ and a set $T : \mathbb{P}B$, the range *restriction* of R to T is denoted by $R \triangleright T$ and is defined as
>
> $$R \triangleright T \stackrel{def}{=} \{(a, b) \bullet a : A; b : B \mid (a, b) \in R \wedge b \in T\}$$
>
> Similarly, the range *co-restriction* is denoted by $R \triangleright\!\!\!- T$ and is defined as
>
> $$R \triangleright\!\!\!- T \stackrel{def}{=} \{(a, b) \bullet a : A; b : B \mid (a, b) \in R \wedge b \notin T\}$$

(**Example 14.5**)

Refer to Example 14.1. Imagine a scenario in which no patient suffers from the illnesses r and t and the database is to be updated accordingly. We can achieve this by modifying *complaints* as

complaints $\triangleright\!\!\!-$ $\{r, t\}$
$=$ *complaints* $\triangleright\!\!\!-$ $\{r, t\}'$
$= \{(A, p), (A, s), (F, q), (G, u)\}$

(**Exercise 14.9** ✳)

1. Refer to Example 14.1.
   (a) Define a new relation from *treatment* by excluding the medicines N, U, X and Y from all treatments.
   (b) Define a new relation from *Patient* to *Illness* using *complaints* by excluding the illnesses that may be treated by medicines V, Y and M.
2. Refer to question 2 of Exercise 14.7 (and also Exercise 12.3).
   (a) Define a relation giving the registration numbers of vehicles and their owners but restricting owners to John, Adam and Rosi only.
   (b) Define a relation giving the vehicles and their owners, but restricting the registration of the vehicles involved to those of a given set S and excluding the owners Gill, Eriko, Carlos and Lars.

(**Exercise 14.10** ✳)

Write the observations on range restriction and co-restriction which are analogous to those made earlier with respect to domain restriction and co-restriction

(14.5) **Relational overriding**

Continuing the theme of the previous section, we see the need for modifying relations in another way, namely by 'reconfiguring' the relationship partially, instead of by eliminating elements from the domain or the range. Returning to Example 14.1, we may envisage a situation which requires updating the record of patients' illnesses in order to account for recovery of some patients from some of the illnesses, their contracting new illnesses or for admissions of new patients. Relational overriding allows for most such modifications in one single operation.

Definition) Relational overriding
___

Given a 'base' relation $R : A \rightarrow B$ and an 'update' relation $S : A \rightarrow B$, the *relational overriding* of R by S is denoted by $R \oplus S$ and is defined as

$$R \oplus S \stackrel{def}{=} (\text{dom } S \lhd R) \cup S$$

Example 14.6)
___

Let the scenario outlined above consist of the following changes:

1. Patient F recovers from illness r but continues to suffer from illness q.
2. Patient C contracts illnesses q and s but recovers at the same time from r.
3. Patient D is admitted suffering from illnesses p and t.
4. Nobody recovers totally. (Note that the total recovery of any patient requires the use of domain subtraction.)
5. The information about patients not mentioned above remains unchanged.

The update relation incorporating all above modifications is

$illnessUpdate = \{(F, q), (C, q), (C, s), (D, p), (D, t)\}$

The relation resulting from updating *complaints* with the above modifications is given by

   complaints $\oplus$ *illnessUpdate*

and its contents may be worked out as

   complaints $\oplus$ *illnessUpdate*
   $= ((\text{dom } illnessUpdate) \lhd complaints) \cup illnessUpdate$
   $= (\{F, C, D\} \lhd complaints) \cup illnessUpdate$
   $= \{(A, p), (A, s), (E, r), (G, s)\} \cup \{(F, q), (C, q), (C, s), (D, p), (D, t)\}$
   $= \{(A, p), (A, s), (E, r), (G, s), (F, q), (C, q), (C, s), (D, p), (D, t)\}$

Exercise 14.11 ✶)
___

1. Refer to Example 14.1. How would you introduce the following changes to the treatments available?

   (a) Medicine M may be prescribed also for illness q.
   (b) Illness t can be treated only with the medicines X and Z.
   (c) There is a new medicine L for illness p.
   (d) There is a new substitute medicine L for illness p.
   (e) Illness u may also be treated with L.

   Work out the content of the resulting relation step by step.

2. Refer to question 2 of both Exercises 14.7 and 14.9 on vehicle ownership and registration. Propose a relation from owners to vehicle registration numbers and modify its value to account for the following two separate occasions of changes in ownership.

(a) First change:
   - Pele disposes of his current vehicles.
   - The new owner of vehicles M2X, J5X, A1A and A5B is Pele.
   - Rosi disposes of her second vehicle while retaining her only remaining vehicle X6J.
   - Yuri acquires his first vehicle B3X.

(b) Second change:
   - Yuri replaces his vehicle by acquiring A5B from Pele.
   - Rosi replaces her vehicle with L3L.

Work out the updated vehicle ownership assuming the initial ownership is as follows:
   - John owns C3A, C2A.
   - Jo owns K2A.
   - Pele owns A5D.
   - Rosi owns L5J, X6J.
   - Peter owns X3M.

Observations

Given arbitrary relations R, S and T,

$$R, S, T : X \leftrightarrow Y$$

then the following hold:

$$R \oplus R = R$$
$$R \oplus (S \oplus T) = (R \oplus S) \oplus T$$

Exercise 14.12 ✳✳✳

Prove the second assertion in the Observations.

Exercise 14.13 ✳✳

Produce a set theoretically valid statement about relations for each of the following expressions by inserting as appropriate a variable denoting a set or a relation, or a symbol denoting an operation on sets or relations in place of each dotted blank. The symbols R, S and T in these expressions are variables standing for arbitrary sets or relations of appropriately typed elements. X denotes an arbitrary type.

1. $(R \oplus S) \oplus T = R \oplus (S \ldots T)$
2. $(R \,\mathring{,}\, S)^{\sim} = S^{\sim} \ldots R^{\sim}$

3. $R \oplus R = \ldots$

4. $(R \lhd S) \cup (R \ntriangleleft S) = \ldots$

5. $(R \rhd S) \rhd T = R \rhd (S \ldots T)$

6. $R(S \cup T) = (\ldots (\ldots)) \cup (\ldots (\ldots))$

7. $(R \, ; \, S) \, ; \, T = R \ldots (S \ldots T)$

8. $\mathrm{id}\, X \, ; \, R = \ldots$

9. $\mathrm{id}(\mathrm{dom}\, R) \ldots R \, ; \, R^{\sim}$

Chapter 15

Properties of binary relations

Topic: Relations

....

Mathematics, rightly viewed, possesses not only truth, but supreme beauty – a beauty cold and austere, like that of sculpture.

Bertrand Russell
British logician and philosopher (1872–1970)

Objectives

On completion of this chapter you should be able to:

- Define reflexivity, symmetry and transitivity and identify relations with such properties.

- Define and identify equivalence relations.

- Define relations inducing partitions.

- Determine equivalence classes and quotients.

- Determine reflexive closure, symmetric closure and transitive closure.

This chapter considers only binary relations defined on sets, rather than relations from a set of values of one type to a set of another type. Such binary relations may exhibit certain very important mathematical properties and, therefore, sit in a class of their own.

The properties concerned are *reflexivity*, *symmetry* and *transitivity*. We encounter them mostly in mathematics, physical sciences and, not surprisingly, computer science. We will see that they are extremely useful for characterizing the underlying structure of important practical problems.

These properties are typically exhibited by products and services which can be substituted for one another. For example, certain automotive spare parts and pharmaceuticals manufactured by different manufacturers can often be substituted for one another. From the customer's point of view, the same applies to services such as flights operated by different airlines. Utilization of such properties in handling information can therefore lead to efficiencies in computer applications which support the relevant commercial activities. Communication patterns in networks and programs with respect to functionality also exhibit these properties. Therefore, we encounter them in computational problems as well.

15.1 Properties of binary relations

Given a binary relation *on a given set*, one can make certain important observations about it based on the following:

1. The extent of elements pairing with themselves.
2. The extent of elements pairing with each other on a reciprocal basis.
3. The extent of elements pairing with each other counting on intermediate pairs.

The extent to which a relation exhibits these characteristics results in several notable properties. These properties fall into three distinct categories:

1. Reflexivity, irreflexivity and non-reflexivity
2. Symmetry and antisymmetry
3. Transitivity

These concepts are explained below.

Definition) Reflexivity
_____

Given a binary relation $R : A \leftrightarrow A$, the extent of *reflexivity* may be characterized by three properties, as follows:

R is *reflexive*	if and only if $(a, a) \in R$ for every element a in A
R is *irreflexive*	if and only if $(a, a) \in R$ for none of the elements a in A
R is *non-reflexive*	if R is neither reflexive nor irreflexive

---

Example 15.1)
_____

Given that,

$$A = \{a, b, c, d, e, f\}$$
$$R : A \leftrightarrow A$$

the following extensions of the relation R illustrate the three concepts on the extent of reflexiveness.

Extension of R	Property
$R = \{e \mapsto e,\ a \mapsto f,\ a \mapsto a,\ d \mapsto b,\ b \mapsto b,$ $f \mapsto a,\ f \mapsto f,\ d \mapsto d,\ a \mapsto c,\ c \mapsto c\}$	R is reflexive
$R = \{a \mapsto f,\ d \mapsto b,\ f \mapsto a,\ a \mapsto c\}$	R is irreflexive
$R = \{e \mapsto e,\ a \mapsto f,\ d \mapsto b,\ b \mapsto b,\ f \mapsto a,$ $d \mapsto d,\ a \mapsto c,\ c \mapsto c\}$	R is non-reflexive

---

Definition Symmetry

Given a binary relation $R : A \leftrightarrow A$, the extent of *symmetry* may be characterized by three properties, as follows:

R is *symmetrical*   if and only if for any two elements $a, b \in A$

$$(a, b) \in R \Rightarrow (b, a) \in R$$

R is *anti-symmetrical*   if and only if for any two elements $a, b \in A$

$$(a, b) \in R \wedge (b, a) \in R \Rightarrow a = b$$

R is *non-symmetrical*   R is neither symmetrical nor antisymmetrical

---

From the Definition we can see that, in symmetric relations, every pair of the form (a, b) in the relation must be accompanied by a dual of the form (b, a). However, in the case of antisymmetric relations, the 'symmetry' is permitted only for pairs of the form (a, a).

Example 15.2

Given that

$$A = \{a, b, c, d, e, f\}$$
$$R : A \leftrightarrow A$$

the following relations illustrate the two concepts on the extent of symmetry.

Extension of R	Property
$R = \{e \mapsto e,\ a \mapsto f,\ c \mapsto a,\ d \mapsto b,\ b \mapsto b,$	R is symmetrical
$\quad c \mapsto f,\ f \mapsto a,\ b \mapsto d,\ f \mapsto c,\ a \mapsto c\}$	
$R = \{e \mapsto e,\ a \mapsto f,\ d \mapsto b,\ b \mapsto a,\ f \mapsto b,$	
$\quad a \mapsto d,\ a \mapsto c,\ c \mapsto c\}$	R is antisymmetrical

Definition Transitivity

Given a binary relation $R : A \leftrightarrow A$, R is said to be *transitive* if and only if for any three elements $a, b, c \in A$,

$$(a, b) \in R \wedge (b, c) \in R \Rightarrow (a, c) \in R$$

Example 15.3

Given that

$$A = \{a, b, c, d, e, f\}$$
$$R : A \leftrightarrow A$$

the following set of pairs

$$R = \{a \mapsto c, \ c \mapsto d, \ a \mapsto d, \ c \mapsto f, \ a \mapsto f, \ f \mapsto d, \ e \mapsto e, \ b \mapsto e,$$
$$e \mapsto b, \ b \mapsto b, \ c \mapsto c\}$$

makes R a transitive relation.

Exercise 15.1 ✳

State the properties that we wish the following relations to possess.

On the domain $\mathbb{Z}$ of integers:
1. *greater-than*
   (Pairs of numbers such that the first number is greater than the second.)

2. *not-less-than*
   (Pairs of numbers such that the first number is not less than the second.)

3. *add-up-to-5*
   (Pairs of numbers such that their sum equals to 5.)

4. *differ-in-5*
   (Pairs of numbers such that their difference equals 5, that is, for any pair (a, b) such that $a - b = 5$.)

On a set P of persons:
5. *is-brother*
   (Pairs of individuals such that one of them is a brother of the other.)

6. *has-same-status-as*
   (Pairs of individuals such that both have the same status or occupy the same position.)

Exercise 15.2 ✳

This is in essence a continuation of Exercise 15.1. If possible, identify the properties relevant to the relations set out in Table 15.1; otherwise explain why.

Exercise 15.3 ✳✳

With reference to Example 14.2,

1. Identify the properties of the relation *net* with elements as enumerated.

2. Assuming that all nodes have the capability to act as forwarding stations, determine pairs of nodes such that the second node in each pair is reachable from the first.

15.2 Equivalence relations

The three properties of reflexivity, symmetry and transitivity give rise to an important class of binary relations, called equivalence relations. Consider, as an

Table 15.1   Relations for Exercise 15.2.

Relation	Property					
	Reflexive	Irreflexive	Non-reflexive	Symmetric	Antisymmetric	Transitive
People related by common birthdays						
People related by being older						
People related by marriage						
People related by parenthood						
People related by superiority						
People enjoying authorizing rights over others as well as themselves						
Siblings						
Equivalent spare parts in automotive industry						
Nodes in communication or transmission networks on the basis of accessibility						
Precisely coded messages in different languages						

example, barter – the direct exchange of goods without any intervening medium of exchange or money. Assume that the exchange rates of different goods are fixed.

Let *Goods* denote a set of 'categories' or 'units' of goods, for example, the following:

Goods = {**2goats**, **3pots**, **1cow**, **5chkn**, **grainSack**. **2chkn**,
      sapphire, **1ozGold**, **1ozDiamond**}

The items of goods that may be exchanged against each other stand in a certain relation. Let us call it *barter*:

barter : *Goods* ↔ *Goods*

In relation to this one may observe an interesting pattern of pairing of goods:

1. An item of each goods category may be exchanged for itself or for an item of the same category. That is, two goats may be exchanged for any two goats. Since this applies to each category of goods, the relation *barter* must be *reflexive*.

2. If an item of a goods category may be exchanged for an item of another category, then it must be the case that the second item is exchangeable for the first one. That is, if two goats may be exchanged for five chickens, then five chickens may be exchanged for two goats. Here we are talking of *barter* being a *symmetric* relation.

3. If an item of a goods category may be exchanged for a second item of another category and that second item may be exchanged for a third item of yet another category, then it must be the case that the first item is exchangeable for the third one. That is, if two goats may be exchanged for five chickens and five chickens may be exchanged for a cow, then two goats may be exchanged for a cow. Thus, we are talking about the *transitivity* of the relation *barter*.

As an example, consider an extension of *barter* of the form indicated below:

barter = {(**2goats**, **5chkn**), (**1cow**, **5chkn**), (**3pots**, **2chkn**)
      (**5chkn**, **2goats**), (**5chkn**, **1cow**), (**2chkn**, **3pots**)
      (**2goats**, **2goats**), (**5chkn**, **5chkn**), (**1cow**, **1cow**), ...}

The pairs enumerated above say that two goats, five chickens, three pots and one cow are all equivalent to one another in terms of their 'purchasing power'.

A relation having the above characteristics is called an *equivalence relation*.

(**Definition**) Equivalence relation

A binary relation R on a set A is said to be an *equivalence relation* if and only if R is reflexive, symmetrical and transitive.

Terminology

Until now we have used the term 'equivalent' only in relation to propositions and formulae in predicate logic. We use the same term here, in the context of equivalence relations, to talk about *objects* which are *roughly the same* from the perspective of a given application. In other words, they are identical with respect to one or more chosen attributes.

Example 15.4

A classic problem that illustrates the concept of equivalence relation is the relationship between spare parts produced by different manufacturers. Consider a group of 'hypothetical' manufacturers called *Lucas*, *Champion* and *Bosch*, specializing in the production of some spare parts. We could represent them as,

[*Parts*]
Lucas, Champion, Bosch : $\mathbb{P}$ *Parts*

Let the parts that they produce be:

$$Lucas = \{L1, L2, L3, L4\}$$
$$Champion = \{C1, C2, C3, C4, C5\}$$
$$Bosch = \{B1, B2, B3\}$$

and let the following also be true:

1. The parts $L1$, $L3$, $C1$ and $C3$ may be used as substitutes for one another.
2. The parts $L4$ and $C5$ may be used as substitutes for each other.
3. The parts $B1$, $B2$ and $C4$ may be used as substitutes for one another.
4. The parts $L2$, $C2$ and $B3$ each have no other substitutes other than themselves.

The immediate reading of above description is that individual spare parts hold in a certain relation like the following:

$$\{(L1, C1), (C1, L1), (C1, C3), (C3, C1), (L1, L3), (L3, L1),$$
$$(L4, C5), (C5, L4), (B2, C4), (B1, B2)\}$$

However, a closer examination would reveal that there must be some further substitutable pairs in this relation on the strength of the above. We have named this complete relation *substitutes*. Its full extension is:

$$substitutes = \{(L1, C1), (C1, L1), (C1, C3), (C3, C1), (L1, L3), (L3, L1),$$
$$(L4, C5), (C5, L4), (B2, C4), (B1, B2), (L1, C3), (C3, L1),$$
$$(C1, L3), (L3, C1), (L3, C3), (C3, L3), (C4, B1), (B1, C4),$$
$$(L1, L1), (L2, L2), (L3, L3), (L4, L4), (C1, C1), (C2, C2),$$
$$(C3, C3), (C4, C4), (C5, C5), (B1, B1), (B2, B2), (B3, B3)\}$$

This set differs from the preceding one by having not only the symmetric pairs but also all transitive and reflexive pairs. It is not difficult to justify the inclusion of these pairs. Thus, *substitutes* is an equivalence relation.

The pairing of parts according to substitutability is also shown in the graph of the relation *substitutes* in Figure 15.1.

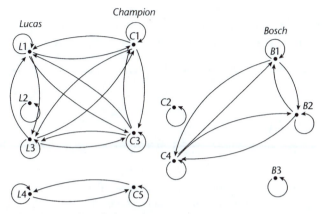

Champion

Lucas

Bosch

Figure 15.1   The relation *substitutes* on spare parts.

Given three relations R_1, R_2 and R_3, all defined on the set $\{a_1, a_2, a_3, a_4, a_5, a_6\}$, determine which of the following relations are equivalence relations.

1. $R_1 = \{(a_1, a_2), (a_5, a_2), (a_1, a_5), (a_3, a_6), (a_5, a_1), (a_2, a_1),$
   $(a_2, a_5), (a_6, a_3), (a_4, a_4)\}$

2. $R_2 = \{(a_1, a_2), (a_5, a_2), (a_1, a_5), (a_3, a_6), (a_5, a_1), (a_2, a_1), (a_2, a_5),$
   $(a_1, a_1), (a_2, a_2), (a_3, a_3), (a_4, a_4), (a_5, a_5), (a_6, a_6)\}$

3. $R_3 = \{(a_1, a_2), (a_5, a_2), (a_1, a_5), (a_3, a_6), (a_5, a_1), (a_2, a_1), (a_2, a_5),$
   $(a_6, a_3), (a_1, a_1), (a_2, a_2), (a_3, a_3), (a_4, a_4), (a_5, a_5), (a_6, a_6)\}$

Consider a set *Prog* of programs $p_1, \ldots, p_{10}$. In general, programs can be equivalent to one another on the grounds of functionality, algorithmic strategies employed, the quality of the code or many other attributes. With respect to, say, the quality of the code, the programs p_1, p_5 and p_7 are of comparable quality. The program p_3 is incomparable with both p_7 and p_4, but is comparable to p_6, while the programs p_2 and p_4 are of the same standing.

1. Produce an equivalence relation expressing the above relationship between programs.

2. Suggest another non-trivial specific instance of an equivalence relation on the same set of programs, classifying them, say, according to their underlying algorithmic features.

3. How would you now determine the programs exhibiting the same quality of code and the same algorithmic features?

Given three integers p, q and m, the integer p is said to be *congruent to q modulo m* provided that m divides $(p - q)$ exactly. A relation denoting this is

$$congruent\ (p,q)\ mod\ m \overset{def}{\Leftrightarrow} m \,|\, (p - q)$$

where *congruent (p,q) mod m* is a ternary relation (predicate) and $m \,|\, n$ stands for 'm divides n exactly'.

1. Give a mathematical definition for $m \,|\, n$.

2. Identify the properties of equivalence relations applicable to the relation *congruent (p,q) mod m* on $\mathbb{Z}$ for some specific m.

3. By fixing m to some small number, indicate the elements of a non-trivial instance of the relation exhibiting the properties mentioned in your answer to question 2.

4. How would you reason formally about your answer to question 2? If you wish, attempt a formal proof.

With reference to Example 14.2 in Chapter 14, generalize the relation *net* in terms of its desirable properties such that:

1. The model caters only for direct connections between immediately accessible processors in the specified directions.

2. The model provides for bidirectional communication capabilities between those adjacent pairs of processors with any link between them.

3. The processors in the model are capable of forwarding messages to other processors in the direction of the arcs.

4. The model exhibits all three capabilities listed above.

15.3 Partitions and equivalence classes

It was quite evident in the spare parts example of the previous section that mutually substitutable parts were in distinct groups. These groups exhibit some rather interesting characteristics. For example, any part may belong to only one group and the groups cover the whole set of parts of interest to us. Such a set of 'groups' is known as a *partition*.

Definition Partition

Given a set P of some subsets of an arbitrary set A, that is,

$$P : \mathbb{P}(\mathbb{P}A)$$

the set P is called a partition of A if and only if the following conditions hold:

1. All sets in P are non-empty, that is

$$\varnothing \notin P$$

2. P is a pairwise disjoint collection of sets.

3. The union of all the elements in the sets which are in P is exactly the set A, that is

$$\bigcup P = A$$

Note

Some mathematicians allow a partition to contain the empty set.

Example 15.5

Referring to Example 15.4, the partition of the spare parts implicit in the informal description of substitutability is shown in Figure 15.2.

It is important to note that the information in Figure 15.2 about the given partition of spare parts is also captured in the relation *substitutes*. In fact, there is a natural link between partitions and equivalence relations. This is because each grouping (set) in the partition may be determined from the equivalence relation, or vice versa. For example, the mutually substitutable parts $L1$, $L3$, $C1$ and $C3$ may be obtained from the relation *substitutes* as the set:

$$\{x \mid x \in (Lucas \cup Champion \cup Bosch) \land (L1, x) \in substitutes\} = \{L1,\ L3,\ C1,\ C3\}$$

This is a typical example of what is termed an *equivalence class*.

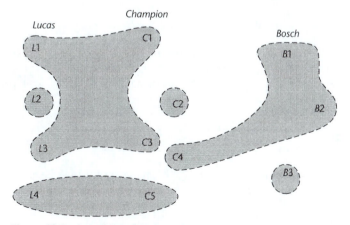

Figure 15.2   A partition of spare parts.

Definition   Equivalence class

Given an equivalence relation R on a set A, associated with each element a of the set A is a set

$$[a] \overset{def}{=} \{x \mid x \in A \land (a, x) \in R\}$$

The set $[a]$ is called the equivalence class of a.

Example 15.6

Referring to Example 15.4, the equivalence classes of the elements in the set $(Lucas \cup Champion \cup Bosch)$ due to *substitutes* are the following:

$$[L1] = [L3] = [C1] = [C3] = \{L1, L3, C1, C3\}$$
$$[L4] = [C5] = \{L4, C5\}$$
$$[B1] = [B2] = [C4] = \{B1, B2, C4\}$$
$$[L2] = \{L2\}$$
$$[C2] = \{C2\}$$
$$[B3] = \{B3\}$$

Observations

It is important to note the following:

1. Every element in A belongs to its own equivalence class. That is, for every $a \in A$,

   $a \in [a]$

2. If two elements in A are related to each other through R, then they share the same equivalence class. That is, for $a, b \in A$,

   $[a] = [b] \Leftrightarrow (a, b) \in R$

3. Each element in A has a unique equivalence class. That is, for every $a, b \in A$,

   $[a] \neq [b] \Leftrightarrow [a] \cap [b] = \varnothing$

The properties listed in the Observations and the properties of partitions discussed earlier exhibit a remarkable similarity. In fact, if all the equivalence classes of a given set are presented as a set of sets, the resulting set is nothing but a partition. One can obtain this partition simply by using the concept *quotient*.

Definition   Quotient

Given an equivalence relation R on a set A, the *quotient* of A by R is denoted by A/R and is defined as the set of equivalence classes of all elements in A. That is,

$$A/R \overset{def}{=} \{[a] \mid a \in A\}$$

Terminology

The partition produced by A/R is said to be *induced* by the equivalence relation R.

Example 15.7

Referring to Example 15.4, the quotient of the set $(Lucas \cup Champion \cup Bosch)$ due to the relation *substitutes* is the following:

$$(Lucas \cup Champion \cup Bosch)/substitutes = \{\{L1, L3, C1, C3\}, \{L4, C5\}, \{B1, B2, C4\},$$
$$\{L2\}, \{C2\}, \{B3\}\}$$

Note that this is exactly the partition shown in Figure 15.2.

Exercise 15.8 ✳ ✳

Return to Exercise 15.5.

1. Give the equivalences classes of the programs $p_1, \ldots, p_{10}$ with respect to the relation on the quality of program code.

2. Determine the quotient of the set *Prog* of programs with respect to the relation on the quality of program code.

3. Determine the same with respect to the relation reflecting close algorithmic features.

4. Partition the set *Prog* of programs such that the programs in each partition exhibit a 'similar' quality of program code and algorithmic features. [Note: Resolve any ambiguity of the word 'similar' by introducing an appropriate assumption.]

Exercise 15.9 ✳ ✳

The symbols a, b, c, d, e, f, g stand for certain countries and the following groups form a set of completely independent closed alliances (for example, military).

Alliance I: a, d, e
Alliance II: b, f

The remaining countries are totally independent. The countries in any alliance enjoy equal rights and fulfil equal obligations.

1. Enumerate the elements (pairs) of a binary relation on the set of countries that induces the above alliances and each independent state on its own as a partition of the given set of countries.

2. Identify the properties of the relation you defined in question 1. What are relations exhibiting such properties together called?

3. Write a mathematical expression for the set of alliances and independent states in terms of the relation you enumerated in question 1 and the set of countries given.

4. Enumerate the elements of a _new_ binary relation on the same set of countries inducing a different partition which corresponds to the independent states joining the Alliance II.

Return to Exercise 15.6. As before, let $p, q \in \mathbb{Z}$.

1. Give some elements of each of the sets [0], [1] and [2] due to *congruent* (p, q) *mod* 3 such that they indicate the composition (make-up) of [0], [1] and [2].

2. What is the difference between the quotients of $\mathbb{Z}$ due to
   (a) *congruent* (p, q) *mod* 3
   (b) *congruent* (p, q) *mod* 5

3. Show informally that the sets [1] and [2] due to *congruent* (p, q) *mod* 3 partition $\mathbb{Z}$.

15.4 Relational closures

Closures are a special kind of relational operation whereby new relations are constructed from old ones, but ensuring that certain properties hold with respect to the result. The properties concerned are reflexivity, symmetry and transitivity, discussed in Section 15.1.

Let us first explore the need for these operations. Consider, for example, the design of a network for data transmission. When the problem is first posed, one may focus on just those links which are considered essential at that stage. Suppose that the designer is given at the outset this initial set of links between adjacent nodes, along with an initial set of nodes. Certain issues the designer may address almost immediately are: (1) whether to allow transmission of data within each node, (2) whether to make each link bidirectional, and (3) whether to make each node a forwarding station to its adjacent nodes. Let us assume that the designer does not wish to achieve these at any cost, but at a reasonable marginal cost. That is, the designer is to make a firm commitment to the original set of links as proposed, and then consider adding the minimum set of facilities (links) in order to achieve the options that he thinks are appropriate. In considering option (2), for instance, he may decide to make the original set of links proposed bidirectional – nothing more and nothing less. The set of links he comes up with in this case may be produced exactly by the mathematical operation of 'symmetric closure'. Similarly, the other options may also be formulated as 'closure' operations.

Description   Relational closures

There are three kinds of closure operations:

    reflexive closure
    symmetric closure
    transitive closure

and each operation is concerned with adding the bare minimum number of pairs of elements to a given binary relation R, but ensuring that, for the resulting relation R',

1. the required property (reflexivity, symmetry or transitivity) holds for R'
2. R' includes R; i.e. $R \subseteq R'$
3. if there is another relation R'' for which (1) and (2) hold, then $R' \subset R''$

Condition (3) in the Description is important to ensure that R' is the smallest relation satisfying the required property. This ensures that we add only the minimum number of pairs necessary.

(**Definition**) Relational closures

Letting $R : A \leftrightarrow A$, *relational closures* may be formally defined in the following manner:

1. Reflexive closure:

   $$R' = R \cup (\text{id } A)$$

2. Symmetric closure:

   $$R' = R \cup R^{\sim}$$

3. Transitive closures (usually denoted by R^+ and R^*):
   (a) irreflexive transitive closure:

   $$R^+ = \bigcup_{i \in 1 \ldots \infty} R^i = R \cup R^2 \cup R^3 \cup R^4 \ldots$$

   (b) Reflexive transitive closure:

   $$R^* = \bigcup_{i \in 0 \ldots \infty} R^i = R^0 \cup R^+$$

   where R^i denotes the ith relational iteration, and $R^0 = \text{id } A$.

(**Example 15.8**)

Let

$$A = \{a, b, c\} \text{ and } R = \{(a, b), (c, a), (c, c)\}$$

Then

1. Reflexive closure:

   $$R' = \{(a, b), (c, a), (a, a), (b, b), (c, c)\}$$

2. Symmetric closure:

   $$R' = \{(a, b), (c, a), (c, c), (b, a), (a, c)\}$$

3. Irreflexive transitive closure:

$$R^+ = \{(a,b),(c,a),(c,c),(c,b)\}$$

Reflexive transitive closure:

$$R^* = \{(a,b),(c,a),(a,a),(b,b),(c,c),(c,b)\}$$

Example 15.9

Let A represent the set of nodes in the network and the relation R on A the initial set of links proposed. Then:

1. The network allowing transmission of data within each and every node will have the links as in the reflexive closure of R.

2. The network with bidirectional links corresponds to the symmetric closure of R.

3. The network allowing reachability of nodes depending on whether intermediate links serve as stepping stones is defined by the transitive closure of R.

Example 15.10

Consider Exercise 14.3 based on the relation *parent*. It is possible to define a new relation *ancestor* consisting of pairs of individuals as follows:

$$ancestor = parent \cup g\_parent \cup gg\_parent \cup ggg\_parent \cup gggg\_parent \cup \ldots$$

where *g_parent*, *gg_parent*, *ggg_parent*, *gggg_parent* and so on are the relations required in the answer to Exercise 14.3. In other words, *ancestor* is the irreflexive transitive closure of *parent*.

Exercise 15.11 ✳

Produce a set theoretically valid statement about relations for each of the following expressions by inserting an appropriate expression in place of each dotted blank. X is such a type and R is a relation on X.

1. $\ldots \subseteq R^+$

2. $(\text{id} \ldots) \subseteq R^*$

3. $R^+ = \ldots \, ; R^*$

Exercise 15.12 ✳✳

Boris, Sergei, Tam and Viktor are weightlifters. Viktor can outlift Tam, but Sergei can outlift Viktor. Tam can outlift Boris, but Sergei can outlift Tam.

1. Which of the statements among (a)–(c) below happen to be true in the light of these statements?
   (a) Both Boris and Sergei can outlift Viktor.
   (b) Viktor can outlift Boris but can't outlift Tam.
   (c) Viktor can outlift Boris by more than he can outlift Tam.

2. Rank the weightlifters according to lifting ability.

3. Characterize the general properties of the underlying mathematical relation.

Your answers must be based on relations.

Exercise 15.13 ✳ ✳

With reference to Example 14.2 in Chapter 14 and continuing Exercises 15.3 and 15.7, extend the functionality of the network described by *net* such that the resulting network has, in addition to those of *net*, the following capabilities separately:

1. All nodes in the model, irrespective of whether they are connected to others or not, are capable of communicating with themselves.

2. The model provides for bidirectional communication capabilities between those adjacent pairs of processors with any link between them.

3. All nodes in the model are capable of forwarding messages to other processors in the direction of the arcs.

4. The model exhibits all three capabilities listed above.

Chapter 16

Functions and their classification

Topic: Functions

....

Structures are the weapons of the mathematician.

Nicholas Bourbaki
(pseudonym)

Objectives

On completion of this chapter you should be able to:

- Define mathematical functions.

- Relate functions to sets and mathematical relations.

- Identify types of functions.

- Understand function application both in continuous and discrete domains.

- Use functions, as well as relations, in specification of simple systems.

- Compare and contrast functional programming and imperative programming.

- Use functions as a way of computing.

Recall question 2 of both Exercises 14.7 and 14.9 on vehicle ownership and registration. There we studied two relationships: one between vehicles and their registration numbers, and the other between vehicle ownership and registration numbers. We treated the information in both these cases as mathematical relations.

An examination of the actual requirements of these relations would reveal that their *abstraction* as relations is incomplete. This is because, according to most national regulations, no vehicle may be legally owned by two persons and that vehicle registrations uniquely identify each vehicle individually. Implicit in this scenario is the notion of *mathematical function*. Functions extend the notion of relation by restricting the association of any object in a given relation to no more than one object.

Along with relations, functions play an important role in almost all areas of computing. This is underlined by two special topics considered in this chapter: formal system specification and functional programming. We are already familiar with formal system specification from our study in Section 12.7 of Chapter 12. Functional programming is a unique paradigm of computation, where functions, specifically the notion of *function application*, serve as the underlying computational mechanism.

16.1 Functions as relations

Functions are a special kind of relations. Therefore, it is appropriate to begin the study of functions by examining the features that distinguish functions from ordinary mathematical relations, which we studied in Chapters 13, 14 and 15. Further-more, the relational view of functions explains better the nature of functions and, as seen shortly, the classification of functions.

Definition) Function
___

A *function* is a relation which associates a unique element in its range for every element in its domain. Thus, given two arbitrary types A and B and a relation f from A to B, that is

$$f : A \leftrightarrow B$$

The relation f is said to be a function if and only if

$$\forall x : A; y, z : B \bullet (x, y) \in f \wedge (x, z) \in f \Rightarrow y = z$$

___

Terminology

- Functions are also known as *mappings* and *transformations*.
- Given an element x in the domain of a function f, the element y in its range associated with x through f is found by the *application* of f to x. The same is stated by the following alternative mathematical notations:

$$f(x) = y \quad \text{and} \quad f\,x = y$$

Notation

A notation used to indicate that a mathematical object f is a function is to declare its type as

$$f : A \nrightarrow B$$

We will return to a more comprehensive set of notations in Section 16.2.

Example 16.1)
___

Two examples of functions drawn from real life are given here.

1. *People and their birthdays*

   One may immediately observe that nobody may have more than one birthday. Therefore, the relation may be characterized as a mathematical function. It may be formally introduced by first introducing two types, *People* and *Date*, for all possible individuals and dates respectively, and then letting the relation concerned be an element of the type

   People ↔ *Date*

Note that the above denotes not just one, but a set of functions.

2. *Library books and their borrowers*
   Following the normal library practice that no book may be borrowed jointly by more than one person, the relation may be seen as a function. Again, this function may be formally introduced as an element of

   Book ↔ *Person*

where *Book* and *Person* are appropriate types.

The following is a more abstract function.

3. Given the following sets *Greek* and *Roman*1

   $Greek = \{\alpha, \beta, \gamma, \phi, \omega, \xi, \zeta, \tau\}$
   $Roman1 = \{p, q, r, s, t, u, v, w\}$

A specific function f from *Greek* to *Roman*1 is given below:

   $f = \{(\alpha, s), (\beta, t), (\gamma, r), (\omega, r), (\xi, q), (\zeta, u)\}$

It relates each element in the set *Greek* to a unique element in the set *Roman*1. Application of f to the element β, that is $f(\beta)$, gives the element t in *Roman*1 associated with β. This example is illustrated in Figure 16.1.

Note

As may be observed in Figure 16.1, there are no diverging arrows from elements in *Greek* to those in *Roman*1 in the graph of the function f. Note, however, that there can be converging arrows.

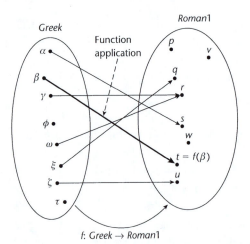

f: Greek → Roman1

Figure 16.1   An example illustrating function application.

(16.2) Classification of functions

Functions come in such a variety of forms in computing that it is often necessary to identify how functions differ in character from one another. Our concern here is not what they represent in real life but their *mathematical structure*. The term 'mathematical structure' implies here more detailed information about the participation of elements of the underlying sets in a given function. This may be seen not only with respect to the extent of participation of elements in the domain or the range of the function, but also with respect to permitted pairings of elements in the function.

The following is a summary of how functions are commonly classified according to their structure. It also incorporates the notation used in the specification language Z for identification of their types. Note that f in Table 16.1 is a function from a set A to a set B.

Table 16.1 Classification of functions.

Function type	Description	Notation
Partial	Domain of f is a subset of A	$f : A \nrightarrow B$
Total	Domain of f is equal to A	$f : A \rightarrow B$
Surjective or onto	Range of f is equal to B	$f : A \twoheadrightarrow B$
Injective or one-to-one	A function whose inverse is also a function	
	(1) Partial version	$f : A \rightarrowtail\!\!\!\!\rightarrow B$
	(2) Total version	$f : A \rightarrowtail B$
Bijective	A function which is both surjective and injective, i.e. onto and one-to-one	$f : A \rightarrowtail\!\!\!\twoheadrightarrow B$
Finite mappings	A function which is a finite set	$f : A \nrightarrow\!\!\!\!\rightarrow B$

A more detailed definition of these function types is given in the remaining subsections.

16.2.1 Partial and total functions

(**Definition**) Partial and total functions

Given two arbitrary types A and B, the set of *partial functions* from A to B is defined as the following set of relations

$$A \nrightarrow B \stackrel{def}{=} \{f : A \leftrightarrow B \mid \forall x : A; y,z : B \bullet (x,y) \in f \wedge (x,z) \in f \Rightarrow y = z\}$$

The set of *total functions* from from A to B is defined as the following set of partial functions

$$A \rightarrow B \stackrel{def}{=} \{f : A \nrightarrow B \mid \text{dom} f = A\}$$

Note that the definition given for the set $A \nrightarrow B$ is identical to the definition of functions given in Section 16.1. This is because partial functions are the most general of all functions.

Note also that any partial function from A to B may be defined for some, all or none of the elements in A. In contrast, total functions from A to B must be defined for all elements of A.

Terminology

A set of functions shown, for example, as $A \nrightarrow B$ is also referred to as a *function space* from A to B.

Notation

We may introduce a partial function f and a total function g from A to B by declaring their types as

$f : A \nrightarrow B$ (f is a partial function from A to B)
$g : A \rightarrow B$ (g is a total function from A to B)

Example 16.2

Imagine a part of a library database concerned with the information about library stocks, namely, the location of books in the library and the books on loan to its users.

In order to deal with locations, let us introduce a new type, *Shelf*, to denote the set of all possible locations for storage of books, and let us assume that the type, *Book*, concerns only the books belonging to the library. The latter may be applicable when dealing with a fixed collection of books.

1. *The information on books and locations*
    One would expect that every library book has a designated storage location. If this information is kept as a relation *store* from *Book* to *Shelf*, *store* must really be a total function:

    $store : Book \rightarrow Shelf$

2. *The information on books on loan*
    On the other hand, the books on loan to users would vary over time and certainly nobody expects all books to be on loan at all times, although this is a possibility. Therefore, if this information is kept as a relation *loans* from *Book* to *Person*, the most appropriate function type is a partial function from *Book* and *Person*. That is,

    $loans : Book \nrightarrow Person$

3. Let us return to the function space from *Greek* to *Roman*1 used for f in Example 16.1. Figures 16.2 and 16.3 show two additional functions from the same function space, one illustrating a partial function and the other a total function.

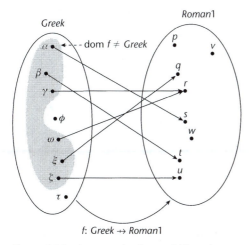

f: Greek ↣ Roman1

Figure 16.2 An example of a partial function.

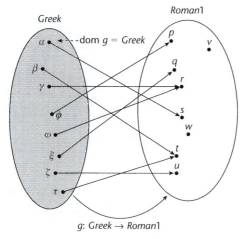

g: Greek → Roman1

Figure 16.3 An example of a total function.

16.2.2 Surjective functions

Surjective functions are in some way a counterpart to total functions. They concern not the extent of elements in the domain but that in the range.

(**Definition**) Surjective functions

Given two arbitrary types A and B, the set of *partial surjective functions* from A to B is defined as the following set of partial functions:

$$A \twoheadrightarrow B \stackrel{def}{=} \{f : A \nrightarrow B \mid \operatorname{ran} f = B\}$$

The set of *total surjective functions* from A to B may be defined as the following set of partial surjective functions:

$$A \twoheadrightarrow B \stackrel{def}{=} \{f : A \nrightarrow B \mid \operatorname{dom} f = A\}$$

Note that any partial surjective function from A to B, as given in the Definition, must be defined for all elements of B, but may be defined, in general, for some of the elements in A. By contrast, total surjective functions from A to B must be defined for all elements of A and for all elements of B. This does not necessarily mean that A and B are of the same size (see, for example, Figure 16.5 in Example 16.3 below).

Notation

We may introduce a partial surjective function s and a total surjective function t from A to B by declaring their types as

$s : A \nrightarrow B$ (s is a partial surjective function from A to B)
$t : A \twoheadrightarrow B$ (t is a total surjective function from A to B)

Example 16.3

1. A building society (an organization lending money to its members for purchasing homes) is to be transformed into an ordinary private bank. The society is considering the following two alternative schemes for distribution of shares of the new bank:
   (a) All (current) society members are to be allocated shares.
   (b) All shares are to be distributed among all society members.

   If the information on share distribution is kept as a function *allocation* from *Share* to *Member* (*Share* and *Member* being appropriate types), then scheme (a) corresponds to a partial surjective function

   allocation : *Share* $\nrightarrow$ *Member*

   whereas scheme (b) corresponds to a total surjective function

   allocation : *Share* $\twoheadrightarrow$ *Member*

   An implication of *allocation* being a partial surjective function is that the society is not obliged to distribute all shares among its members, whereas the total version imposes this constraint.

2. Let *Roman2* and *Roman3* be two new sets, such that

   Roman2 = $\{r, s, t\}$
   Roman3 = $\{p, q, r, s, t, u\}$

   Figure 16.4 presents an example of partial surjective function s from *Greek* to *Roman2*, while Figure 16.5 presents a total surjective function t from *Greek* to *Roman3*.

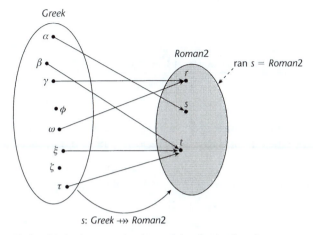

Figure 16.4   An example of a partial surjective function.

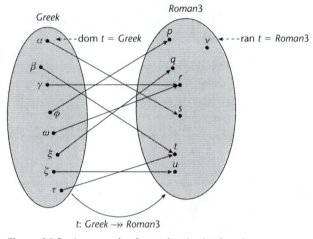

Figure 16.5   An example of a total surjective function.

16.2.3   Injective and bijective functions

Injective and bijective functions require their inverse relations to be functions too. As a consequence, the elements both in the domain and in the range of the function must have unique counterparts on either side.

(**Definition**)   Injective functions

Given two arbitrary types A and B, the set of *partial injective functions* from A to B is defined as the following set of partial functions from A to B:

$$A \rightarrowtail B \stackrel{def}{=} \{ f : A \rightarrow B \mid f^{\sim} \in B \rightarrow A \}$$

Terminology

Injective functions are also called *one-to-one functions* and sometimes just *one–one functions*. This is because there is a one-to-one correspondence between the elements of the domain and the elements of the range of the function.

Note

There are neither diverging arrows nor converging arrows in the graph of an injective function (see, for example, Figures 16.6 and 16.7 in Example 16.4 below).

Partial injective functions also have their counterparts to total functions and surjective functions. They are called, respectively, total injective functions and bijective functions.

(**Definition**)   Total injective functions and bijective functions
_____

Given two arbitrary types A and B, the set of *total injective functions* from A to B is defined as the following set of partial injective functions:

$$A \rightarrowtail B \stackrel{def}{=} \{f : A \rightarrowtail B \mid \text{dom } f = A\}$$

The set of *bijective functions* from from A to B is defined as the following set of injective functions:

$$A \rightarrowtail\!\!\!\rightarrow B \stackrel{def}{=} \{f : A \rightarrowtail B \mid \text{ran } f = B\}$$
$$= A \rightarrowtail B \cap A \twoheadrightarrow B$$

Note that any partial injective function from A to B may be defined for some, all or none of the elements in B. By contrast, bijective functions from A to B must be defined for all elements of B.

Notation

We may introduce a partial injective function i, a total injective function j and a bijective function b from A to B as follows:

$i : A \rightarrowtail B$ (i is a partial injective function from A to B)
$j : A \rightarrowtail B$ (j is a total injective function from A to B)
$b : A \rightarrowtail\!\!\!\rightarrow B$ (c is a bijective function from A to B)

(**Example 16.4**)
_____

1. Let us consider the example on motor vehicles and their registration numbers. The registration information is perhaps best kept as a function *registration* from, say, a type, *Reg*, denoting all possible registration numbers, to a type, *Vehicle*, denoting all possible motor vehicles. The type of this function depends on the actual requirements. In this respect, consider the following cases:

(a) Why might *registration* be a partial injective function?
Each registration number must identify a unique vehicle, while there must also be a unique identification for each vehicle. This would imply an injective function for *registration*.

$$registration : \; Reg \rightarrowtail Vehicle$$

This, however, does not require that every vehicle should have a registration number. This may be what is required if the authorities wish to maintain some vehicles, for example, the vehicles used by the official elite, out of the vehicle registration system.

(b) Why might *registration* be a bijective function?
On the other hand, the authorities may wish that every vehicle must be under the vehicle registration system. This would require *registration* to be a bijective function. That is,

$$registration : \; Reg \rightarrowtail\!\!\!\rightarrow Vehicle$$

(c) A case for a total injective function.
It is unreasonable to make *registration* a total injective function since this would imply the use of all conceivable registration numbers. However, it is easily seen that the inverse function of *registration* in (b) above is a total injective function:

$$registration^{\sim} : \; Vehicle \rightarrowtail Reg$$

2. Let us consider two functions from *Greek* to *Roman3* and from *Greek* to *Roman1*. Examples of a partial injective function *i* from *Greek* to *Roman3* and a bijective function *b* from *Greek* to *Roman1* are illustrated in Figures 16.6 and 16.7. Note that in the case of the bijective function *b*,

$$\#(\mathrm{dom}\; b) = \#(\mathrm{ran}\; b) = \#Greek = \#Roman1$$

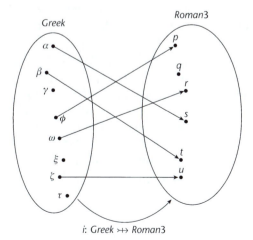

i: Greek ⤖ Roman3

Figure 16.6   An example of a partial injective function.

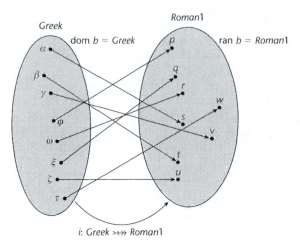

Figure 16.7 An example of a bijective function.

Abstraction of many relationships in real life may correspond to functions. Functions may in turn have specific characteristics, which may be captured by different function types.

Exercise 16.1 ✻ ✻

1. Based on your own understanding, identify which of the relations in Table 16.2 are better represented as functions. If applicable, identify the types appropriate to them. Give your reasons.

2. Give the most specific type for each of the relations listed in Table 16.2.

Exercise 16.2 ✻ ✻ ✻

Below is an extract from a puzzle called 'Death in the Decanter' (from Madachy (1979)). Using appropriate sets, relations and functions, describe it mathematically. Indicate clearly the eligibility of the club members for drinks, constraints on their consumption of drinks and the facts related to their actual consumption.

Buharin, Brezinsky, Chernov, Chikarin, Petrovsky, Semenov and Wilensky of the Bottle Club hold their annual 'booze-up', the drinks being beer, brandy, chianti, cider, port, sherry and whisky. In conformity with the rules of the club, each person samples exactly three different kinds of drinks, but nothing beginning with the initial of his own name. After the party, three genuine corpses are found under the table among the seven drunks. An investigation shows that one of the drinks had been maliciously tampered with. The following facts also come to light:

(a) The three victims among them sampled all seven drinks.
(b) The brandy drinker among the victims refused sherry.
(c) The port drinkers outnumbered the whisky drinkers by one.
(d) The person having the same initial as the drink sampled by all three victims drank chianti.
(e) There was one drink sampled by all three victims and Chernov.

Table 16.2 Relations for Exercise 16.1.

Relation from/on:	Function classification				
	Partial $\leftrightarrow$	Total $\rightarrow$	Injective $\rightarrowtail$	Surjective $\twoheadrightarrow$	Bijective $\rightarrowtail\hspace{-8pt}\rightarrow$
People to their birthdays					
Vehicles to their legal owners					
Vehicles to their registration numbers					
Books to their authors					
Books in a given library to their identifications					
Countries of the world to their capitals					
Countries of the world to their current prime ministers					
Computer user-names to their passwords					
Telephone numbers to households					
Companies to their VAT (value added tax) registration numbers					
Adjacent railway stations on a train route					
Trains to their departure times from a railway station					
Any empty relation					

(16.3) Functions as expressions

Our study has so far been restricted to functions in discrete domains. As a result, we were able to treat them as sets of pairs, that is, as binary relations. This gave us the impression that function application amounts to retrieval of information 'recorded' or hidden in a function. This operational view is not far off from the notion of a function found in databases.

However, it is not always feasible to represent information in this manner. Consider, for example, a function that relates numbers to their squares. Since numbers form an infinite domain, it is impossible to enumerate this function. Instead we must resort to set comprehension. Thus, we may define the function concerned in two alternative forms as:

$$square = \{(x, y) \bullet x, y : \mathbb{Z} \mid y = x^2\}$$
$$= \{(x, x^2) \bullet x : \mathbb{Z}\}$$

on the domain of $\mathbb{Z}$. Another example is:

$$hypotenuse = \{((x, y), z) \bullet x, y, z : \mathbb{R} \mid x > 0 \wedge y > 0 \wedge z > 0 \wedge z^2 = x^2 + y^2\}$$

which has the type $\mathbb{R} \times \mathbb{R} \nrightarrow \mathbb{R}$. This function is intended for computing the hypotenuse of a right-angled triangle, knowing the lengths of its other two sides. We also consider the lengths of sides to be strictly positive numbers.

Although we can define any function in this manner, it can sometimes be cumbersome. An alternative is to define them as expressions:

$$square \quad : \mathbb{Z} \rightarrow \mathbb{Z}$$
$$square(x) = x^2$$

and

$$hypotenuse : \mathbb{R} \times \mathbb{R} \nrightarrow \mathbb{R}$$
$$\forall x, y : \mathbb{R} \bullet x > 0 \wedge y > 0 \wedge hypotenuse(x, y) = z, \quad \text{where} \quad z > 0 \wedge z^2 = x^2 + y^2$$

The first defines the function *square* explicitly, while the second defines *hypotenuse* implicitly. A more conventional expression for hypotenuse is the following:

$$hypotenuse(x, y) = \sqrt{x^2 + y^2}$$

provided that the square root operator $\sqrt{}$ always returns the positive square root.

In the latter kind of representation of functions, function application is not merely 'retrieval' of some hidden or stored information but involves some kind of computation or 'evaluation'.

Example 16.5

The following are some further examples illustrating the use of expressions for defining functions.

$f(x, y) = x + y$	The function that adds two numbers
$f(x) = \sin(x)$	The function that computes the sine value of its argument
$f(x) = 7x^5 + 12x^4 + 3x^2 - 5x - 4$	The function that computes the given polynomial with some fixed coefficients with respect to its argument x
$f(y) = \int_0^y x^2 \, dx$	The function that computes the integral of x^2 from 0 to y
$f(x) = \ln x$	The function that computes the natural logarithm (to the base e) of its argument x

There are many function 'lookalikes'. These are not really functions but relations, often used in the style of functions by choosing a particular element in the range related to the 'argument' of the function.

Example 16.6

$\sqrt{x}$ The 'function' that computes the square root of a number. Note that any positive real number may have two square roots. (The same applies to negative real numbers and complex numbers when operating in the domain of complex numbers.)

$\arccos(x)$ The 'function' that computes the arc-cosine (the inverse of cosine) value of its argument. Note that, in general,

$$\arccos\left(\tfrac{1}{2}\right) = \pm\tfrac{1}{3}\pi + 2k\pi$$

for $k = 0, 1, \ldots, \infty$.

1. Identify the types appropriate to the functions listed in Table 16.3, giving your reasons.

2. Give the most specific type for each of the functions listed in Table 16.3.

Consider the board games draughts (also called checkers), chess, and snakes and ladders. As they progress, the state of these games can be modelled using functions, relations, and so on. Each of these games has an initial state and usually many intermediate states and, eventually, reaches a final state, giving rise to a winner. In the case of snakes and ladders, there can be more than one winner, emerging from some of the intermediate states at different times. The state of the board in draughts and chess alters with every move of a piece on the board chosen directly by the player. In the case of snakes and ladders, the move of pieces is determined by the throw of a die by one player at a time.

Suggest appropriate functions, relations and sets for modelling each of the three games. In the case of functions, identify their types and characterize those properties which cannot be captured by types by additional predicates.

16.4 Function composition

Recall relational composition covered in Chapter 14. Here is another way to look at it but with regard to functions.

Table 16.3 Functions for Exercise 16.3.

Function	Function classification				
	Partial $\leftrightarrow$	Total $\longrightarrow$	Injective $\rightarrowtail$	Surjective $\twoheadrightarrow$	Bijective $\rightarrowtail\!\!\!\twoheadrightarrow$
$f(x) = x + 2$ on $\mathbb{N}$					
$f(x) = x + 2$ on $\mathbb{Z}$					
$f(x) = x + 2$ on $\mathbb{R}$					
$f(x) = x^2$ on $\mathbb{N}$					
$f(x) = x^2$ on $\mathbb{Z}$					
$f(x) = x^2$ on $\mathbb{R}$					
$f(x) = x^3$ on $\mathbb{Z}$					
$f(x) = x^3$ on $\mathbb{R}$					
$f(x) = \sqrt[3]{x}$ on $\mathbb{Z}$					
$f(x) = \sqrt[3]{x}$ on $\mathbb{R}$					
$f(x) = \dfrac{1}{x}$ on $\mathbb{N}$					
$f(x) = \dfrac{1}{x}$ on $\mathbb{Z}$					
$f(x) = \dfrac{1}{x}$ on $\mathbb{R}$					
$f(x) = \sin^2(x) + \cos^2(x)$ on $\mathbb{R}$					
$f(x, y) = x + y$ from $\mathbb{R}^2$ to $\mathbb{R}$					
$f(x, y, z) = \dfrac{x + y + z}{3}$ on $\mathbb{R}^3$ to $\mathbb{R}$					
$f(r) = \pi \times r^2$ on $\mathbb{R}$ (area of circle)					
$f(n) = n! = n \times (n - 1) \times \ldots \times 2 \times 1$ on $\mathbb{N}$					

Definition   Function composition

Given two functions of the types $f : X \nrightarrow Y$ and $g : Y \nrightarrow Z$ for some sets X, Y and Z, *function composition* $f \,\fatsemi\, g$ (or $g \circ f$) may be viewed as

$$(f \,\fatsemi\, g)(x) \stackrel{\text{def}}{=} (g \circ f)(x) \stackrel{\text{def}}{=} g(f(x))$$

provided that $x \in \text{dom } f$ and $f(x) \in \text{dom } g$.

Notation

The expression $g(f(x))$ is the origin of the notation $g \circ f$; in both of them f and g have the same order of appearance.

Exercise 16.5 ✳✳

Let

$$f(x) = x^2$$

and let the function y be defined in the following alternative forms:

1. $y = f(x)$
2. $y = f(x - 2)$
3. $y = f(2x + 1)$
4. $y = f(2x - 1) + 3$
5. $y = f\left(\dfrac{1}{x - 1}\right)$

Define, for each case, the function y

(a) as an expression involving x only;

(b) as a composition of two or more functions.

Identify the domains of the above functions, if y is a function defined on

(c) $\mathbb{N}$

(d) $\mathbb{Z}$

(e) $\mathbb{R}$

Exercise 16.6 ✳✳

Consider a simple bank. (Note that this exercise relies also on general relations.)

1. Suggest mathematical relations and functions appropriate for representing the following, and identify their types.
   (a) Account numbers and personal account holders.
   (b) Personal account holders and their addresses.
   (c) Accounts and their current balance.

2. Using the above, answer the following:
   (a) Given a specific individual *a*, write an expression giving the balance in *a*'s account.
   (b) Write an expression giving the names and addresses of those whose current balance is below a certain specified amount *n*.
   (c) Given a set of pairs, where each pair associates an individual with his/her new balance, write an expression giving the updated current balance of all accounts.

3. State the following formally.
   (a) The bank keeps the addresses of each and every customer.
   (b) The bank does not allow overdrafts beyond a certain credit limit *odLimit*.
   (c) The maximum number of customers of the bank is limited to a certain predefined number *customerLimit*.

16.5 An application: more on formal system specification

Let us return to the specification of the library considered as an example in Section 12.7. Because of our limited acquaintance with set theory then, the specification covered just the basic features of the library. With our familiarity with relations and functions, it is possible now to extend this exercise further to deal with other more interesting features of the library such as records of lending, location of individual books, an author catalogue, a subject catalogue using keywords and so on.

16.5.1 An informal specification

Below is a brief description of additional system requirements. Let us assume that the library system includes the following:

1. A record of loans, giving information about books and their borrowers.

2. A storage record, indicating whether any given book is out on loan, is available for borrowing or belongs to the reference collection, as well as where it is kept.

3. An author catalogue.

The lending facility is limited to registered users only. As before, only non-reference books may be borrowed. No book may be borrowed jointly by more than one person at a time. There is a fixed upper limit on the number of books that any user is allowed to borrow. The storage record covers all books in the library stock. The author catalogue covers only the books in the library, but the stock may contain items such as reports without an author.

16.5.2   System parameters

Systems are sometimes defined with respect to some predefined parameters. These are related to various physical parameters of the system such as size, capacity and range of application. Basically, as far as specifications are concerned, these parameters are some unspecified constants. The parameters are defined in the Z notation in the following style:

$\mid Book\_Limit : \mathbb{N}_1$

This is intended as a parameter defining the limit imposed in our example on the number of books users are permitted to borrow. Such parameters are defined outside schemata and apply globally in a given specification.

16.5.3   Specification of subsystems

In comparison with real ones, the system implied by the requirements in Section 16.5.1 is still a simple system. However, it is not a trivial one from the computational point of view and does not lend itself to an immediate solution.

Following the well known axiom in computing, 'divide and conquer', let us decompose the system into a number of smaller subsystems. When this decomposition is inspired by the desire to see, on one hand, that each subsystem addresses a coherent subset of requirements of the system as a whole and, on the other, that the coupling between subsystems is minimal with respect to any dependencies on each other's information, we call it a *modular decomposition*. *Modularity* is another important banner in computing. Modular decompositions result in modular designs, which are easier to understand as well as to implement. Modular designs results in modular products, consisting of components which mirror function and communicate via well understood interfaces. In service, modular products are easy to maintain and can be easily adapted to other applications.

Unlike in the case of designing totally new things, modular development of a system such as a library information system has the benefit of knowledge about existing systems.

If we are to follow the ideas of modular development strictly, we should also define the schemas specifying the operations on the relevant states. However, this requires some of the more advanced schema operations, which are outside the scope of our brief study. Therefore, Example 16.7 confines itself to the definition of the general state of the system concerned only.

Example 16.7

Referring to our example, three subsystems containing (1) loan information, (2) storage information and (3) author catalogue information is hardly a surprising decomposition. The state of each subsystem may be defined by a separate schema. The schemas *Loans*, *Store* and *Authors* formalize their general states.

Loans subsystem

```
┌─ Loans ─────────────────────────────────────────────────
│
│   Lib_Stock      (an included schema)  ⎫
│   users          : 𝔽 Person            ⎪
│   borrowers      : Book ⇸ Person        ⎬  ... (signature part)
│   loan_count     : Person ⇸ ℕ           ⎭
│ ───────────────────────────────────────
│   users = dom loan_count               ⎫
│   on_loan = dom borrowers              ⎪  (an extended
│   ran loan_count ⊆ {0 .. Book_Limit}    ⎬   predicate
│   ran borrowers = dom (loan_count ▷ {0})⎭        part)
│
└──────────────────────────────────────────────────────────
```

In addition to what is conveyed by *Lib_Stock* – a schema defined in Example 12.10 – *Loans* has three components:

users	The set of registered users of the library
borrowers	A partial function recording books on loan and their borrowers
loan_count	A partial function maintaining a count of loans to different users

and further relationships between pairs of them. It is important to question why *borrowers* and *loan_count* have to be partial functions, and not relations or functions of any other type. For example, if *borrowers* is introduced simply as a relation, then it would allow any book to be lent to more than one borrower at the same time, thus contravening one of the informally stated requirements. Through the choice of an appropriate type of mathematical structure for a component, that is, by stating whether the component is a simple set, a relation or a function of specific type such as an injective function, the signature part of a specification captures some of the system requirements immediately. The rest of the requirements, applicable at the given level of abstraction, are captured by means of predicates in the predicate part.

Among others, the predicate part of *Loans* conveys that the count of books lent to different users ranges from 0 to whatever number is specified by the global parameter *Book_Limit* and that only those users with at least one loan are considered as borrowers. Obviously, the schema *Loans* conveys more information than what is explicitly stated there, not least because of what it inherits from *Lib_Stock*.

Author catalogue subsystem

```
┌─ Authors ───────────────────────────────────────────────
│
│   stock      : 𝔽 Book
│   authors    : Book ↔ Person
│ ───────────────────────────────────────
│   dom authors ⊆ stock
│
└──────────────────────────────────────────────────────────
```

The schema *Authors*, which defines a very basic author catalogue, consists of two components: *stock*, with the meaning as defined in *Lib_Stock*, and a relation *authors* giving the information on books and their authors. It is a general relation since a book can have multiple authors and some authors may have written more than one book. The only predicate in the schema states that the author catalogue covers only those books in the library and that not all books necessarily have an author – one of the informally stated requirements.

Storage subsystem

```
┌─ Store ──────────────────────────────────────────────
│  Lib_Stock
│  availability : Book ↦ Status
│  shelf        : Book ↦ Location
├──────────────────────────────────────────────────────
│  stock = dom availability
│  ∀b : Book •
│     availability(b) = In ⇔ b ∉ on_loan ∧ b ∉ ref_coll
│     availability(b) = Out ⇔ b ∈ on_loan
│     availability(b) = Ref ⇔ b ∈ ref_coll
│  on_shelf = dom shelf
└──────────────────────────────────────────────────────
```

By means of two partial functions *availability* and *shelf*, the schema *Store* provides respectively the information on book status and the information on where the books are kept. Once again, question the appropriateness of these mathematical structures.

The first predicate states that the status record *availability* must cover every book in the library stock. The second predicate elaborates on *availability* by specifying the status values to be recorded against each book. The third predicate requires that the function *shelf*, which records where individual books are kept, covers all books in *on_shelf*.

16.5.4 Extended library specification

The schemas *Loans*, *Authors* and *Store*, which play the role of specifications of three subsystems introduced earlier, can now be integrated to produce the specification of the system as a whole. This is done using schema inclusion.

```
┌─ Lib_Sys ────────────────────────────────────────────
│  Loans   ⎫
│  Authors ⎬ ........................... (included schemas)
│  Store   ⎭
└──────────────────────────────────────────────────────
```

In the absence of additional predicates as in the given case, the same may be achieved by schema conjunction.

It is instructive to compare this schema against its expanded version, which is

---
_Lib_Sys_ _____

stock, on_loan,
on_shelf, ref_coll : $\mathbb{F}$ Book
users   : $\mathbb{F}$ Person
borrowers   : Book $\leftrightarrow$ Person
authors   : Book $\leftrightarrow$ Person
loan_count   : Person $\nrightarrow \mathbb{N}$
availability   : Book $\nrightarrow$ Status
shelf   : Book $\nrightarrow$ Location

    (Book categories))
stock = on_loan $\cup$ on_shelf
on_loan $\cap$ on_shelf = $\varnothing$
ref_coll $\subseteq$ on_shelf

    (Information on users and borrowers)
users = dom loan_count
on_loan = dom borrowers
ran loan_count $\subseteq \{0 \ldots Book\_Limit\}$
ran borrowers = dom (loan_count $\rhd \{0\}$)

    (Catalogue information)
dom authors $\subseteq$ stock

    (Availability and storage)
stock = dom availability
$\forall b : Book \bullet$
   availability(b) = **In** $\Leftrightarrow b \notin on\_loan \wedge b \notin ref\_coll$
   availability(b) = **Out** $\Leftrightarrow b \in on\_loan$
   availability(b) = **Ref** $\Leftrightarrow b \in ref\_coll$
on_shelf = dom shelf

The expanded version of _Lib_Sys_ shows the extent of information conveyed by the first version in a concise and more comprehensible manner. This illustrates the power of the schema language in terms of expressiveness when used in a modular way.

(**Exercise 16.7** ✳ ✳)
_____

1. Explain the significance of each line of mathematical text in the expanded version of the schema _Lib_Sys_.

2. Clearly identifying pre- and postconditions, define state transformations on *Lib_Sys* in the expanded form such that they formalize the operations for the following.
   (a) Lending a book from the library.
   (b) Disposing of a collection of books from the library stock.

(16.6) An application: functional programming

16.6.1   What does functional programming offer?

Functional programming is a paradigm of programming where *programs* consist entirely of mathematical functions. There are a number of important attractions for adopting functions as the only 'mechanism' of computation. These are as follows.

1. Programs are often initially conceived as *black-boxes*, that is, as abstract descriptions of what is required in terms of an *input/output relation* (see Figure 16.13). The notion of a black-box matches closely that of mathematical function because:
   (a) as functions, (deterministic) programs produce a unique output for each input;
   (b) neither black-boxes nor functions are concerned with the internal mechanisms that produce the output (result) from the input (arguments);
   (c) neither notion is concerned with efficiency and other performance measures since these are considerations which take prominence as the development process of a program progresses towards implementation.
   Note that there are differences between the two notions too. For instance, implicit in the black-box representation is a temporal delay in producing the output from the input once it becomes available. By contrast, the notion of a mathematical function is a 'time-less' relation between the elements in the domain and the range.
   Therefore, at higher levels of abstraction, where efficiency and detailed temporal behaviour are not a concern, functional programs could serve as high-level abstractions of programs. Since functional languages themselves are formal languages that implement the notion of a mathematical function, such functional programs could also be seen as specifications.

2. A mathematical function has no notion of *state* and, therefore, different occurrences of the same variable at different places in a mathematical definition mean the same thing. (Recall from our discussion in Section 7.2 that the phrase 'same variable' refers to the same *free variable* within a given scope).

Figure 16.8   Programs as black-boxes.

Obviously, this is not the case in imperative programs. For example, different *x*s in the following program fragment mean different values:

```
begin
var
        x : integer;
        ⋮
        x := 4;
        ⋮
        x := 5;
        ⋮
        x := x + 1;
        ⋮
end
```

For example, consider the truth of *x* being an even number, which is true in one place and is, or could be, false elsewhere.

A characteristic of a variable, or for that matter of an expression, having the same meaning everywhere within the given context of mathematical text is called *referential transparency*. As shown in the above example, this is not so in imperative programs. Referential transparency is a property crucial in mathematical reasoning outlined in previous chapters. As evident from the *refinement calculus* discussed in Section 9.7, lack of referential transparency complicates reasoning about imperative programs considerably.

Functional programming languages adhere to referential transparency rigourously and, as a result, inherit the kind of mathematical reasoning discussed in Chapter 10 on mathematical induction and in Section 19.3 on *equational reasoning*, as well as in Chapters 4, 5 and 9 when dealing with proofs in logic.

Thanks to adherence to referential transparency, there is no notion of *assignment* in functional languages. Once defined, a variable or expression has the same meaning everywhere within the context of a given program. The lack of an assignment command in functional languages is often seen as a feature that distinguishes functional languages from imperative languages.

3. The point made above on assignment in imperative languages has a wider relevance. This lies not merely in the linguistics, but in the reliance of imperative programs on *side-effects* on the state of the underlying machine as a way of computing. This requires the programmer to define fully the *control structure* of an imperative program, that is, the order in which various commands are to be executed. In situations where the programmer's prime concern is the exploration of different solutions to a given problem, this could be a distraction as well as a burden.

Being in essence scripts of mathematical text as we write them on paper, functional programs remove this burden completely. A programmer working in the functional paradigm can instead concentrate on how to decompose a problem, how to put the solutions together, how to justify the correctness of the program, and so on. A functional program is able to sort out the order of function evaluation by itself.

4. Problem decomposition is a strategy common to all paradigms of programming. The development of a program of reasonable size as a monolithic entity is difficult and error-prone, and invariably results in programs which are incomprehensible even soon after development and in programs whose behaviour is difficult to predict. Programming as a discipline has learned from past lessons and has evolved through such approaches as structured programming to more mature ideas of *modularization*, enabling and encouraging programmers to think of large programs in terms of more manageable small programs. Modularization has also given rise to increased productivity and such long-term benefits as software libraries and, hence, software reuse.

   Having taken modularization on board, we have to choose a scheme for modularizing programs. Here, functional programming proposes the attractive proposition of using *function composition*, discussed in Section 16.4, as a basis for modularization, whereby complex functions can be broken into simpler functions, which are put together later by function composition. Functional programming also provides for another way to build complex functions from simpler functions elegantly. This is based on the concept of a *higher-order function* – a function which takes other functions as arguments. Basically, this allows the definition of new functions capable of performing specialized tasks on complex data structures using, on one hand, general abstract higher-order functions and, on the other hand, functions on basic data types.

   A functional program is thus a collection of functions, where the *main function*, in other words, the *main program*, is built from other functions using such constructors as function composition and higher-order functions. What is noteworthy is not just their capability to build more complex functions, but their mathematical underpinnings, enabling mathematical reasoning about the correctness of complex functions.

5. The need for *higher-order functions*, which take other functions as arguments, introduces a desirable uniformity to functional languages. As a result, functional languages make no distinction between *data* and *functions*. This means that all functions, in other words, programs, can be manipulated and reasoned about in the same manner as data, and vice versa.

Despite the above justifications, treatment of programs as mathematical functions requires some caution. First, no programming language guarantees that programs written in it always terminate. This is because it is easy to end up, unintentionally, in programs which could enter endless loops. Such potentially non-terminating programs too have their mathematical counterparts under the guise of *partial functions*. Therefore, programmers need to be aware of the possibility of partial functions in functional programs and of the possible consequences.

In comparing programs and functions above, item 1 was careful to qualify the kind of program so compared to deterministic ones. Some examples of non-deterministic programs are those corresponding to 'function lookalikes' mentioned in Section 16.3.

Non-determinism arises quite often in program development. First, the design of a system recognizes that the environment is independent and is outside its control and, therefore, that the system must be prepared to cope with all possible environmental actions. Secondly, even in cases where environmental behaviour is eventually made deterministic, the relevant information may be lacking at early stages of design. Non-determinism is also a means of leaving greater freedom to the implementer and preventing premature commitments to particular design choices at the early stages of development. The above are some of the reasons justifying non-deterministic programs. Since mathematically non-deterministic programs are relations, strictly speaking, they cannot be expressed in functional languages.

16.6.2   Basic concepts

Like all programming languages, functional languages provide the following:

1. Some *basic data types* such as numbers, characters and Boolean values and ways to manipulate them with operators such as $=, \neq, +, -, <, \leqslant$ and so on in the case of numbers, $=, \neq, <, \leqslant$, and so on in the case of characters, and $=, \neq, <, \leqslant, \neg, \wedge, \vee$, and so on in the case of Boolean values.

2. More complex *derived data types* such as pairs, functions and lists and ways to manipulate them.

3. The capability for defining other types of values by the programmer.

The expressions are sequences of symbols, representing constants (values), variables, functions and operators. Apart from being syntactically correct, expressions must conform with permissible types. The type of an expression is deducible from its constituents. Being functions themselves, operators on values such as numbers too have types. Such types are given in the style

$$+ \quad :: \quad num \rightarrow num \rightarrow num$$

Note that *num* denotes the type for an implementation of numbers, and the operator $+$ has been introduced in the form of a *curried function*, explained below.

A function is defined in the form of a set of equations, which may involve a case analysis using conditions. Defining functions can be enhanced by using local definitions. This is illustrated in the definition of *sqrt* below with the use of a `where`-clause.

16.6.3   An example – calculation of hypotenuse

Sections 16.6.3–16.6.7 contain an example illustrating some of the basic ideas of functional programming by implementing as a functional program the function defined in Section 16.3 for computing the length of the hypotenuse of a right-angled triangle. This program is based largely on Bird and Wadler (1998) and Abelson *et al.* (1985). Except for the symbols used for basic types, the exposition follows the general syntax of the language given in Bird and Wadler.

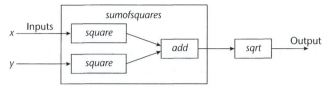

Figure 16.9   Strategy in calculating hypotenuse.

Given the lengths of its other two sides, calculation of the length of the hypotenuse of a right-angled triangle requires first the calculation of the sum of squares of the lengths of its other two sides, and then the square root of the latter. This strategy is depicted in Figure 16.9, where each box represents a function named as labelled.

16.6.4   ## Some subsidiary functions

Function definitions may include type declarations, but this is not essential since the types of functions can often be inferred from the function body. The notation used here for function type does not make the distinctions made in Section 16.2 between different types of function, such as partial, injective and so forth. Below is a function *square* for computing the square of a number. Its body uses the operator $\times$ on numbers, which is a basic type.

$$square \quad :: \quad num \rightarrow num$$
$$square \; x = x \times x$$

A function may have more than one expression defining it, that is, different expressions for different sets of values of its arguments. This can be catered for by attaching a condition against each expression. The function *abs* given below, which computes the absolute value of a number, demonstrates the use of two alternative definitions, one for negative values of its argument x and the other for its non-negative values.

$$abs \quad :: num \rightarrow num$$
$$abs \; x = -x, \qquad \texttt{if} \;\; x < 0$$
$$\quad\;\; = x, \qquad\quad \texttt{otherwise}$$

The function *square* is a unary function, but there can be functions of higher arities. For the sake of generality, however, such functions are often written as *curried functions*. The function *add* given below is not different from +, except that it can take arguments at different times.

$$add \qquad :: \; num \rightarrow num \rightarrow num$$
$$add \; x \; y = x + y$$

The function *add* takes each of its arguments one at a time in the order indicated by arrows; *add* also allows its partial application to arguments. For an $x \in num$, *add x* denotes a function from the function space

$$num \rightarrow num$$

For example, *add* 3 is the function which adds 3 to its argument. For a further $y \in num$, the function *add* may be applied fully to both its arguments as in *add x y*, in which case *add* returns the final result, which is $x + y$.

Functions can make use of other simpler functions. In this respect, the function *sumofsquares*, which computes the sum of squares of its two arguments, is an example:

> *sumofsquares*   :: *num* → *num* → *num*
> *sumofsquares x y* = *add* (*square x*) (*square y*)

16.6.5   Square root function

There is no readily available formula for calculating the square root of a number. A definition of the form

> *sqrt*   :: *num* → *num*
> *sqrt x* = *y*
>   where $y \geqslant 0$
> $x =$ *square y*

is not a solution, but in effect an alternative to the specification written in the more familiar style

> $sqrt(x) = y \Leftrightarrow square(y) = x$

Furthermore, there is no exact solution for *sqrt* since there are numbers such as 2, the square roots of which are irrational numbers. Therefore, we cannot implement *sqrt* accurately so that it satisfies its specification exactly for all values of its argument. However, it is possible to obtain an approximate solution by successive approximation, that is, by first guessing an initial approximation for *y* and then iteratively improving current approximation until a desired accuracy is reached.

A well known approach to solving an equation for its roots is *Newton's method* of successive approximation. Given an equation of the form

> $f(y) = 0$

and that y_i is an approximation to one of its roots, according to Newton's method,

$$y_{i+1} = y_i - \frac{f(y_i)}{f'(y_i)}$$

where $f'(y)$ is the differential of $f(y)$, is considered a better approximation. In the given case, since we are looking for a *y* such that $y^2 = x$, the equation $f(y) = 0$ takes the form

> $y^2 - x = 0$

It follows from the above that $f'(y) = 2y$, since differentiation of f is with respect to *y* only. Therefore

$$y_{i+1} = y_i - \frac{y_i^2 - x}{2y_i}$$

$$= \frac{y_i \times 2y_i - y_i^2 + x}{2y_i}$$

$$= \frac{y_i^2 + x}{2y_i}$$

$$= \frac{y_i + \dfrac{x}{y_i}}{2}$$

Given that y_i is the ith approximation to $sqrt(x)$, its $(i+1)$th approximation may be determined as

$$y_{i+1} = \frac{y_i + \dfrac{x}{y_i}}{2}$$

The above can be 'coded' as the function

$$\textit{improve} \quad :: \quad \textit{num} \to \textit{num} \to \textit{num}$$
$$\textit{improve } x\ y = (y + x/y)/2 \qquad \text{if } y > 0$$

Let us examine how the above definition improves each approximation in successive calls, first in the case of evaluation of square root of the irrational number 2:

(first approximation $y_1 = 1$;
subsequent approximations: y_2, y_3, etc.)

improve 2	1	$= (1 + 2/1)/2$	$= 1.5$	(y_2)
improve 2	1.5	$= (1.5 + 2/1.5)/2$	$= 1.416667$	(y_3)
improve 2	1.416667	$= (1.416667 + 2/1.416667)/2$	$= 1.414216$	(y_4)
improve 2	1.414216	$= (1.414216 + 2/1.414216)/2$	$= 1.414214$	(y_5)

Then, in the case of 9 having an exact solution, which is 3:

(first approximation $y_1 = 2$;
subsequent approximations: y_2, y_3, etc.)

improve 9	2	$= (2 + 9/2)/2$	$= 3.25$	(y_2)
improve 9	3.25	$= (3.25 + 9/3.25)/2$	$= 3.009615$	(y_3)
improve 9	3.009615	$= (3.009615 + 9/3.009615)/2$	$= 3.000015$	(y_4)

This illustrates the effectiveness of Newton's method. The intention is that the process of successive approximation terminates once an acceptable accuracy is reached. Let ε denote the acceptable tolerance on deviation of the approximate solution from the specification. In other words, we are relaxing the specification of *sqrt* as

$$sqrt(x) = y \Rightarrow abs(square(y) - x) \leqslant \varepsilon$$

Satisfaction of the above condition can be checked using a function *satis* in the programming language

$$\textit{satis} \quad :: \quad \textit{num} \to \textit{num} \to \textit{bool}$$
$$\textit{satis } x\ y = abs(y^2 - x) < eps$$

where $eps :: num$. For example, eps could have a value such as $eps = 0.001$.

As mentioned under item 5 in Section 16.6.1, functions are not different from other data types and can play the role of data to other higher-order functions. The function *until*, which keeps applying some function f to x, unless the predicate p is satisfied by x, is such a higher-order function:

$$until \qquad :: (\alpha \to bool) \to (\alpha \to \alpha) \to \alpha \to \alpha$$
$$until\ p\ f\ x = x, \qquad\qquad\qquad \texttt{if}\ p\ x$$
$$\qquad\quad = until\ p\ f\ (f\ x), \qquad \texttt{otherwise}$$

The function *until* is significant in two other respects. First, it is a *polymorphic function* – a function parametrized with respect to an arbitrary type α. Instantiation of every occurrence of α consistently with a specific type such as *num* or *Char* (*Char* being the set of ASCII characters) yields a typed version of *until*, appropriate to the instantiating type. For example, if the actual arguments supplied for the formal arguments p, f and x in *until* are of the following types:

$$p :: num \to bool$$
$$f :: num \to num$$
$$x :: num$$

then the function *until* will be of the type

$$until :: (num \to bool) \to (num \to num) \to num \to num$$

Note that it is not necessary to instantiate α with a specific type every time when *until* is used, because, as mentioned earlier, type information can be inferred from the types of the actual arguments. Polymorphic functions are therefore a general way of defining functions so that they can be used across several types, thus contributing to reusability of functions.

Secondly, *until* is a *recursive function*, as defined informally in Section 10.3.2. Note that recursion could give rise to the problem of non-termination mentioned earlier and, therefore, when using the function *until* it is necessary to make sure that the actual arguments used for p and x are such that the predicate $p\ x$ eventually becomes true as, otherwise, recursion will never end.

Finally, we define the *sqrt* as

$$sqrt\ x = until\ (satis\ x)\ (improve\ x)\ x$$

or, alternatively, as *sqrt'*

$$sqrt' \quad :: num \to num$$
$$sqrt'\ x = until\ satis\ improve\ x$$
$$\qquad\quad \texttt{where}$$
$$\qquad\qquad\qquad satis\ y = abs(y^2 - x) < eps$$
$$\qquad\qquad\qquad improve\ y = (y + x/y)/2$$

where, through the use of the clause `where`, functions *satis* and *improve* have been made definitions which are local to the function *sqrt'*. Note, for example, that the function

$$satis\ y = abs(y^2 - x) < eps$$

appearing as a local definition of *sqrt'*, has only one argument, namely, y. The variable x occurring free there refers to the formal argument x of *sqrt'*.

16.6.6   Calculation of the hypotenuse

The functions developed in Sections 16.6.4–16.6.5 can be used now to define the function *hypotenuse* for calculating the hypotenuse of a right-angled triangle using the lengths of its other two sides. This is defined below using function composition, where the dot plays the role of the function composition operator '∘' introduced in Section 16.4.

> *hypotenuse*   :: *num* → *num* → *num*
> *hypotenuse a b* = (*sqrt* . *sumofsquares a*) *b*

16.6.7   Reduction

This is an appropriate moment to show how a functional program evaluates expressions. This is an issue related to efficiency of programs and to implementation of functional languages and, therefore, as mentioned earlier, is not of any relevance from the problem-solving point of view. However, the topic is of both practical and theoretical interest.

The process of *evaluation* of the value of an expression in functional programming is known as *reduction*. The term 'reduction' is more appropriate in one important respect, because it conveys straight away the idea that the so-called *values* in programs are in fact not values themselves, but their representations. Thus, values themselves are *expressions*, albeit the simplest ones, or the most convenient ones, which the language designers have chosen. In this sense, evaluation is the reduction of an expression to its simplest form, by successively replacing its various subterms by other equivalent expressions, given either in function definitions or as part of definition of the language. In practical terms, therefore, reduction is the replacement of a subterm of an expression by an equivalent expression. An expression is said to be in *canonical* or *normal* form if it cannot be further reduced. An example of canonical form is the representation of a number such as 5 or a pair of values of some primitive data types.

In terms of the number of options, the process of reduction of a given expression is not unique. This is illustrated in the following example, reducing the expression *square* (2 + 3).

Reduction of innermost expression first	**Reduction of outermost expression first**
square (2 + 3)	*square* (2 + 3)
= *square*(5)	= (2 + 3) × (2 + 3)
= 5 × 5	= 5 × (2 + 3)
= 25	= 5 × 5
= 25	= 25

Although in this particular case the difference in complexity of the two computations is practically insignificant, the example points to both opportunities and dangers in the way that reduction is conducted. The advantage that the innermost reduction above has over outermost reduction can be reversed, and amplified, by a different example, based on the following functions:

$$first\,(x, y) = x$$
$$infinity \quad = 1 + infinity$$

Now consider the reduction of *first* (5, *infinity*).

Reduction of innermost expression first	**Reduction of outermost expression first**
first(5, infinity)	first(5, infinity)
= first(5, 1 + infinity)	= 5
= first(5, 1 + 1 + infinity)	
= first(5, 1 + 1 + 1 + infinity)	
⋮	

This example illustrates that, although a more immediate solution could be within reach, the process of innermost reduction can unnecessarily end up in an infinite loop. Thus, the two reduction strategies can have profound differences in terms of the final outcome and each can have both advantages and disadvantages over the other. A clear advantage offered by the outermost reduction is that the evaluation always successfully terminates if the expression is reducible to its canonical form.

Terminology

* The strategy based on outermost reduction is commonly known as *lazy evaluation* since no term (expression) is reduced unless it is absolutely essential. Another term for the same idea is *normal order evaluation* because of its ability to reduce a term to its normal form if there is one.

* The strategy based on innermost reduction is known as *eager evaluation* because of the eagerness of the evaluation process to press ahead with every required computation that is possible at a given time.

(**Example 16.8**)

Let us see how the function *hypotenuse* is evaluated when its two arguments happen to be 3 and 4. In the order of function composition, evaluation begins with *sumofsquares*.

$$hypotenuse\ 3\ 4$$
$$= sqrt\ (sumofsquares\ 3\ 4)$$
$$= sqrt\ (add\ (square\ 3)\ (square\ 4))$$
$$= sqrt\ (add\ (3 \times 3)\ (square\ 4))$$
$$= sqrt\ (add\ (3 \times 3)\ (4 \times 4))$$
$$= sqrt\ (add\ 9\ (4 \times 4))$$
$$= sqrt\ (9 + 16)$$
$$= sqrt\ 25$$

The result obtained by evaluating *sumofsquares* is then passed to *sqrt*, which is immediately reduced to an expression involving *until*. The first recursive call of *until* progresses as follows:

$sqrt$ 25 = $until$ ($satis$ 25) ($improve$ 25) 25

$$= \begin{cases} 25, & \text{if } (satis\ 25)\ 25 \\ until\ (satis\ 25)\ (improve\ 25)\ ((improve\ 25)\ 25), & \texttt{otherwise} \end{cases}$$

$$= \begin{cases} 25, & \text{if } abs(25^2 - 25) < 0.001 \\ until\ (satis\ 25)\ (improve\ 25)\ ((improve\ 25)\ 25), & \texttt{otherwise} \end{cases}$$

$$= \begin{cases} 25, & \text{if } 600 < 0.001 \\ until\ (satis\ 25)\ (improve\ 25)\ ((improve\ 25)\ 25), & \texttt{otherwise} \end{cases}$$

Since its termination condition is not satisfied, *until* then enters is second recursive call.

$= until$ ($satis$ 25) ($improve$ 25) (($improve$ 25) 25)
$= until$ ($satis$ 25) ($improve$ 25) ((25 + 25/25)/2)
$= until$ ($satis$ 25) ($improve$ 25) 13

$$= \begin{cases} 13, & \text{if } (satis\ 25)\ 13 \\ until\ (satis\ 25)\ (improve\ 25)\ ((improve\ 25)\ 13), & \texttt{otherwise} \end{cases}$$

$$= \begin{cases} 13, & \text{if } abs(13^2 - 25) < 0.001 \\ until\ (satis\ 25)\ (improve\ 25)\ ((improve\ 25)\ 13), & \texttt{otherwise} \end{cases}$$

$$= \begin{cases} 13, & \text{if } 144 < 0.001 \\ until\ (satis\ 25)\ (improve\ 25)\ ((improve\ 25)\ 13), & \texttt{otherwise} \end{cases}$$

Since its termination condition is still not satisfied, *until* then enters is third recursive call.

$= until$ ($satis$ 25) ($improve$ 25) (($improve$ 25) 13)
$= until$ ($satis$ 25) ($improve$ 25) ((13 + 25/13)/2)
$= until$ ($satis$ 25) ($improve$ 25) 7.4615

$$= \begin{cases} 7.4615, & \text{if } (satis\ 25)\ 7.4615 \\ until\ (satis\ 25)\ (improve\ 25)\ ((improve\ 25)\ 7.4615), & \texttt{otherwise} \end{cases}$$

$$= \begin{cases} 7.4615, & \text{if } abs(7.4615^2 - 25) \\ & \quad < 0.001 \\ until\ (satis\ 25)\ (improve\ 25)\ ((improve\ 25)\ 7.4615), & \texttt{otherwise} \end{cases}$$

$$= \begin{cases} 7.4615, & \text{if } 30.6746 < 0.001 \\ until\ (satis\ 25)\ (improve\ 25)\ ((improve\ 25)\ 7.4615), & \texttt{otherwise} \end{cases}$$

Analogously, as indicated below, as long as its termination condition is not satisfied *until* carries on with further recursive calls.

$= until$ ($satis$ 25) ($improve$ 25) (($improve$ 25) 7.4615)
$= until$ ($satis$ 25) ($improve$ 25) ((7.4615 + 25/7.4615)/2)
$= until$ ($satis$ 25) ($improve$ 25) 5.4060

$$\vdots$$

(after three more recursive calls)

$$\vdots$$

$= 5.000023178254$

Exercise 16.8 ✳

By tracing its first three steps, show how the function *sqrt* works when its argument has the value 3.

Exercise 16.9 ✳✳

The function *until* defined in Section 16.6.5 can be used for other purposes. Define the predicates and functions necessary for using it for the following purposes.

1. Locating the next multiple of 5 greater than a given number.
2. Locating the first prime number after a given number.

Show how your solution works for one of the above when the argument to *until* has the value 8.

Exercise 16.10 ✳✳✳

Generalize the solution developed in Section 16.6.5 so that it can compute the roots of any numerical function *f*.

Chapter 17

Numbers

Topic: Mathematical data types

'Can you do addition?' the White Queen asked.
'What's one and one and one and one and one and one and one and one and one and one?'
'I don't know,' said Alice. 'I lost count.'

Lewis Carroll
English logician, mathematician and novelist (1832–98)
(in *Through the Looking Glass*)

Objectives

On completion of this chapter you should be able to:

- Define sets of numbers forming a contiguous stretch.

- Describe natural numbers and integers.

- Prove basic properties of congruence.

- Describe the relationship between different systems of numbers.

- Represent numbers in binary notation and interpret them in decimal representation.

- Assess the range and accuracy of implementation of numbers in computers.

Despite being a highly abstract concept, numbers are indispensable to human thought and activities and we learn about them early in our life. Starting with *natural numbers* ($\mathbb{N}$) in preschool learning, we come in contact with other kinds of numbers in later stages of learning, namely, *integers* ($\mathbb{Z}$), *rational numbers* ($\mathbb{Q}$), *real numbers* ($\mathbb{R}$) and *complex numbers* ($\mathbb{C}$). These number systems enable the solution of different kinds of problems in science and engineering, often with no other conceivable alternative. Despite this vital role, history has witnessed various prejudices against the acceptance of some of these number systems.

17.1 Natural numbers

Motivation for our study of natural numbers is twofold. First, natural numbers are of great interest in their own right. In addition to being the most fundamental and basic system of counting, natural numbers lie at the heart of mathematics. Number theory, where natural numbers occupy a highly prominent place, has even been dubbed the '*Queen of Mathematics*'. Secondly, by being the most fundamental of all data types, they provide one of the most fascinating insights into the construction of other data types frequently encountered in computer science. Not surprisingly, theoretical studies of abstract data types often begin with a study of natural numbers.

17.1.1   Some notations

The set of natural numbers may be constructed mathematically using a distinguished element called *zero*, denoted commonly by the Hindu–Arabic *numeral '0'*, and a function *succ* – the *successor function*. Informally, the successor function maps every natural number to its successor, and may be shown as follows:

$$succ \ = \ \{0 \mapsto 1, \ 1 \mapsto 2, \ 2 \mapsto 3, \ 3 \mapsto 4, \ 4 \mapsto 5, \ldots\}$$

A complementary function is the *predecessor function*, denoted by *pred*. Being the inverse of *succ*, *pred* maps every natural number except *zero* to its predecessor. It may be shown as follows:

$$pred \ = \ \{1 \mapsto 0, \ 2 \mapsto 1, \ 3 \mapsto 2, \ 4 \mapsto 3, \ 5 \mapsto 4, \ldots\}$$

Subsets of natural numbers forming a contiguous segment are commonly shown using dots for intermediate numbers. Thus, following the $\mathbb{Z}$ notation, the set of natural numbers from 2 to 6 may be denoted as:

$$2..6 \ = \ \{2, 3, 4, 5, 6\}$$

Similarly

$$5.. = \{5, 6, 7, \ldots\}$$
$$.. \, 4 = \{0, 1, 2, 3, 4\}$$

The above notation can be formally defined as:

$$\_ \, .. \, \_ \; : \quad \mathbb{N} \to \mathbb{P} \, \mathbb{N}$$
$$.. \, \_ \; : \quad \mathbb{N} \to \mathbb{P} \, \mathbb{N}$$
$$\_ \, .. \, \_ \; : \quad \mathbb{N} \times \mathbb{N} \to \mathbb{P} \, \mathbb{N}$$

with the following meanings:

$$\forall \, m, n : \mathbb{N} \bullet$$
$$m, .. = \{i : \mathbb{N} \mid i \geqslant m\}$$
$$.. \, , n = \{i : \mathbb{N} \mid i \leqslant n\}$$
$$m, .. \, , n = \{i : \mathbb{N} \mid m \leqslant i \leqslant n\}$$

17.1.2   Definition of natural numbers

Mathematical understanding of natural numbers is founded on the notion of function. This explains why we deferred our study of natural numbers until now.

In the previous subsection we indicated that the natural numbers can be constructed mathematically from a unique natural number *zero* and using the successor function *succ*. Let us examine here the nature of this function.

Let us begin our study by questioning first why *succ* has to be a function in the first place. Figures 17.1 and 17.2 illustrate this point by indicating possible 'circularities' (for example, between *eerht* and *ruof* in Figure 17.1) and 'competitors' for *zero* in $\mathbb{N}$ (for example, at *owt* in Figure 17.2), if it were not a function.

Succ being just a function is not sufficient either. If it were, it could, as shown in Figure 17.3, have a loop around *zero*, thus making *zero* a 'black hole', preventing the rest of the natural numbers ever being reached. Thus, it must be the case that *zero* $\notin$ ran *succ*.

Furthermore, if *succ* is a mere function, it could still range past some natural numbers, leaving 'gaps' in $\mathbb{N}$, as between *eno* and *owt* in Figure 17.4.

The scenarios shown in Figures 17.1, 17.2 and 17.4 may be excluded by qualifying *succ* to be an injective function. Could, then, the set of natural numbers $\mathbb{N}$ be defined in such a way that it contains *zero* and the elements reachable by a certain injective function *succ* such that the following holds? That is,

$$\{zero\} \cup \text{ran } succ \subseteq \mathbb{N}$$

However, this is still not satisfactory. Figure 17.5 illustrates an injective function satisfying all the aforementioned and yet containing some 'islands of junk' in $\mathbb{N}$. The only way to exclude such junk in $\mathbb{N}$ is to insist that *succ* is an injective function defined only on those elements which are reachable from *zero*.

In addition, however, we must make sure of the infinite nature of $\mathbb{N}$ and, in particular, that the set of numbers we are aiming at consists of the whole of $\mathbb{N}$, as otherwise we could easily end up picking up one of its infinite subsets. Remember, there are many other infinite subsets of $\mathbb{N}$, such as the set of even numbers. Our aim must therefore be to pick the largest possible subset of $\mathbb{N}$, which, by being the

Figure 17.1 One reason why *succ* is a function.

Figure 17.2 Another reason why *succ* is a function.

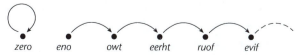

Figure 17.3 Why *zero* should not be reachable by *succ*.

Figure 17.4   Why *succ* is an injective function.

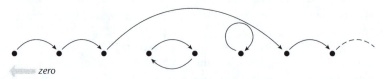

Figure 17.5   Why every element in $\mathbb{N}$ must be reachable from *zero*.

'largest' subset, must be $\mathbb{N}$ itself. Thus, in defining $\mathbb{N}$, our argument takes the following form.

Let S be a subset of $\mathbb{N}$ with two important characteristics:

1. *Zero* is an element of S, that is,

    $zero \in S$

2. For every element in S, its successor is also in S, that is,

    $\forall n \bullet n \in S \Rightarrow succ\ n \in S$

Could S be the $\mathbb{N}$ we require? Obviously, the answer is affirmative. Thanks to the manner of definition of $\mathbb{N}$, our reasoning has an inductive flavour. By virtue of *zero* being in S, *succ* 0 (the number denoted by the numeral 1) must be in S, and by virtue of that, the number denoted by the numeral 2 must be in S, and so forth. S must then be identical to $\mathbb{N}$; neither will it have 'missed' any natural numbers nor will it have retained any unnecessary 'junk'.

A conclusion of our exploration into the realms of natural numbers is that the set of natural numbers has to be characterized by the triple (*zero*, $\mathbb{N}$, *succ*) where $\mathbb{N}$ itself plays the role of a 'carrier' of natural numbers. The point is that it is meaningless to talk about $\mathbb{N}$ without its other partners *zero* and *succ*. As seen above, all three components in the above triple are subjected to further constraints. The following definition summarizes our discussion

(**Definition**)   Natural numbers
___

A basic mathematical abstraction of the set of *natural numbers* is the triple

$$(zero,\ \mathbb{N},\ succ) \tag{17.1}$$

where

$$zero \in \mathbb{N} \tag{17.2}$$
$$succ \in \mathbb{N} \rightarrowtail \mathbb{N} \tag{17.3}$$

Furthermore,

1. *zero* is not reachable by *succ*, that is,

   $$zero \notin \text{ran } succ \tag{17.4}$$

2. *zero* and other elements reachable by *succ* are in $\mathbb{N}$, that is,

   $$\{zero\} \cup \text{ran } succ \subseteq \mathbb{N} \tag{17.5}$$

3. Every subset S of $\mathbb{N}$ consisting of *zero* and the successors of all elements of S reachable by *succ* is exactly $\mathbb{N}$. That is,

   $$\forall S : \mathbb{PN} \bullet (zero \in S \wedge \forall n \bullet n \in S \Rightarrow succ\ n \in S) \Rightarrow S = \mathbb{N} \tag{17.6}$$

17.1.3   ## Numerals

The above Definition helps us to identify different numbers in the following manner:

zero, succ(zero), succ(succ(zero)), succ(succ(succ(zero))),
  succ(succ(succ(succ(zero)))), . . .

and to understand how they relate to each other.

Numbers are abstract objects and, in the process of counting, we are often able to relate them to the world around us. However, since there are infinitely many of them, numbers as conceived above do not lend themselves easily as a basis of calculation or as an object of mathematical study. This is because the successor function itself does not provide us with a convenient way to represent numbers. Obviously, the above form of writing numbers can be simplified, for example, by letting n' as an abbreviation for $succ(n)$ – the successor of n, resulting in

zero, zero', zero'', zero''', zero'''', . . .

However, this does not make a great deal of difference. What is required is a scheme with a richer set of symbols to denote a few numbers and the ability to generate expressions denoting the rest in a systematic manner. The numbers can then be written down as a sequence of symbols and be interpreted according to a *positional principle*, whereby the individual symbols are assigned numerical weights (in multiples of a 'base') depending on their position in the sequence. This approach is discussed further in Section 17.6.1 when dealing with representation of numbers in computers.

The lack of a practical way to write numbers using *succ* is overcome by *numerals*. Different civilizations have invented different systems of numerals. Ancient civilizations such as Babylonians and Egyptians had their own systems of numerals. Roman numerals and Chinese numerals are still in use to varying degrees. The most prevalent system of numerals currently is, of course, Hindu-Arabic numerals, based on the familiar symbols: 0, 1, 2, . . ., 9.

17.1.4   Operations on natural numbers

Knowing natural numbers as described above is not enough. Knowing what they are is inextricably linked with what we can do with them. Therefore, an understanding of their use through such operations as addition and multiplication is just as important.

Since we have been dealing with numbers as if we know nothing about them *a priori*, we need to deal with these operations in the same manner. However, as with the properties of the function *succ*, we are free to state a minimal amount of our intuitive expectations as *axioms*. For example, writing 0 for *zero* and letting n' denote *succ*(n), with the two assertions

$$m + 0 = m \qquad\qquad (17.7)$$
$$m + n' = (m + n)' \qquad\qquad (17.8)$$

it is possible to characterize adequately the notion of *addition*. However, there are many other properties which do not follow immediately from the above, and yet we know them to be true of $+$. These include

$$0 + m = m \qquad\qquad (17.9)$$
$$m + n = n + m \qquad\qquad (17.10)$$
$$l + (m + n) = (l + m) + n \qquad\qquad (17.11)$$

The problem is, therefore, how to derive them.

At the core of our understanding of natural numbers are the *axioms* (17.2)–(17.6). Properties such as (17.7) and (17.8) are additional axioms specific to operations, in this case, to $+$. The axioms (17.2)–(17.6) are of special significance in deriving the third category of properties such as (17.9) and (17.10), because they, in particular, (17.2) and (17.6), serve as the basis of mathematical induction – the kind of reasoning we came across in Chapter 10 in relation to infinite sets with some ordering. Mathematical induction thus enables reasoning about natural numbers themselves.

Example 17.1
_____

Proof of property (17.9), that is,

$$P(m) \stackrel{def}{\Leftrightarrow} 0 + m = m$$

Base case

Proof of $P(0)$:

$$0 + 0 = 0 \qquad P(m) \text{ for } m = 0$$
$$\Leftrightarrow 0 = 0 \qquad \text{axiom (17.7)}$$
$$\Leftrightarrow \textbf{\textit{true}} \qquad \text{identity}$$

Inductive case

Induction hypothesis: Assume $P(k)$, that is,

$$0 + k = k$$

Inductive proof: Prove P(k′), that is,

$$0 + k' = k'$$

k′ being the successor of k. Proof of the above:

1. $0 + k = k$ assumption (induction hypothesis)
2. $(0 + k)' = k'$ succ being a function, axiom (17.3)
3. $0 + k' = k'$ from 1 and 2, axiom (17.8)

Hence, the proof of (17.9)

Exercise 17.1 ✳✳✳

Prove the property (17.10) on commutativity of +, that is,

$$m + n = n + m$$

17.2 Integers

If, at our disposal, is only the set of natural numbers, with addition as one of its operations, a question such as 'What could be the number which gives 3 upon addition of 5?' is totally outside its confines. This is a limitation of natural numbers and has given rise to an extended set of numbers called *integers*. The set of integers can be shown in the familiar notation as

$$\mathbb{Z} = \{\ldots, -3, -2, -1, 0, 1, 2, 3, 4, \ldots\}$$

Integers differ from natural numbers in that they provide us with a way to count items in two directions, namely, *positive* and *negative* directions defined with respect to a *datum* designated by *zero* and, with that, a way to define the difference between any two numbers irrespective of their magnitudes.

17.2.1 Integers as an algebra

Integers can be defined as an *algebra* in an *axiomatic* manner. An *algebra* is basically one or more non-empty sets of values and a finite collection of operations on these sets. We came across the notion of *axiom* in relation to *theories* in Section 1.5 of Chapter 1. Axioms are statements which we take for granted. They express some of the fundamental properties of the operations. Obviously, there are various consequences of axioms concerning other (unstated) properties of the operations; they form the *theorems* of the theory concerned. A more complete discussion on how to define algebras in this manner may be found in Chapter 19 in relation to Boolean algebra.

Integers may be treated as an algebra by characterizing axiomatically the fundamental operations on integers. Two ideal candidates, in this respect, are + denoting addition and × denoting multiplication.

In what follows, wherever they are not quantified, a, b and c below are arbitrary integers; 1 and 0 are two distinguished elements in $\mathbb{Z}$.

Terminology

Given that $\odot$ is a binary operator like $+$ and $\times$ introduced above, an element i is said to be a *right identity element* for $\odot$ if it results in

$$x \odot i = x$$

for every element x in the set concerned.

The remainder of this subsection introduces the axioms necessary for defining integers as an algebra.

Closure

As mentioned above, $+$ and $\times$ are operations *on* $\mathbb{Z}$, that is, their results are also integers. In other words, $\mathbb{Z}$ is *closed* under addition and multiplication.

$$\forall a, b \bullet a, b \in \mathbb{Z} \Rightarrow a + b \in \mathbb{Z} \wedge a \times b \in \mathbb{Z} \qquad \textbf{(17.12)}$$

Identity elements

$$a \times 1 = a \qquad \textbf{(17.13)}$$
$$a + 0 = a \qquad \textbf{(17.14)}$$

According to these two properties and the terminology introduced earlier, 0 plays the role of *right identity element* for $+$ and 1 for $\times$.

We are already familiar with properties such as commutativity, and so on, from our study of logic and sets. Those related to logic may be found in Section 4.2 and those on sets in Section 12.3. Below is an analogous list of properties relevant to integers.

Commutativity

$$a \times b = b \times a \qquad \textbf{(17.15)}$$
$$a + b = b + a \qquad \textbf{(17.16)}$$

Associativity

$$a \times (b \times c) = (a \times b) \times c \qquad \textbf{(17.17)}$$
$$a + (b + c) = (a + b) + c \qquad \textbf{(17.18)}$$

Distributivity

$$a \times (b + c) = (a \times b) + (a \times c) \qquad \textbf{(17.19)}$$

Thus, multiplication distributes over addition, but not vice versa.

Additive inverse

$$\forall a \in \mathbb{Z} \bullet \exists \bar{a} \in \mathbb{Z} \bullet a + \bar{a} = 0 \qquad\qquad (17.20)$$

The common notation for $\bar{a}$ is $-a$ and is called the *additive inverse* of a. This allows the definition of subtraction as

$$a - b \stackrel{def}{=} a + (-b) \qquad\qquad (17.21)$$

This property basically introduces negative numbers as well as the notion of *subtraction*, thus making integers different from natural numbers.

Cancellation

$$\forall a, b, c \in \mathbb{Z} \bullet a \times c = b \times c \wedge c \neq 0 \Rightarrow a = b \qquad\qquad (17.22)$$

That is, a non-zero multiplier in an equality may be cancelled out.

As usual with axiomatic definitions, in formulating the axioms, we have relied on our intuitive understanding and everyday experience only. As mentioned above, axioms are a minimal set of facts that we are prepared to admit as fundamental properties. All other observations concerning various properties have to be derived as logical consequences of the axioms. This is illustrated below with examples and exercises.

Example 17.2

Proof of $(-1) \times a = -a$:

1.	$1 + \bar{1} = 0$	additive inverse of 1, axiom (17.20)
2.	$a \times (1 + \bar{1}) = a \times 0$	from 1, multiplication by a
3.	$a \times 1 + a \times \bar{1} = a \times 0$	from 2, distributivity, axiom (17.19)
4.	$a + a \times \bar{1} = a \times 0$	from 3, identity, axiom (17.13)
5.	$a + \bar{1} \times a = a \times 0$	from 4, commutativity, axiom (17.15)
6.	$a + \bar{1} \times a = 0$	from 5 (see Exercise 17.2)
7.	$\bar{a} + a + \bar{1} \times a = \bar{a} + 0$	from 6, addition of $\bar{a}$
8.	$a + \bar{a} + \bar{1} \times a = \bar{a} + 0$	from 7, commutativity, axiom (17.16)
9.	$0 + \bar{1} \times a = \bar{a} + 0$	from 8, additive inverse, axiom (17.20)
10.	$\bar{1} \times a + 0 = \bar{a} + 0$	from 9, commutativity, axiom (17.16)
11.	$\bar{1} \times a = \bar{a}$	from 10, identity, axiom (17.14) twice
12.	$(-1) \times a = -a$	from 11, definition of $-x$ as $\bar{x}$

Example 17.3

Proof of $-(a \times b) = a \times (-b)$

1.	$a \times b + \overline{a \times b} = 0$	additive inverse; axiom (17.20)
2.	$a \times \bar{b} + a \times b + \overline{a \times b} = a \times \bar{b} + 0$	from 1, addition of $a \times \bar{b}$

3. $a \times (\bar{b} + b) + \overline{a \times b} = a \times \bar{b} + 0$ from 2, distributivity, axiom (17.19)

4. $a \times (b + \bar{b}) + \overline{a \times b} = a \times \bar{b} + 0$ from 3, commutativity, axiom (17.16)

5. $a \times 0 + \overline{a \times b} = a \times \bar{b} + 0$ from 4, additive inverse, axiom (17.20)

6. $0 + \overline{a \times b} = a \times \bar{b} + 0$ from 5 (see Exercise 17.2)

7. $\overline{a \times b} + 0 = a \times \bar{b} + 0$ from 6, commutativity, axiom (17.16)

8. $\overline{a \times b} = a \times \bar{b}$ from 7, identity, axiom (17.14) twice

9. $-(a \times b) = a \times (-b)$ from 8, definition of $-x$ as $\bar{x}$

Exercise 17.2 ✳ ✳

Given that a, b and c are integers, prove the following.

1. $a \times 0 = 0$ (a property already used in Examples 17.2 and 17.3)
2. $-(a + b) = (-a) + (-b)$
3. If $n + a = n + b$ then $a = b$

Exercise 17.3 ✳ ✳

Using appropriate definitions, prove that

$$(a + b)^2 = a^2 + 2ab + b^2$$

17.2.2 Congruence

Let us revisit Exercises 15.6 and 15.10. There we introduced a ternary relation *congruent* such that, given three integers p, q and m, the integer p is said to be *congruent to q modulo m* provided that m divides $(p - q)$ exactly. We expressed the same as

$$congruent\ (p, q)\ mod\ m \overset{def}{\Leftrightarrow} m \mid (p - q)$$

where $m \mid n$ stands for 'm divides n' exactly. Congruency of integers in the above manner is commonly given by the notation

$$p \equiv q\ (mod\ m) \overset{def}{\Leftrightarrow} m \mid (p - q)$$

(Note that often the symbol $\equiv$ is also used for equivalence.) Following the answer to Exercise 15.6, let us restate the properties of congruence modulo m. Congruence modulo m is

1. Reflexive – That is, for every $p \in \mathbb{Z}$

$$p \equiv p\ (mod\ m)$$

2. Symmetrical – That is, for every $p, q \in \mathbb{Z}$

$$p \equiv q\ (mod\ m) \Rightarrow q \equiv p\ (mod\ m)$$

3. Transitive – That is, for every $p, q, r \in \mathbb{Z}$

$$p \equiv q\ (mod\ m) \wedge q \equiv r\ (mod\ m) \Rightarrow p \equiv r\ (mod\ m)$$

Arithmetical operations addition, subtraction and multiplication on integers may be performed on any congruence without affecting it. Thus, if $p \equiv q$ *(mod m)*, then:

$$p + r \equiv q + r \ (mod \ m)$$
$$p - r \equiv q - r \ (mod \ m)$$
$$p \times r \equiv q \times r \ (mod \ m) \tag{17.23}$$

Exercise 17.4 ✳✳

1. Prove the congruences (17.23) hold, provided that $p \equiv q$ *(mod m)*.

2. Demonstrate that the above form of congruence does not hold for division.

Notation

The following is a notation

$a \oplus_m b$
$a \ominus_m b$
$a \otimes_m b$

used, respectively, for addition, subtraction and multiplication of integers modulo a given integer m. For example, $4 \oplus_5 8 = 2$.

17.3 A tour through other number systems

In order to give an overall picture of numbers, we outline below other number systems. Our discussion is not intended to give the reader a working knowledge about the subject, merely an appreciation of the relationship between various number systems.

17.3.1 Rational numbers

Analogous to how integers were brought about by the need for an additive inverse, rational numbers arise from the desirability of having a *multiplicative inverse* $\bar{a}$ for any integer a. As usual, $\bar{a}$ for every integer a other than 0 needs to be defined as

$$a \times \bar{a} = 1$$

In this case, however, we cannot ensure that $\bar{a}$ is always in $\mathbb{Z}$. To demonstrate this, consider, for example, 5 for a, in which case $\bar{a}$ equals $\frac{1}{5}$ and is not an integer.

On the other hand, there is a vital real need for a 'multiplicative inverse' in our ordinary life. Some examples are the necessity of dividing a whole number of things into parts, or stating with accuracy the degree of 'wholeness' of partially completed processes. Typical examples of the latter are partially built things, visible phases of the moon, and so on.

This limitation can be overcome by adopting axioms (17.13)–(17.21) used in defining integers, and then augmenting them with a new axiom.

Multiplicative inverse

$$\forall a \in \mathbb{Q} \bullet a \neq 0 \Rightarrow (\exists \bar{a} \in \mathbb{Q} \bullet a \times \bar{a} = 1) \qquad \textbf{(17.24)}$$

The system of numbers resulting from axioms (17.13)–(17.21) taken in conjunction with the above axiom is known as the *rational numbers*, denoted by $\mathbb{Q}$. Note that an axiom corresponding to (17.22) on cancellation is unnecessary in $\mathbb{Q}$ since cancellation in this sense follows as a consequence of (17.24). In the new number system, except when $b = 0$, the term $a \times \bar{b}$ makes perfect sense, whereas this is not the case, in general, in integers.

The rational numbers are commonly written as *fractions* in the style $\frac{a}{b}$, where both the numerator a and the denominator b are integers. Note that this is just a representation and that any rational number, abstractly speaking, is an ordered pair of integers. It is also a common convention to write the rational number $\frac{a}{1}$ in the style of an integer a.

Representation of rational numbers as fractions using integers enables the definition of *addition* and *multiplication* of rational numbers in terms of their counterparts on integers. Without making the distinction between the operations on the two sets explicit, addition and multiplication of rational numbers can be defined as

$$\frac{a}{b} + \frac{c}{d} = \frac{a \times d + b \times c}{b \times d} \qquad \textbf{(17.25)}$$

$$\frac{a}{b} \times \frac{c}{d} = \frac{a \times c}{b \times d} \qquad \textbf{(17.26)}$$

Note that $+$ and $\times$ on the left-hand side of the above equalities are the operations for addition and multiplication of rational numbers, whereas the same symbols on the right-hand side are the corresponding operations on integers.

It is easy to verify that properties of commutativity, associativity and distributivity (of multiplication over addition) hold for addition and multiplication of rational numbers as defined by (17.25) and (17.26). Similarly, it may be verified that the additive identity in this representation is $\frac{0}{1}$, or simply 0, and the additive inverse (the negative) of $\frac{a}{b}$ is $\frac{a}{b}$, or simply $\frac{-a}{b}$. The multiplicative identity becomes $\frac{1}{1}$, or simply 1, and the multiplicative inverse of any non-zero rational number $\frac{a}{b}$ is $\frac{b}{a}$, written also as $\left(\frac{a}{b}\right)^{-1}$.

17.3.2   Real numbers

The development of mathematics, as well as science, inevitably brought about the need for solving algebraic equations producing numbers other than integers and rational numbers. A well known example belonging to neither category is $\sqrt{2}$, encountered, for example, in calculations of the length of the hypotenuse of an isosceles right-angled triangle. Obviously, there are other examples, such as $\sqrt{3}$, π and e, belonging to the same category.

The fact that $\sqrt{2}$ is not a rational number is a particularly interesting example. Being the 'historically first' irrational number, $\sqrt{2}$ did not win favour even from the great Greek mathematician Pythagoras and, worse still, for its discoverer it appears to have cost his life at Pythagoras's hands. More about this may be found in Singh (1997). The reasoning behind the finding that $\sqrt{2}$ is an irrational number illuminates, yet again, the value of proof. This is because no other form of reasoning, whether experimental or computational, is a viable alternative in this case. The proof is as follows.

Obviously, $\sqrt{2}$ must be a root of the equation $x^2 = 2$. Let us assume that $x \in \mathbb{Q}$ and that x can be represented as a fraction $\frac{a}{b}$ expressed in terms of the 'lowest' possible integers, that is, a and b have no common factors. A consequence of this assumption is that

$$\left(\frac{a}{b}\right)^2 = 2$$
$$\Leftrightarrow a^2 = 2 \times b^2$$

leading to the conclusion that a^2, and hence a as well, are even integers. If a is an even integer, then it must be possible to represent a as the product $2 \times c$, involving an integer c, which upon its substitution in the above leads to

$$(2 \times c)^2 = 2 \times b^2$$
$$\Leftrightarrow 4 \times c^2 = 2 \times b^2$$
$$\Leftrightarrow 2 \times c^2 = b^2$$

The above points to the inevitable conclusion that b too must then be an even integer. Thus, the assumption of x being a rational number leads to the conclusion that both a and b are divisible by 2, which contradicts that they have no common factors. (Recall that this kind of proof strategy is known as *proof by contradiction*, discussed in Section 5.7.5.)

This shows that $\sqrt{2}$ has no place in the number systems we have studied so far and can be accommodated only in a new number system. The numbers in this system are called the *real numbers*, $\mathbb{R}$. However, one of our major difficulties now is the lack of a representation scheme for numbers such as $\sqrt{2}$ and $\sqrt{3}$. In the case of rational numbers we managed to represent them as fractions, but in the case of irrational numbers this cannot be done, except in the form of *limits* of an infinite sequence of ever converging rational numbers. Thus, for example, $\sqrt{2}$ may be thought of as the number corresponding to the limit of the sequence of rational numbers

$$\frac{14}{10}, \frac{141}{100}, \frac{1414}{1000}, \frac{14142}{10000}, \dots \tag{17.27}$$

It is possible to characterize real numbers algebraically. Here, real numbers borrow all axioms applicable to rational numbers. These axioms take the following form:

1. $\mathbb{R}$ is *closed* under addition and multiplication, that is, these operations use and produce no numbers other than those in $\mathbb{R}$.

2. Addition and multiplication in $\mathbb{R}$ are commutative and associative.

3. Multiplication in $\mathbb{R}$ distributes over addition.

4. $\mathbb{R}$ has an additive identity, an additive inverse for its every number, a multiplicative identity, and a multiplicative inverse for its every non-zero number.

Any algebraic structure possessing the above properties is known in mathematics as a *field*. In this sense, both rational numbers and real numbers constitute fields. In order to distinguish between these two number systems, we need an additional axiom, but its introduction requires some new terminology.

Ordering of numbers and ordered fields

The notion of ordering here is intended to convey what is meant by one number being greater or less than another number. For this, let us identify a subset $\mathbb{R}^+$ of $\mathbb{R}$, representing the set of strictly *positive* real numbers. $\mathbb{R}^+$ can be defined such that

$$\forall a, b \in \mathbb{R}^+ \bullet a + b \in \mathbb{R}^+ \wedge a \times b \in \mathbb{R}^+ \tag{17.28}$$
$$\forall a \in \mathbb{R} \bullet a \in \mathbb{R}^+ \oplus a = 0 \oplus (-a) \in \mathbb{R}^+ \tag{17.29}$$

where $\oplus$ stands here for exclusive 'or'. Condition (17.28) asserts that $\mathbb{R}^+$ itself is closed under addition and multiplication. Condition (17.28) eliminates 0 and negative real numbers from $\mathbb{R}^+$.

With the above, the relations $<$ (less than), $>$ (greater than), $\leqslant$ (less than or equal to) and $\geqslant$ (greater than or equal to) can be defined as

$$\forall a, b \in \mathbb{R} \bullet a < b \Leftrightarrow b + (-a) \in \mathbb{R}^+ \tag{17.30}$$
$$\forall a, b \in \mathbb{R} \bullet a > b \Leftrightarrow a + (-b) \in \mathbb{R}^+ \tag{17.31}$$
$$\forall a, b \in \mathbb{R} \bullet a \leqslant b \Leftrightarrow a < b \vee a = b \tag{17.32}$$
$$\forall a, b \in \mathbb{R} \bullet a \geqslant b \Leftrightarrow a > b \vee a = b \tag{17.33}$$

A field equipped with an ordering relation such as $<$ or $>$ given above is said to be an *ordered field*.

Lower bounds and completely ordered fields

Given a non-empty set of numbers S of an ordered field, a number a is said to be a *lower bound* of S, if $a \leqslant x$ for all $x \in S$. In this case, S is said to be *bounded below* by a. A lower bound a of S is said to be a *greatest lower bound* of S, if a is greater than or equal to all lower bounds of S. An ordered field is said to be a *completely ordered field*, if its every non-empty subset of numbers, which is bounded below, has a greatest lower bound.

This brings us to the final axiom, which distinguishes $\mathbb{R}$ from $\mathbb{Q}$, namely, complete ordering.

Complete ordering

$\mathbb{R}$ constitutes a completely ordered field. $\tag{17.34}$

Let us consider briefly how the above axiom distinguishes $\mathbb{R}$ from $\mathbb{Q}$. Consider, for example, the set of numbers

$$S = \{x \mid x^2 > 2\}$$

In this case, the greatest lower bound of S is denoted by $\sqrt{2}$, which, as shown by (17.27), can be approximated by numbers in $\mathbb{Q}$, but is not in $\mathbb{Q}$. This makes $\mathbb{Q}$ not a completely ordered field. However, by definition, the number $\sqrt{2}$ is in $\mathbb{R}$.

17.3.3 Complex numbers

As seen above, every new number system we have considered attempts to fill a gap in the capability of a previous one. The gap being considered here is shown, for example, by the innocent-looking equation $x^2 + 1 = 0$, which poses the perplexing question as to the meaning of $\sqrt{-1}$. Thus, in addition to real numbers, algebraic equations have led us also to *complex numbers*, $\mathbb{C}$. The number $\sqrt{-1}$, denoted conventionally by 'i', has secured a special place in complex numbers. It enables the representation of every complex number in the form of $a + bi$, in terms of a pair of real numbers a and b.

A characteristic feature of integers, rational numbers and real numbers is the existence of negative numbers and the ordering of numbers as captured, for example, by (17.30)–(17.33). It is possible to view this geometrically in terms of a continuous one-dimensional *real axis* pointing in two opposite directions: positive and negative. Obviously, integers and rational numbers do not occupy all points in this axis, whereas real numbers do.

Complex numbers generalize this geometric representation to a two-dimensional space defined by two orthogonal axes: *real axis* and *imaginary axis*. In this representation, a complex number may be shown in two alternative ways: in terms of Cartesian coordinates a and b measured along the real and imaginary axes, or in terms of polar coordinates r and θ measured respectively as the length (*absolute value*) and angle (*argument* or *phase*) of the *radius vector* (measured from the real axis). This is shown in Figure 17.6. The two representations are related through

$$a + bi = r(\cos\theta + i\sin\theta)$$

When b happens to be 0, complex numbers in the above form are indistinguishable from real numbers. On the other hand, when a happens to be 0,

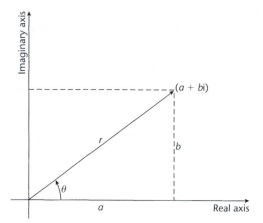

Figure 17.6 Geometrical representations of complex numbers.

the corresponding complex numbers represent numbers of the form $\sqrt{-2}$, $\sqrt{-3.5}$, $\sqrt{-0.3333}$ and so on.

Analogous to the abstract representation of rational numbers as a pair of integers, a complex number may thus be viewed abstractly as a pair of real numbers, albeit measured along two different kinds of axis. This allows manipulation of complex numbers by means of operations on $\mathbb{R}$. For example, addition and multiplication $\mathbb{C}$ may be defined in terms of those on $\mathbb{R}$ as

$$(a + b\mathrm{i}) + (c + d\mathrm{i}) = (a + c) + (b + d)\mathrm{i}$$
$$(a + b\mathrm{i}) \times (c + d\mathrm{i}) = (ac - bd) + (bc + ad)\mathrm{i}$$

17.4 Dense vs sparse sets

Sets with an ordering such as $<$ can be either *dense* or *sparse*. A *dense set* is a set in which, between any two elements in the set, there is always a third element. In this sense, the sets of rational numbers $\mathbb{Q}$ and real numbers $\mathbb{R}$ are dense sets. The sets of natural numbers $\mathbb{N}$ and integers $\mathbb{Z}$ are called, on the other hand, *sparse sets*.

17.5 Countability

Despite both being dense sets, there is a distinction between $\mathbb{Q}$ and $\mathbb{R}$, namely, in that $\mathbb{Q}$ is countable and $\mathbb{R}$ is not. Countability is a term usually applied to infinite sets. A set is said to be *countable* if all its elements can be put into a one-to-one correspondence with the elements in $\mathbb{N}$. Countability of $\mathbb{Q}$ is a surprising result because, if we start counting the rational numbers lying within a given interval of numbers from one end to the other, we never seem to be able to finish counting them even within that stretch, never mind the rest. Cantor, the German mathematician who founded set theory, however, discovered an ingenious method of counting the elements of $\mathbb{Q}$ without ever missing any of its elements. This is illustrated in Figure 17.7. In the process, each and every rational number can be mapped to a unique natural number. Cantor also showed that it is impossible to list the real numbers in numerical order and, therefore, that $\mathbb{R}$ is *uncountable*, or *non-denumerable*.

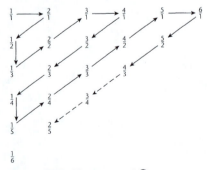

Figure 17.7 How to count $\mathbb{Q}$.

17.6 Numbers in computers

17.6.1 Representation of numbers in computers

Digital computers perform mathematical operations in binary arithmetic, based on the notion of a *binary digit*, or *bit* for short. A binary digit can take only two values, which are usually denoted by 0 and 1. At the physical level, 0 and 1 correspond to electrical pulses of two distinct voltages. Computers represent numbers as patterns of bits and store each number in memory in units of *words*, a word being an array of fixed number of bits in computer memory. The number of bits in each word varies from computer to computer and takes values such as 8, 16, 32. An 8-bit word is usually referred to as a *byte*. As a result, a word may consist of one or more bytes. Depending on the size of their values, numbers may require more than one byte for their representation. The same applies to situations when working in words, resulting in single-length words, double-length words and so on.

The familiar *decimal system* of numbers uses ten digits and permits the representation of numbers in the form

5389.762

relying implicitly on the polynomial

$$\underbrace{5 \times 10^3 + 3 \times 10^2 + 8 \times 10^1 + 9 \times 10^0}_{\text{integral part}} + \underbrace{7 \times 10^{-1} + 6 \times 10^{-2} + 2 \times 10^{-3}}_{\text{fractional part}}$$

as a way of conveying its meaning. The number 10 serves as the *base* in this case and, therefore, the decimal system is also known as *base 10 notation*. An alternative term for base is *radix*. The base 10 notation has come about from the 'computer at our finger tips', but other civilizations have used different numbers as the base in their counting. Thus, binary notation is a special case of this approach, adopted in computing especially for internal representation of numbers. Note that binary notation is not the only representation used in computing; *octal* (base 8 notation using 0, 1, 2, 3, 4, 5, 6, 7 as its digits) and *hexadecimal* (base 16 notation using 0, 1, 2, 3, 4, 5, 6, 7, 8, 9, A, B, C, D, E, F as its digits) systems are special-purpose representations used by computers for output of numbers and other kinds of information in a concise form. In order to avoid the possible confusion of numbers written using the same numerals (typically in Hindu–Arabic numerals) but in different representations, their base is often indicated by writing it as a subscript. Thus 563_{10} is a number in the decimal representation, whereas 563_8 is a number in the octal representation. Note that 563_8

$$563_8 = 5 \times 8^2 + 6 \times 8^1 + 3 \times 8^0 = 320 + 48 + 3 = 371_{10}$$

and is thus 371 in the decimal representation. This shows that the same sequence of numerals in different representations could denote different numbers.

In general, digital representation of numbers may employ r digits as the base, permitting, for example, the representation of a number with n digits in its integral part and m digits in its fractional part as:

polynomial $d_{n-1}r^{n-1} + d_{n-2}r^{n-2} + \ldots + d_0r^0 + d_{-1}r^{-1} + d_{-2}r^{-2} + \ldots + d_{-m}r^{-m}$
representation

$$
\underbrace{\overset{\downarrow}{d_{n-1}} \quad \overset{\downarrow}{d_{n-2}} \quad \ldots \quad \overset{\downarrow}{d_0}}_{\text{integral part}} \quad \underbrace{\overset{\downarrow}{d_{-1}} \quad \overset{\downarrow}{d_{-2}} \quad \ldots \quad \overset{\downarrow}{d_{-m}}}_{\text{fractional part}}
$$

digital representation

As a result, each digit among $d_{n-1}, d_{n-2}, \ldots, d_1, d_0, d_{-1}, \ldots, d_{-m}$ in this case stands for one of the chosen r digits. Thus

10011011101

is a binary representation and

40A97ED320B1

is a hexadecimal representation.

17.6.2   Binary representation of integers

A good insight into how numbers are represented in computers may be obtained by examining the case of integers.

Conversion to and from decimals

It is obvious that a decimal integer may be converted into binary representation by successively dividing it by 2 and collecting remainders, for example:

```
2) 963   (remainders)
2) 481      1
2) 240      1
2) 120      0
2)  60      0
2)  30      0
2)  15      0
2)   7      1
2)   3      1
2)   1      1
     0      1          Thus, 963₁₀ = 111100011₂
```

Thus, $963_{10} = 1111000011_2$

Conversely, a binary number may be converted into its equivalent decimal representation by representing it as a polynomial. Thus

$$
\begin{aligned}
110100101_2 &= 1 \times 2^8 + 1 \times 2^7 + 0 \times 2^6 + 1 \times 2^5 + 0 \times 2^4 + 0 \times 2^3 + 1 \times 2^2 \\
&\quad + 0 \times 2^1 + 1 \times 2^0 \\
&= 1 \times 256 + 1 \times 128 + 0 \times 64 + 1 \times 32 + 0 \times 16 + 0 \times 8 \\
&\quad + 1 \times 4 + 0 \times 2 + 1 \times 1 \\
&= 256 + 128 + 32 + 4 + 1 = 421_{10}
\end{aligned}
$$

Exercise 17.5 ✳

1. Give the binary representations of the following integers. (a) 398_{10}, (b) 436_8, (c) 762_{10}, (d) 762_8.

2. Give the decimal representations of the following integers (a) 10011011, (b) 11010111, (c) 11111111, (d) 10000111.

Representation of negative integers

Depending on the technique used in arithmetical operations, it is necessary to distinguish between positive and negative integers in their representations. A straightforward way is to reserve a special *sign bit* in the binary representation of each integer in order to indicate its sign. Conventionally, a 0 in the sign bit plays the role of a flag for positive numbers and 1 for negative numbers. This is known as the *signed-magnitude* representation.

With this approach, in subtracting a larger integer from a smaller integer, it is necessary first to swap the two operands, then carry out the subtraction and finally set the sign bit of the result to 1. The same applies to addition, since the addition of numbers with opposite signs, as well as numbers with negative signs, requires a different sequence of steps. These manipulations could be time-consuming, resulting in inefficient implementation of computer arithmetic.

A widely used alternative is the *two's complement* representation of negative integers. The motivation for this should become clearer shortly. Two's complement of a binary number is that obtained by adding 1 to its *complement*, that is, the number obtained by swapping all 1s in its representation to 0s and, likewise, all 0s to 1s. For example, the complement of 01011001 is 10100110 and its two's complement is 10100111. In this representation, given a binary number x, $-x$ is represented by two's complement of x, that is

$$-x = \bar{x} + 1$$

where $\bar{x}$ is x's complement.

Exercise 17.6 ✳

1. Give the integers and their representations that can be accommodated in four consecutive bits in sign-magnitude representation.

2. Give the integers and their representations that can be accommodated in four consecutive bits in two's complement representation. Is there a bit which plays the role of the sign bit in this representation?

3. Generalizing the above, give the range of integers that can be accommodated in an N-bit two's complement representation.

Binary addition and subtraction in sign-magnitude representation

Binary arithmetic is similar to decimal arithmetic. Binary addition and binary subtraction use the ideas of *carry* and *borrow* as in decimal arithmetic. This is illustrated below.

Addition

In decimal representation

```
      3 6 8 1 2
   +  2 5 3 7 9
      6 2 1 9 1
(carry)  1 1    1
```

In binary representation

```
        1 0 0 1 1
    +   1 1 0 0 1
        0 1 1 0 0
(carry) 1      1 1
```

Subtraction   (smaller number from a larger number in conventional way)

In decimal representation

```
(borrow)      10     9 10
           3² 4 7⁶ 0 5
        -  2  5 3  7 9
           9  3 2  6
```

In binary representation

```
(borrow)        1 1 2
           1⁰ 0 0 0 1
        -  0  1 0 1 1
           0  0 1 1 0
```

Binary subtraction in two's complement representation

The form of representation could have important implications on complexity in computer arithmetic and, for that matter, in any computation. A good example illustrating this is the subtraction of binary numbers. It is clear from the example above that the manual style of doing subtraction is not the ideal way for computers because it may require (depending on their magnitude) interchanging operands and taking care of the sign in the result. Two's complement representation helps to avoid this.

Consider an 8-bit number x. Let its binary representation be 00101101. Let us examine why its two's complement, 11010011, is equivalent to $-x$. First note that x's complement is

$$\bar{x} = 11010010$$

leading to the fairly obvious result

$$x + \bar{x} = 11111111 = 2^8 - 1$$

which, as shown above, is $2^8 - 1$ in the standard interpretation of 8-bit representation. Addition of 1 to $x + \bar{x}$ results in

$$x + \bar{x} + 1 = \boxed{1}\ 00000000 = 2^8$$

The above is equal to 2^8 only in theory. In practice, however, it is equal to 0. This is because the highlighted $\boxed{1}$ in the above is lost due to the fixed length of the representation. Thus, in practice we have

$$x + \bar{x} + 1 = 00000000 = 0$$

giving

$$-x = \bar{x} + 1$$

Table 17.1   Three different representations of 9 subtracted from 3.

Decimal	Binary representation			
	Sign-magnitude		Two's complement	
	(borrow)			
	1 2			
3	0 $\cancel{1}^0$ 0 0 1	(9)	0 0 0 1 1	(3)
− 9	− 0 0 0 1 1	(3)	+ 1 0 1 1 1	(−9)
−6	1 0 1 1 0	(−6)	1 1 0 1 0	(−6)
			1 1 1	
			(carry)	

which lets us represent −x as two's complement of x. Note that this is a consequence of the fixed length of memory cells used to store numbers.

The main advantage of two's complement representation is that it allows us to perform subtraction as addition, thereby eliminating the need for additional manipulations required by subtraction. In practical terms, this amounts to eliminating the need for special circuits for doing subtraction.

Table 17.1 illustrates the subtraction of 9 from 3 in three different representations: in the familiar decimal representation, sign-magnitude binary representation and two's complement binary representation.

Exercise 17.7 ✳✳✳

In N-bit two's complement representation, the sum of two integers could be outside the range established in the answer to Exercise 17.6. In this case, the addition is said to produce an *overflow*. Discuss the circumstances under which an overflow can take place.

We expect the second iteration (repeated computation) of two's complement applied to an integer to produce the same integer. Investigation of this requires a knowledge of sequences, a topic addressed in Chapter 18, and hence it is deferred until Exercise 18.6.

Shift operations and binary multiplication and division

A shift of the digital representation of an integer by a digit either to the left or to the right usually amounts to multiplication or division of the given integer by the number serving as the base. For example, a shift of 00010110 by one digit to the left results in 00101100. In decimal representation, this amounts to multiplication of 22 by 2, resulting in 44. On the other hand, a shift of 00010110 by one digit to the right results in 00001011, amounting to division of 22 by 2 resulting in 11.

The above interpretation of shift as multiplication or division assumes that no bit is lost at the extreme ends in the process of shifting. Obviously, this is not the case in general. Shift of bit patterns with no regard to the significance of this loss is called *logical shift*. When dealing with bit patterns that represent numbers, shift operations that model arithmetical operations must take care of features that are significant in numbers. They include preservation of the sign bit, 'downstream' propagation of the sign bit in right shifts and rounding of numbers to account for lost bits. The following examples illustrate the need for such measures.

Logical shift of a bit pattern by one digit to the right may be shown as

$$10000000_2 \longrightarrow 01000000_2$$

If the above two bit patterns stand for numbers in two's complement representation, the shift is equivalent in decimal arithmetic to

$$-2^7 \longrightarrow 2^6$$

which does not correspond to division by 2. The division by 2 in this case should really result in -2^6. This can be achieved in arithmetic only by adding 2^6 to -2^7, that is

$$-2^7 + 2^6 = 2^6(-2 + 1) = -2^6$$

Therefore, *arithmetical shift*, that is, the shift producing the right arithmetical result, should take the form

$$10000000_2 \longrightarrow 11000000_2$$

In other words, the sign bit needs to be propagated down the bit pattern if the right shift is to model division in arithmetic faithfully. The process can be repeated. Thus, division by 2^4 can be shown as four consecutive right shifts

$$10000000_2 \longrightarrow 11000000_2 \longrightarrow 11100000_2 \longrightarrow 11110000_2 \longrightarrow 11111000_2$$

As in the case of the earlier single shift, the above is to be justified by

$$\begin{aligned} -2^7 + 2^6 + 2^5 + 2^4 + 2^3 &= 2^3(-2^4 + 2^3 + 2^2 + 2^1 + 1) \\ &= 2^3(-16 + 8 + 4 + 2 + 1) \\ &= -2^3 \end{aligned}$$

Thus

$$11111000_2 = -2^3_{10}$$

The above shows that 1s following the sign bit of a negative integer in two's complement can be represented as an *exponent* of 2. We use this fact later when dealing with the accuracy of implementation of real numbers.

Now let us consider appropriate ways of dealing with the loss of bits. Taking no measures at all against loss amounts to *truncation*. Alternatively, the lost bit may be added to the new least significant bit. In a right shift over several places, 1 is added to the surviving integer, depending on whether the discarded fraction is greater than 0.5 in the decimal representation, or ignored otherwise.

Multiplication and division of integers by 2 may be carried out by shifting the binary representations either leftwards or rightwards, so long as the possibility of losing the bits in the extreme positions is appropriately taken care of. This allows carrying out the remaining arithmetical operations, namely, multiplication and division, as a combination of multiplications or divisions by 2, and additions.

17.6.3   Binary representation of real numbers

When dealing with numbers with a fractional part, their representation as a sequence of digits itself does not indicate the position of the *radix point*, which separates the integral and fractional part. This information is kept elsewhere. Note that, at implementation level, a representation concerns not only how numbers are stored but also how they are manipulated by algorithms (operations). In general, the representation may assume that the radix point resides between the two extreme digit positions.

Fixed point number representation assumes that the radix point resides between two fixed adjacent digit positions. It is an appropriate representation for calculations involving fractional parts of constant length, that is, calculations dealing exclusively with quantities such as time, money, etc. By contrast, *floating point number* representation is intended for calculations of numbers with considerable variations in magnitude, typically in scientific calculations.

Fixed point representation

In general, the radix point in fixed point representation can be anywhere within the radix. The further it is to the right, the smaller is the number of digits used in the fractional part and, hence, the accuracy of the number. A major disadvantage of having a variable radix point is the need for keeping track of its position. This involves properly aligning the radix point of operand numbers prior to performing arithmetical operations such as addition. Two common approaches to fix the radix point are to assume it be immediately to the right of the least significant digit (rightmost digit) or, alternatively, immediately to the left of the most significant digit (leftmost digit). These two options treat the number concerned as an integer or as a fraction respectively.

Floating point representation

Fixed point representation is suitable for dealing with numbers of a limited range. This can be seen through the range of integers that can be represented by binary representations – a problem considered in Exercise 17.6. In the case of 16-bit representation of integers, this range is approximately between $\pm 2^{15}$, or $\pm 3.28 \times 10^4$, and in the case of 32-bit representation $\pm 2^{31}$, or $\pm 2.15 \times 10^9$. Although such a range may be adequate in most applications used in commerce and business, as well as in the solution of simple scientific problems, it is too narrow a range when dealing with sophisticated and complex scientific calculations. This limitation is overcome by representing numbers in the form

$M \times B^e$

where, M is known as the *mantissa*, B as the *base* and e as the *exponent*. Some examples in this representation are 0.4673×10^{-16}, 010.11×2^{011} and 0.1011×2^{011}, the first in the decimal representation and the latter two in the binary representation.

The floating point representation offers two major advantages. In programming terms, there is no longer a need to keep track of the radix point and to make sure that different operands are properly aligned when performing arithmetical operations. In addition, the floating point representation allows the coverage of a wider range of numbers – greatly extending the limits of numerical computing.

In computer implementation of the above representation of real numbers, the base is usually fixed and is not recorded as a part of individual floating numbers. For efficient implementation of computer arithmetic, the exponent is limited to integers. On the other hand, the mantissa can be given, in general, as a number in a fixed point representation, where the radix point is allowed to *float* between the two possible extreme positions – hence, the name. Obviously, when dealing with a specific number, the position of the radix point and the exponent are not independent of each other. This dependency is best shown, for example, as in

$$0.4673 \times 10^{-16} = 46.73 \times 10^{-18} = 0.004673 \times 10^{-14}$$

in the familiar decimal representation. As seen in the following example,

$$00110101011100110000000 \times 2^2$$
$$= 00000110101011100110000 \times 2^5$$
$$= 00000000110101011100110 \times 2^8$$

the same is generally true in binary representation. Exceptions are when the most significant bit, or the least significant bit, happens to be a 1, with the consequent loss of bits with the shift of bits leftwards, or rightwards, due to the fixed length of the representation.

This brings us to question of the most 'optimal' fixed point representation of mantissa. From the point of view of *accuracy*, the optimal representation in a given radix is the representation which accommodates the largest number of digits. In binary representations where the mantissa is stored as a fraction, this corresponds

1. in the case of positive numbers, to bit patterns with a 1 in the secondmost left bit position;

2. in the case of negative numbers, to bit patterns with a 0 in the secondmost left bit position.

In relation to both cases, note that the leftmost bit is reserved as a sign bit. In relation to (2), note our earlier observation that 1s following immediately after the sign bit of a negative integer can be represented as an exponent of 2. This explains why, in the case of negative numbers, a 0 must occupy the secondmost left bit position.

The bit patterns of floating point numbers cannot be shifted arbitrarily; the dependence between radix point in the mantissa and the exponent needs to be

Table 17.2 The range of values that can be accommodated in the mantissa.

Sign of mantissa	Range of mantissa in 24-bit representation as a fraction	Decimal value
Positive	From 010000000000000000000000 to 011111111111111111111111	$2^{-1} = 0.5$ $2^{-1} + 2^{-2} + \ldots + 2^{-23} \approx 1$
Negative	From 100000000000000000000000 to 101111111111111111111111	
	That is, from 100000000000000000000000 $- 2^1$ (definition of two's complement; note that the fractional part starts at the second digit) to 101111111111111111111111 $= -(\overline{101111111111111111111111} - 1)$ $= -(\overline{101111111111111111111110})$ $= -(010000000000000000000001)$	$2^0 - 2^1 = -1$ $-(2^{-1} + 2^{-23}) \approx -0.5$

properly taken care of. Once this is done in accordance with (1) and (2) above, a floating point number is said to be *normalized*.

Now let us consider the *range* of values that can be accommodated in normalized floating point numbers. First, the range of values in the mantissa. This is presented in Table 17.2. Now, let us consider the contribution of the exponent to the range of values that can be accommodated in floating point representation. Taking an 8-bit exponent as an illustration, we note that in two's complement the exponent has a range of -128 to 127.

With a 24-bit mantissa and an 8-bit exponent, 32-bit floating point representation thus covers two disjointed ranges of numbers:

1. From -2^{127} to -0.5^{-128} (or, approximately, from -1.7×10^{38} to -1.47×10^{-39}).
2. From 0.5^{-128} to 2^{127} (or, approximately, from 1.47×10^{-39} to 1.7×10^{38}).

Exercise 17.8 ✳ ✳ ✳

Assess the range and accuracy of real numbers implemented in a 64-bit representation with a 16-bit exponent.

17.6.4 Abstract number systems and their machine representation

As a computational system, the real number system may be seen as a structure

$$(\mathbb{R}, +, -, \times, \div)$$

in which, the binary operations share the type

$$\odot : \mathbb{R} \times \mathbb{R} \to \mathbb{R}$$

the symbol $\odot$ denoting any one of the operations $+$, $-$, $\times$ or $\div$. By contrast, machine implementations of the real number system have restrictions, resulting in a different structure

$$(\mathbb{M}, +, -, \times, \div)$$

with the operations $+$, $-$, $\times$ and $\div$ each having a different type definition as indicated by

$$\boxdot : \mathbb{M} \times \mathbb{M} \to \mathbb{M}$$

Note that $\mathbb{M}$ is a proper finite subset of $\mathbb{R}$, which takes into account the fact that computer implementation of real numbers is constrained by the *word length* used for their internal representation. The relationship between the computer implementation $\boxdot$ of an arithmetical operation $\odot$ can be given as

$$\boxdot = \mathbb{M} \times \mathbb{M} \triangle (\odot ; \ round)$$

where *round* is a function of type $\mathbb{R} \to \mathbb{M}$, which maps every real number to a unique number in the machine representation. Thus, the concrete implementation $\boxdot$ of each of the abstract mathematical operations $\odot$ on $\mathbb{R}$ is constrained in its domain to machine implementable numbers and the results are likewise approximated by machine implementable numbers.

Exercise 17.9 ✳ ✳

Using a graph, illustrate the above relationship between numbers in the abstract sense and their implementation in computers.

Chapter 18

Sequences and bags

Topic: Mathematical data types

A place for everything and everything in its place.

Mrs Beeton
(1836–65)
(in *Book of Household Management*; attributed to Samuel Smiles)

Objectives

On completion of this chapter you should be able to:

- Define sequences as functions.
- Define operations on sequences and demonstrate how they work for specific arguments.
- Define bags (multi-sets) as functions.
- Define operations on bags and demonstrate how they work for specific arguments.

Sequences and *bags* are two data types frequently used in formal specification. Except for minor differences in associated operations, sequences are close to *lists* in functional and other declarative programming languages. As their mathematical representations, this chapter introduces two further special kinds of set, both based on the notion of function.

18.1 Sequences as sets

We have seen that elements in ordinary sets have no order. In this respect, we introduced in Chapter 13 the notions of tuples and product sets for dealing with sets whose elements possess some internal order. Tuples may, in general, consist of elements drawn from different domains of values. A deficiency of tuples, as we have presented them here, is that there is no machinery to manipulate them.

In many practical situations, for example, when dealing with queues, strings of characters (files, textual documents) and so on, there is a need to place elements drawn from a single set in some order and to be able to manipulate them. For such purposes, let us define an abstract data type called *sequences*. The definition of an abstract data type involves

1. an appropriate mathematical structure such as a set or a relation, and

2. a collection of operations on it.

In ordinary mathematics, sequences are introduced in the following manner:

4, 8, 6, ...

This is a sequence of numbers, whose first term is 4, second is 8, third is 6, and so on. A sequence is thus a mapping from a segment of $\mathbb{N}_1$. This is strictly a partial mapping, because we require sequences to be finite mappings in order to be able to perform such operations as concatenation (joining) of two or more sequences in the construction of a new one, or reversing the order of elements in a sequence. Thus, sequences are sets and, hence, all operations applicable to sets, relations and functions remain applicable to sequences.

Definition Sequences

Given an arbitrary type X, *sequences* of elements drawn from X are functions belonging to the set

$$\{f : \mathbb{N}_1 \nrightarrow X \mid \text{dom } f = 1..\# f\}$$

where $\mathbb{N}_1 = \mathbb{N} - \{0\}$.

Since X is a *generic* type, a sequence may be a sequence of numbers, of characters, of files or, in general, of values of any type.

The set in the Definition, the elements of which represent sequences, is regarded as the type

$$\text{seq } X \stackrel{def}{=} \{f : \mathbb{N}_1 \nrightarrow X \mid \text{dom } f = 1..\# f\}$$

Example 18.1

Using the above definition, the sequence

3, 6, 9, 9, 15, 1

may be represented as

$$\{(1,3), (2,6), (3,9), (4,9), (5,15), (6,1)\}$$

The following is a syntactically equivalent notation for the same

$$\langle 3, 6, 9, 9, 15, 1\rangle$$

introduced purely for convenience.

Example 18.2

A symbolic sequence such as

$$\langle \textit{Albert, Mike, Silva, Rita}\rangle$$

can be written as the set

$$\{(1, \textit{Albert}), (2, \textit{Mike}), (3, \textit{Silva}), (4, \textit{Rita})\}$$

18.2 Operations on sequences

Below are some commonly used operations on sequences:

1. A primitive constructor called *cons* for extending a sequence by inserting an element at the head of the sequence.

2. A binary constructor '_ ⌢ _' for appending (concatenating) two sequences.

3. Accessor operations called *head* and *tail*, respectively, for extracting the element at the head or the tail end of a sequence.

4. Accessor operations called *front* and *last*, respectively, for extracting the front end of a sequence or the last element of a sequence.

5. A modifier called *rev* for reversing a sequence.

6. An operator for removing some elements from a sequence and forming a compacted sequence from the resulting 'sequence'.

The following are the mathematical definitions of some of the above operations. Letting X be an arbitrary (*generic*) type, the constructor *cons* in (1) above may be defined as:

$$cons : X \rightarrow \text{seq } X \rightarrow \text{seq } X$$
$$\forall a : X; S : \text{seq } X \bullet$$
$$cons\ a\ S = \{1 \mapsto a\} \cup (pred_{\S}\ S)$$

where *pred* is the predecessor function introduced in Section 17.1. The concatenation operator in (2) can be defined as:

$$\_ \frown \_ : \text{seq } X \rightarrow \text{seq } X \rightarrow \text{seq } X$$
$$\forall S_1, S_2 : \text{seq } X \bullet$$
$$S_1 \frown S_2 = S_1 \cup (pred^{\#S_1}_{\S}\ S_2)$$

The accessor functions in (3) and (4) are:

$$head, last : \text{seq } X \nrightarrow X$$
$$tail, front : \text{seq } X \nrightarrow \text{seq } X$$
$$\forall S : \text{seq } X \mid S \neq \varnothing \bullet$$
$$head\ S = (S\ 1)$$
$$last\ S = (S\ (\#S))$$
$$tail\ S = S \circ (\{0\} \lhd succ)$$
$$front\ S = \{\#S\} \lhd S$$

where *succ* is the successor function introduced on Section 17.1. Note that since S is a function $(S\ 1)$ in the above means the first element S. The function *rev* in (5) is:

$$rev : \text{seq } X \rightarrow \text{seq } X$$
$$\forall S : \text{seq } X \bullet$$
$$rev\ S = \{i \mapsto (\#S - i + 1) \mid i \in 1..\#S\}_{\S}\ S \qquad \textbf{(18.1)}$$

Example 18.3

This example illustrates some the above operations. Let *Char* represent the set of characters, with elements $'a'$, $'b'$, ..., for alpha characters and $\triangledown$ for the space character. Let s and t be the following sequences of characters:

$S, T : \text{seq } Char$
$S = \langle c, o, l, d, \triangledown \rangle$
$T = \langle d, r, i, n, k \rangle$

(Note that individual characters in sequences are not enclosed within quotation marks for clarity.) These sequences may be manipulated as follows by some of the operations introduced in this section.

$$
\begin{aligned}
head\ S &= head\ \langle c, o, l, d, \triangledown \rangle \\
&= \langle c, o, l, d, \triangledown \rangle\ 1 \\
&= (\{(1, c), (2, o), (3, l), (4, d), (5, \triangledown)\}\ 1) \\
&= c
\end{aligned}
$$

$$
\begin{aligned}
tail\ S &= tail\ \langle c, o, l, d, \triangledown \rangle \\
&= \langle c, o, l, d, \triangledown \rangle \circ (\{0\} \triangleleft succ) \\
&= \{(1, c), (2, o), (3, l), (4, d), (5, \triangledown)\} \circ (\{0\} \triangleleft \{(0, 1), (1, 2), (2, 3), \ldots\}) \\
&= \{(1, c), (2, o), (3, l), (4, d), (5, \triangledown)\} \circ \{(1, 2), (2, 3), (3, 4), \ldots\}) \\
&= \{(1, o), (2, l), (3, d), (4, \triangledown)\} \\
&= \langle o, l, d, \triangledown \rangle
\end{aligned}
$$

$$
\begin{aligned}
S \frown T &= S \cup (pred^{\#S}\,;\, T) \\
&= S \cup (pred^S\,;\, \langle d, r, i, n, k \rangle) \\
&= S \cup (\{5 \mapsto 0, 6 \mapsto 1, 7 \mapsto 2, \ldots\}\,;\, \{1 \mapsto d, 2 \mapsto r, 3 \mapsto i, 4 \mapsto n, 5 \mapsto k\} \\
&= S \cup (\{6 \mapsto d, 7 \mapsto r, 8 \mapsto i, 9 \mapsto n, 10 \mapsto k\} \\
&= \{1 \mapsto c, 2 \mapsto o, 3 \mapsto l, 4 \mapsto d, 5 \mapsto \triangledown\} \cup \\
&\qquad (\{6 \mapsto d, 7 \mapsto r, 8 \mapsto i, 9 \mapsto n, 10 \mapsto k\} \\
&= \{1 \mapsto c, 2 \mapsto o, 3 \mapsto l, 4 \mapsto d, 5 \mapsto \triangledown, 6 \mapsto d, 7 \mapsto r, 8 \mapsto i, 9 \mapsto n, 10 \mapsto k\} \\
&= \langle c, o, l, d, \triangledown, d, r, i, n, k \rangle
\end{aligned}
$$

Given two sequences of characters R and S,

$R = \langle a, m, e \rangle$
$S = \langle r, i, c, a \rangle$

where, as in the previous example, the symbols $'a'$, $'b'$, ... $'z'$ written in lower case represent the character set, work out the values of the following, giving all intermediate steps.

1. *front S*

2. *cons s R*

3. $R \frown S$

4. $rev\ (R \frown S)$

Exercise 18.2 ✻

Produce a set theoretically valid statement about sequences for each of the following expressions by inserting, as appropriate, a variable denoting a sequence, or a symbol (or name) denoting an operation on sequences, in place of each dotted blank. The symbols p, q, r and s in these expressions are variables standing for arbitrary sequences of elements drawn from some given type X and x is an arbitrary element of X.

1. $(p \frown q) \frown r = \ldots \frown (\ldots \frown r)$

2. $(\ldots \frown p) = p$

3. $(\ldots (cons\ x\ p)) = p$

4. $p \neq \langle\rangle \Rightarrow (cons\ (head\ p)\ (\ldots\ p)) = p$

5. $(rev\ (p \frown q) = (rev \ldots) \frown (rev \ldots)$

6. $rev(rev\ s) = \ldots$

7. $(\#(p \frown q) = \# \ldots + \# \ldots$

8. $s \neq \langle\rangle \Rightarrow (front\ s) \frown (\ldots\ s) = s$

Observation

The valid statements produced in the answer to Exercise 18.2 are laws about sequences.

Exercise 18.3 ✻ ✻ ✻

Prove any two of the statements produced in answer to Exercise 18.2.

Exercise 18.4 ✻ ✻

S_1 and S_2 are sequences of characters each containing a unique occurrence of each of their characters.

1. Identify the classification of S_1 and S_2 as functions.

2. Write an expression for the relation relating every pair of positions in the two sequences with a common character.

3. Given that $S_1 = \langle s,\ u,\ b,\ m,\ i,\ t \rangle$, illustrate how the definition for *rev* given in (18.1) works for *rev* S_1.

Exercise 18.5 ✻ ✻ ✻

1. Define mathematically an operation referred to as *zip*, which interleaves alternately the first n characters in the two sequences, n being the length of the shorter sequence. For example, for the sequences

$$S_1 = \langle g,\ e,\ t,\ t,\ o \rangle$$
$$S_2 = \langle r,\ a,\ ! \rangle$$

zip S_1 S_2 gives the following:

$$zip\ S_1\ S_2 = \langle g.\ r,\ e,\ a,\ t,\ !\rangle$$

Illustrate how your definition works for *zip* S_1 S_2.

2. Write a general expression for the sequence containing characters common to both sequences but in the order that they appear in S_1.

Exercise 18.6 ✳✳✳

Let us return to the discussion in Section 17.6.2 on the use of *two's complement* as a convenient binary representation of both positive and negative integers. Show that the second iteration of two's complement applied to an integer produces the same integer. Are there circumstances when this might not be the case?

18.3 Bags

Bags or multi-sets are collections of objects where multiple occurrences of objects are allowed. This kind of situation arises when one chooses to ignore minor, or less important, distinctions between objects. Set theoretically, these may be viewed as a special kind of set, namely, as mappings from a given (finite) domain of interest, say a set A, to $\mathbb{N}$.

Definition   Bags

Given an arbitrary type X, all possible *bags* of elements drawn from X are members of the set

$$\{f : X \nrightarrow \mathbb{N}_1\}$$

From the Definition, the type for bags of element type X may therefore be given as

$$bag\ X \stackrel{def}{=} X \nrightarrow \mathbb{N}_1$$

Thus, both sequences and bags are mappings between a given domain of interest and $\mathbb{N}$, but differ in the direction of the mapping.

For example, the following is a bag represented set theoretically.

$$b = \{(\textbf{apple}, 3),\ (\textbf{pear}, 6),\ (\textbf{plum}, 9),\ (\textbf{kiwi}, 9)\}$$

The elements in a bag may be enumerated using the notation $[\![\ldots]\!]$. Thus, the elements in the above bag may be shown as

$$b = [\![\textbf{apple}, \textbf{pear}, \textbf{plum}, \textbf{kiwi}]\!]$$

without indicating the actual number of instances of each element. The number of instances of elements in a given bag is given by a special function called *count*, which is described below. Note that the notation $[\![\ ]\!]$ denotes the empty bag.

18.4 Operations on bags

The special functions and operations on bags are as follows. The function *count* is defined as:

$$count : \text{bag } X \rightarrowtail (X \to \mathbb{N})$$
$$\forall b : \text{bag } X \bullet$$
$$count\ b = \{(x,0) \mid x \in X\} \oplus b$$

The relational overriding operation $\oplus$ in this definition ensures that *count* returns 0 if any given element is not in the bag b, but otherwise the number recorded against it in the function b. The infix version of the above function is

$$\_\,\sharp\,\_ : \text{bag } X \times X \to \mathbb{N}$$
$$\forall\ b : \text{bag } X; x : X \bullet$$
$$b \sharp\ x = count\ b\ x$$

Other useful relations concern bag membership and sub-bags. The bag membership relation says whether any given element x is in a given bag b or not. It may be defined as:

$$\_\,\mathsf{E}\,\_ : X \leftrightarrow \text{bag } X$$
$$\forall\ b : \text{bag } X; x : X \bullet$$
$$x \mathsf{E} b \Leftrightarrow x \in \text{dom } b$$

Similarly, the sub-bag relation may be defined as:

$$\_\,\sqsubseteq\,\_ : X \leftrightarrow \text{bag } X$$
$$\forall\ b, c : \text{bag } X \bullet$$
$$b \sqsubseteq c \Leftrightarrow (\forall\ x : X \bullet b \sharp\ x \leqslant c \sharp\ x)$$

That is, a bag b is a sub-bag of a bag c if and only if the number of occurrences of every element of X in b is less than or equal to the number of its occurrences in c.

Another important operation on bags is union of two bags:

$$\_\,\uplus\,\_ : \text{bag } X \times \text{bag } X \to \text{bag } X$$
$$\forall\ b, c : \text{bag } X; \ x : X \bullet$$
$$(b \uplus c) \sharp\ x = b \sharp\ x + c \sharp\ x$$

defined here implicitly using the infix count operation. Similarly, one may define an operation for taking the difference of two bags:

$$\_\,\uplus\,\_ : \text{bag } X \times \text{bag } X \to \text{bag } X$$
$$\forall\ b, c : \text{bag } X; \ x : X \bullet$$
$$(b \uplus c) \sharp\ x = max\{b \sharp\ x - c \sharp\ x, 0\}$$

where *max* is a function returning the maximum of a given set of natural numbers.

Example 18.4

Let b be a bag with the following elements:

$$b = \{(\textbf{\textit{apple}}, 3), (\textbf{\textit{pear}}, 6), (\textbf{\textit{plum}}, 4), (\textbf{\textit{kiwi}}, 9)\}$$
$$c = \{(\textbf{\textit{apple}}, 1), (\textbf{\textit{orange}}, 3), (\textbf{\textit{plum}}, 4), (\textbf{\textit{mango}}, 4)\}$$
$$d = \{(\textbf{\textit{orange}}, 3), (\textbf{\textit{plum}}, 1)\}$$

The following illustrates the effect of the above functions (operations) when applied as shown to the bags b, c and d.

$$count\ b = \{(\textbf{apple}, 3), (\textbf{pear}, 6), (\textbf{plum}, 4), (\textbf{kiwi}, 9),$$
$$(\textbf{orange}, 0), (\textbf{mango}, 0), (\textbf{banana}, 0),$$
$$\ldots (0\text{ for all other fruits})\ldots\}$$

$$count\ b\ \textbf{plum} = 4$$
$$count\ b\ \textbf{papaya} = 0$$
$$b \sharp \textbf{pear} = count\ b\ \textbf{pear} = 6$$
$$b \uplus c = \{(\textbf{apple}, 4), (\textbf{pear}, 6), (\textbf{plum}, 8), (\textbf{kiwi}, 9), (\textbf{orange}, 3), (\textbf{mango}, 4)\}$$
$$b \sqcup c = \{(\textbf{apple}, 2), (\textbf{pear}, 6), (\textbf{kiwi}, 9)\}$$
$$\textbf{apple} \sqin b$$
$$\textbf{orange} \not\sqin b$$
$$d \sqsubseteq c$$
$$c \not\sqsubseteq b$$

Exercise 18.7 ✳✳✳

An electronic mailing system keeps a record of the number of mail items intended for different addresses of its users.

1. Propose an appropriate mathematical data structure for recording this information.
2. Describe mathematically the effect of updating the record with the arrival of a new mail intended for a user.
3. Describe mathematically the effect of removing mail intended for a number of addresses from the mailing system.
4. Define a predicate for checking whether there is any mail intended for a group of addresses.
5. Describe mathematically the effect of an operation giving the number of mail items in the mailing system intended for a particular address.
6. Assert that the number of mail items intended for the specific address mr_nice should not exceed a predefined number p.
7. Assert that users are restricted to a maximum of m mail items in every user address, m being a predefined number.
8. Assert that the capacity of the mailing system as a whole is limited to a predefined number n.
9. Describe mathematically the effect of merging the records of two existing mailing systems.

Exercise 18.8 ✳✳✳

Produce a set theoretically valid statement about bags for each of the following expressions by inserting, as appropriate, a variable denoting a bag, a symbol (or name) denoting an operation or a relation on bags, or a logical connective, in place of each dotted blank. The symbols b, c and d in these expressions are variables standing for arbitrary bags of elements drawn from some given type X.

1. $[\,] \sqsubseteq \ldots$
2. $b \sqsubseteq c \ldots c \sqsubseteq b \Rightarrow b = c$
3. $b \sqsubseteq c \wedge c \sqsubseteq d \Rightarrow b \ldots d$
4. $b \uplus [\,] = \ldots$
5. $b \uplus c = c \ldots b$
6. $(b \uplus c) \uplus d = b \ldots (c \ldots d)$
7. $b \cup [\,] = \ldots$
8. $[\,] \uplus b = \ldots$
9. $(b \uplus c) \uplus c = \ldots$
10. $\mathrm{dom}(b \uplus c) = \ldots c \cup \ldots b$
11. $b \ldots c \Rightarrow \mathrm{dom}\, c \subseteq \mathrm{dom}\, b$

Observation

The statements produced in the answer to Exercise 18.8 are laws about bags.

Example 18.5

Let us prove the law (the statement (3) in Exercise 18.8).

$$a \sqsubseteq b \wedge b \sqsubseteq c \Rightarrow a \sqsubseteq c$$

Proof:

$\forall\, a, b, c : \mathrm{bag}\, X \bullet$

1. $a \sqsubseteq b \wedge b \sqsubseteq c$	assumption
2. $a \sqsubseteq b$	from 1, $\wedge\_E$
3. $b \sqsubseteq c$	from 1, $\wedge\_E$
4. $\forall\, x : X \bullet a \sharp x \leqslant b \sharp x$	from 2, definition of sub-bag
5. $\forall\, x : X \bullet b \sharp x \leqslant c \sharp x$	from 3, definition of sub-bag
6. $a \sharp x \leqslant b \sharp x$	from 4, $\forall\_E$
7. $b \sharp x \leqslant c \sharp x$	from 5, $\forall\_E$
8. $a \sharp x \leqslant c \sharp x$	from 6 & 7, transitivity of $\leqslant$
9. $\forall\, x : X \bullet a \sharp x \leqslant c \sharp x$	from 8, $\forall\_I$
10. $a \sqsubseteq c$	from 9, definition of sub-bag
11. $a \sqsubseteq b \wedge b \sqsubseteq c \Rightarrow a \sqsubseteq c$	from 1 & 10, $\Rightarrow\_I$

Exercise 18.9 ✳✳✳

Prove the validity of any two statements in the answer to Exercise 18.8.

Chapter 19

Boolean algebra

Topic: Logic and sets

··

If you want to understand function, study structure.

Francis Harry Compton Crick
British biophysicist and Nobel prize laureate (b. 1916)

Objectives

On completion of this chapter you should be able to:

- Explain in terms of its constituents what Boolean algebra is.

- List key properties of operations associated with Boolean algebra.

- Prove the above properties.

- Interpret Boolean algebra as propositional logic.

- Interpret Boolean algebra as an algebra of sets.

- Describe the commonality between set theory and propositional logic as Boolean algebra.

This chapter is devoted to a study of the inherent link between set theory and logic. It also illustrates what are *formal systems*, which is a topic of considerable interest in computing. The reader may gain a good appreciation of the material by reading sections other than Section 19.3, which is devoted to proofs.

At the outset of Chapter 11, we mentioned the close relationship that exists between logic and set theory. Section 12.3 underlined this relationship further by highlighting the relationship between certain set theoretic laws and their counterparts in logic. This similarity is really a reflection of the similarity in structure between, on the one hand, the logical formulae written using propositions and logical connectives $\land$, $\lor$ and $\neg$ and, on the other hand, the set theoretic formulae written using sets and set theoretic operations $\cap$, $\cup$ and the absolute complement.

In this chapter we intend to extract this similarity in the form of an *algebra*. An algebra is also referred to as a *structure*, that is, something that consists of a number of rather specific components. Typically, one of the components of an algebra is a set and others are various operations intended either for manipulating the elements of the given set or for making various observations about them. There are different kinds of algebra. Our concern here is with *Boolean algebra*.

19.1 What is Boolean algebra?

Boolean algebra is a set S, consisting of two distinguished elements denoted by 1 and 0, together with three operations exhibiting some specific properties. These operations are: one unary operation, denoted by $^-$ and two binary operations, denoted by $+$ and $\times$. The three operations take as arguments, and return as results, only elements of S. According to the terminology introduced in Section 13.3, such operations are defined *on* the set S. The nature of these operations should be clear from the study of *relations* in Chapter 13 and, more importantly, *functions* in Chapter 20.

19.1.1 Structure of Boolean algebra

As an algebraic structure, Boolean algebra is a sextuple:

$$(S, 0, 1, +, \times, ^-)$$

Inspired by number theory, the elements 0 and 1 are usually referred to as 'zero' and 'unity' respectively. Similarly, let us read $\times$ as 'multiplication' and $+$ as 'addition'. Let us also borrow from set theory the term 'complement' for $^-$. Despite our familiarity with them in number theory, the symbols 0, 1, $+$ and $\times$ should not be taken to mean their usual meanings. In fact, for the time being we attach no meanings at all to them and our intention is to interpret them later in different ways.

Although our primary aim here is to understand the relationship between logic and set theory, Boolean algebra serves as a good vehicle for the study of *formal deductive systems* (see Section 1.5 for a related discussion). With this in mind, we first present the axioms of Boolean algebra which we take for granted and then consider their consequences as theorems.

19.1.2 Axioms in Boolean algebra

The properties that must be exhibited by $^-$, $+$ and $\times$ may be stated as follows using some arbitrary elements a, b and c of the set S.

Zero and unity as identity elements

$$a \times 1 = a \tag{19.1}$$

$$a + 0 = a \tag{19.2}$$

According to the above two properties, 0 plays the role of *right identity element* for $+$ and 1 the same for $\times$. A definition of this term may be found in Section 17.2 in relation to the discussion on integers.

Commutativity

$$a \times b = b \times a \tag{19.3}$$

$$a + b = b + a \tag{19.4}$$

Note the similarity of the above commutation properties with those in arithmetic if we treat $\times$ as multiplication and $+$ as addition of numbers.

Distributivity

$$a \times (b + c) = (a \times b) + (a \times c) \tag{19.5}$$

$$a + (b \times c) = (a + b) \times (a + c) \tag{19.6}$$

Here we part with number theory because the property (19.6) does not hold there. In order to demonstrate the invalidity of (19.6) in number theory, consider the following counterexample:

$$
\begin{aligned}
& 3 + (4 \times 5) = (3 + 4) \times (3 + 5) \\
\Leftrightarrow\ & 3 + 20 = 7 \times 8 \\
\Leftrightarrow\ & 23 = 56 \\
\Leftrightarrow\ & \textit{false}
\end{aligned}
$$

Relationship of elements with their complements

$$a \times \bar{a} = 0 \tag{19.7}$$

$$a + \bar{a} = 1 \tag{19.8}$$

These properties also describe the relationship of the complement $^{-}$ with the operations $\times$ and $+$.

Size of S

S has at least two distinct elements. $\tag{19.9}$

19.2 Theorems in Boolean algebra

The treatment of the above properties of $^{-}$, $+$ and $\times$ as axioms leads to other interesting properties, which may be proved as theorems. Below is a selection of theorems about Boolean algebra. Proof of some of these theorems follows in Section 19.3 and others are given as exercises.

Idempotence

$$a \times a = a \tag{19.10}$$

$$a + a = a \tag{19.11}$$

Cross identity elements

$$a \times 0 = 0 \qquad \text{(19.12)}$$

$$a + 1 = 1 \qquad \text{(19.13)}$$

Distinctness of zero and unity

$$0 \neq 1 \qquad \text{(19.14)}$$

Note that we have not insisted explicitly that 0 and 1 are distinct. This follows as a consequence of the axioms given above.

Uniqueness of zero and unity

The elements 0 and 1 in S are each unique.   **(19.15)**

This follows as a consequence of the axioms given above.

Double complement

$$\bar{\bar{a}} = a \qquad \text{(19.16)}$$

A doubly complemented element is identical to the original element.

Associativity

$$a + (b + c) = (a + b) + c \qquad \text{(19.17)}$$

$$a \times (b \times c) = (a \times b) \times c \qquad \text{(19.18)}$$

De Morgan's properties

$$\overline{(a \times b)} = \bar{a} + \bar{b} \qquad \text{(19.19)}$$

$$\overline{(a + b)} = \bar{a} \times \bar{b} \qquad \text{(19.20)}$$

A selection of other properties

$$\bar{0} = 1 \qquad \text{(19.21)}$$

$$\bar{1} = 0 \qquad \text{(19.22)}$$

$$a \times (a + b) = a \qquad \text{(19.23)}$$

$$a + (a \times b) = a \qquad \text{(19.24)}$$

$$\bar{a} \times (a \times b) = 0 \qquad \text{(19.25)}$$

$$\bar{a} + (a + b) = 1 \qquad \text{(19.26)}$$

$$a \times (\bar{a} \times \bar{b}) = 0 \qquad \text{(19.27)}$$

$$a + (\bar{a} + \bar{b}) = 1 \qquad \text{(19.28)}$$

$$a = b \quad \text{if} \quad a \times c = b \times c \qquad \text{(19.29)}$$

$$\text{and} \quad a + c = b + c$$

19.3 Proof of theorems

In this section, we prove a few of the theorems given in the previous section. Some theorems may be proved directly from axioms but some proofs inevitably rely on other theorems. (Note that the order of presentation of the theorems in the previous section does not necessarily follow the dependencies in their proof.) Since we do not intend to prove all theorems, in such cases we assume that the subsidiary theorems for a given proof have been previously proved.

Example 19.1

Proof of uniqueness of zero – property (19.15)

Let us consider two zeros 0_1 and 0_2 both satisfying the following defining property:

$$a + 0_1 = a \tag{19.30}$$

$$a + 0_2 = a \tag{19.31}$$

Since a is an arbitrary element, each of the above may be instantiated with 0_1 or 0_2. Instantiation of (19.30) with 0_2 and (19.30) with 0_1 leads to

$$0_2 + 0_1 = 0_2 \tag{19.32}$$

$$0_1 + 0_2 = 0_1 \tag{19.33}$$

which, by the commutation property (19.4), leads in turn to

$$0_1 = 0_2$$

Example 19.2

Proof of idempotence – property (19.11)

a	RHS of (19.11)
$= a + 0$	identity element of $+$, axiom (19.2)
$= a + (a \times \bar{a})$	complement, axiom (19.7)
$= (a + a) \times (a + \bar{a})$	distributivity, axiom (19.6)
$= (a + a) \times 1$	complement, axiom (19.8)
$= a + a$	identity element of $\times$, axiom (19.1)

Example 19.3

Proof of $a + (a \times b) = a$ – property (19.24)

$a + (a \times b)$	LHS of (19.24)
$= (a \times 1) + (a \times b)$	identity element of $\times$, axiom (19.1)
$= a \times (1 + b)$	distributivity, axiom (19.5)
$= a \times (b + 1)$	commutativity, axiom (19.4)
$= a \times 1$	cross identity elements, property (19.13)
$= a$	identity element of $\times$, axiom (19.1)

Proof of (19.23) follows analogously.

Example 19.4

Proof of De Morgan's property (19.19)

The proof is based on the following observations:

$$(\bar{a} + \bar{b}) \times (a \times b) = 0 = \overline{(a \times b)} \times (a \times b) \qquad \textbf{(19.34)}$$

$$(\bar{a} + \bar{b}) + (a \times b) = 1 = \overline{(a \times b)} + (a \times b) \qquad \textbf{(19.35)}$$

which, together with property (19.29), yield the desired De Morgan's property:

$$\overline{(a \times b)} = \bar{a} + \bar{b}$$

This leads us to two subgoals:

$$(\bar{a} + \bar{b}) \times (a \times b) = 0 \qquad \textbf{(19.36)}$$

$$(\bar{a} + \bar{b}) + (a \times b) = 1 \qquad \textbf{(19.37)}$$

Subgoal (19.36) may be proved as:

$$(\bar{a} + \bar{b}) \times (a \times b)$$ LHS of (19.36)
$$= (a \times b) \times (\bar{a} + \bar{b})$$ commutativity, axiom (19.3)
$$= ((a \times b) \times \bar{a}) + ((a \times b) \times \bar{b})$$ distributivity, axiom (19.5)
$$= (\bar{a} \times (a \times b)) + (\bar{b} \times (a \times b))$$ commutativity, axiom (19.3)
$$= (\bar{a} \times (a \times b)) + (\bar{b} \times (b \times a))$$ commutativity, axiom (19.3)
$$= 0 + 0$$ property (19.25)
$$= 0$$ identity element of +, axiom (19.2)

Subgoal (19.37) may be proved as:

$$(\bar{a} + \bar{b}) + (a \times b)$$ LHS of (19.37)
$$= ((\bar{a} + \bar{b}) + a) \times ((\bar{a} + \bar{b}) + b)$$ distributivity, axiom (19.6)
$$= (a + (\bar{a} + \bar{b})) \times (b + (\bar{b} + \bar{a}))$$ commutativity, axiom (19.4)
$$= 1 + 1$$ property (19.28)
$$= 1$$ cross identity elements, property (19.13)

The above proofs of the required subgoals conclude the proof of De Morgan's property (19.19).

Example 19.5

Proof of associativity given by property (19.17)

$$(a + b) + c$$ RHS of (19.17)
$$= ((a + b) + c) \times 1$$ identity element of $\times$, axiom (19.1)

$$= ((a + b) + c) \times (a + \bar{a})$$ complements, axiom (19.8)
$$= (((a + b) + c) \times a) + (((a + b) + c) \times \bar{a})$$ distributivity, axiom (19.5)

$$= (a \times ((a+b)+c)) + (\overline{a} \times ((a+b)+c)) \qquad \text{commutativity, axiom (19.3)}$$
$$= ((a \times (a+b)) + (a \times c)) + (\overline{a} \times ((a+b)+c)) \qquad \text{distributivity, axiom (19.5)}$$
$$= (a + (a \times c)) + (\overline{a} \times ((a+b)+c)) \qquad \text{property (19.23)}$$
$$= a + (\overline{a} \times ((a+b)+c)) \qquad \text{property (19.24)}$$
$$= a + ((\overline{a} \times (a+b)) + (\overline{a} \times c)) \qquad \text{distributivity, axiom (19.5)}$$
$$= a + (((\overline{a} \times a) + (\overline{a} \times b)) + (\overline{a} \times c)) \qquad \text{distributivity, axiom (19.5)}$$
$$= a + (((a \times \overline{a}) + (\overline{a} \times b)) + (\overline{a} \times c)) \qquad \text{commutativity, axiom (19.3)}$$
$$= a + ((0 + (\overline{a} \times b)) + (\overline{a} \times c)) \qquad \text{complements, axiom (19.7)}$$
$$= a + (((\overline{a} \times b) + 0) + (\overline{a} \times c)) \qquad \text{commutativity, axiom (19.4)}$$
$$= a + ((\overline{a} \times b) + (\overline{a} \times c)) \qquad \text{identity element of } +,$$
$$\text{axiom (19.2)}$$

$$= a + (\overline{a} \times (b+c)) \qquad \text{distributivity, axiom (19.5)}$$
$$= a + ((\overline{a} \times (b+c)) + 0) \qquad \text{identity element of } +,$$
$$\text{axiom (19.2)}$$

$$= a + (0 + (\overline{a} \times (b+c))) \qquad \text{commutativity, axiom (19.4)}$$
$$= a + ((a \times \overline{a}) + (\overline{a} \times (b+c))) \qquad \text{complements, axiom (19.7)}$$
$$= a + ((\overline{a} \times a) + (\overline{a} \times (b+c))) \qquad \text{commutativity, axiom (19.3)}$$
$$= a + (\overline{a} \times (a + (b+c))) \qquad \text{distributivity, axiom (19.5)}$$
$$= a + ((a + (b+c)) \times \overline{a}) \qquad \text{commutativity, axiom (19.3)}$$
$$= (a \times (a + (b+c))) + ((a + (b+c)) \times \overline{a}) \qquad \text{property (19.23)}$$
$$= ((a + (b+c)) \times a) + ((a + (b+c)) \times \overline{a}) \qquad \text{commutativity, axiom (19.3)}$$
$$= (a + (b+c)) \times (a + \overline{a}) \qquad \text{distributivity, axiom (19.5)}$$
$$= (a + (b+c)) \times 1 \qquad \text{complements, axiom (19.8)}$$
$$= a + (b+c) \qquad \text{identity element of } \times,$$
$$\text{axiom (19.1)}$$

(Exercise 19.1 ✳✳✳)

Prove a selection of theorems yet to be proved.

(19.4) **Propositional interpretation of Boolean algebra**

As mentioned earlier, the components in the Boolean algebra described above have not been given any meaning. Its presentation has essentially dealt with the syntactic form of the algebra with no reference to semantics. However, with the associated deductive system, its syntactic structure has enabled the proof of formulae which follow logically from the chosen axioms.

Abstract treatment of mathematical structures in this manner results in very general theories, which can be interpreted in different ways in the study of different fields. Let us demonstrate this by interpreting the Boolean algebra with respect to propositional logic and sets.

In relation to propositional logic, this interpretation takes the form shown in Table 19.1.

Table 19.1   The Boolean algebra interpreted with respect to propositional logic.

Boolean algebra	Propositional interpretation
S	Collection of all propositional formulae
a, b, c	Propositional variables
0	Contradictory propositional formulae as represented by **false** (see Section 3.6)
1	Tautological propositional formulae as represented by **true** (see Section 3.6)
$-$	Propositional connective $\neg$
$\times$	Propositional connective $\wedge$
$+$	Propositional connective $\vee$
$=$	Propositional connective $\Leftrightarrow$

Under this interpretation, all axioms and theorems of the Boolean algebra become logically true propositions or tautologies. Furthermore, since under this interpretation the main connective in every formula is the material equivalence $\Leftrightarrow$, all axioms and theorems of the Boolean algebra express logical equivalences or laws of logic, such as those presented in Section 4.2.

Despite the choice made in the above table, $=$ may be interpreted alternatively as the symbol $\Longleftrightarrow$ denoting the logical equivalence directly. The choice of $\Leftrightarrow$ or $\Longleftrightarrow$ for $=$ would depend on whether we wish to treat $=$ as a component of the Boolean algebra or as a symbol outside it.

Note that the propositional interpretation given above corresponds only to a part of the logical system we studied. This is because we have omitted the connective $\Rightarrow$ and its reasoning aspects. Omission of $\Rightarrow$ is immaterial in the case of propositional logic since certain propositional connectives, including $\Rightarrow$, are really abbreviations for slightly longer formulae written in terms of other connectives.

19.5   Set interpretation of Boolean algebra

Our second interpretation of Boolean algebra is with respect to sets. Here too we omit certain parts of set theory but, unlike in the case of propositional logic discussed above, one of these omissions is worthy of special note. In particular, the interpretation omits altogether the symbol $\in$ denoting set membership, which is a fundamental set theoretic concept. In order to highlight this omission, let us refer to the part of set theory considered in our interpretation as the *algebra of sets*.

In relation to this algebra of sets, the interpretation takes the form shown in Table 19.2.

Table 19.2   The Boolean algebra interpreted with respect to sets.

Boolean algebra	Interpretation in algebra of sets
S	Collection of all sets
a, b, c	Variables denoting sets
0	The empty set $\varnothing$
1	The universal set U
$-$	The absolute complement $'$
$\times$	Set intersection $\cap$
$+$	Set union $\cup$
$=$	Set equality $=$

Under this interpretation, all axioms and theorems of the Boolean algebra become laws about sets, such as those given in Section 12.3.

(19.6) Significance of Boolean algebra

Although our brief study of Boolean algebra has been primarily aimed at a better appreciation of the underlying concepts of logic and set theory, Boolean algebra is important in its own right in many branches of computing. Our study of digital circuits in Chapters 2 and 4 is one such application. The kind of treatment given here for Boolean algebra should also provide an insight into formal theories. This kind of approach is an established approach to specification of abstract data types, where it is known as the *algebraic approach to specification*. The latter is an alternative to the approach outlined in Chapters 12 and 16 using the specification notation Z. The latter approach is known as the *model-oriented approach to specification*. More about these approaches may be found in Section 12.7 and Section 16.5.

Chapter 20

Lambda abstraction of functions

Topic: Functions

In a symbol there is concealment and yet revelation; here therefore, by Silence and by Speech acting together, comes a double significance.

Thomas Carlyle
British historian (1795–1881)

Objectives

On completion of this chapter you should be able to:

- Represent functions in curried form.

- Define functions as λ-functions.

- Work out the result of a substitution of variables in an expression.

- Replace bound variables in λ-functions as β-reduction.

- Work out application of λ-functions as β-reduction.

- Simplify λ-functions by means of β-reduction.

- Perform reductions in applicative order and normal order.

This chapter covers a form of function abstraction called *λ-functions* – a branch of mathematical logic having a profound influence on theoretical aspects of computing. In particular, λ-functions serve as the basis of functional programming, discussed in Section 16.6, and feature in formal specification languages such as the Z notation. An implementation of λ-functions may also be found in the programming language Lisp.

20.1 Curried functions

The concept of a *curried function* is due to Schönfinkel but it is named after H. B. Curry, who is credited with the rediscovery and extensive use of Schönfinkel's work in this area.

According to our study of functions so far, any function takes all its arguments at once and returns the result. A typical example is the operator for addition

$$\_ + \_ : \mathbb{N} \times \mathbb{N} \rightarrow \mathbb{N}$$

which takes a pair of numbers and returns their sum. Although it takes two numbers, it is important to realize that this function really takes only one object as its argument, which just happens to be a pair of numbers.

By contrast, one can invent a *curried* version of the above function which takes the two numbers in turn, as if on separate occasions, and returns a result each time the function is applied to a number. Let the curried counterpart of the above function be called *add*. It has the following type

$$add : \mathbb{N} \rightarrow (\mathbb{N} \rightarrow \mathbb{N})$$

or, alternatively,

$$add : \mathbb{N} \rightarrow \mathbb{N} \rightarrow \mathbb{N}$$

The above two notations make the point that function arrows associate to the right. On the other hand, the function application associates to the left, that is:

$$add\ x\ y = ((add\ x)\ y)$$

As a result of the above two associative rules on function arrows and function application, when *add* is applied to a particular number, say 5, it returns an intermediate function of the type

$$\mathbb{N} \rightarrow \mathbb{N}$$

such that the intermediate function automatically adds 5 to whatever number is fed to it as its argument. As a consequence, when both arguments are supplied, *add* behaves exactly like '+' . An advantage of curried functions is that they allow *partial application* of functions and, thus, the definition of new functions from old ones. For example, the function which always adds 5 to its argument may be defined as below by partially applying *add* to 5.

$$add5 : \mathbb{N} \rightarrow \mathbb{N}$$
$$add5 = add\ 5$$

(20.2) Infix operators

Curried functions can also be used in relation to mathematical operators such as $\_ + \_$ for addition given in *infix* style. Because of our familiarity with them, statements about properties of infix operators are more intelligible than those dealing with other styles, and thus help reasoning. They consist of place-holders, indicated by underscores '_', for arguments but with no clear indication as to where different arguments fit in. Curried functions, together with the notation introduced below, help to clarify this ambiguity.

Unlike _+_, some of the binary infix operators are non-commutative functions, where swapping of variables alters the meaning completely. Therefore, it is important to make sure that the right argument is inserted at the right place. An example of a non-commutative operator is _−_ for subtracting numbers; another is the relational overriding operator _⊕_, defined in Section 14.5. There are operators with no symbol at all. An example is the operator for raising a number to a power, as exemplified by 2^3 for raising the number 2 to the power 3.

When defining infix operators in the style of curried functions, we may clarify the position of the operands by using labelled underscores '$\underline{i}$' indicating the place of the ith argument, the order being determined by the syntax. As an example, let us consider in this notation a curried 'non-customary' version of subtraction operation:

$$\underline{2} - \underline{1} : \mathbb{N} \to \mathbb{N} \to \mathbb{N}$$

where, for example, $\underline{2}$ indicates the place intended for the second argument. The above is non-customary in the sense that it subtracts the number given first from the second one. Its application to the numbers 3 and 5 in that order may be evaluated as

$$((\underline{2} - \underline{1})3) \, 5 = (\underline{2} - 3) \, 5 = 5 - 3 = 2$$

Note that $(\underline{2} - 3)$ is a function on $\mathbb{N}$, which subtracts 3 from its argument.

20.3 Function names

Let us examine here the reasons for using names for functions. One reason is that some functions are so frequently used in mathematics, science and engineering that they need some convenient, commonly agreed means for referring to them. Typical examples are functions such as *sine* and *cosine* in trigonometry and the logarithmic function *log* in algebra. Another reason is that function names provide us with a way to indicate the role of arguments of the function in its definition. This becomes useful in trying to convey, or understand, the meaning of an expression such as

$$\textit{diff}\,(\textit{square } a)(\textit{square } b) \tag{20.1}$$

Note that *diff* and *square* in the above denote the functions

$$
\begin{aligned}
\textit{diff} \quad &:: \mathbb{N} \to \mathbb{N} \to \mathbb{N} \\
\textit{square} \quad &:: \mathbb{N} \to \mathbb{N} \\
\textit{diff } x \, y &= x - y \\
\textit{square } x &= x \times x
\end{aligned}
$$

If a and b are constants, say, 5 and 4 respectively, then the expression (20.1) has a value, which is 9. On the other hand, a and b could be free variables, in which case the context determines the meaning of the expression (20.1). Alternatively, one of the variables in (20.1) could be a free variable and the other a kind of 'bound' variable, in effect making (20.1) a function. Since the variables of the

Table 20.1   Roles of the variables in the function *diffofsquares*.

Role of variables informally	Role of variables made explicit
a is a free variable and *b* is a formal parameter	*diffofsquares b = diff(square a)(square b)*
a is a formal parameter and *b* is a free variable	*diffofsquares a = diff(square a)(square b)*
Both *a* and *b* are formal parameters	*diffofsquares a b = diff(square a)(square b)*
Both *a* and *b* are formal parameters	*diffofsquares b a = diff(square a)(square b)*

latter kind are formal parameters of the function, it is important to indicate the status, and hence the role, of variables being used. In the case of (20.1), there are a number of different possibilities, which can be shown by inventing a function name *diffofsquares* (for difference of squares) and considering the possibilities as enumerated in Table 20.1.

It can be seen from Table 20.1 that introduction of function names indirectly helps to clarify the role of variables in function definitions.

20.4 Lambda abstraction

Despite the above benefits gained by naming functions, the concept of a λ-*function* provides us with a way to dispense with function names. Thus, it is a form of function abstraction, where the emphasis is on the essence of a function, that is, what it 'does' to its arguments, and not how it is referred to. Using λ-abstraction it becomes unnecessary to name functions unless function names are necessary on other grounds. This makes sense when functions are defined on a one-off basis, for example, when a function is used only as an argument to another function. Another situation is where a function is used in a secondary role as in

$$\forall b : \text{bag } X \bullet count\ b = \underbrace{(\lambda x : X \bullet 0)}_{\text{secondary function}} \oplus b$$

which is an alternative definition to that given in Section 18.4 when discussing bags. As a result, λ-functions are basically a kind of 'anonymous function'. As it dispenses with function names, λ-abstraction provides us with an alternative way to indicate the role of individual variables.

Lambda-functions are introduced according to the following syntax:

$$\lambda \langle \text{variable} \rangle \bullet \langle \text{function\_body} \rangle \tag{20.2}$$

or according to the more general syntax:

$$\lambda \langle \text{signature} \rangle \mid \langle \text{constraint} \rangle \bullet \langle \text{function\_body} \rangle \tag{20.3}$$

The symbol λ in λ-functions is a flag indicating that what follows is a function without a name. The term 'variable' indicates the place of a single variable,

Table 20.2   The functions of Table 20.1 as λ-functions (for Example 20.1).

λ-abstraction	Role of variables
$\lambda\, b \bullet diff(square\ a)(square\ b)$	a is a free variable and b is a formal parameter.
$\lambda\, a \bullet diff(square\ a)(square\ b)$	a is a formal parameter and b is a free variable.
$\lambda\, a,\ b \bullet diff(square\ a)(square\ b)$	Both a and b are formal parameters; a is the first and b is the second.
$\lambda\, b,\ a \bullet diff(square\ a)(square\ b)$	Both a and b are formal parameters; b is the first and a is the second.

whereas 'signature' is a list of variable declarations, possibly with their types. 'Constraint' is a predicate constraining the values of variables. Lambda-functions are curried functions and, therefore, the order of variables listed in 'signature' conforms with the order expected in curried functions. 'Function_body' is a term (an expression) defining the result to be returned.

Example 20.1

Referring to expression (20.1), functions enumerated in Table 20.1 may be distinguished from one another in terms of the λ-functions listed in Table 20.2.

Notation

Note that in Example 20.1 we have used a common abbreviation, according to which the following are identical (equivalent) to each other:

$$\lambda\, a, b \bullet diff(square\ a)(square\ b)$$
$$\stackrel{def}{=} \lambda\, a \bullet (\lambda\, b \bullet diff(square\ a)\ (square\ b))$$
$$\stackrel{def}{=} \lambda\, a \bullet \lambda\, b \bullet diff(square\ a)\ (square\ b) \tag{20.4}$$

Example 20.2

Here are some functions which behave identically when they are fully applied.

$f(x) = x + 2$ on $\mathbb{N}$	$\lambda x : \mathbb{N} \bullet x + 2$
$f(x) = \sqrt[3]{x}$ on $\mathbb{Z}$	$\lambda x : \mathbb{Z} \mid (n \in \mathbb{Z} \wedge n^3 = x) \bullet n$
$f(x, y) = x + y$ from $\mathbb{R}^2$ to $\mathbb{R}$	$\lambda x, y : \mathbb{R} \bullet x + y$
$f(x, y) = \sqrt{x^2 + y^2}$ from $\mathbb{R}^2$ to $\mathbb{R}$	$\lambda x, y : \mathbb{R} \bullet (x^2 + y^2)^{\frac{1}{2}}$
$f(x, y) = \sqrt{x + y}$ from $\mathbb{R}^2$ to $\mathbb{R}$, if $x + y \geqslant 0$	$\lambda x, y : \mathbb{R} \mid x + y \geqslant 0 \bullet (x + y)^{\frac{1}{2}}$

Exercise 20.1 ✳

Define the types of the named functions (on the left) and λ-functions (on the right) in the above example.

Example 20.3

The following examples illustrate how function application works in the case of λ-functions.

$$(\lambda x : \mathbb{N} \bullet x + 2)\ 5 = 5 + 2 = 7$$
$$(\lambda x : \mathbb{Z} \mid n \in \mathbb{Z} \wedge n^3 = x \bullet n)\ 27 = 3$$
$$(\lambda x : \mathbb{Z} \mid n \in \mathbb{Z} \wedge n^3 = x \bullet n)\ 28 = \text{'undefined'}$$
$$(\lambda x, y : \mathbb{R} \bullet y + x)\ 7 = \lambda y : \mathbb{R} \bullet y + 7$$
$$(\lambda x, y : \mathbb{R} \bullet (x^2 + y^2)^{\frac{1}{2}})\ 5 = \lambda y : \mathbb{R} \bullet (5^2 + y^2)^{\frac{1}{2}}$$

Exercise 20.2 ✳

1. Define the types of the values or expressions resulting from the application of the λ-functions in Example 20.3.

2. Define the λ-versions for the following functions.
   (a) $f(x) = x + 2$ on $\mathbb{Z}$
   (b) $f(x) = x^2$ on $\mathbb{Z}$
   (c) $f(x) = x^3$ on $\mathbb{R}$
   (d) $f(x) = \sqrt[3]{x}$ on $\mathbb{R}$
   (e) $f(x) = \dfrac{1}{x}$ on $\mathbb{R}$
   (f) $f(x) = \dfrac{1}{x} + \sqrt{x}$ on $\mathbb{R}$
   (g) $f(x, y) = \sin^2(x) + \cos^2(y)$ from $\mathbb{R}^2$ to $\mathbb{R}$
   (h) $f(x, y, z) = \dfrac{x + y}{z}$ from $\mathbb{R}^3$ to $\mathbb{R}$
   (i) $f(r) = \pi \times r^2$ on $\mathbb{R}$ (for computing the area of a circle)

This section introduced two versions of syntax for λ-functions, namely, in the forms (20.2) and (20.3). Among them, (20.3) is the syntax followed by specification languages such as the Z notation and incorporates, among other things, built-in syntactic features, type declarations and additional symbols. This is too complex for the remainder of our study, which deals with reasoning about λ-functions. We restrict ourselves, therefore, to λ-functions of the form (20.2).

20.5 Lambda calculus

20.5.1 Motivation

Consider the λ-functions and their application to arguments shown in Table 20.3.

Table 20.3 Application of some λ-functions.

Function application	Result	Comment
$\lambda x \bullet x\ a$	a	$\lambda x \bullet x$ is the *identity function*
$\lambda x \bullet y\ a$	y	$\lambda x \bullet y$ is the *constant function* always returning y
$((\lambda\ a,\ b \bullet diff(square\ a)(square\ b))4)5$	9	The given function is identical to $\lambda x \bullet 9$

The purpose of Table 20.3 is to show that certain expressions involving λ-functions are identical to one another and correspond to already familiar concepts. In order to reason about such identities, we need a λ-*calculus*. Our account of λ-calculus relies on the following sources: Hein (1996), Henson (1987) and Hindley and Seldin (1986).

20.5.2   Syntax of lambda calculus

The λ-calculus we study considers λ-functions in the simple form (20.2). In other words, it is not equipped to deal with the elaborate extensions to λ-calculus made with types and so on. For this reason, the resulting system is referred to as *pure λ-calculus*.

Lambda-calculus is a *formal system* such as propositional logic covered in Chapter 3 and Boolean algebra covered in Chapter 19. Our study of λ-calculus, therefore, naturally relies on the experience gained in Chapter 3 on propositional logic as a formal system.

(Definition)   Lambda-terms

As a formal system, λ-calculus consists of λ-*terms*. These are as follows:

1. All variables and constants are λ-terms. These are called *atoms*.
2. If M and N are λ-terms, then $(M\ N)$ is also a λ-term. With reference to a term of the form $(M\ N)$, $(M\ N)$ is said to be an *application of M to N*.
3. If M is a λ-term and x is a variable, then $(\lambda x \bullet M)$ is also a λ-term. In this case, $(\lambda x \bullet M)$ is said to be an *abstraction*, because we form a function out of a term (expression).

Excessive parentheses may be omitted by following the convention that application of λ-terms associates to the left. According to this convention, the λ-term '$P\ Q\ R\ S$' is to be interpreted as

$(((P\ Q)R)S)$

Note also that we treat $(\lambda x \bullet P\ Q)$ as $((\lambda x \bullet P)Q)$.

Notation

1. We use the symbol $\equiv$ for identity of λ-terms syntactically, that is, when dealing with terms with no concern for what they represent. The symbol $=$ is reserved, as usual, for identity of objects such as numbers, sets, functions and so on.

2. Furthermore, note that we continue to use the abbreviations introduced in (20.4).

Note

The Definition of syntax of λ-terms excludes numbers, other primitive types of values such as truth values, built-in operators such as $+$, $\times$, etc., and other function symbols such as *diff* and *square* we used earlier. The power of λ-calculus lies in the fact that these can be constructed from the λ-terms introduced in the Definition. Later on we will consider an example illustrating this.

Example 20.4

Table 20.4 lists some λ-terms.

Table 20.4   Some λ-terms.

λ-terms	Explanation
x	x is a variable (an atom) and, therefore, according to (1) in the syntax Definition, it is a λ-term
y	As above, since y is a variable
$\lambda x \bullet x$	x is a λ-term as well as a variable and, therefore, according to (3), $(\lambda x \bullet x)$ is a λ-term
$\lambda x \bullet y$	y is a λ-term and x is a variable, and therefore, according to (3), $(\lambda x \bullet y)$ is a λ-term
$(((\lambda x \bullet x\, \lambda x \bullet y)x)a)$	It is a λ-term because:
	$(((\underbrace{\lambda x \bullet x}_{\substack{\text{abstraction.}\\\text{see (3)}}}\quad \underbrace{\lambda x \bullet y}_{\substack{\text{abstraction.}\\\text{see (3)}}})x)a)$
	$\underbrace{\phantom{\text{application, see (2)}}}_{\text{application, see (2)}}$
	$\underbrace{\phantom{\text{application, see (2)....}}}_{\text{application, see (2)....}}$
$(\lambda x \bullet y(\lambda x \bullet x\, a))$	It is a λ-term because:
	$(\underbrace{\lambda x \bullet y}_{\text{abstraction}}\quad (\underbrace{\lambda x \bullet x}_{\text{abstraction}}\, a))$
	$\underbrace{\phantom{\text{application}}}_{\text{application}}$
	$\underbrace{\phantom{\text{application}}}_{\text{application}}$
	This λ-term represents a *function composition*

Exercise 20.3 ✳

Identify λ-terms among the following.

1. $x\ y$
2. $\lambda x \bullet y\ x$
3. $\lambda x \bullet \lambda z\ y \bullet x\ z$
4. $\lambda x \bullet (x\ x)\ \lambda x \bullet (x\ x)$
5. $\lambda x \bullet \lambda y \bullet x$
6. d
7. $\lambda x \bullet \lambda \lambda y \bullet x$
8. $x\ \lambda x \bullet (\lambda y \bullet y)\ x$
9. $\lambda x \bullet (x(x\ y))\ N$, where N is an arbitrary λ-term.
10. $\lambda x \bullet x\ x\ y\ N$, where, as above, N is an arbitrary λ-term.

20.5.3 Bound and free variables

The notions of *bound* and *free variables* in λ-calculus are similar to those discussed in Chapter 7. Similarities, as well as differences, are as follows:

1. The role of quantifiers $\forall$ and $\exists$ is played by the symbol λ.
2. The role of variables and constants in predicate logic is played by variables and constants in λ-calculus, that is, by atoms.
3. When determining the scope of λ-terms in the absence of parentheses, particularly in the case of terms involving any λ, left associativity of application of λ-terms mentioned in Section 20.5.2 must be taken into account.
4. In pure λ-calculus there are no counterparts to predicate symbols.

Because of the above similarities, our discussion relies on that in Chapter 7 on variable status in predicate logic.

Description) Bound and free variables

An occurrence of a variable x in a λ-term M is a *bound variable* if and only if it occurs within a part of M having the form $\lambda x \bullet N$. Otherwise, the particular occurrence of x is said to be *free*.

Exercise 20.4 ✳

Identify bound and free variables in the λ-terms listed in Exercise 20.3.

20.5.4   Transformation of lambda terms

Reasoning about λ-terms is based on their transformation to other λ-terms. The most basic way to transform a term to another is replacement of a variable by a λ-term.

(**Description**)   Substitution of variables
_____

The notation

$$E[x/M]$$

denotes the λ-term obtained by replacing all free occurrences of the variable x in the λ-term E by the λ-term M.

Here we encounter the kind of problem we encountered in Section 9.5 of Chapter 9. It concerns the possible clash of variable names in the term M with those in E in the process of substitution. As in predicate logic, injudicious substitutions can thus lead to conclusions contrary to our intuition. In this respect, the rules clarifying what constitutes the 'judicious substitutions' are given in the Observations.

(**Observations**)
_____

Here are some rules on substitution of variables. Given that E, F, M are λ-terms,

1. $x[x/M] \equiv M$

2. $y[x/M] \equiv y$ provided that $x \neq y$

3. $(E\ F)[x/M] \equiv ((E[x/M])\ (F[x/M]))$

4. $(\lambda x \bullet E)[x/M] \equiv \lambda x \bullet E$

5. $(\lambda y \bullet E)[x/M] \equiv \lambda y \bullet (E[x/M])$

   provided that: (a) $x \neq y$, and
   　　　　　　　　(b) y is not free in M, or
   　　　　　　　　(c) x is not free in E.

6. $(\lambda y \bullet E)[x/M] \equiv \lambda z \bullet (E[y/z][x/M])$

   provided that: (a) $x \neq y$, and
   　　　　　　　　(b) y is free in M, and
   　　　　　　　　(c) x is free in E, and
   　　　　　　　　(d) z is a fresh free variable, that is, z is free neither in E nor in M.

As mentioned above, the six rules are designed to avoid incorrect reasoning about λ-terms. Some are fairly intuitive, but others, especially rules (5) and (6), are not so. In order to illustrate their relevance, consider the following example, namely, the function

$$\lambda x \bullet y \qquad\qquad\qquad\qquad\qquad \textbf{(20.5)}$$

which is a constant function always returning y as its result, and another version of the same

$$\lambda z \bullet y \qquad\qquad\qquad\qquad\qquad \textbf{(20.6)}$$

Since x in (20.5) and z in (20.6) are bound variables and, therefore, have no relevance as far as the meaning is concerned, both (20.5) and (20.6) represent the same constant function. Therefore, we would expect any substitution to preserve the fundamental character of the function. However, the substitution

$$[y/z] \qquad\qquad\qquad\qquad\qquad \textbf{(20.7)}$$

could be problematic. That is, of course, if we disregard the proposed substitution rules. Now, although the functions which we are dealing with are identical, and the actual substitutions too are identical, indiscriminate application of rule (6) would lead to

$$\underbrace{(\lambda x \bullet y)}_{E}\underbrace{[y/z]}_{x/M} \equiv \underbrace{\lambda x \bullet z}_{E[x/M]} \qquad\qquad \textbf{(20.8)}$$

$$\underbrace{(\lambda z \bullet y)}_{E}\underbrace{[y/z]}_{x/M} \equiv \underbrace{\lambda z \bullet z}_{E[x/M]} \qquad\qquad \textbf{(20.9)}$$

Note the difference: (20.8) results in a constant function returning z as its result, whereas (20.9) results in the identity function. Obviously, something is wrong.

Now let us perform the same substitution, but obeying the substitution rules (1)–(6). The relevant rules are (5) and (6) only. In the case of the substitution proposed on the left-hand side of (20.8), note that:

1. $x \neq y$.
2. The variable x is not free in the term z, which plays the role of M.
3. The variable y is free in the term y, which plays the role of E.

Since the above satisfies the conditions attached to it, rule (5) is applicable and yields the term shown on the right-hand side of (20.8).

On the other hand, in the case of the substitution proposed on the left-hand side of (20.9), we have:

1. $x \neq y$.
2. The variable z is free in the term z, which plays the role of M.
3. The variable y is free in the term y, which plays the role of E.

These violate the conditions attached to rule (5) but satisfy the conditions attached to rule (6). So, it is rule (6) which is applicable. In order to apply it, however, we need a variable which is not free in either E or M, that is, a variable outside $\{z, y\}$. Let it be p. Rule (6) then leads to:

$$\underbrace{(\lambda z \bullet y)}_{E} \underbrace{[y/z]}_{x/M} \equiv \lambda p \bullet \underbrace{(y[z/p][y/z])}_{(E[y/z][x/M])} \qquad \text{rule (6)}$$

$$\equiv \lambda p \bullet y[y/z] \qquad \text{rule (2)}$$

$$\equiv \lambda p \bullet z \qquad \text{rule (1)} \qquad\qquad \textbf{(20.10)}$$

resulting in a constant function. This outcome agrees with our intuition since the variable being replaced by z is y, which is in the body of the function.

Example 20.5

$$(\lambda y \bullet x \; (\lambda x \bullet x))[x/(\lambda y \bullet x \; y)]$$

$$\equiv ((\lambda y \bullet \underbrace{x}_{E})[x/\underbrace{(\lambda y \bullet x \; y)}_{M}] \; (\lambda x \bullet x)[x/(\lambda y \bullet x \; y)]) \qquad \text{rule (3)}$$

$$\equiv (\lambda p \bullet x[y/p][x/(\lambda y \bullet x \; y)] \; (\lambda x \bullet x)[x/(\lambda y \bullet x \; y)]) \qquad \text{rule (6)}$$

$$\equiv (\lambda p \bullet x[x/(\lambda y \bullet x \; y)] \; (\lambda x \bullet x)[x/(\lambda y \bullet x \; y)]) \qquad \text{rule (2)}$$

$$\equiv (\lambda p \bullet (\lambda y \bullet x \; y) \; (\lambda x \bullet x)[x/(\lambda y \bullet x \; y)]) \qquad \text{rule (1)}$$

$$\equiv (\lambda p \bullet (\lambda y \bullet x \; y) \; (\lambda x \bullet x)) \qquad \text{rule (4)}$$

Example 20.6

Consider now a slight alteration of the terms in Example 20.5.

$$(\lambda y \bullet \underbrace{(x \; (\lambda x \bullet x))}_{E}) \; [x/\underbrace{(\lambda y \bullet (x \; y))}_{M}]$$

$$\equiv (\lambda y \bullet (x \; (\lambda x \bullet x))[x/(\lambda y \bullet (x \; y))]) \qquad \text{rule (5)}$$

$$\equiv (\lambda y \bullet (x[x/(\lambda y \bullet (x \; y))] \; (\lambda x \bullet x)[x/(\lambda y \bullet (x \; y))])) \qquad \text{rule (3)}$$

$$\equiv (\lambda y \bullet ((\lambda y \bullet (x \; y)) \; (\lambda x \bullet \underbrace{x}_{E})[x/\underbrace{(\lambda y \bullet (x \; y))}_{M}])) \qquad \text{rule (1)}$$

$$\equiv (\lambda y \bullet ((\lambda y \bullet (x \; y)) \; (\lambda x \bullet x))) \qquad \text{rule (4)}$$

Exercise 20.5 ✳ ✳

Justifying each step, perform the following substitutions.

1. $(y \; (\lambda z \bullet x \; y))[x/(\lambda y \bullet z \; y)]$
2. $(y \; (\lambda z \bullet (x \; y)))[x/(\lambda y \bullet (z \; y))]$

20.5.5 ## Application of lambda functions

The result of applying a λ-function to its argument can be worked out by replacing the formal parameter of the function in the function body with the λ-term playing the role of the argument. Therefore, rules on how to transform λ-terms by substitution have direct relevance in determining the result of application of λ-functions. However, as we have seen already, substitutions cannot be made arbitrarily, but according to precise rules. Sometimes, this could involve transformation or manipulation of λ-functions first into an appropriate form prior to making the substitution suggested above. There are three different ways to manipulate λ-functions, known as *conversion* or *reduction*.

Alpha conversion

Alpha conversion, also known as α-*reduction*, is a rule on how to change bound variables in λ-functions.

(**Description**) Alpha conversion
_____

Given that the variable y does not occur free in E, the function $\lambda x \bullet E$ can be reduced to the function $\lambda y \bullet E[x/y]$. The same is stated formally as:

$$\lambda x \bullet E \xrightarrow{\alpha} \lambda y \bullet E[x/y] \tag{20.11}$$

where $\xrightarrow{\alpha}$ denotes the α-conversion.

Note that the symbol $\xrightarrow{\alpha}$ in (20.11) denotes a relation on λ-terms, which is reflexive, symmetrical and transitive.

Notation

We denote the converse of $\xrightarrow{\alpha}$ by $\xstyle{\not\xrightarrow{\alpha}}$. Thus, $M \not\xrightarrow{\alpha} N$ means that M cannot be reduced to N by an α-conversion.

(**Example 20.7**)
_____

Alpha conversion permits/forbids the following reductions:

$$\lambda x \bullet x \xrightarrow{\alpha} \lambda y \bullet y$$

$$\lambda x \bullet y \xrightarrow{\alpha} \lambda z \bullet y$$

$$\lambda x \bullet y \not\xrightarrow{\alpha} \lambda y \bullet y$$

Beta conversion

Beta conversion or β-*reduction* is the rule that characterizes function application. Let us consider how to evaluate the function application

$$(\lambda x \bullet E \ M)$$

In this case, the substitution

$$E[x/M]$$

seems to give the result we expect from function application. However, this requires that the substitution process does not bind any variable inadvertently.

(Description) Beta conversion

Given that the substitution of M for x in E does not introduce any new occurrence of variable binding, $\lambda x \bullet E\ M$ can be reduced to the term $E[x/M]$. This is stated formally as:

$$\lambda x \bullet E\ M \xrightarrow{\beta} E[x/M] \tag{20.12}$$

where $\xrightarrow{\beta}$ denotes the β-conversion.

(Example 20.8)

$$((\lambda x \bullet (x\ y))\ (\lambda x \bullet (x\ y)))$$

$$\xrightarrow{\beta} (x\ y)[x/\lambda x \bullet (x\ y)]$$

$\equiv (x[x/(\lambda x \bullet (x\ y))]\ y[x/(\lambda x \bullet (x\ y))])$ subs. rule (3)

$\equiv ((\lambda x \bullet (x\ y))\ y[x/(\lambda x \bullet (x\ y))])$ subs. rule (1)

$\equiv ((\lambda x \bullet (x\ y))\ y)$ subs. rule (2)

$\xrightarrow{\beta} (x\ y)[x/y]$

$\equiv (y\ y)$ subs. rule (1)

There are cases where reductions may never terminate. Example 20.9 gives one such instance.

(Example 20.9)

$$(\lambda x \bullet (x\ x)\ (\lambda x \bullet (x\ x)))$$

$$\xrightarrow{\beta} (x\ x)[x/\lambda x \bullet (x\ x)]$$

$\equiv (x[x/(\lambda x \bullet (x\ x))]\ x[x/(\lambda x \bullet (x\ x))])$ subs. rule (3)

$\equiv ((\lambda x \bullet (x\ x))\ (\lambda x \bullet (x\ x)))$ subs. rule (1)

$$\vdots$$

$\xrightarrow{\beta} ((\lambda x \bullet (x\ x))\ (\lambda x \bullet (x\ x)))$ repeating the above

$$\vdots$$

$\xrightarrow{\beta} ((\lambda x \bullet (x\ x))\ (\lambda x \bullet (x\ x)))$ repeating the above again

(Exercise 20.6 ✱✱)

Examine the reducibility of the following term.

$$((\lambda x \bullet (x\ x\ y))\ (\lambda x \bullet (x\ x\ y)))$$

Eta conversion

Eta conversion or *η-reduction* is a rule which forces equivalence of λ-terms of the form $\lambda x \bullet (E\ x)$ and E when x is not free in E.

Description) Eta conversion

Given that x does not occur free in E, $\lambda x \bullet (E\ x)$ can be reduced to the term E. This is stated formally as:

$$\lambda x \bullet (E\ x) \xrightarrow{\eta} E \tag{20.13}$$

where $\xrightarrow{\eta}$ denotes the η-conversion.

The reasoning underlying the η-conversion may be seen from the following application $(\lambda x \bullet (E\ x)F)$, which reduces to $(E\ F)$.

Example 20.10

The η-conversion given below reduces as

$$\lambda y \bullet \underbrace{(((\lambda y \bullet (x\ y))\ (\lambda x \bullet x))\ y)}_{y \text{ is not free.}} \xrightarrow{\eta} ((\lambda y \bullet (x\ y))\ (\lambda x \bullet x))$$

20.5.6   Reducibility and normal form

Various conversion rules allow simplification of λ-terms. In particular, a λ-term of the form $(\lambda x \bullet E\ M)$ can be simplified by β-conversion to $E[x/M]$. For this reason, a term of the form $(\lambda x \bullet E\ M)$ is called a *β-redex*, that is, a *reducible expression* by β-conversion, or simply, a *redex*. A term is said to be in *normal form* if it does not contain any β-redex, that is, if it cannot be further reduced by β-conversion.

However, not every λ-term has a normal form. This is because some terms involve non-terminating chains of reductions.

Example 20.11

λ-term	Whether in *normal form*
x	Yes
$(x\ y)$	Yes
$\lambda x \bullet x$	Yes
$\lambda x \bullet (x\ x)$	Yes
$\lambda x \bullet x\ a$	No, by definition
$((\lambda x \bullet x)\ (\lambda x \bullet a\ y))$	No, reasons as indicated
$(\lambda x \bullet (x\ x)(\lambda x \bullet (x\ x)))$	No, because it leads to an infinite sequence of reductions (see Example 20.9)

20.5.7   Reduction orders

Our discussion here is related to that in Section 16.6.7 with reference to evaluation order of functions in functional programming. As there, some λ-terms may be reduced into simpler forms in several different ways. In this respect, there are two reduction orders of λ-terms as well: the *innermost reduction* and the *outermost reduction*. A redex is said to be an *innermost redex* if it does not contain any further redex. On the other hand, a redex is said to be an *outermost redex* if it is not a part of any other redex.

Terminology

- The outermost and innermost reduction orders are also known as *normal* and *applicative order reductions*, respectively.

- A sequence of reductions is said to be a *normal order reduction sequence* if at every stage the outermost redex is reduced. On the other hand, a sequence of reductions is said to be an *applicative order reduction sequence* if, at every stage, the leftmost of the innermost redexes is reduced.

Example 20.12

Consider the reduction of the following term:

$$(\lambda x \bullet x \; \underbrace{(\lambda y \bullet y \; a)}_{\text{innermost}})$$
$$\underbrace{}_{\text{outermost}}$$

As indicated above, there are both an outermost redex and an innermost redex. Let us begin with the reduction of the outermost redex.

$$\underbrace{(\lambda x \bullet x \; (\lambda y \bullet y \; a))}_{\text{outermost}}$$
$$\xrightarrow{\beta} x[x/(\lambda y \bullet y \; a)]$$
$$\equiv \underbrace{(\lambda y \bullet y \; a)}_{\text{outermost}} \qquad\qquad \text{subs. rule (1)}$$
$$\xrightarrow{\beta} y[y/a]$$
$$\equiv a \qquad\qquad \text{subs. rule (1)}$$

Now let us start the reduction from the innermost redex.

$$(\lambda x \bullet x \; \underbrace{(\lambda y \bullet y \; a)}_{\text{innermost}}))$$
$$\xrightarrow{\beta} (\lambda x \bullet x \; y[y/a])$$
$$\equiv \underbrace{(\lambda x \bullet x \; a)}_{\text{innermost}} \qquad\qquad \text{subs. rule (1)}$$
$$\xrightarrow{\beta} x[x/a]$$
$$\equiv a \qquad\qquad \text{subs. rule (1)}$$

Example 20.13

Here is a more complex reduction than that in Example 20.12, illustrating again the normal and applicative order reduction sequences. In the first normal order sequence, let us consistently keep reducing the outermost redex, as follows.

$$\underbrace{((\lambda x \bullet (\lambda y \bullet y\ x)z)p)}_{\text{outermost}}$$

$$\overset{\beta}{\rightarrow} ((\lambda y \bullet y\ x)z)[x/p]$$

$\equiv ((\lambda y \bullet y\ p)[x/p]\ z[x/p])$	subs. rule (3)
$\equiv ((((\lambda y \bullet y)[x/p])\ p[x/p])\ z[x/p])$	subs. rule (3)
$\equiv ((\lambda y \bullet y[x/p]\ p[x/p])\ z[x/p])$	subs. rule (5)
$\equiv ((\lambda y \bullet y\ p[x/p])\ z[x/p])$	subs. rule (2)
$\equiv ((\lambda y \bullet y\ p)\ z[x/p])$	subs. rule (2)
$\equiv \underbrace{((\lambda y \bullet y\ p)\ z}_{\text{outermost}})$	subs. rule (2)

$$\overset{\beta}{\rightarrow} (y\ p)[y/z]$$

$\equiv (y[y/z]\ p[y/z])$	subs. rule (3)
$\equiv (z\ p[y/z])$	subs. rule (1)
$\equiv (z\ p)$	subs. rule (2)

In the second applicative order reduction sequence of the same, let us consistently keep reducing the innermost redex.

$$((\lambda x \bullet \underbrace{(\lambda y \bullet y\ x)\ z}_{\text{innermost}})p)$$

$$\overset{\beta}{\rightarrow} ((\lambda x \bullet y[y/x]\ z)p)$$

$\equiv \underbrace{((\lambda x \bullet x\ z)p}_{\text{innermost}})$	subs. rule (1)

$$\overset{\beta}{\rightarrow} (x[x/z]\ p)$$

$\equiv (z\ p)$	subs. rule (1)

As in functional programming, depending on the reduction strategy, there could be a considerable difference in the length of reduction sequence of a given term. This is evident in Example 20.13. A major advantage of normal order reduction is, however, that it reduces a term to its normal form if the latter exists, whereas applicative order reduction could enter an infinite reduction sequence and, thereby, never reach the normal form of the term concerned. This can be illustrated by adjoining a term such as that in Example 20.9 with a non-terminating chain of reductions to another term, as in the following:

$$(\lambda x \bullet y\ (\dots \text{non-terminating inner redex} \dots))$$

In this particular case, the adoption of the applicative order reduction strategy (reduction of the inner redex first) could be a fatal mistake for the reduction process.

(Example 20.14)

For brevity, let $(N\ N)$ represent a non-terminating inner redex. The normal order reduction sequence delivers the normal form of the term in one reduction step:

$\underbrace{(\lambda x \bullet y\ (N\ N))}_{\text{outermost}}$

$\qquad \overset{\beta}{\rightarrow} y[x/(N\ N)]$ outermost reduction

$\qquad \equiv y$ rule (2)

However, the applicative order reduction sequence will never end:

$(\lambda x \bullet y\ \underbrace{(N\ N)}_{\text{innermost}}\ )$

$\qquad \overset{\beta}{\rightarrow} (\lambda x \bullet y\ \underbrace{(N\ N)}_{\text{innermost}}\ )$ innermost reduction

$\qquad \qquad \vdots$

$\qquad \overset{\beta}{\rightarrow} (\lambda x \bullet y\ \underbrace{(N\ N)}_{\text{innermost}}\ )$ innermost reduction

Example 20.14 has examined the capability of both strategies to deliver the normal form, if it exists, and found that normal order reduction is superior on this count. Suppose that we are dealing with a term which has no danger of entering into a non-terminating reduction sequence in an inner redex. In this case, would the two strategies lead to the same normal form? This seems to be the case in Examples 20.12 and 20.13, but the question is whether this is always the case. The answer is yes. Without going into any detail, we just mention the existence of two well known results called *Church–Rosser theorems* justifying both these claims, that is:

1. The result of β-reduction sequences of a term is independent of the reduction order. In other words, normal forms are unique.

2. If a term has a normal form, then the normal order reduction sequence can reach it.

(20.6) Modelling mathematical objects

In Section 20.5.2 we noted that λ-calculus is powerful enough to represent different types of values. Let us consider in this section how this can be done just for truth values. Truth values can be represented as the following λ-terms:

$$true = \lambda x \bullet \lambda y \bullet x \qquad\qquad\qquad\qquad \textbf{(20.14)}$$

$$false = \lambda x \bullet \lambda y \bullet y \qquad\qquad\qquad\qquad \textbf{(20.15)}$$

The appropriateness of the above terms as truth values may be tested against how they model the conditional:

if P then M else N **(20.16)**

written in the style of a programming command. Mathematically, the above is a triple. In the notation of λ-calculus it takes the form

$(P\ M\ N)$ **(20.17)**

where P is a term which reduces to either *true* or *false*. Our expectation is that

true M N = M
false M N = N

As can be seen from (20.14), when P happens to be reducible to *true*, we have:

$$
\begin{aligned}
\textit{true M N} &\equiv \lambda x \bullet \lambda y \bullet x\ M\ N \\
&\equiv ((\lambda x \bullet (\lambda y \bullet x)\ M)\ N) &&\text{association of application} \\
&\xrightarrow{\beta} ((\lambda y \bullet x)[x/M]\ N) \\
&\equiv (\lambda y \bullet x[x/M]\ N) &&\text{rule (5)} \\
&\equiv (\lambda y \bullet M\ N) &&\text{rule (1)} \\
&\xrightarrow{\beta} M[y/N] &&\text{rule (5)} \\
&\equiv M &&\text{rule (5), assuming that } y \text{ is not free in } M
\end{aligned}
$$

On the other hand, when P happens to be reducible to *false*, we have:

$$
\begin{aligned}
\textit{false M N} &\equiv ((\lambda x \bullet (\lambda y \bullet y)\ M)\ N) \\
&\xrightarrow{\beta} ((\lambda y \bullet y)[x/M]\ N) \\
&\equiv ((\lambda y \bullet y)\ N) &&\text{rule (2)} \\
&\xrightarrow{\beta} y[y/N] \\
&\equiv N &&\text{rule (1)}
\end{aligned}
$$

Thus, according to the above case analysis, the terms (20.14), (20.15) and (20.17) faithfully represent the conditional. Likewise, other Boolean operators such as *and, or* and *not* may be represented as λ-terms.

Exercise 20.7 ✳✳✳

Suggest λ-terms for the Boolean operators *and, or* and *not*, and verify their appropriateness. You may use here the definition given in (20.17) for the conditional.

Outline answers to exercises

Exercise 1.2

Let the following symbols denote the propositions involved.

W	**Mechanical work is done.**
M	**The force moves an object,** or
	The object is moved (*by a force*).
P	**A force is the push needed to move *the object*.**
T	**A force is the pull needed to move *the object*.**
A	**The man is asked to lift the heavy object onto a shelf.**
L	**The man lifts the heavy object onto a shelf.**
H	**The object is too heavy for the man to lift.**
D	**The man *has done* useful work,** or
	The man *has done much work* (strains much).

where words in *italic* signify some modifications. The argument in *symbolic form* is:

W whenever M, where P or T.
W only if M – for example, when A and L.
If H (…then it is not the case that …) D, no matter S.

Exercise 2.1

1. No, it is not a proposition; it is a command.

2. No, because it is an exclamation.

3. Yes, although it is a false proposition!

Exercise 2.2

Connectives are shown in *italic* and prime propositions in **bold**.

1. **Edmund Hillary conquered Mount Everest** *and* **Tenzing Norgay conquered Mount Everest.**

2. **Edmund Hillary and Tenzing Norgay were the first to conquer Mount Everest.**

3. **Indochina lies within the tropics** *and* **Indochina has hot summers** *but* **the winters in the northern parts of Indochina are cool.**

Exercise 2.4

Prime propositions:

Symbol	Meaning
S	Spending increases.
E	Economy overheats.
D	Excess demand increases.
A	Inflation rises.
B	Inflation falls.
C	There are tax cuts.
I	Interest rate rises.

Then

1. $E \Leftrightarrow D$
2. $(\neg A) \Rightarrow (\neg D)$
3. $B \Rightarrow C$
8. $A \vee (\neg A)$

Exercise 2.5

If we translate this into logic, we get $\neg p \wedge (q \Rightarrow \neg r)$, where p is *'The bar-staff mean to offend'*, q is *'The bar-staff think you are over 18'*, and r is *'The bar–staff ask for identification'*. Considering formulae with appropriate truth values for p, q and r, we get $\neg$ **false** $\wedge$ (**false** $\Rightarrow \neg$ **false**) which works out to be 'true'. The sentence amounts to a polite but humorous notice indirectly addressed to the under 18s.

Exercise 2.7

1. The meaning of this sentence really depends on your definition of fun. It is therefore imprecise.
2. This is both ambiguous and imprecise. 'Funny' can mean either peculiar or amusing – this is ambiguity. Whichever meaning is taken, 'funny' is a relative term – this is imprecision.
3. This is a precise and unambiguous sentence.

Exercise 3.2

1. (a) $p \vee \neg q \Rightarrow r$
   (b) $\neg p \Leftrightarrow q \Rightarrow r$
2. (a) $((\neg p) \wedge (\neg q)) \Rightarrow (\neg r)$
   (b) $(\neg p) \wedge (q \Rightarrow r)$

Exercise 3.3

5. In the following truth table, let A represent (i.e. A is equivalent to) the formula $A \overset{def}{\Leftrightarrow} p \vee (q \wedge r) \Rightarrow (p \wedge q) \vee r$.

p	q	r	$q \wedge r$	$p \wedge q$	$p \vee (q \wedge r)$	$(p \wedge q) \vee r$	A
T	T	T	T	T	T	T	T
T	T	F	F	T	T	T	T
T	F	T	F	F	T	T	T
T	F	F	F	F	T	F	F
F	T	T	T	F	T	T	T
F	T	F	F	F	F	F	T
F	F	T	F	F	F	T	T
F	F	F	F	F	F	F	T

Exercise 3.4

p	q	$p \vee q$	$p \wedge q$	$\neg (p \wedge q)$	$(p \vee q) \wedge \neg (p \wedge q)$
T	T	T	T	F	F
T	F	T	F	T	T
F	T	T	F	T	T
F	F	F	F	T	F

Exercise 3.5

Construct a truth table for each of the formulae: $\neg p \wedge (q \Rightarrow \neg r)$ and $\neg p \wedge (q \Leftrightarrow \neg r)$. This should show that the answer to Exercise 2.5 can be true for three cases:

	Case		
	1	2	3
p (*The bar-staff mean to offend*)	F	F	F
q (*The bar-staff think you are over 18*)	T	F	F
r (*The bar-staff ask for identification*)	F	T	F

whereas the answer to Exercise 2.6 is true only for two cases:

	Case	
	1	2
p (*The bar-staff mean to offend*)	F	F
q (*The bar-staff think you are over 18*)	T	F
r (*The bar-staff ask for identification*)	F	T

Exercise 3.8

2. Input/output table for the digital circuit in Figure 3.5:

A	B	C	O
0	0	0	0
0	0	1	0
0	1	0	0
0	1	1	0
1	0	0	0
1	0	1	1
1	1	0	1
1	1	1	1

Exercise 3.9

1. A recognizer with two inputs: see Figure A.1(a).
2. A recognizer with three inputs: see Figure A.1(b).

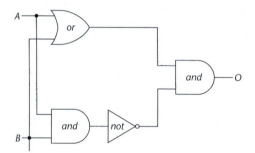

Figure A.1(a)   A solution for question 1 of Exercise 3.9

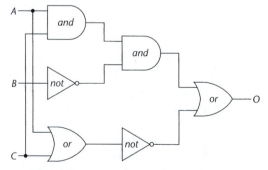

Figure A.1(b)   A solution for question 2 of Exercise 3.9

Exercise 3.11

5. Some points we might make are:

   (a) Both syntax and semantics are equally important.
   (b) In order to argue about the meaning of a sentence, the sentence has to be correctly written in the first place.
   (c) A language without semantics is just gibberish.
   (d) A language without syntax is inconceivable.
   (e) The richness of a language depends on the richness of the syntax.
   (f) Poor form and style of syntax make text less readable. A limited vocabulary and limited set of syntactic constructs make any language less expressive.
   (g) The syntax is extremely important for making any sense of very long formulae in any formal language. Here is a very typical example taken from number theory. One cannot make an obvious distinction between the meaning of two numbers such as:

   (i) 100136745891289864324092387
   (ii) 100136745891289864324092388

   except by appealing to syntax. We see that the number given in (ii) is greater than that in (i) by one. This is the only sense of their magnitudes we can make of them, and that relies purely on their syntax.

Exercise 4.1

3. $\neg (p \wedge q) \Longleftrightarrow \neg p \vee \neg q$

p	q	$p \wedge q$	$\neg (p \wedge q)$	$\neg p$	$\neg q$	$\neg p \vee \neg q$
T	T	T	F	F	F	F
T	F	F	T	F	T	T
F	T	F	T	T	F	T
F	F	F	T	T	T	T

Columns 4 and 7 are identical.

Exercise 4.2

3. $p \wedge (q \wedge r) \Longleftrightarrow (p \wedge q) \wedge r$

Proof:

$p \wedge (q \wedge r)$
$\Longleftrightarrow p \wedge \neg \neg (q \wedge r)$ — negation law
$\Longleftrightarrow p \wedge \neg (\neg q \vee \neg r)$ — De Morgan's law
$\Longleftrightarrow \neg \neg (p \wedge (\neg (\neg q \vee \neg r)))$ — negation law
$\Longleftrightarrow \neg (\neg p \vee \neg (\neg (\neg q \vee \neg r)))$ — De Morgan's law
$\Longleftrightarrow \neg (\neg p \vee (\neg q \vee \neg r))$ — negation law
$\Longleftrightarrow \neg ((\neg p \vee \neg q) \vee \neg r)$ — associativity
$\Longleftrightarrow \neg (\neg (p \wedge q) \vee \neg r)$ — De Morgan's law
$\Longleftrightarrow \neg \neg (p \wedge q) \wedge \neg \neg r$ — De Morgan's law
$\Longleftrightarrow (p \wedge q) \wedge r$ — negation law (twice)

Exercise 4.6

Note that some of the sentences can be ambiguous.

1. Sentence (a) translates to $\neg C \Rightarrow (B \vee W)$. Sentence (b) translates to $(\neg C \wedge \neg B) \Rightarrow W$. So we have to prove that

$$\neg C \Rightarrow (B \vee W) \Longleftrightarrow (\neg C \wedge \neg B) \Rightarrow W$$

Proof:

$\neg C \Rightarrow (B \vee W)$
$\Longleftrightarrow \neg (\neg C) \vee (B \vee W)$ implication law
$\Longleftrightarrow C \vee (B \vee W)$ negation law
$\Longleftrightarrow (C \vee B) \vee W$ associativity
$\Longleftrightarrow \neg (\neg C \wedge \neg B) \vee W$ De Morgan's law
$\Longleftrightarrow (\neg C \wedge \neg B) \Rightarrow W$ implication law

Exercise 4.7

Here we must distinguish between logical expressions and programming commands. In a command such as

if A then S_1

containing a subcommand S_1, let us treat S_1 differently from conditions such as A by writing $\boxed{S_1}$ instead of S_1. With this convention, we write, for example,

$A \Rightarrow \boxed{S_1}$

The point is that the program name should appear only on its own, as the 'consequence' of an implication, or as a disjunct. We will avoid writing formulae of the form $A \wedge \boxed{S_1}$. The answer to (1) is:

true $\Rightarrow \boxed{S_1}$
$\Longleftrightarrow \neg$ **true** $\vee \boxed{S_1}$
$\Longleftrightarrow$ **false** $\vee \boxed{S_1}$
$\Longleftrightarrow \boxed{S_1}$

requiring the execution of just S_1.

Exercise 4.9

$(B \wedge C) \vee (A \wedge C) \vee (A \wedge B)$	formula derived in Example 4.6 for the circuit in Figure 3.3
$\Longleftrightarrow (B \wedge C) \vee (A \wedge C) \vee (A \wedge B) \vee (A \wedge B)$	idempotence
$\Longleftrightarrow \neg \neg (B \wedge C) \vee \neg \neg (A \wedge C)$ $\vee \neg \neg (A \wedge B) \vee \neg \neg (A \wedge B)$	negation
$\Longleftrightarrow \neg (\neg (B \wedge C) \wedge \neg (A \wedge C))$ $\vee \neg (\neg (A \wedge B) \wedge \neg (A \wedge B))$	De Morgan's law
$\Longleftrightarrow \neg ((\neg (B \wedge C) \wedge \neg (A \wedge C))$ $\wedge (\neg (A \wedge B) \wedge \neg (A \wedge B)))$	De Morgan's law

The above corresponds to the digital circuit in Figure A.2 and is functionally equivalent to the one in Figure 3.3.

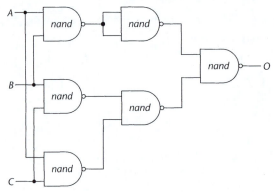

Figure A.2   A digital circuit for the patient monitoring system using only *nand* gates

Exercise 5.4

The lines 5–10 of the proof required in question 1 are as follows:

5.	$\neg C \lor D$	from 4, $\lor\_I$
6.	A	from 3 & 5, $\Rightarrow \_E$ (*modus ponens*)
7.	$\neg B$	from 1 & 6, $\Rightarrow \_E$ (*modus ponens*)
8.	$\neg B \land \neg C$	from 4 & 7, $\land\_I$
9.	$\neg (B \lor C)$	from 8, De Morgan's law
10.	D	from 2 & 9, $\lor\_E$

Exercise 5.5

1. First, we identify the prime propositions:

   p You give your order by telephone.
   q You give your order by fax.
   r We deal with it promptly.
   s We deal with it efficiently.
   t Your goods arrive the next day.
   u We use Zippo couriers.

   The form of the argument is thus:

   $(p \lor q) \Rightarrow r \land s$
   $(r \lor u) \Rightarrow t$
   Therefore, $p \Rightarrow t$

   Finally, we prove the validity of the argument:

1.	$(p \lor q) \Rightarrow r \land s$	premise
2.	$(r \lor u) \Rightarrow t$	premise
3.	p	assumption
4.	$p \lor q$	from 3, $\lor\_I$

5.	$r \land s$	from 1 & 4, $\Rightarrow$ _E (*modus ponens*)
6.	r	from 5, $\land$_E
7.	$r \lor u$	from 6, $\lor$_I
8.	t	from 2 & 7, $\Rightarrow$ _E (*modus ponens*)
9.	$p \Rightarrow t$	from 3–8, $\Rightarrow$ _I

Exercise 5.7

First, we identify the prime propositions:

Symbol	Meaning
D	There is a **delay** in the descent of the buggy to the Martian surface.
C	**Clocks** of the robot are misaligned.
P	There is a **power** shortage in the robot.
B	Solar **batteries** are fully drained during the Martian night.
M	Commands from **Mission Control** reach the robot.

Various premises and claims of the argument form three different arguments:

Documented statements:
Axiom (a) $(C \Rightarrow P) \Rightarrow D$
Axiom (b) $C \Rightarrow \neg M \land D$
Axiom (c) $B \lor D \Rightarrow P$

Various claims: On the grounds of (a), (b) and (c):
1. D
2. $(B \lor D) \land C$
3. P

Claims (1) and (3) are true, whereas (2) is false. Below are the relevant formal justifications for (1) and (2).
Proof of (1):

1.	$(C \Rightarrow P) \Rightarrow D$	premise: axiom (a)
2.	$C \Rightarrow \neg M \land D$	premise: axiom (b)
3.	$\neg (\neg C \lor P) \lor D$	from 1, implication (twice)
4.	$(\neg \neg C \land \neg P) \lor D$	from 3, De Morgan's law
5.	$(C \land \neg P) \lor D$	from 4, double negation
6.	$(C \lor D) \land (\neg P \lor D)$	from 5, distributivity
7.	$C \lor D$	from 6, $\land$_E
8.	$\neg C \lor (\neg M \land D)$	from 2, implication
9.	$(\neg C \lor \neg M) \land (\neg C \lor D)$	from 8, distributivity
10.	$\neg C \lor D$	from 9, $\land$_E
11.	$(C \lor D) \land (\neg C \lor D)$	from 7 & 10, $\land$_I
12.	$(C \land \neg C) \lor D$	from 11, distributivity
13.	**false** $\lor D$	from 12, contradiction
14.	D	from 13, simplification

Refutation of (2): An assignment of truth values showing that the claim (2) as a conclusion happens to be false when the axioms (a), (b) and (c) are true.

Prime propositions					Axiom (a)	Axiom (b)	Axiom (c)	Claim (2)
D	C	P	B	M	$(C \Rightarrow P) \Rightarrow D$	$C \Rightarrow \neg M \wedge D$	$B \vee D \Rightarrow P$	$(B \vee D) \wedge C$
T	F	T	F	T	T	T	T	F

Exercise 6.1

1. $cold(x)$, $country(x)$
2. $country(x)$, $warm(x)$, $resort(x)$

Exercise 6.2

1. Everybody is an adult or a child.
2. Everybody is an adult or there are some children.
6. If nobody is short then everybody is a clever child.

Exercise 6.3

1. (a) $(\forall x \bullet tall(x)) \wedge (\exists x \bullet child(x))$
   (d) $\forall x \bullet (adult(x) \Rightarrow tall(x)) \wedge (adult(x) \Rightarrow \neg clever(x))$

Exercise 6.4

1. (a) $\forall x \bullet first\_year(x) \wedge student(x) \Rightarrow clever(x)$
   (b) $\neg \exists x \bullet clever(x) \wedge \neg hardworking(x)$
   (f) $\forall x \bullet \neg lazy(x) \Leftrightarrow hardworking(x)$

Exercise 6.6

1. John is short and someone is cleverer than John and is respected by Jane.
2. If everybody loves tall people then tall people are respected by everybody.

Exercise 6.7

1. $\neg \exists x \bullet \exists y \bullet loves(x, y) \wedge \neg respects(x, y)$
3. $\neg \exists x \bullet \exists y \bullet cleverer(x, y) \wedge \neg clever(x)$

Exercise 6.8

Suitable predicates are x *supplies* y meaning that the store x supplies the store y, and x *in* p meaning that the store x is located at the place p.

1. $\forall x \bullet \forall y \bullet x$ *supplies* $y \wedge x$ *in* **London** $\Rightarrow \neg y$ *in* **London**
3. $\neg \exists x \bullet x$ *in* **Grimsby** $\wedge \exists y \bullet y$ *in* **Halifax**

Exercise 6.10

In all cases below, the value y is not to be altered.

1. Set the value of x to $y + 1$ (in the conventional terminology of programming, assign $y + 1$ to x).
2. Increase the value of x in excess of y, provided that x is initially less than y.
3. Set the value of x to the sum of its initial value and the value of y, provided that x is initially less than y.

Exercise 6.11

In (5) below, *rightangled* is a new Boolean valued program variable taking only one of the two values: TRUE and FALSE.

5. *rightangled* : [**true**, *rightangled* = TRUE $> 0 \wedge b > 0 \wedge c > 0 \wedge$
$$(a^2 = b^2 + c^2 \vee b^2 = a^2 + c^2 \vee c^2 = a^2 + b^2)]$$

6. x, y : [**true**, $(a \neq 0 \wedge b \neq 0 \wedge c = x_0 \Rightarrow x/y = a/b) \wedge$
$$(a = 0 \vee b = 0 \vee c \neq x_0 \Rightarrow x + y = 0)]$$

7. x, y : [$a \neq 0 \wedge b^2 - 4ac \geqslant 0, a \times x^2 + b \times x + c = 0 \wedge$
$$a \times y^2 + b \times y + c = 0 \wedge (x = y \Leftrightarrow b^2 - 4ac = 0)]$$

Exercise 6.12

We continue to use the predicates in Example 6.11. Program specifications are:

1. x : [**true**, y loves $x \wedge y$ respects $x \wedge \neg x$ cleverer y]
2. x : [$\neg x$ cleverer y, y loves $x \wedge y$ respects x]

Exercise 7.1

1. All employers employ at least one smart, clever employee.
2. All employers are clever if they employ smart employees.
3. All employers employ at least one smart employee and x is clever.
6. If everyone employs y then there is someone who is smart and clever.

Exercise 7.2

1. $\forall x \bullet \exists y \bullet employs\,(y, x) \Rightarrow smart(x)$
2. $\forall x \bullet \exists y \bullet employs\,(y, x) \wedge smart(x) \Rightarrow clever(y)$

Exercise 7.3

1. (a) $\forall \frac{1}{x} \bullet \exists \frac{1}{y} \bullet employs\left(\frac{1}{x}, \frac{1}{y}\right) \Rightarrow smart\left(\frac{1}{y}\right) \wedge clever\left(\frac{1}{y}\right)$

   (b) $\forall \frac{1}{x} \bullet \exists \frac{1}{y} \bullet employs\left(\frac{1}{x}, \frac{1}{y}\right) \Rightarrow smart\left(\frac{1}{y}\right) \wedge clever\left(\frac{1}{y}\right)$

Exercise 7.4

1. $\exists\,{}^1_x \bullet {}^{free}_y$ *taller_than* ${}^1_x$

2. $\exists\,{}^1_x \bullet \exists\,{}^1_y \bullet {}^1_x$ *taller_than* ${}^1_y \land {}^1_y$ *taller_than* ${}^{free}_y$

Exercise 7.5

We assume that *Actor* represents the set of all possible actors and *Item* the set of all possible items.

1. $\forall x : Actor \bullet \exists y : Item \bullet rich(x) \land valuable(y) \Rightarrow collects(x, y)$
2. $\forall x : Item \bullet valuable(x) \Rightarrow \exists y : Item \bullet superior(x, y)$

Exercise 7.6

In the following answers *x reg y* means that *x* is registered for *y*.

1. $\forall x : Person \mid x$ *attends* **CS** $\bullet \neg\, x$ *attends* **Maths** $\lor x$ *reg* **Maths**
2. $\exists x : Person \mid x$ *attends* **CS** $\land x$ *reg* **Maths** $\bullet \neg\, x$ *attends* **Maths**

Exercise 7.7

1. $\overbrace{\forall x, y : Lecturer \bullet sarcastic(x) \lor cynical(y)}$
   Interpretation: All lecturers are sarcastic or cynical.

3. $\overbrace{\forall x : Lecturer \mid sarcastic(x) \bullet \exists y : Student \bullet annoyed(y)}$

   Interpretation: For every sarcastic lecturer there is an annoyed student.

Exercise 8.1

1.

x	$male(x)$	$\neg\,male(x)$	$kind(x)$	$\neg\,male(x) \Rightarrow kind(x)$	$\forall x : H \bullet \neg\,male(x) \Rightarrow kind(x)$
Adam	T	F	F	T	--
Eve	F	T	T	T	--
Rosalyn	F	T	F	F	--
Pele	T	F	F	T	--
Mario	T	F	T	T	--
					F

Exercise 8.2

1.

x	male(x)	greedy(x)	kind(x)	¬ kind(x)	greedy(x)∨ male(x)∧ ¬ kind(x)	(greedy(x)∨ male(x) ∧ (greedy(x) ∨¬ kind(x))	∃x : H •
Adam	T	T	F	T	T	T	–
Eve	F	F	T	F	F	F	–
Rosalyn	F	F	F	T	T	F	–
Pele	T	T	F	T	T	T	–
Mario	T	F	T	F	F	F	–
							F

Exercise 9.1

1. $\sin(x) = \frac{1}{2}$ — x is an unknown

2. $\sin^2(x) + \cos^2(x) = 1$ — x is a genuine variable

3. $\sin^2(x) + \cos^2(y) = 1$ — x could be a genuine variable and y an unknown, or vice versa. Both cannot be genuine variables simultaneously

5. $\dfrac{a}{b} = \dfrac{c}{d} \Rightarrow a \times d = b \times c$ — a, b, c and d are all genuine variables. Neither b nor d can be zero

9. $ax^2 + bx + c = 0 \Rightarrow$

$$x = \frac{-b + \sqrt{b^2 - 4ac}}{2a}$$

$$\vee\, x = \frac{-b - \sqrt{b^2 - 4ac}}{2a}$$

a is a genuine variable ranging over real numbers excluding zero, b, c are genuine variables ranging over real numbers, and x is an unknown ranging, in general, over complex numbers.

Exercise 9.2

1. Definition of the predicate $prime(x)$ is left for the reader. The predicate $consecutive\_primes(i, j)$ may be defined such that

$$\forall i, j : \mathbb{N} \bullet consecutive\_primes(i, j) \Rightarrow$$
$$(i \neq j \wedge prime(i) \wedge prime(j) \wedge (\forall k : \mathbb{N} \bullet i \leqslant k \leqslant j \wedge prime(k) \Rightarrow k = i \vee k = j))$$

(a) $\forall n : \mathbb{N} \bullet even(n) \Rightarrow (\exists i, j : \mathbb{N} \bullet i > j \wedge prime(i) \wedge prime(j) \wedge n = i - j)$

(b) $\forall n : \mathbb{N} \bullet even(n) \Rightarrow (\exists i, j : \mathbb{N} \bullet consecutive\_primes(i, j) \wedge n = i - j)$

Exercise 9.4

1.
1.	$\forall x \bullet (p(x) \vee r(x) \Rightarrow \neg q(x))$	premise
2.	$\exists x \bullet \neg (\neg p(x) \wedge \neg r(x))$	premise
3.	$\neg (\neg p(x) \wedge \neg r(x))$	from 2, $\exists\_E$
4.	$\neg \neg p(x) \vee \neg \neg r(x)$	from 3, De Morgan

5. $p(x) \vee r(x)$	from 4, $\neg \_E$
6. $p(x) \vee r(x) \Rightarrow \neg q(x)$	from 1, $\forall\_E$
7. $\neg q(x)$	from 5 & 6, $\Rightarrow \_E$
8. $\exists x \bullet \neg q(x)$	from 7, $\exists\_I$

Exercise 9.5

1. Proof of logical implication

1. $\forall x \bullet (p(x) \Rightarrow q(x))$	assumption
2. $\forall x \bullet p(x)$	assumption
3. $p(y)$	from 2, $\forall\_E$
4. $p(y) \Rightarrow q(y)$	from 1, $\forall\_E$
5. $q(y)$	from 3 & 4, $\Rightarrow \_E$
6. $\forall x \bullet q(x)$	from 5, $\forall\_I$
7. $(\forall x \bullet p(x)) \Rightarrow (\forall x \bullet q(x))$	from 2 & 6, $\Rightarrow \_I$
8. $(\forall x \bullet p(x) \Rightarrow q(x)) \Rightarrow (\forall x \bullet p(x) \Rightarrow \forall x \bullet q(x))$	from 1 & 7, $\Rightarrow \_I$

No premises used, so the result is a logical implication.

2. Show the equivalence by showing separately the two implications.

3. The formula required to prove is equivalent to

$$\forall x \bullet \exists y \bullet \neg p(x, y) \Rightarrow \forall x, y \bullet \neg p(x, y)$$

Its invalidity can be shown by providing a counterexample. Let, for example, $p(\_, \_)$ be the predicate $\_ \geqslant \_$ on the domain of natural numbers. Then the above says

$$\forall x \bullet \exists y \bullet x < y \Rightarrow \forall x, y \bullet x < y$$

LHS is true since for any natural number one can find another which is greater than the first. However, the RHS is false since the predicate $\_ < \_$ is not universally true on $\mathbb{N}$. Hence, the given formula is invalid.

Exercise 9.7

This is not a problem that fits well into predicate logic. We propose a solution which works here, but with a warning that the approach is not to be treated as a general approach.

Let us first introduce a rather unusual predicate

$$Q(x, p)$$

with the informal meaning that 'the person x is permitted to ask whether the proposition p is true'. It is unusual in the sense that Q is a predicate which could take another predicate or a proposition p as an argument. For this reason, we need to exercise some care in its usage. Let us introduce two related predicates $Q^Y(x, p)$ and $Q^N(x, p)$ so that

$$Q(x, p) \Leftrightarrow Q^Y(x, p) \vee Q^N(x, p) \tag{A.1}$$

with $Q^Y(x, p)$ for questions to which the correct answers are yes and $Q^N(x, p)$ for questions to which the correct answers are no. Let *Person* and *Formula* be two distinct sets (types) with the meanings as indicated by the chosen words.

Let us introduce two 'conventional' predicates: $opt(x)$ meaning that the person x is an optimist and $psm(x)$ meaning that the person x is a pessimist.

The discipline of asking questions, the truth of various propositions and the status of the persons are related in the following manner:

$\forall x : Person; \; p : Formula \bullet$

$$Q^Y(x, p) \Rightarrow opt(x) \tag{A.2}$$
$$Q^N(x, p) \Rightarrow psm(x) \tag{A.3}$$
$$Q^Y(x, p) \Rightarrow p \tag{A.4}$$
$$Q^N(x, p) \Rightarrow \neg p \tag{A.5}$$
$$opt(x) \Leftrightarrow \neg psm(x) \tag{A.6}$$
$$opt(x) \vee psm(x) \tag{A.7}$$

Let us refer to formulae (A.1–A.7) as axioms of the theory of the 'world without realists'.

1. No one is permitted to ask the above question. Here is a proof substantiating it. Note that x represents an arbitrary individual.

1.	$Q(x, psm(x))$	assumption
2.	$Q^Y(x, psm(x)) \vee$ $Q^N(x, psm(x))$	from 1 & axiom (A.1)
3.	$Q^Y(x, psm(x))$	assumption
4.	$opt(x)$	from 3 & axiom (A.2)
5.	$psm(x)$	from 3 & axiom (A.4)
6.	$\neg opt(x)$	from 5 & axiom (A.6)
7.	$opt(x) \wedge \neg opt(x)$	from 4 & 6; $\wedge\_I$
8.	*false*	from 7, contradiction
9.	$\neg Q^Y(x, psm(x))$	from 3 & 8, $\neg\_I$
10.	$Q^N(x, psm(x))$	assumption
11.	$psm(x)$	from 10 & axiom (A.3)
12.	$\neg psm(x)$	from 10 & axiom (A.5)
13.	$psm(x) \wedge \neg psm(x)$	from 11 & 12, $\wedge\_I$
14.	*false*	from 13, contradiction
15.	$\neg Q^N(x, psm(x))$	from 10 & 14, $\neg\_I$
16.	$\neg Q^Y(x, psm(x)) \wedge \neg Q^N(x, psm(x))$	from 9 & 15, $\wedge\_I$
17.	$\neg (Q^Y(x, psm(x)) \vee Q^N(x, psm(x)))$	from 16, De Morgan
18.	*false*	from 2 & 17, contradiction
19.	$\neg Q(x, psm(x))$	from 1 & 18, $\neg\_I$

2. This is a question which could be asked by either type.

3. The speaker is a pessimist and the person P must be an optimist.

4. The speaker is an optimist and the other person is a pessimist.

Exercise 9.8

The following are some possible refinements.

1. $prog_1 \sqsubseteq prog_3$ – Strengthening of *post*. Formal justification:

$$n^3 = n \wedge n \geqslant 0 \overset{?}{\Rightarrow} qn^3 = n \equiv \textbf{true} \quad \text{(follows immediately from } \wedge \text{ elimination)}$$

2. $prog_1 \sqsubseteq prog_4$ – Weakening of *pre*

$$n < 0 \overset{?}{\Rightarrow} q \; \textbf{true} \equiv \textbf{true} \quad \text{(conclusion being identically true)}$$

3. $prog_1 \sqsubseteq prog_6$ – Strengthening of *post*. Its justification requires:

$$n^3 = abs(n) \overset{?}{\Rightarrow} n^3 = n$$

The above is a logical implication and can be substantiated by a following proof.

Exercise 10.2

3. Proof by induction of:

$$P(n) \overset{def}{\Leftrightarrow} \sum_{i=1}^{n} \frac{1}{i^2} \leqslant 2 - \frac{1}{n}$$

Note that, in contrast to questions 1 and 2 of this exercise, our conjecture here does not propose an explicit definition for the function $\sum_{i=1}^{n} \frac{1}{i^2}$.

Recursive definition for the underlying function:

$$\sum_{i=1}^{1} \frac{1}{i^2} = 1$$

$$\sum_{i=1}^{n} \frac{1}{i^2} = \frac{1}{n^2} + \sum_{i=1}^{n-1} \frac{1}{i^2}$$

Base case

Proof of $P(1)$:

$$\sum_{i=1}^{1} \frac{1}{i^2} \leqslant 2 - \frac{1}{1} \qquad \qquad P(n) \text{ for } n = 1$$

$$\Leftrightarrow 1 \leqslant 2 - 1 \qquad \qquad \text{arithmetic and recursive definition}$$
$$\Leftrightarrow 1 \leqslant 1 \qquad \qquad \text{arithmetic}$$
$$\Leftrightarrow \textbf{true} \qquad \qquad \text{number theory}$$

Inductive case

Induction Hypothesis: Assume

$$\sum_{i=1}^{k} \frac{1}{i^2} \leqslant 2 - \frac{1}{k}$$

Inductive proof: Prove

$$\sum_{i=1}^{k+1} \frac{1}{i^2} \leqslant 2 - \frac{1}{k+1}$$

Proof:

1. $\displaystyle\sum_{i=1}^{k} \frac{1}{i^2} \leqslant 2 - \frac{1}{k}$ assumption (induction hypothesis)

2. $\displaystyle\sum_{i=1}^{k+1} \frac{1}{i^2} = \frac{1}{(k+1)^2} + \sum_{i=1}^{n} \frac{1}{i^2}$ recursive definition

3. $\displaystyle\sum_{i=1}^{k+1} \frac{1}{i^2} \leqslant \frac{1}{(k+1)^2} + 2 - \frac{1}{k}$ from 1 & 2

4. $\displaystyle\sum_{i=1}^{k+1} \frac{1}{i^2} \leqslant 2 - \frac{k^2+k+1}{k(k+1)^2}$ from 3, algebra

5. $\displaystyle\sum_{i=1}^{k+1} \frac{1}{i^2} \leqslant 2 - \frac{k^2+k}{k(k+1)^2} - \frac{1}{k(k+1)^2}$ from 4, algebra

6. $\displaystyle\sum_{i=1}^{k+1} \frac{1}{i^2} \leqslant 2 - \frac{1}{k+1} - \frac{1}{k(k+1)^2}$ from 5, algebra

7. $\displaystyle\sum_{i=1}^{k+1} \frac{1}{i^2} \leqslant 2 - \frac{1}{k+1}$ from 6, since $\frac{1}{k(k+1)^2} > 0$

Hence, the proof.

Exercise 10.3

Proof of

$$F_{n+m-2} = F_n F_{m-1} + F_{n-1} F_{m-2}$$

for all natural numbers $n, m \geqslant 2$. Let

$$P(n,m) \stackrel{def}{\Leftrightarrow} F_{n+m-2} = F_n F_{m-1} + F_{n-1} F_{m-2}$$

Base case:

Proof of $P(n,2)$; i.e. for $m = 2$:

$F_n F_1 + F_{n-1} F_0$	RHS of $P(n,2)$ (i.e. $m = 2$)
$= F_n \times 1 + F_{n-1} \times 0$	definition of F_0 and F_1
$= F_n$	arithmetic
$= F_{n+2-2}$	an identity

Thus

$$F_{n+m-2} = F_n F_{m-1} + F_{n-1} F_{m-2} \quad \text{for } m = 2$$

That is, $P(n, 2)$ is true. Therefore, the first requirement of the principle of mathematical induction is satisfied.

Inductive case

Induction hypothesis: Assume $P(n, k)$ to be true. Since $m = k$ here

$$F_{n+k-2} = F_n F_{k-1} + F_{n-1} F_{k-2}$$

Inductive proof: Prove $P(n, k + 1)$ to be true, that is,

$$F_{n+k-1} = F_n F_k + F_{n-1} F_{k-1}$$

Proof:

F_{n+k-1}	LHS of the above equality
$= F_{n+k-2} + F_{n+k-3}$	definition of F_{n+k-1}
$= F_n F_{k-1} + F_{n-1} F_{k-2} + F_n F_{k-2} + F_{n-1} F_{k-3}$	induction hypothesis for F_{n+k-2} and F_{n+k-3}
$= F_n(F_{k-1} + F_{k-2}) + F_{n-1}(F_{k-2} + F_{k-3})$	commutativity of $+$ and distributivity of $\times$ over $+$
$= F_n F_k + F_{n-1} F_{k-1}$	recursive definition of F_k and F_{k-1}

Hence, the proof by induction for $P(n, m)$ for all $n, m \geqslant 2$.

Exercise 10.5

The following concerns only performance based on comparisons. For any given i, the algorithm makes $C(i)$ comparisons:

$$C(i) = \begin{cases} i - 1 & \text{maximum} \\ 1 & \text{minimum} \\ \dfrac{i}{2} & \text{on average} \end{cases}$$

The total number of comparisons made by the algorithm for all *is* is:

$$C_{max}(n) = \sum_{i=2}^{n} (i - 1) = \frac{n^2 - n}{2} \qquad O(n^2)$$

$$C_{min}(n) = \sum_{i=2}^{n} 1 = n - 1 \qquad O(n)$$

$$C_{ave}(n) = \sum_{i=2}^{n} \frac{i}{2} = \frac{n^2 + n - 2}{4} \qquad O(n^2)$$

An analogous estimate may be made with respect to performance based on moves (assignments of array elements).

Exercise 11.1

1. The intended meaning of the names given to sets used should be clear from the context.

   (a) *Primary_Colours* = {**red**, **yellow**, **blue**}
   Primary_Colours = {$x \mid x \in Colour \wedge isPrimary(x)$}
   where *Colour* is the set of all colours and *isPrimary(x)* is a predicate defining primary colours.

   (f) *Triangular_Nums* = {1, 3, 6, 10, 15, 21, 28}
   Triangular_Nums = {$t \mid \exists n \bullet t = n \times (n+1)/2 \wedge 1 \leqslant t \leqslant 30$}

2. The compositions of sets asked for in (c) and (e) in question 1 are not definite.

Exercise 11.2

2. The sets concerned are:
   $squares1to20 = \{1,\ 4,\ 9,\ 16\}$
   $roofNums = \{1,\ 1+3,\ 1+3+5,\ 1+3+5+7\} = \{1,\ 4,\ 9,\ 16\}$

   and are obviously identical.

3. The above two sets are identical even if extended to infinity. As an informal proof, it may be observed that each 'roof' may be stretched to a square as shown in Figure A.3. Therefore, we are speaking about the same set.

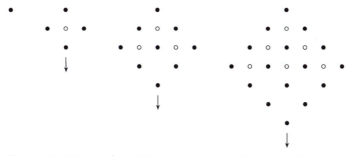

Figure A.3   Diagram for solution to question 3 of Exercise 11.2

Exercise 11.3

1. The predicate $\varphi(x)$:
   (a) $\varphi(x) \Leftrightarrow rich(x)$
   (b) $\varphi(n) \Leftrightarrow \exists k : \mathbb{N} \bullet k \times 20 = n \wedge 0 \leq n \leq 100$

2. Let *Country* be the set of all countries and *Europe*, *EU*, *Africa*, *Mediterranean* and *UN* be the sets of countries with the obvious meanings. Assume also the following predicates:

east_of_L(c, n)	The country c is east of Longitude n°.
north_of_Med(c)	The country c is north of the Mediterranean sea.

   (a) {$x \mid x \in Country \wedge x \in Europe \wedge east\_of\_L(x, 5^{\circ})$} $\subseteq EU$
   (b) *Mediterranean* $\not\subseteq EU$
   (c) $EU \subseteq UN$

Exercise 11.4

2. $\mathbb{P}\{\{1,2\}, \{5\}, \{2,3\}\} = \{\varnothing, \{\{1,2\}\}, \{\{5\}\}, \{\{2,3\}\},$
$$\{\{1,2\}, \{5\}\}, \{\{1,2\}, \{2,3\}\}, \{\{5\}, \{2,3\}\},$$
$$\{2,3\}\}, \{\{1,2\}, \{5\}, \{2,3\}\}\}$$

Exercise 11.5

This can be proved by mathematical induction. Note that (1) this exercise requires the knowledge of set theoretic operations to be covered in Chapter 12, and (2) the data we are dealing with are sets, which can be ordered on the basis of size of sets. The proofs involve two operations: $\#$ and $\mathbb{P}$. Their properties are as follows:

$$\#\varnothing = 0$$
$$\#\{x\} = 1$$
$$\#(A \cup B) = \#A + \#B - \#(A \cap B)$$
$$\mathbb{P}\varnothing = \{\varnothing\}$$
$$\mathbb{P}(A \cup \{x\}) = \mathbb{P}\, A \cup \{a \cup \{x\} \mid a \in \mathbb{P}\, A\}, \text{ provided that } x \notin A$$

We omit the proof of the base case. Proof of the inductive case is as follows.

Induction hypothesis

$$\#(\mathbb{P}A) = 2^{\#A}$$

Let $\#A = n$ for some n.

Inductive proof: Consider an element $x \notin A$. Obviously, $\#(A \cup \{x\}) = n + 1$. Now prove

$$\#(\mathbb{P}(A \cup \{x\})) = 2^{\#(A \cup \{x\})}$$

The proof is:

$\#(\mathbb{P}\,(A \cup \{x\}))$	
$= \#(\mathbb{P}\, A) + \#\{\{x\} \cup a \mid a \in \mathbb{P}\, A\} - $	
$\quad \#(\mathbb{P}\, A \cap \{\{x\} \cup a \mid a \in \mathbb{P}\, A\})$	definitions given above
$= \#(\mathbb{P}\, A) + \#\{\{x\} \cup a \mid a \in \mathbb{P}\, A\}$	since the sets in the intersection are disjoint
$= \#(\mathbb{P}\, A) + \#(\mathbb{P}\, A)$	since the subsets containing x correspond exactly to the elements of $\mathbb{P}\, A$.
$= 2 \times \#(\mathbb{P}A)$	arithmetic
$= 2 \times 2^n$	induction hypothesis
$= 2^{n+1}$	arithmetic
$= 2^{\#(A \cup \{x\})}$	since $\#(A \cup \{x\}) = n + 1$

Exercise 12.2

1. *foreign* $\cap$ *languages*
2. *languages* $\cap$ *literary* $= \varnothing$

5. *foreign* ∩ *literary* ≠ ∅ ⇒ *foreign* ∩ *literary* ⊆ *poetry*

6. *biographies* ∩ *fiction* = ∅

8. *fiction* = ∅ ⇒ *literary* = ∅

Exercise 12.3

Let there be a type, *Vehicle*, and let us introduce certain subsets of *Vehicle* as,

popular, luxury, commercial, family,
sports, expensive, RollsRoyces, limousines   : ℙ *Vehicle*

The answers are:

2. *commercial* ∪ *family* ⊆ *luxury'*

3. *luxury* − *sports* ≠ ∅

5. *popular* ∩ *sports* ∩ *expensive'* ≠ ∅

6. *expensive* ∩ *luxury* − *RollsRoyces*

8. (*family* ∪ *commmercial*)'

Exercise 12.4

Referring to Exercise 6.3:

1. Let there be a type

Person

and let us introduce certain subsets of *Person* as

tall, children, adults, clever, short : ℙ *Person*

The answers are:

(a) *Person* = *tall* ∧ *children* ≠ ∅
(b) *short* ∩ *adults* ≠ ∅ ⇒ *tall* ∩ *children* ⊆ *clever'*

Exercise 12.5

1 (a) $A \cup (B \cap C) = (A \cup B) \cap (A \cup C)$
    Consider an arbitrary element x in $A \cup (B \cap C)$,

$x \in A \cup (B \cap C)$
$\Leftrightarrow x \in A \vee x \in (B \cap C)$ defn of union
$\Leftrightarrow x \in A \vee (x \in B \wedge x \in C)$ defn of intersection
$\Leftrightarrow (x \in A \vee x \in B) \wedge (x \in A \vee x \in C)$ distributivity (logic)
$\Leftrightarrow x \in A \cup B \wedge x \in A \cup C$ defn of union
$\Leftrightarrow x \in (A \cup B) \cap (A \cup C)$ defn of intersection

Hence, the proof.

2. (a) Consider an arbitrary element x in $A \cap B$. We need to prove that

$$x \in A \cap B \Rightarrow x \in A$$

The proof is as follows:

1. $x \in A \cap B$ assumption
2. $x \in A \wedge x \in B$ from 1, defn of intersection
3. $x \in A$ from 2, $\wedge\_E$
4. $x \in A \cap B \Rightarrow x \in A$ from 1 & 3, $\Rightarrow \_I$

Exercise 12.6

The argument written set theoretically is:

1. $commercial \cup family \subseteq luxury'$ premise
2. $sports \cap commercial = \emptyset$ premise
3. $sports \cap family \neq \emptyset$ premise
$\overline{sports \cap luxury' \neq \emptyset}$ Conclusion

Proof of validity is left to the reader.

Exercise 12.8

1. The solution given in the following schema covers only the primary operation. An operation for lending a book from the library.

```
┌─Lend₀────────────────────────────────
│   ΔLib_Stock
│   book? : Book
├──────────
│   book? ∈ stock − ref_coll − on_loan
│   on_loan' = on_loan ∪ {book?}
│   on_shelf' = on_shelf − {book?}
│   ref_coll' = ref_coll
└────────────────────────────────────
```

Exercise 13.2

Let us introduce a new relation

$lovesAnimal : H \leftrightarrow A$

with the informal meaning that $(x, y) \in lovesAnimal$ if and only if the person x loves the animal y.

1. $hasPet \cup treats$

2. $hasPet - treats$

5. $(hasPet \cup lovesAnimal) \cap treats$

6. $hasPet \cap lovesAnimal' \cap treats$

Exercise 13.3

Let us introduce the following types:

$[Year, Country]$

with the obvious meanings. We will continue to use the set H and A used in examples.

1. $liveStockLimit : \mathbb{P}(H \times A \times \mathbb{N})$

   with the meaning that $(x, y, n) \in liveStockLimit$ if and only if the farmer x is permitted to keep n animals of species y.

2. $treatmentRecord : \mathbb{P}(H \times A \times \mathbb{N} \times Year^2)$

   with the meaning that $(x, y, n, a, b) \in treatmentRecord$ if and only if the veterinary surgeon x has treated n animals of species y between the years a and b inclusively.

Exercise 13.4

We use the relation $lovesAnimal$ introduced in the answer to Exercise 13.2.

1. $hasPet \cap treats \neq \varnothing$
4. $hasPet \subseteq lovesAnimal$
5. $lovesAnimal \subseteq hasPet$
8. $hasPet \subseteq lovesAnimal \cup treats$

Exercise 13.5

Let us introduce the following types:

$[Person, Book]$

and the relations

$author, favourite : Person \leftrightarrow Book$

$(x, y) \in author$ if and only if the person x is the author of the book y. On the other hand, $(x, y) \in favourite$ if and only if the book y is a favourite book of the reader x.

1. $favourite \cap author = \varnothing$
2. $favourite \neq \varnothing \Rightarrow author \neq \varnothing$
4. $favourite' \cap author \neq \varnothing$

Exercise 13.6

2. dom $(hasPet - treats) \cap$ dom $treats$
3. dom $(hasPet \cap lovesAnimal)$
5. (dom $(hasPet \cup lovesAnimal)) \cap$ (dom $treats$)

Exercise 13.7

For the proof of $(R^\sim)^\sim = R$ we need to prove that

$$(x, y) \in (R^\sim)^\sim \Leftrightarrow (x, y) \in R$$

for any x and y of appropriate types. The proof is:

$(x, y) \in (R^\sim)^\sim$
$\Leftrightarrow (y, x) \in R^\sim$ definition of inverse
$\Leftrightarrow (x, y) \in R$ definition of inverse

Exercise 14.1

1. *medication* = {*(Jo, paracetamol), (Yuri, omeprazole),*
                     (Yuri, paracetamol), (Rio, insulin),
                     (Tom, salbutamol), (Hilary, antihistamine)}

2. Let us introduce a new relation

     notPermitted : Illness $\leftrightarrow$ Medicine

such that $(x, m) \in$ *notPermitted* if and only if the medicine m is not permitted as a treatment for the illness x. The required solution *noGood* is

     noGood : Patient $\leftrightarrow$ Medicine

with the meaning that $(p, m) \in$ *noGood* is true if and only if the patient p should not be treated with the medicine m. The relation *noGood* may be defined as

     noGood = complaints $\fatsemi$ notPermitted

3. *treatment$^\sim \fatsemi$ notPermitted*

4. *treatment $\fatsemi$ (notPermitted$^\sim$)*

Exercise 14.2

A proof outline of only one of the laws, namely

$$R \fatsemi (S \fatsemi T) = (R \fatsemi S) \fatsemi T$$

We intend to prove that

$$(x, z) \in R \fatsemi (S \fatsemi T) \Leftrightarrow (x, z) \in R \fatsemi (S \fatsemi T)$$

for some arbitrary x and z.

$(x, z) \in R \fatsemi (S \fatsemi T)$
$\Leftrightarrow \exists y \bullet (x, y) \in R \wedge (y, z) \in (S \fatsemi T)$ defn of $\fatsemi$
$\Leftrightarrow \exists y \bullet (x, y) \in R \wedge (\exists t \bullet (y, t) \in S \wedge (t, z) \in T)$ defn of $\fatsemi$
       $\vdots$
$\Leftrightarrow (x, z) \in (R \fatsemi S) \fatsemi T$ defn of $\fatsemi$

Exercise 14.3

$g\_parent = \{(\textit{John, Adam}), (\textit{John, Eve}), (\textit{David, Leo}),$
$\qquad\qquad (\textit{David, Jo}), (\textit{David, Rosi}), (\textit{Mary, Adam}),$
$\qquad\qquad (\textit{Mary, Eve}), (\textit{Mary, Ann}), (\textit{Pele, Ann}),$
$\qquad\qquad (\textit{Jo, Lincoln}), (\textit{Jo, Ono}) (\textit{Rosi, Lincoln}),$
$\qquad\qquad (\textit{Rosi, Ono})\}$
$gg\_parent = \{(\textit{David, Adam}), (\textit{David, Eve}),$
$\qquad\qquad\quad (\textit{David, Ann}), (\textit{Mary, Lincoln}), (\textit{Mary, Ono}),$
$\qquad\qquad\quad (\textit{Pele, Lincoln}), (\textit{Pele, Ono})\}$
$ggg\_parent = \{(\textit{David, Lincoln}), (\textit{David, Ono})\}$
$gggg\_parent = \varnothing$

Exercise 14.4

Proof of $R^{m+n} = R^m \,;\, R^n$ by induction. Induction over one of the variables is sufficient since $R^{m+n} = R^{n+m}$. We choose m.

Base case

Proof for $m = 0$:

R^{m+n}
$= R^{0+n}$ for base case: $m = 0$
$= R^n$ arithmetic
$= \text{id } A \,;\, R^n$ a property of id
$= R^0 \,;\, R^n$ defn of R^0
$= R^m \,;\, R^n$ for base case: $m = 0$

Base case proven.

Inductive case

Induction hypothesis: $R^{m+n} = R^m \,;\, R^n$
Inductive proof: Prove $R^{(m+1)+n} = R^{m+1} \,;\, R^n$

The proof:

$R^{(m+1)+n}$
$= R \,;\, R^{m+n}$ defn of $R^{(m+1)+n}$
$= R \,;\, (R^m \,;\, R^n)$ induction hypothesis
$= (R \,;\, R^m) \,;\, R^n$ associativity of $;$
$= R^{m+1} \,;\, R^n$ defn of R^{m+1}

Induction step proven. Hence, the complete proof.

Exercise 14.5

1. The individuals receiving the medicines N, V, X and Z are:

$medication^{\sim}(\!|\{N, V, X, Z\}|\!) = \{A, C, E, F\}$

3. Nodes reachable in three or more steps from nodes a, d, f and i are:

$(net^3 \cup net^4 \cup net^5)(\!| \{a, d, f, i\} |\!)$
$= (\{(a, a), (b, b), (c, c), (d, d), (d, b), (e, e), (f, f), (f, a), (f, h), (e, c), (g, c), (g, e),$
$\quad (d, c), (f, b), (e, a), (g, a), (g, h), (f, c), (e, b), (g, b)\})(\!| \{a, d, f, i\} |\!)$
$= \{a, d, b, f, h, c\}$

Exercise 14.7

2. Let us introduce the types *Vehicle*, *NumberPlate*, and *Person*.
   (a) A relation for recording vehicles and their registration numbers:

   $$registration : Vehicle \leftrightarrow NumberPlate$$

   A relation for recording vehicle registration numbers and vehicle owners is:

   $$owner : NumberPlate \leftrightarrow Person$$

   (b) $((luxury \cap sports) \cup RollsRoyces) \lhd registration$
   (c) $(commercial \cup limousines) \lhd registration$

Exercise 14.11

2. We use a relation *ownership* from *Person* to *numberPlate* instead of *owner*˜.
   (a) First change:
   $$update_1 = \{(Pele, M2X), (Pele, J5X), (Pele, A1A), (Pele, A5B),$$
   $$(Rosi, X6J), (Yuri, B3X)\}$$

   (b) Second change:
   $$update_2 = \{(Yuri, A5B), (Rosi, L3L)\}$$

   Initial ownership:
   $$ownership = \{(John, C3A), (John, C2A), (Jo, K2A), (Pele, A5D), (Rosi, L5J),$$
   $$(Rosi, X6J), (Peter, X3M)\}$$

   (c) New ownership:
   Let *ownership'* be the new ownership relation:

   $$ownership' = ownership \oplus update_1 \oplus update_2$$
   $$= ownership \oplus (update_1 \oplus update_2)$$

   Work out first $update_1 \oplus update_2$:

   $update_1 \oplus update_2$
   $= \{(Pele, M2X), (Pele, J5X), (Pele, A1A), (Pele, A5B), (Rosi, L3L), (Yuri, A5B)\}$

   ownership'
   $= \{(John, C3A), (John, C2A), (Jo, K2A), (Peter, X3M), (Pele, M2X),$
   $\quad (Pele, J5X), (Pele, A1A), (Pele, A5B), (Rosi, L3L), (Yuri, A5B)\}$

Exercise 15.1

Properties desired in the given relations are:

1. _greater-than_   Irreflexive, not symmetrical, not antisymmetrical, transitive
3. *add-upto-5*   Irreflexive, symmetrical, not antisymmetrical, non-transitive
5. _is-brother_   Irreflexive, symmetrical (if *P* consists of males only), transitive

Exercise 15.2

Relation	Property					
	Reflexive	Irreflexive	Non-reflexive	Symmetric	Antisymmetric	Transitive
People related by common birthdays	Yes	No	No	Yes	No	Yes
People related by being older	No	Yes	No	No	No	Yes
People related by marriage	No	Yes	No	Yes	No	No
People related by parenthood	No	Yes	No	No	No	No
People related by superiority	No	Yes	No	No	No	Yes

Exercise 15.5

1. $qualityR = \text{id } Prog \cup \{(p_1, p_5),\ (p_5, p_1),\ (p_1, p_7),\ (p_7, p_1),\ (p_5, p_7),$
$(p_7, p_5),\ (p_3, p_6),\ (p_6, p_3),\ (p_2, p_4),\ (p_4, p_2)\}$

2. $algorithmR = \text{id } Prog \cup \{(p_3, p_6),\ (p_6, p_3),\ (p_3, p_8),\ (p_8, p_3),\ (p_6, p_8),\ (p_8, p_6),$
$(p_2, p_4),\ (p_4, p_2),\ (p_2, p_9),\ (p_9, p_2),\ (p_4, p_9),\ (p_9, p_4)\}$

3. $qualityR \cap algorithmR = \text{id } Prog \cup \{(p_3, p_6),\ (p_6, p_3),\ (p_2, p_4),\ (p_4, p_2)\}$

Exercise 15.6

1. $m \mid n \Leftrightarrow \exists k \bullet n = m \times k$
2. All three properties: reflexivity, symmetry and transitivity.

4. A proof for the answer to (2). Let us deal with the three properties separately.
  (a) Reflexivity. We have to show that for every $p \in \mathbb{Z}$, the predicate
      congruent (p, p) *mod m* is identically true. The proof is:

   $\quad$ *congruent* (p, p) *mod m*
   $\quad \Leftrightarrow\ m \mid (p - p) \qquad$ defn of $m \mid n$
   $\quad \Leftrightarrow\ m \mid 0 \qquad\qquad$ arithmetic
   $\quad\ \ \Leftrightarrow\ \mathbf{true} \qquad\qquad$ arithmetic

  (b) Symmetry. We have to show that for every $p, q \in \mathbb{Z}$, the predicate,

   $\quad$ *congruent* (p, q) *mod m* $\Rightarrow$ *congruent* (p, q) *mod m*

   is identically true. Instead, we show something which is even stronger.

   $\quad$ *congruent* (p, q) *mod m*
   $\quad \Leftrightarrow\ m \mid (p - q) \qquad\qquad$ defn of $m \mid n$
   $\quad \Leftrightarrow\ m \mid (q - p) \qquad\qquad$ a property of exact division
   $\quad \Leftrightarrow$ *congruent* (q, p) *mod m* $\quad$ defn of $m \mid n$

  (c) Transitivity. It requires that

   $\quad$ *congruent* (p, q) *mod m* $\wedge$ *congruent* (q, r) *mod m* $\Rightarrow$ *congruent* (p, r) *mod m*

   is identically true. The proof is left for the reader.

Exercise 15.8

1. Equivalences classes of the programs in relation to quality of program code:

$$[p_1] = [p_5] = [p_7] = \{p_1, p_5, p_7\}$$
$$[p_2] = [p_4] = \{p_2, p_4\}$$
$$[p_3] = [p_6] = \{p_3, p_6\}$$
$$[p_8] = \{p_8\}$$
$$[p_9] = \{p_9\}$$
$$[p_{10}] = \{p_{10}\}$$

2. *Prog/qualityR* $= \{\{p_1, p_5, p_7\}, \{p_2, p_4\}, \{p_3, p_6\}, \{p_8\}, \{p_9\}, \{p_{10}\}\}$

3. *Prog/algorithmR* $= \{\{p_3, p_6, p_8\}, \{p_2, p_4, p_9\}, \{p_1\}, \{p_7\}, \{p_5\}, \{p_{10}\}\}$

4. *Prog/(qualityR* $\cap$ *algorithmR)* $=$
$$\{\{p_3, p_6\}, \{p_2, p_4\}, \{p_1\}, \{p_5\}, \{p_7\}, \{p_8\}, \{p_9\}, \{p_{10}\}\}$$

Exercise 15.12

1. Let the set of weightlifters be

   $W = \{$*Boris, Sergei, Tam, Viktor*$\}$

Now define a relation *outlift* on *W* as

$outlift : W \leftrightarrow W$

$outlift = \{Viktor \mapsto Tam, Sergei \mapsto Viktor, Tam \mapsto Boris, Sergei \mapsto Tam\}$

and find the transitive closure

$outlift^{+} = \{Viktor \mapsto Tam, Sergei \mapsto Viktor, Tam \mapsto Boris,$
$Sergei \mapsto Tam, Viktor \mapsto Boris, Sergei \mapsto Boris\}$

Note that $outlift^{+}$ represents transitive closure of *outlift* (see Chapter 15).

(a) 'Both Boris and Sergei can outlift Viktor' is false since

$\{Boris \mapsto Viktor, Sergei \mapsto Viktor\} \not\subseteq outlift^{+}$

(c) 'Viktor can outlift Boris by more than he can outlift Tam' is true since

$Viktor \mapsto Boris \in outlift^{2}$
$\{Viktor \mapsto Tam, Tam \mapsto Boris\} \subseteq outlift^{1}$

2. The ranking of the weightlifters is given by the following subset of $outlift^{+}$

$\{Sergei \mapsto Viktor, Viktor \mapsto Tam, Tam \mapsto Boris\}$

Exercise 16.1

1. and 2. Identification of functions among relations.

Question 1						Question 2
Relation from/on:	Function classification					
	Partial $\nrightarrow$	Total $\rightarrow$	Injective $\rightarrowtail$	Surjective $\twoheadrightarrow$	Bijective $\rightarrowtail\!\!\!\twoheadrightarrow$	
Countries of the world to their capitals		✓	✓	✓	✓	$\rightarrowtail\!\!\!\twoheadrightarrow$
Countries of the world to their current prime ministers	✓		✓	✓	✓	$\rightarrowtail\!\!\!\twoheadrightarrow$
Computer user names to their passwords		✓	✓	✓	✓	$\rightarrowtail\!\!\!\twoheadrightarrow$
Telephone numbers to households	✓					$\nrightarrow$
Adjacent railway stations on a train route	✓		✓			$\rightarrowtail$

Exercise 16.2

Let *Char* stand for the set of characters used, *Name* the set of individuals and *Drink* the set of drinks. According to the problem,

$Name = \{Buharin, Brezinsky, Chernov, Chikarin, Petrovsky, Semenov, Wilensky\}$
$Drink = \{beer, brandy, chianti, cider, port, sherry, whisky\}$

Assume that the following functions are given:

$DrinkInitial : Drink \rightarrow Char$
$NameInitial : Name \rightarrow Char$

The eligibility for drinks, restrictions on consumption and the actual consumption may be defined as relations

$eligibility, \ restrictions, \ actual : Name \leftrightarrow Drink$

Also, introduce the set

$victims : \mathbb{F} \ Name$

Some general constraints are:

$actual \subseteq restrictions \subseteq eligibility$

The relation *eligibility* may be defined as:

$eligibility = \{(a, b) \bullet a : Name; \ b : Drink \mid NameInitial(a) \neq DrinkInitial(b)\}$

Drinking is restricted to exactly three drinks, that is,

$\forall a : Name \bullet \#(\{a\} \lhd restrictions) = 3$

There were only three victims, that is,

$\#victims = 3$

The following are the facts related to actual consumption:

(a) $actual \ (\!| \ victims \ |\!) = Drink$

(c) $\#(actual \rhd \{port\}) = \#(actual \rhd \{whisky\}) + 1$

(d)   Let p be the person referred to in the English sentence.

$\exists d : Drink \bullet \forall q : Name \ \bullet q \in victims \land (q, d) \in actual \land (p \in victims \land$
$NameInitial(p) = DrinkInitial(d) \land (p, chianti) \in actual)$

Exercise 16.3

Question 1						Question 2
Function	Function classification					
	Partial $\rightarrowtail$	Total $\rightarrow$	Injective $\rightarrowtail$	Surjective $\twoheadrightarrow$	Bijective $\rightarrowtail\!\!\!\twoheadrightarrow$	
$f(x) = x^3$ on $\mathbb{Z}$		✓	✓			$\rightarrowtail\!\!\!\twoheadrightarrow$
$f(x) = x^3$ on $\mathbb{R}$		✓	✓	✓	✓	$\rightarrowtail\!\!\!\twoheadrightarrow$
$f(x) = \sqrt[3]{x}$ on $\mathbb{Z}$	✓		✓			$\twoheadrightarrow$
$f(x) = \sqrt[3]{x}$ on $\mathbb{R}$		✓	✓	✓	✓	$\rightarrowtail\!\!\!\twoheadrightarrow$

Exercise 16.4

Functions in the board game *chess*. The kinds of pieces are:

$Kind = \{\textbf{king}, \textbf{queen}, \textbf{rook}, \textbf{bishop}, \textbf{knight}, \textbf{pawn}\}$

which belong to two different colours

$Colour = \{\textbf{black}, \textbf{white}\}$

With these we can define the Cartesian product

$Men = Colour \times Kind$

The elements of the cartesian product represent the kinds of men of the two colours. Let us introduce a constant *Size* as:

$Size : \mathbb{N}$
$Size = 8$

giving a measure of the board. This enables the definition of the squares in the board as

$Position = (1, \,.. \, Size) \times (1, \,.. \, Size)$

The positions occupied by individual tokens can be defined as a function

$chess\_board : Position \rightarrowtail Men$

The rest of the development is left for the reader.

Exercise 16.6

First, the types *Person, Account,* and *Address* with the obvious meanings.
1. (a) Account numbers and personal account holders:

$$accounts : Account \rightarrowtail\!\!\!\!\rightarrow Person$$

   (b) Personal account holders and their addresses:

$$addresses : Person \leftrightarrow Address$$

   (c) Accounts and their current balance:

$$balance : Account \rightarrow\!\!\!\!\!\rightarrow \mathbb{R}^+$$

   where $\mathbb{R}^+$ denotes the set of non-negative real numbers.

2. (a) The balance in a's account is $balance(a)$.
   (b) The names and addresses of those whose current balance is below the amount n is:

$$(accounts^\sim \mathbin{\mathring{,}} balance^\sim (\!|\{x \bullet x : \mathbb{R} \mid 0.0 \leqslant x < n\}|\!)) \lhd addresses$$

   (c) Given a function,

$$update : Account \rightarrow\!\!\!\!\!\rightarrow \mathbb{R}^+$$

   consisting of pairs of individuals and their new balances, the updated current balance of all accounts is:

$$balance \oplus update$$

Exercise 17.1

This may be proved by mathematical induction. As the base case, first show that

$$m + 0 = 0 + m$$

where the result (17.9) may become useful. Then adopting

$$m + n = n + m$$

as the induction hypothesis, prove

$$m + n' = n' + m$$

Exercise 17.2

2. Proof of $-(a + b) = (-a) + (-b)$

   1. $a + b + \overline{a + b} = 0$ additive inverse, axiom (17.20)
   2. $\bar{a} + \bar{b} + a + b + \overline{a + b} = \bar{a} + \bar{b} + 0$ from 1, addition of $\bar{a} + \bar{b}$
   3. $a + \bar{a} + b + \bar{b} + \overline{a + b} = \bar{a} + \bar{b} + 0$ from 2, commutativity, axiom (17.16) thrice
   4. $0 + 0 + \overline{a + b} = \bar{a} + \bar{b} + 0$ from 3, additive inverse, axiom (17.20) twice

5. $0 + \overline{a + b} = \overline{a} + \overline{b} + 0$ from 4, identity, axiom (17.14)

6. $\overline{a + b} + 0 = \overline{a} + \overline{b} + 0$ from 5, commutativity, axiom (17.16)

7. $\overline{a + b} = \overline{a} + \overline{b}$ from 6, identity, axiom (17.14)

8. $-(a + b) = (-a) + (-b)$ from 6, definition of $-x$ as $\overline{x}$

Exercise 17.3

First, introduce the numeral 2 and the notations for xy and x^2 as

$$2 \stackrel{def}{=} 1 + 1$$

$$xy \stackrel{def}{=} x \times y$$

$$x^2 \stackrel{def}{=} x \times x$$

Proof:

$(a + b) \times (a + b)$	LHS of the formula to be proved
$= (a + b) \times a + (a + b) \times b$	distributivity, axiom (17.19)
$= a \times (a + b) + b \times (a + b)$	commutativity, axiom (17.15)
$= a \times a + a \times b + b \times a + b \times b$	distributivity, axiom (17.19)
$= a \times a + a \times b + a \times b + b \times b$	commutativity, axiom (17.15)
$= a \times a + a \times b \times 1 + a \times b \times 1 + b \times b$	identity, axiom (17.13) twice
$= a \times a + (a \times b) \times (1 + 1) + b \times b$	distributivity, axiom (17.19)
$= a \times a + (1 + 1) \times (a \times b) + b \times b$	commutativity, axiom (17.15)
$= a \times a + 2 \times (a \times b) + b \times b$	definition of the numeral 2
$= a^2 + 2ab + b^2$	definitions of square x^2 and product xy given above

Exercise 17.7

Consider two integers i_1 and i_2. The overflow can be detected by observing whether there has been a *carry* into or out of the sign bit.

Case 1: $i_1 > 0$ and $i_2 > 0$. Overflow takes place if and only if a 1 has been carried into the sign bit. If this happens, the stored representation corresponds to a negative integer, which is obviously incorrect. This can be seen in the example

$$01011 + 01001 = 10100$$

which, in decimal representation, reads as

$$11 + 9 = -12$$

Note that it is not possible for a carry to take place out of the sign bit since both i_1 and i_2 are assumed to be positive and, hence, their sign bits are both 0s.

Case 2: i_1 and i_2 are of different signs. No overflow can take place in this case.

Case 3: $i_1 < 0$ and $i_2 < 0$. Overflow takes place if and only if:

(a) a 1 has not been carried into the sign bit, and

(b) a 1 has been carried out of the sign bit.

This can be seen in the example

$$10010 + 11000 = 01010$$

which, in decimal representation, reads as

$$(-14) + (-8) = 10$$

which is obviously incorrect. On the other hand, if a carry into the sign bit has taken place, a carry out of the sign bit does not amount to an overflow. This can be seen in the case of

$$11010 + 11000 = 10010$$

which, in decimal representation, reads as

$$(-6) + (-8) = -14$$

which is correct.

Exercise 17.9

See Figure A.4.

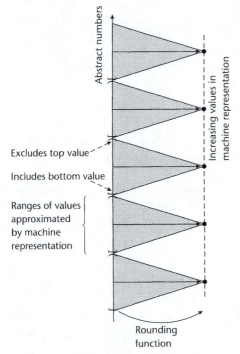

Figure A.4   Approximation of abstract numbers by machine representation

Exercise 18.1

3. Note that $\#R = 3$. Therefore:

$$pred^{\#R} = pred^3$$
$$= \{(3,0),(4,1),(5,2),(6,3),\ldots\}$$
$$pred^{\#R}\,;\,S = \{(3,0),(4,1),(5,2),(6,3),\ldots\}\,;\,\{(1,r),(2,i),(3,c),(4,a)\}$$
$$= \{(4,r),(5,i),(6,c),(7,a)\}$$
$$R \frown S = R \cup (pred^{\#R}\,;\,S)$$
$$= \{(1,A),(2,m),(3,e)\} \cup \{(4,r),(5,i),(6,c),(7,a)\}$$
$$= \langle a,\ m,\ e,\ r,\ i,\ c,\ a\rangle$$

Exercise 18.5

1. Mathematical definition of zip:

$$zip\ S_1\ S_2 = 1..2 \times min(\#S_1, \#S_2) \vartriangleleft$$
$$(((\{(2 \times i - 1, i) \mid i \in \mathbb{N}_1\}\,;\,S_1) \cup$$
$$(\{(2 \times i, i) \mid i \in \mathbb{N}_1\}\,;\,S_2))$$

$$zip\ \langle g,\ e,\ t,\ t,\ o\rangle\ \langle r,a,!\rangle$$
$$= 1..2 \times min(5,3) \vartriangleleft ((\{(2 \times i - 1, i) \mid i \in \mathbb{N}_1\}\,;$$
$$\langle g,\ e,\ t,\ t,\ o\rangle) \cup$$
$$(\{(2 \times i, i) \mid i \in \mathbb{N}_1\}\,;$$
$$\langle r,a,!\rangle))$$
$$= 1..6 \vartriangleleft ((\{(1,1),(3,2),(5,3),(7,4),(9,5),\ldots\}\,;$$
$$\{(1,g),(2,e),(3,t),(4,t),(5,o)\}) \cup$$
$$(\{(2,1),(4,2),(6,3),(8,4),\ldots\}\,;$$
$$\{(1,r),(2,a),(3,!)\}))$$
$$\vdots$$
$$= \{(1,g),(2,r),(3,e),(4,a),(5,t),(6,!)\}$$
$$= \langle g,r,e,a,t,!\rangle$$

Exercise 18.6

This requires the knowledge of binary representation of integers – the topic of Section 17.6.2. First, let us consider how the addition of 1 to an integer ripples through its binary representation. Consider an integer i in N–bit representation as a sequence of bits of length N. Let us partition i's representation into two sequences x and y:

$$i = x \frown y$$

such that an addition of 1 affects all the bits in y but none of the bits in x. Note that for this to happen the first element of y must be a 0 but all others 1s. Thus, the addition of 1 to i may be seen as

$$i + 1 = x \frown swap(y)$$

where $swap$ is a function on sequences of bits which interchanges 0s and 1s in its argument. For any sequence of bits z, $swap(z)$ can be defined as the function composition

$$swap(z) = \{0 \mapsto 1, 1 \mapsto 0\} \circ z$$

It is worth observing that

$$swap(x \frown y) = swap(x) \frown swap(y)$$
$$swap(swap(x)) = x$$

The complement $\bar{a}$ of an integer a is

$$\bar{a} = swap(a)$$

Two's complement of a may be found by first partitioning a into two subsequences x and y:

$$a = x \frown y$$

such that the first element of y is a 1 but all others are 0s. Two's complement $\hat{a}$ of a is then

$$\hat{a} = swap(x) \frown y$$

Repeated computation of two's complement of a twice is then

$$\widehat{(\hat{a})} = \widehat{\bar{a} + 1}$$
$$= \widehat{swap(x) \frown y}$$
$$= \overline{swap(x) \frown y} + 1$$
$$= swap(swap(x)) \frown swap(y) + 1$$
$$= swap(swap(x)) \frown swap(swap(y))$$
$$= x \frown y$$
$$= a$$

The above is correct except for one extreme case.

Exercise 18.7

Let *Address* be a type consisting of all possible addresses of the users.

1. *mail_count, mail_count'* : bag *Address*

   where *mail_count'* signifies the value of *mail_count* soon after the operation.

2. *mail_count'* = *mail_count* ⊎ ⟦*new* ↦ 1⟧

   where *new* ∈ *Address* is the address of the newly arrived message.

3. *mail_count'* = *dispose* ◁ *mail_count*

   where *dispose* : ℙ *Address* is the set of addresses to be removed.

8. $(\biguplus\{[\![special \mapsto m]\!] \bullet x : Address \mid x \mapsto m \in mail\_count\})\, \sharp special \leqslant n$

where $special : Address$ is a specially chosen unique address and $\biguplus$ is a 'generalized' version of bag union operation $\uplus$ applicable to sets of bags.

Exercise 19.1

Below are proofs of some of the theorems given in Section 19.3.

Proof of $\bar{a} \times (a \times b) = 0$ – property (19.25):

0	RHS of (19.25)
$= a \times \bar{a}$	complements, axiom (19.7)
$= \bar{a} \times a$	commutativity, axiom (19.3)
$= \bar{a} \times (a + (a \times b))$	property (19.24)
$= (\bar{a} \times a) + (\bar{a} \times (a \times b))$	distributivity, axiom (19.5)
$= 0 + (\bar{a} \times (a \times b))$	complements, axiom (19.7)
$= (\bar{a} \times (a \times b)) + 0$	commutativity, axiom (19.4)
$= \bar{a} \times (a \times b)$	identity element of +, axiom (19.2)

Proof of Property (19.29):

The proof is based on two assumptions:

1. $a \times c = b \times c$

2. $a + c = b + c$

which are both conditions qualifying property (19.29).

a	LHS of property (19.29)
$= a \times (a + c)$	property (19.23)
$= a \times (b + c)$	assumption (2)
$= (a \times b) + (a \times c)$	distributivity, axiom (19.5)
$= (a \times b) + (b \times c)$	assumption (1)
$= (a \times b) + (c \times b)$	commutativity, axiom (19.3)
$= (a + c) \times b$	distributivity, axiom (19.5)
$= (b + c) \times b$	assumption (2)
$= b$	property (19.23)

Proof of associativity property (19.18):

$(a \times b) \times c$	RHS of property (19.18)
$= \overline{\overline{((a \times b) \times c)}}$	double complement, property (19.16)
$= \overline{\overline{(a \times b)} + \bar{c}}$	De Morgan's property (19.19)
$= \overline{(\bar{a} + \bar{b}) + \bar{c}}$	De Morgan's property (19.19)
$= \overline{\bar{a} + (\bar{b} + \bar{c})}$	associativity, property (19.17)
$= \overline{\bar{a} + \overline{(b \times c)}}$	De Morgan's property (19.19)
$= \overline{\overline{a \times (b \times c)}}$	De Morgan's property (19.19)
$= a \times (b \times c)$	double complement, property (19.16)

Exercise 20.2

1. The types of functions in Example 20.3 are: $\mathbb{N}$, $\mathbb{Z}$, $\mathbb{Z}$ (though undefined), $\mathbb{R} \to \mathbb{R}$ and $\mathbb{R} \nrightarrow \mathbb{R}$ respectively.

2. λ versions of functions:
   (a) $\lambda x : \mathbb{Z} \bullet x + 2$
   (b) $\lambda x : \mathbb{Z} \bullet x^2$
   (c) $\lambda x : \mathbb{R} \bullet x^3$
   (e) $\lambda x : \mathbb{R} \mid x \neq 0 \bullet \dfrac{1}{x}$
   (f) $\lambda x : \mathbb{R} \mid x > 0 \bullet \dfrac{1}{x} + \sqrt{x}$
   (g) $\lambda x, y : \mathbb{R} \bullet \sin^2(x) + \cos^2(y)$

Exercise 20.3

1. $x\, y$ is identical to $(x\, y)$ and is a λ-term.

2. $\lambda x \bullet y\, x$ is identical to $((\lambda x \bullet y)x)$ and is a λ-term.

3. The sequence of symbols $\lambda z\, y$ in $\lambda x \bullet \lambda z\, y \bullet x\, z$ violates the syntax rules and, therefore, this is not a λ-term.

4. $\lambda x \bullet (x\, x)\, \lambda x \bullet (x\, x)$ is identical to $((\lambda x \bullet (x\, x))\, (\lambda x \bullet (x\, x)))$ and is a λ-term.

Exercise 20.4

1. Both x and y are free.

2. Both x and y are free.

8. $\overset{\text{free}}{x}\ \lambda\ \overset{\text{bound}}{x}\ \bullet (\lambda\ \overset{\text{bound}}{y}\ \bullet\ \overset{\text{bound}}{y}\ )\ \overset{\text{free}}{x}$

9. $\lambda\ \overset{\text{bound}}{x}\ \bullet (\ \overset{\text{bound}}{x}\ (\ \overset{\text{bound}}{x}\ \overset{\text{free}}{y}\ ))N$

Exercise 20.5

1. $(y\ (\lambda z \bullet x\, y))[x/(\lambda y \bullet z\, y)]$

$\equiv (y[x/(\lambda y \bullet z\, y)]\ (\lambda z \bullet x\, y)[x/(\lambda y \bullet z\, y)])$ rule (3)

$\equiv (y\ (\lambda z \bullet x\, y)[x/(\lambda y \bullet z\, y)])$ rule (2)

$\equiv (y\ ((\lambda z \bullet \underbrace{x}_{E}\,)[x/\underbrace{(\lambda y \bullet z\, y)}_{M}]\ y[x/(\lambda y \bullet z\, y)]))$ rule (3)

$\equiv (y\ (\lambda p \bullet x[z/p][x/(\lambda y \bullet z\, y)]\ y[x/(\lambda y \bullet z\, y)]))$ rule (6)

$\equiv (y\ (\lambda p \bullet x[x/(\lambda y \bullet z\, y)]\ y[x/(\lambda y \bullet z\, y)]))$ rule (2)

$\equiv (y\ (\lambda p \bullet (\lambda y \bullet z\, y)\ y[x/(\lambda y \bullet z\, y)]))$ rule (1)

$\equiv (y\ (\lambda p \bullet (\lambda y \bullet z\, y)\ y))$ rule (2)

Exercise 20.6

$((\lambda x \bullet (x\ x\ y))\ (\lambda x \bullet (x\ x\ y)))$

$\xrightarrow{\beta} (x\ x\ y)[x/(\lambda x \bullet (x\ x\ y))]$

$\equiv (x[x/(\lambda x \bullet (x\ x\ y))]\ x[x/(\lambda x \bullet (x\ x\ y))]\ y[x/(\lambda x \bullet (x\ x\ y))])$ subs rule (3)

$\equiv ((\lambda x \bullet (x\ x\ y))\ (\lambda x \bullet (x\ x\ y))\ y)$ subs rules (1) & (2)

$\quad\vdots$

$\xrightarrow{\beta} ((\lambda x \bullet (x\ x\ y))\ (\lambda x \bullet (x\ x\ y))\ y\ y)$ repeating the above

$\quad\vdots$

$\xrightarrow{\beta} ((\lambda x \bullet (x\ x\ y))\ (\lambda x \bullet (x\ x\ y))\ y\ y\ y)$ repeating the above again

References

Abelson H., Sussman G. J. and Sussman J. (1985). *Structure and Interpretation of Computer Programs*. Harvard MA: MIT Press.

Andrews D. and Ince D. (1991). Harvard MA: *Practical Formal Methods with VDM*. New York: McGraw-Hill.

Bird R. and Wadler P. (1988). *Introduction to Functional Programming*. Hemel Hempstead: Prentice Hall.

Dijkstra E. W. (1976). *A Discipline of Programming*. Hemel Hempstead: Prentice Hall.

Diller A. (1990). *Z – An Introduction to Formal Methods*. Chichester: Wiley.

Dunham W. (1994). *The Mathematical Universe*. Chichester: John Wiley & Sons.

Hayes I. (1993). *Specification Software Development using VDM*. Hemel Hempstead: Prentice Hall.

Hein J. L. (1996). *Theory of Computation – An Introduction*. Sudbury, Massachusetts: Jones and Bartlett.

Henson M. C. (1987). *Elements of Functional Languages*. Oxford: Blackwell Scientific Publications.

Hindley J. R. and Seldin J. P. (1986). *Introduction to Combinators and λ-Calculus*. Cambridge: Cambridge University Press.

Jones C. B. (1986). *Systematic Software Development in VDM*. Hemel Hempstead: Prentice Hall.

Jones C. B. and Shaw R. C. (1990). *Case Studies in Systematic Software Development*. Hemel Hempstead: Prentice Hall.

Kahane H. (1973). *Logic and Philosophy – A Modern Introduction*. Belmont, California: Wadsworth.

Mackay A. (1991). *A Dictionary of Scientific Quotations*. Bristol: Adam Hilger.

Madachy J. S. (1979). *Madachy's Mathematical Recreations*. New York: Dover Publications.

Morgan C. (1994). *Programming from Specifications*. Hemel Hempstead: Prentice Hall.

Polya G. (1954). *Induction and Analogy in Mathematics*. Princeton University Press.

Potter B., Sinclair J. and Tills T. (1991). *An Introduction to Formal Specification and Z*. Hemel Hempstead: Prentice Hall.

Singh S. (1997). *Fermat's Last Theorem*. London: Fourth Estate.

Spivey M. (1992). *The Z Notation*. Hemel Hempstead: Prentice Hall.

Wirth N. (1986). Algorithms and Data Structures. Englewood Cliffs NJ: Prentice Hall.

Woodcock J. and Davies J. (1996). *Using Z – Specification, Refinement and Proof*. Hemel Hempstead: Prentice Hall.

Index